MASTERING
LOTUS 1-2-3®

Featuring Release 2.01

Programming books from boyd & fraser

Structuring Programs in Microsoft BASIC
BASIC Fundamentals and Style
Applesoft BASIC Fundamentals and Style
Complete BASIC: For the Short Course
Fundamentals of Structured COBOL
Advanced Structured COBOL: Batch and Interactive
Comprehensive Structured COBOL
Pascal
WATFIV-S Fundamentals and Style
VAX Fortran
Fortran 77 Fundamentals and Style
Learning Computer Programming: Structured Logic, Algorithms, and Flowcharting
Structured BASIC Fundamentals and Style for the IBM® PC and Compatibles
C Programming
dBASE III PLUS® Programming

Also available from boyd & fraser

Database Systems: Management and Design
Using Pascal: An Introduction to Computer Science I
Using Modula-2: An Introduction to Computer Science I
Data Abstraction and Structures: An Introduction to Computer Science II
Fundamentals of Systems Analysis with Application Design
Data Communications for Business
Data Communications Software Design
Microcomputer Applications: Using Small Systems Software
The Art of Using Computers
Using Microcomputers: A Hands-On Introduction
A Practical Approach to Operating Systems
Microcomputer Database Management Using dBASE III PLUS®
Microcomputer Database Management Using R:BASE System V®
Office Automation: An Information Systems Approach
Microcomputer Applications: Using Small Systems Software, Second Edition
Mastering Lotus 1-2-3®
Using Enable™: An Introduction to Integrated Software
PC-DOS®/MS-DOS® Simplified
Artificial Intelligence: A Knowledge-Based Approach

Shelly, Cashman, and Forsythe books from boyd & fraser

Computer Fundamentals with Application Software
Workbook and Study Guide to accompany Computer Fundamentals with Application Software
Learning to Use SUPERCALC®3, dBASE III®, and WORDSTAR® 3.3: An Introduction
Learning to Use SUPERCALC®3: An Introduction
Learning to Use dBASE III®: An Introduction
Learning to Use WORDSTAR® 3.3: An Introduction
BASIC Programming for the IBM® Personal Computer
Workbook and Study Guide to accompany BASIC Programming for the IBM® Personal Computer
Structured COBOL — Flowchart Edition
Structured COBOL — Pseudocode Edition
Turbo Pascal Programming

MASTERING
LOTUS 1-2-3®

Featuring Release 2.01

H. Albert Napier
Rice University and
Napier & Judd, Inc.

Philip J. Judd
Napier & Judd, Inc.

Copyright 1988
Boyd & Fraser Publishing Company
Boston

■ DEDICATION

This book is dedicated to our families in appreciation of their support and patience.

■ CREDITS

Publisher: Thomas K. Walker
Editor: Sarah Grover
Production Editor: Pat Donegan
Director of Production: Becky Herrington
Director of Manufacturing: Erek Smith
Composition: Rebecca Evans & Associates
Cover Artwork: Mark A. Wiklund
Cover Design: Becky Herrington
Interior Design: Rebecca Evans & Associates

Manufactured in the United States of America

Lotus 1–2–3, Lotus, and 1–2–3 are registered trademarks of Lotus Development Corporation
IBM PC and PC-DOS are registered trademarks of International Business Machines
dBASE III PLUS is a registered trademark of Ashton-Tate
R:BASE System V is a registered trademark of Microrim, Inc.
Paradox Release 2.0 is a registered trademark of ANsa Software

Library of Congress Cataloging-in-Publication Data

Napier, H. Albert, 1944-
    Mastering Lotus 1-2-3 / H. Albert Napier, Philip J. Judd.
        p.   cm.
    ISBN 0-87835-310-0
    1. Lotus 1-2-3 (Computer program) 2. Electronic spreadsheets.
3. Business--Data processing.   I. Judd, Philip J., 1953-
II. Title.
HF5548.4.L67N36 1988
005.36'9--dc19   88-2381
                                                               CIP

CONTENTS

Chapter Two

Creating a Worksheet (Spreadsheet) 37

Chapter Three
Building an Analysis Model

Chapter Four
Useful Lotus Commands   147

Chapter Five

Creating and Using a Template

Chapter Six

Combining Information Between Spreadsheets

Chapter Seven
Introduction to Macros 243

Chapter Eight

Special Functions in Lotus 1–2–3   265

Chapter Nine
Creating and Printing a Graph   317

Chapter Ten

Overview of Database Capabilities   371

PREFACE

■ INTRODUCTION

Today, there are literally millions of people using personal computers. One of the most popular uses of personal computers, sometimes referred to as microcomputers, is for creating spreadsheets. A spreadsheet is typically completed on what are called "columnar pad" sheets of paper. Spreadsheets are used extensively in accounting, financial analysis and many other business planning and analysis situations.

There are many software packages that can be purchased to create spreadsheets. The most popular software package available for preparing spreadsheets on microcomputers is Lotus 1–2–3. This software package is published by Lotus Development Corporation.

■ OBJECTIVES OF THIS BOOK

This book was developed specifically for an introductory course in microcomputers or spreadsheet analysis that utilizes IBM PC, IBM PC compatibles or other personal computers on which Lotus 1–2–3 can be used. The objectives of this book are as follows:

1. To acquaint the reader with the process of using microcomputers to solve spreadsheet problems.
2. To teach the fundamentals and cover some advanced topics of Lotus 1–2–3.
3. To teach good problem solving techniques for situations in which spreadsheet solutions are appropriate.
4. To develop an exercise-oriented approach that allows the user to learn by example.
5. To encourage independent study and assist those individuals that are working alone to learn how to use Lotus 1–2–3.
6. To teach Lotus 1–2–3 using practical types of problems.

■ LEVEL OF INSTRUCTION

This book is designed to introduce individuals to Lotus 1–2–3. It is pedagogically designed. First, the user learns the basic skills needed to create a spreadsheet; subsequent chapters then build upon the concepts previously presented. A variety of practical examples assist the beginning user in understanding how Lotus 1–2–3 can be used. This book is written for individuals with little or no personal computer experience. The book is characterized by its continuity, simplicity, and practicality.

This book does not replace the Lotus 1–2–3 manual that accompanies the software package. Used in conjunction with the Lotus 1–2–3 manual, this book will give an individual a complete understanding of the capabilities of Lotus 1–2–3.

■ AUTHORS' EXPERIENCE

The authors have worked with microcomputers since they were introduced. More than 10,000 people have participated in microcomputer training courses for which the authors have been responsible. Insights from this experience are implicit throughout the book. In addition, the authors have more than 30 years experience in teaching and consulting in the field of information systems and data processing.

■ LOTUS AUTHORIZED TRAINING COMPANY

The authors' consulting company, Napier & Judd, Inc., is a Lotus Authorized Training Company. The company's materials, instructors and facilities have been evaluated and approved by Lotus Development Corporation. Only a small number of companies in the United States and Canada have been designated as a Lotus Authorized Training Company. This book is based on materials that have been used in the company's training activities in which more than 7,000 participants have been trained on Lotus 1–2–3.

■ ORGANIZATION/FLEXIBILITY

The book is organized in a manner that takes the student through the fundamentals of Lotus 1–2–3 and then builds upon the solid foundation to cover more advanced subjects. The book is useful for classroom courses, training classes, or individual learning.

In Chapter One, the Lotus 1–2–3 package is described and some typical applications are indicated. The process of loading the software package is specified. The various parts of the 1–2–3 worksheet (spreadsheet) screen are explained. Various ways for moving around the worksheet are indicated. The structure of the menu system used by 1–2–3 is illustrated.

The second chapter contains a *step-by-step* process for creating a spreadsheet. The student learns to build and print a spreadsheet. Operations such as: entering labels, numbers and formulas; copying numbers, formulas and labels; widening columns; inserting rows; entering headings; selecting formats for numeric data; saving and retrieving a spreadsheet; and correcting for rounding errors are included.

Users may wish to use 1–2–3 for sensitivity analysis. Chapter Three illustrates an effective way to design a spreadsheet that can be used for "what-if" sensitivity analysis. This chapter also provides the user with an opportunity to reinforce the topics covered in Chapter Two.

Chapter Four covers a variety of useful Lotus commands. Some of the topics covered include: holding a cell constant in a formula; using percent formats; freezing titles; creating windows; checking the status of the worksheet; inserting and deleting columns and rows; hiding columns from view; creating page breaks; suppressing zeros in a worksheet, controlling recalculation in a spreadsheet; erasing cells; moving cells; miscellaneous file commands; using the system command; correcting and editing errors; and using label prefixes.

In Chapter Five, the process for building and using "template" spreadsheets is discussed. A template is a spreadsheet that is constructed and saved as a "shell" for creating future spreadsheets that contain the same formulas and/or format.

Many practical applications of spreadsheets require that information be combined from one or more spreadsheets into one or more other spreadsheets. The process for combining information from several spreadsheets into another spreadsheet is illustrated in Chapter Six.

In many organizations, the same steps are applied to the development of a spreadsheet each time it is used. For example, an organization may summarize the budget expenditures of three departments into one spreadsheet. In 1–2–3, a *macro* can be developed that instructs the computer to repeat the steps automatically rather than have an individual enter the set of steps each time the spreadsheets are summarized. Students are introduced to the process of creating and using macros in Chapter Seven.

There are many pre-programmed functions available in 1–2–3. In Chapter Eight, many of these functions in Lotus are discussed and illustrated. Functions for statistical analysis, financial analysis, date and time, and for specifying computations based on conditions are included.

Graphs can be prepared using 1–2–3. In Chapter Nine, students learn to create and print a graph. The following types of graphs are covered: bar, line, pie, stacked bar, and XY.

While 1–2–3 is not a database management system, "database like" operations can be applied to data in a spreadsheet. The sorting and querying capabilities of 1–2–3 are explained in Chapter Ten.

In many situations, individuals need to document their spreadsheets. Chapter Eleven includes an explanation of the simple "text processing" capabilities of Lotus 1–2–3.

Appendix A includes basic information on PC-DOS for individuals who need to learn basic DOS commands to perform tasks such as formatting a disk and copying a file from one disk to another. Appendix B contains an outline or "tree" of most of the 1–2–3 menu options.

■ DISTINGUISHING FEATURES

The distinguishing features of this book include the following:

Proven Materials

This book is based on proven materials that have been used in college and university classes as well as training seminars. More than 7,000 individuals have learned to use 1–2–3 using materials upon which this book is based. For example, the authors have been responsible for training more than 4,000 members of the Texas Society of CPAs using materials similar to the ones in this book.

Featuring Lotus 1–2–3 Release 2.01

This text features Lotus 1–2–3 release 2.01, with exercises and examples that will also run under earlier versions of 1–2–3.

Comprehensive Coverage

Students learn the basics as well as advanced topics of 1–2–3. Major topics covered include: creating and printing spreadsheets, templates, combining spreadsheets, macros, special functions, graphics, and database.

Learning through Examples

The book is designed for students to learn through examples rather than learn a series of commands. The materials are built around a series of example problems. Commands are learned for one example. The commands are reinforced and new commands are learned on subsequent examples. The example problems are logically related and integrated throughout the book.

Step-by-Step Instructions and Screen Illustrations

All examples include step-by-step instructions for the student to use. Screen illustrations are used extensively to assist the student in learning to use 1–2–3.

Extensive Exercises

At the end of each chapter, there are exercises that provide comprehensive coverage of the topics introduced in the chapter. Answers for many of the exercises are provided for student use.

Templates

Most experienced users of 1–2–3 make extensive use of templates. This book covers the process of building and using templates.

Macros

As people gain experience using 1–2–3, they often begin to use macros. Much of the power of 1–2–3 is really available to users of macros. This book introduces students to the process of building and using macros. Students create macros and then execute the macros.

Graphics

One of the most powerful options available in 1–2–3 is graphics. Graphs can be very useful in business analysis and presentations. Students learn how to create and print bar, line, stacked bar, XY and pie graphs.

Database Capabilities

While 1–2–3 is not a database management system, it does have some database like commands that can be applied to data in a spreadsheet. Students learn how to sort data and do queries on information that is included in a spreadsheet.

Appendix on DOS

Some students need an introduction to the use of PC-DOS. The book provides an appendix that includes some basic PC-DOS operations and commands.

Emphasis on Business and Organizational Problem Solving

The book includes many example problems that are similar to spreadsheets that may be encountered in a business or other type of organization.

What You Should Know

Each chapter includes a list of key concepts that emphasizes what students should learn in the chapter.

■ ACKNOWLEDGEMENTS

We would like to thank and express our appreciation to the many fine and talented individuals who have contributed to the completion of this book. We have been fortunate to have a group of reviewers whose constructive comments have been helpful in completing the book. Special thanks go to: Augusta Chadwick, Los Angeles Valley College; Elaine Daly, Oakton Community College; Priscilla Grocer, Briston Community College; Prasad Kilari, University of Wisconsin/Superior; Margaret Marx, Tunxis Community College; Thomas McKee, Belmont College; and Paul Ross, Millersville University.

No book is possible without the motivation and support of an editorial staff. Therefore, we wish to acknowledge with greatest appreciation the following people at Boyd & Fraser: Sarah Grover, editor, for the opportunity to write this book and for her constant encouragement; Donna Villanucci, who provided great assistance in the editing process; and the production staff for assistance in completing the book.

We appreciate the assistance provided by Janie Connelly of Napier & Judd, Inc. in the preparation of the initial drafts of the book.

Houston, Texas   H. Albert Napier
January 1988   Philip J. Judd

CHAPTER ONE

GETTING STARTED WITH THE LOTUS 1–2–3 SOFTWARE PACKAGE

OBJECTIVES

In this chapter, the student will learn to:

- Load the Lotus 1–2–3 program into the computer
- Identify the basic features of the 1–2–3 spreadsheet screen
- Move the cell pointer around the spreadsheet
- Use the 1–2–3 menu
- Identify the use of the function keys in 1–2–3

CHAPTER OVERVIEW

This book assumes that the reader has little or no knowledge of Lotus 1–2–3. In this chapter, individuals are introduced to the capabilities of 1–2–3. Typical applications of 1–2–3 are indicated. The hardware requirements for using 1–2–3 are specified. The process for loading the software into a personal computer is explained. The basic items that appear on the 1–2–3 worksheet screen are discussed. The process of moving around the 1–2–3 worksheet is illustrated. The Lotus 1–2–3 menu structure is explained and illustrated. The process of entering information into a spreadsheet is discussed. Finally, an overview of the special functions associated with the function keys is presented.

WHAT IS LOTUS 1–2–3?

Lotus 1–2–3 is an integrated software package. The term integrated means that Lotus has more than one basic capability. Lotus 1–2–3 can be used for creating spreadsheets (interchangeably referred to as worksheets), creating graphs, and manipulating information within and between spreadsheet files. In this book, it is assumed that individuals are using Lotus 1–2–3 Release 2.01. However, if an individual is using an earlier version of Lotus 1–2–3, most of the material presented in this book is still applicable.

An example of a worksheet appears in Figure 1–1. In the next chapter, students are shown how to create and print this spreadsheet. Figure 1–2 is a graph that includes some information from the worksheet in Figure 1–1.

Figure 1–1

```
                          ABC COMPANY
                            BUDGET


                   QTR1     QTR2     QTR3     QTR4   YR TOTAL

      SALES        60,000   61,200   62,424   63,672  247,296

      EXPENSES
        SALARIES   35,000   35,500   36,200   37,000  143,700
        RENT        9,000    9,000    9,000    9,000   36,000
        TELEPHONE   1,000    1,050    1,103    1,158    4,311
        OFFICE SUPPLIES 750    800      850      900    3,300
        MISCELLANEOUS 1,000  1,030    1,061    1,093    4,184
                   --------  -------- -------- --------
        TOTAL EXPENSES 46,750  47,380   48,214   49,151  191,495
                   --------  -------- -------- --------
      GROSS PROFIT 13,250   13,820   14,210   14,521   55,801
                   ========  ======== ======== ========  ========
```

Up to six items such as SALES can appear on a graph. Graphs other than bar charts can be developed.

Figure 1–2

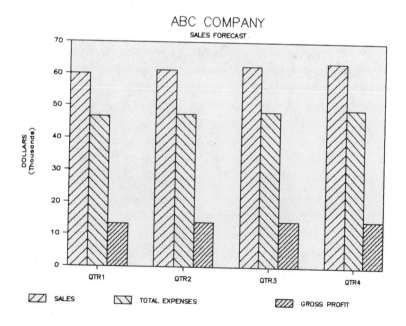

Lotus 1–2–3 can also be used to perform operations on a file. For example, information in a file can be sorted by various criteria. Figure 1–3 is a file that has information on salaries for a group of individuals that is not sorted in any particular order.

Figure 1–3

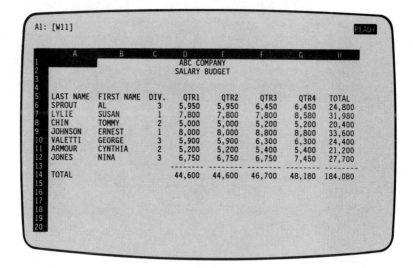

Sometimes it is desirable to sort the information into a particular order. In Figure 1–4, the data that appears in Figure 1–3 has been sorted in ascending order by division number.

Figure 1–4

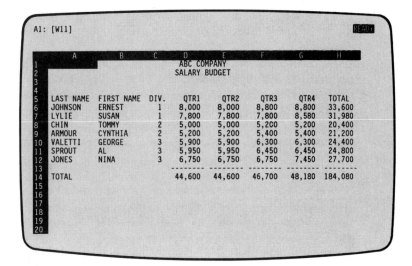

■ TYPICAL APPLICATIONS

Lotus 1–2–3 is used in many organizations as well as for personal use. Some examples of applications of Lotus 1–2–3 include:

> Advertising expense forecast
> Balance sheet forecasts
> Budgets
> Cash flow analysis
> Checkbook balancing
> Depreciation schedules
> Household expenses
> Income statement forecasts
> Income tax projections
> Income tax records
> Inventory forecasting
> Job bids and costing
> Sports analysis
> Stock portfolio analysis and records

■ HARDWARE REQUIREMENTS

To use Lotus 1–2–3, a user must have a microcomputer with a minimum of 256K of main memory. It is recommended that the user have two floppy disk drives or one floppy disk drive and a hard disk. A monochrome or color monitor can be used with Lotus

1–2–3. A color monitor is particularly useful if an individual wants to see better quality graphics. It may be necessary to purchase a graphics card in order to view graphics on the screen.

A printer is also necessary. A dot matrix printer provides the capability of printing spreadsheets as well as graphs. Most letter quality and laser printers do not provide a full range of graphics printing capabilities. If high quality graphics are desired, a plotter is necessary.

Blank diskettes that have been appropriately formatted are also needed. These diskettes can be used to store spreadsheets and graphs on files to be used at a later time.

■ SOFTWARE REQUIREMENTS

The Lotus 1–2–3 diskettes on which the software is stored are needed. The software package includes 4 diskettes. The diskettes are labeled: System Disk, Backup System Disk, PrintGraph Disk, and Utility Disk. The PC-DOS system (often referred to as simply DOS) software disk is also needed. If a hard disk is used, the DOS software and the Lotus software can be stored on the hard disk to expedite the processing of the software. To install the DOS and 1–2–3 software properly on the hard disk, see the DOS reference manuals that come with the personal computer being used and the Lotus 1–2–3 reference manuals that come with the Lotus 1–2–3 software.

■ LOADING THE LOTUS 1–2–3 SOFTWARE PACKAGE

Before attempting to load Lotus 1–2–3 into the memory of the microcomputer, all connections need to be checked. Make sure the monitor and printer are properly installed. The power cord should be connected to an appropriate electric outlet.

To turn on or "boot" the computer:

Insert	the DOS System disk in drive A
Turn on	the computer

The power switch is typically located on the right side panel of the processing unit or on the front of the processing unit.

After a number of seconds, the following message will appear on the screen:

```
Current date is Tue 1-01-1980
Enter new date (mm-dd-yy):
```

When prompted, as indicated above, to enter the new date:

Type   today's date using a mm-dd-yy format (you do not need
                to input the day of the week)

Press   ⏎

Figure 1–5 illustrates the process of entering a date.

Figure 1–5

```
Current date is Tue  1-01-1980
Enter new date (mm-dd-yy): 07/27/87
```

Note that Figure 1–5 shows the screen before the ⏎ key is pressed.
    Now the system will display the default time on the screen and ask that the user enter the correct time. When prompted to enter the new time:

Type   the present time using the international time format, e.g.
                8:01 for 8:01 a.m. or 13:05 for 1:05 p.m.

Press   ⏎

The results of entering the time and pressing the ⏎ key appear in Figure 1–6.

Figure 1–6

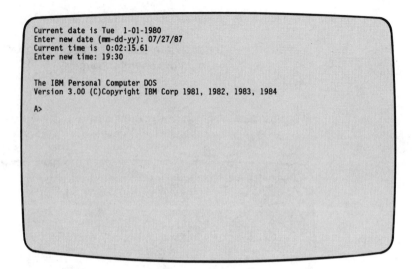

```
Current date is Tue  1-01-1980
Enter new date (mm-dd-yy): 07/27/87
Current time is  0:02:15.61
Enter new time: 19:30


The IBM Personal Computer DOS
Version 3.00 (C)Copyright IBM Corp 1981, 1982, 1983, 1984

A>
```

Note that additional information appears on the screen indicating that the DOS system has been loaded.

To load Lotus 1–2–3:

Remove	the DOS System disk from drive A
Insert	the Lotus 1–2–3 System disk in drive A
Type	LOTUS ↵

Lotus 1–2–3 takes the user to the initial Lotus menu. The initial menu for 1–2–3 appears in Figure 1–7.

Figure 1–7

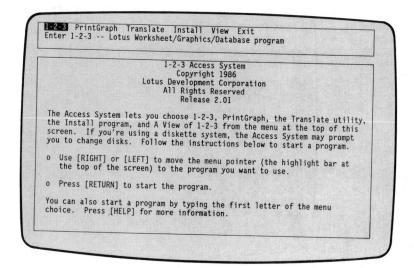

The menu at the top of the screen has the sets of characters 1–2–3, PrintGraph, Translate, Install, View and Exit. Notice that the characters 1–2–3 are highlighted with a rectangle. Below 1–2–3 appears the message "Enter 1–2–3—Lotus Worksheet/Graphics/Database program" indicating that this program will be entered if the 1–2–3 option is selected from the menu.

The menu structure will be illustrated in more detail later in this chapter. To select the "Enter 1–2–3—Lotus Worksheet/Graphics/Database program":

Press   ⏎

A message asking the user to Please wait . . . then appears on the screen followed in a few seconds by the Lotus 1–2–3 logo and some copyright information. A blank worksheet like the one in Figure 1–8 then appears on the screen in another few seconds.

Figure 1–8

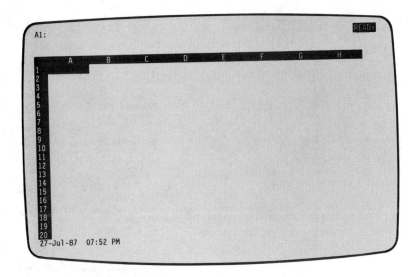

THE LOTUS 1–2–3 SPREADSHEET (WORKSHEET) SCREEN

Figure 1–8 is the standard form of the initial **worksheet** used by Lotus when it is loaded. The terms **spreadsheet** and **worksheet** are used interchangeably in this book. It is a grid-like structure consisting of rows and columns. Figure 1–9 is a worksheet screen after the main menu of Lotus 1–2–3 has been placed on the screen.

Figure 1–9

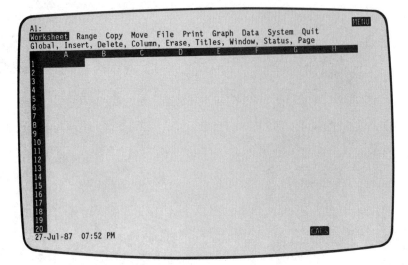

In this section various items that appear on the worksheet screen in Figure 1–9 are discussed.

Row Numbers

On the left border of the worksheet on the screen is a set of numbers called **row numbers.** Note that there are 20 rows appearing on the screen. There are a total of 8,192 rows available in the worksheet.

Column Letters

Across the top border of the worksheet on the screen is the set of letters A through H. These are the **column letters.** There are 256 columns in the worksheet. The columns are identified with the letters A through Z, AA through AZ, BA through BZ and so forth until the letter IV is reached.

Cell

A **cell** is the area on a worksheet that occurs at the intersection of a column and a row. For example, the area where column A intersects with row 1 is called cell A1. Data can be stored in a cell. Initially, each cell is wide enough to display 9 characters.

Cell Pointer

Notice on the screen that cell A1 is highlighted by a rectangular form. The item highlighting cell A1 is called the **cell pointer.** The cell pointer can be moved from cell to cell in the worksheet. Whenever information is input to the worksheet, it is placed in the cell highlighted by the cell pointer.

Current Cell

The **current cell** is highlighted by the cell pointer. The next data entry or operation affects this cell.

Cell Address

The location of a cell is called the **cell address.** A cell address is defined by a column letter followed by a row number. For example B2 is the cell address for the cell that occurs at the intersection of column B and row 2.

Control Panel

Above the worksheet at the top of the screen is an area called the **control panel.** The control panel consists of three lines. The first line has the cell address for the current cell, the contents of the cell, and some other information that is discussed later in the book. Notice at the top left side of the screen, there is a cell address. Assuming you have a blank worksheet and the cell pointer is in cell A1, then the cell address area on the first line of the control panel will say A1: and there will be blank spaces immediately to the right.

The second line of the control panel displays the current data when the contents of a cell are being created or edited. It is also used to display the main Lotus 1–2–3 menu when the command key (the / key) is pressed.

The third line of the control panel is used to display either a submenu or a one line description of the command item currently highlighted on the second line of the control panel.

Mode Indicator

The **mode indicator** appears in the top right corner of the control panel area of the worksheet. It indicates the current operating mode. For example, it may say READY indicating that 1–2–3 is ready to input information or create a formula. If it says MENU, then a menu appears on the screen and a selection can be made from the menu.

Status Indicator

The **status indicator** specifies the condition of certain keys or of the program. For example, if the Caps Lock key is pressed the characters CAPS will appear in the right corner below the worksheet indicating that all alphabetic characters subsequently used are automatically capitalized. To remove the CAPS specification, an individual needs only to press the Caps Lock key again and the CAPS indicator no longer appears on the screen.

Date and Time Indicator

At the bottom left side of the screen the date and time appear. Assuming the current date and time have been entered properly, the current date and time should appear. Lotus 1–2–3 has an option that allows the user to suppress the date and time indicator from view.

◼ MOVING AROUND THE SPREADSHEET

As indicated earlier in this chapter, the cell pointer is the highlighted rectangle on the screen that indicates the location on the worksheet. The cell address of the cell pointer's location always appears in the top left corner of the worksheet. In this section, methods to move the cell pointer on the worksheet are discussed and illustrated.

Using the Arrow Keys to Move the Cell Pointer

The arrow keys, which are the basic keys used to move the cell pointer from cell to cell on the worksheet, are located on the right side of the keyboard (see Figure 1–10). The arrow keys are placed either on the numeric keypad (sometimes called "the ten key") or they may be in separate location.

Figure 1–10

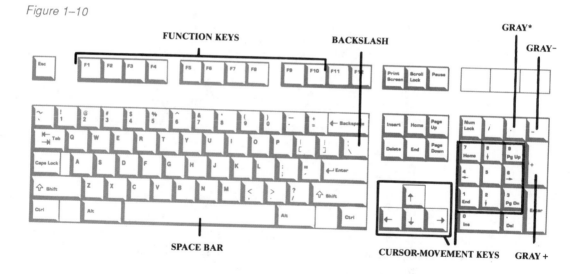

To illustrate the use of the arrow keys:

Locate the arrow keys

Press the key with the arrow pointing to the right seven times.

The key with the arrow pointing to the right is called the "right arrow" key. As illustrated in Figure 1–11, the cell pointer is now in cell H1. This fact is indicated on the first line of the control panel. The process of moving around the screen is sometimes called "scrolling".

Figure 1–11

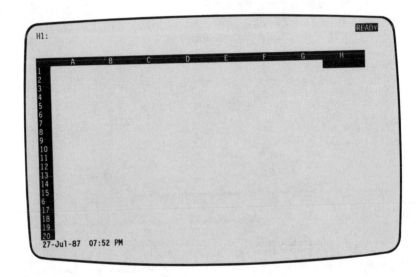

To move the cell pointer to cell I1:

Press the right arrow key one time

As illustrated in Figure 1–12, the cell pointer has been moved to Column I and Column A has disappeared. 1–2–3 can only display a total of 72 characters on the screen and no portion of a column is displayed unless the entire column can be shown on the screen.

Figure 1–12

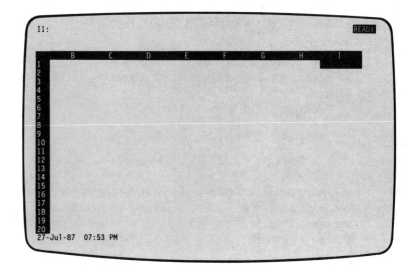

To move to cell A1:

Locate   the left arrow key

Press   the left arrow key eight times or until the cell pointer
              appears in cell A1

If the left arrow key is pressed too many times, a "beep" sound will be heard indicating that the user is trying to move to the left of column A. Anytime the "beep" sound occurs, it indicates that a user is trying to perform some type of operation that is not permitted at that point.

To move the cell pointer rapidly:

Locate   the down arrow key

Press   the down arrow key and hold it down

After the cell pointer has moved down 20 or 30 rows stop depressing the down arrow key.

To return the cell pointer to cell A1:

Locate   the up arrow key

Press   the up arrow key until the cell pointer appears in cell A1

A "beep" sound may be heard if the up arrow key has been depressed too long.

Using the [PgDn] and [PgUp] Keys to Move the Cell Pointer

The cell pointer key can be moved up and down one screen at a time using the [PgUp] and [PgDn] keys. [PgDn] stands for "Page Down" and [PgUp] means "Page Up". These keys permit a 1–2–3 user to move the cell pointer up and down the screen 20 rows at a time.

To use the [PgDn] key:

Locate   the [PgDn] key

Press   the [PgDn] key

Assuming that the cell pointer was in cell A1 prior to pressing the [PgDn] key, then the cell pointer is now in cell A21. See Figure 1–13. If the cell pointer was not in cell A1, then the cell pointer is now in a cell that is 20 rows farther down in the worksheet from the cell it was in prior to pressing the [PgDn] key.

Figure 1–13

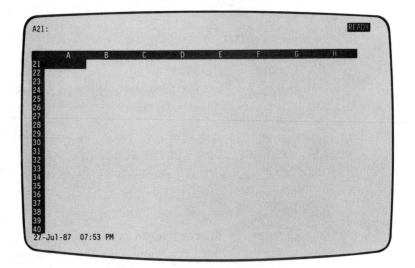

To use the [PgUp] key:

Locate   the [PgUp] key

Press   the [PgUp] key

Assuming that the cell pointer was in cell A21 prior to pressing the [PgUp] key, the cell pointer should now be in cell A1. If the cell pointer was not in cell A21, then the cell pointer is now 20 rows up in the worksheet.

Using the Tab Key to Move the Cell Pointer

The cell pointer can be moved to the right or left one screen at a time using the Tab key.

To move the cell pointer one screen to the right:

Make	sure the cell pointer is in cell A1
Locate	the Tab key (it is usually to the left of the letter Q)
Press	the Tab key

As illustrated in Figure 1–14, the cell pointer has been moved to the right one screen and now appears in cell I1.

Figure 1–14

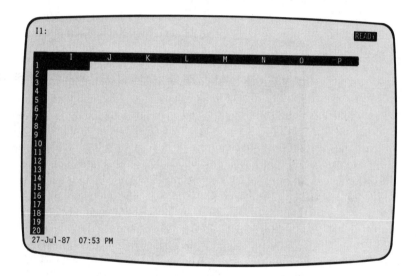

To move the cell pointer one screen to the left:

Make	sure the cell pointer is in cell I1
Locate	the Tab key
Hold	a Shift key down
Press	the Tab key

The cell pointer has been moved to cell A1 or one screen to the left. The shift key is marked with the ⇑ sign or with the word Shift. There are two shift keys on a keyboard.

Using the [GoTo] Key (the F5 Function Key) to Move the Cell Pointer

Sometimes it is necessary to move the cell pointer to a particular cell in the worksheet. For example, to move the cursor to cell IV8192:

Make	sure the cell pointer is in cell A1
Locate	the F5 function key (the F5 key is usually on the left side of the keyboard or at the top of keyboard)
Press	the F5 key

As displayed in Figure 1–15, the screen now has a message in the control panel prompting the user to enter the cell address desired.

Figure 1–15

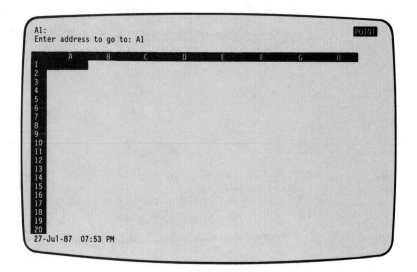

Type	IV8192 ↵

Figure 1–16 illustrates the entering of cell address IV8192.

Figure 1-16

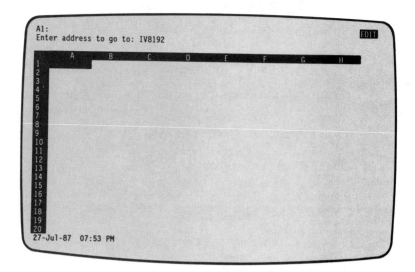

Press   ↵

As illustrated in Figure 1-17, the cell pointer is now in cell IV8192.

Figure 1-17

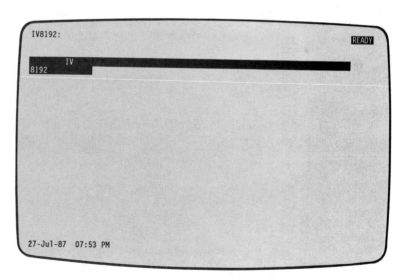

Cell IV8192 is the cell in the bottom right corner of the worksheet. In other words, column IV is the last column in the worksheet and row 8192 is the last row in the worksheet.

Using the Home Key to Move the Cell Pointer

The cell pointer can be moved to the top left corner by pressing the Home key. To illustrate the use of the Home key:

Locate the Home key (it is usually on the numeric/directional keypad or on the right side of the keyboard)

Press the Home key

The cell pointer is now in cell A1.

■ LOTUS 1–2–3 MENU STRUCTURE

Earlier in this chapter, the menu structure was mentioned. In this section, the menu structure is discussed and illustrated.

To display the main 1–2–3 menu:

Press the slash (/) key

The main 1–2–3 menu is now on the screen. Notice the word MENU now appears in the Mode indicator. See Figure 1–18.

Figure 1–18

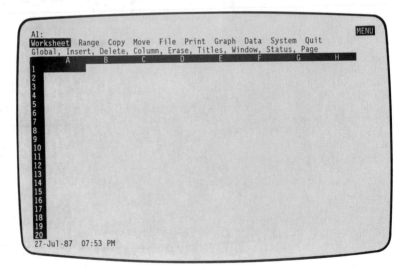

The menu appears on the second line of the control panel. The Worksheet option on the menu is highlighted. The submenu that will be used if the Worksheet option is selected appears on the third line of the control panel.

Other options on the main menu include Range, Copy, Move, File, Print, Graph, Data, System, and Quit. The options are used to perform a variety of operations on a worksheet. Many of these operations are illustrated in the remainder of this book.

To remove the Main menu from the screen:

Press   the Esc key

Esc stands for escape. It can be used to "back up" one level in the menu structure. In this situation, since the main menu is displayed on the screen, the main menu will disappear.

Using the Menu Structure

To illustrate the use of the menu structure, information is entered in cell A1 and then the worksheet is erased.

To specify some information to be entered in cell A1:

Make   sure the cell pointer is in cell A1
Type   Lotus

The word Lotus now appears on the second line of the control panel. Notice that when the first character is typed the word LABEL appears in the Mode indicator indicating that a label is being entered. See Figure 1–19.

Figure 1–19

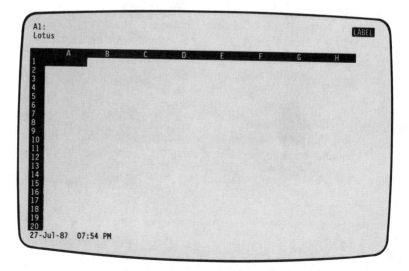

To enter the information in cell A1:

Press ↵

The word Lotus now appears in cell A1. See Figure 1–20.

Figure 1–20

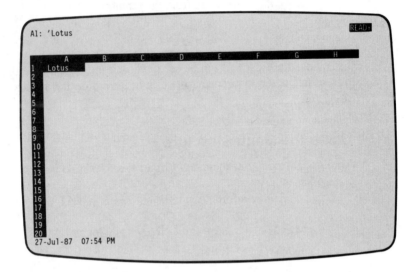

Note that all labels are "left justified" in a cell. In other words, the characters begin at the left most position in the cell. When a number is entered, the Mode indicator says VALUE and the number is "right justified" in the cell when the ↵ is pressed; that is, the number appears in the right most portion of the cell.

Notice that the characters 'Lotus appear next to the cell address A1 on the first line in the control panel. The ' is the symbol that means label in 1–2–3 and Lotus is the information stored in cell A1.

To erase the entire worksheet:

Press the / key

At this point the main menu appears on the screen as it appears in Figure 1–21. The menu structure works by moving the menu pointer to the menu option that is desired and pressing the ↵ key.

Figure 1-21

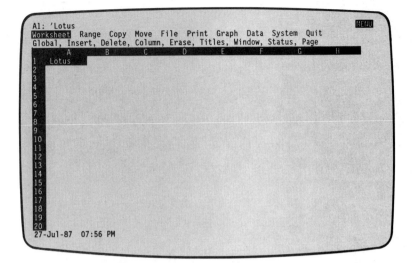

The menu pointer is a rectangular shape that is similar to the cell pointer. It is used to highlight the options on a menu. Since it is desired to use the Worksheet option, the cell pointer does not need to be moved and the ↵ key can be pressed.

Press ↵

The submenu that previously appeared on the third line of the control panel now appears on the second line of the control panel and becomes the menu that is in use. See Figure 1-22. Note that the menu pointer is on the word Global.

Figure 1–22

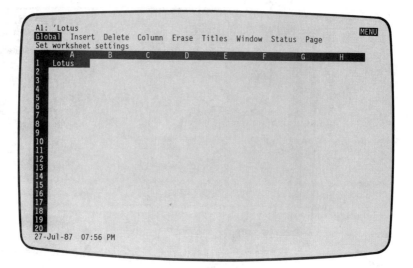

The next step in the process of erasing the worksheet on the screen is to move the menu pointer to the Erase menu option. See Figure 1–23.

To move the menu pointer to the Erase option:

Press   the right arrow key until the menu pointer is on the word Erase

Figure 1–23

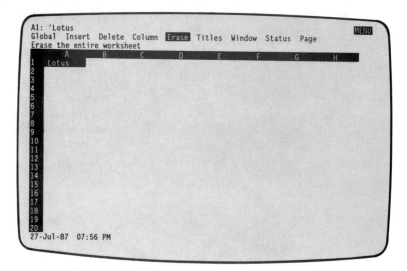

To complete the process of erasing the worksheet:

Press   ↵

Figure 1–24 illustrates that 1–2–3 gives the user the option of making sure it is desirable to erase the worksheet. If the ↵ is pressed while the No option is highlighted, then 1–2–3 returns to the READY mode and the worksheet is **not** erased.

Figure 1–24

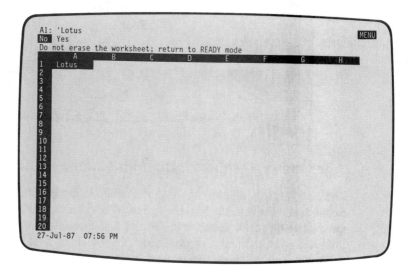

The final steps in the process for erasing the worksheet are:

Press   the right arrow key to move the menu pointer to the word Yes. Notice the explanation of the option on the third line of the control panel that indicates the worksheet will be erased if the Yes menu option is selected.

Press   ↵

A blank worksheet now appears on the screen. The screen should appear exactly like the one in Figure 1–25.

Figure 1–25

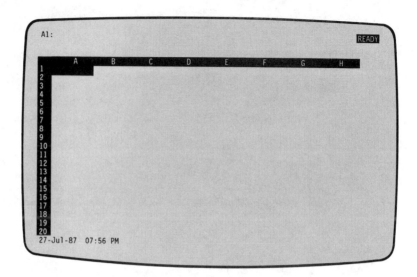

Alternative Method for Using the Menu Structure

The standard way of using the menu structure is explained in the previous section. Recall that when a menu is on the screen, to select a particular menu option, the user must move the menu pointer to the appropriate menu option and press the ↵ key. In this section, an alternative approach for using the menu structure is illustrated.

To illustrate the alternative method, the process for erasing a worksheet is repeated. To place the word Lotus in cell A1:

Make	sure the cell pointer is in cell A1
Type	Lotus ↵

The screen should now look like Figure 1–26.

Figure 1–26

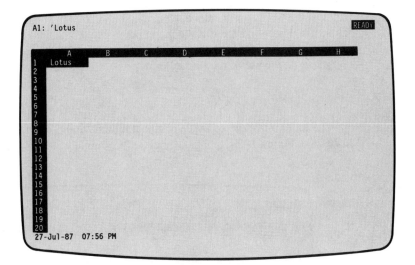

To begin the process of erasing the screen:

Press   the command key (the / key)

The slash key is referred to as the **command key** because the initial set of command options appear as the main menu. The screen should now look like Figure 1–27.

Figure 1–27

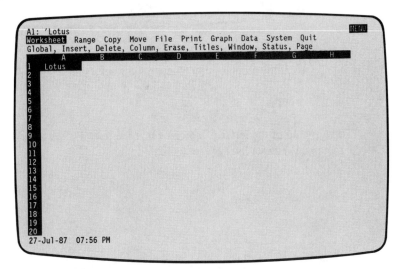

Look at the words on the menu. Notice that none of the words start with the same first character. Rather than move the menu pointer to the desired menu option, a user can press the letter on the keyboard corresponding to the first letter of the word in the menu. To illustrate the use of the first letter:

Type W

The letter W activates the Worksheet option on the main menu. The screen now looks like Figure 1–28.

Figure 1–28

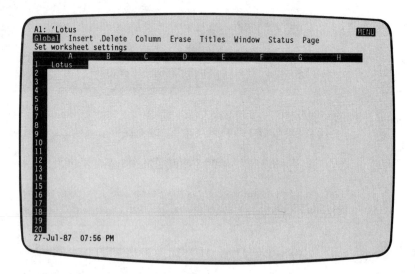

To select the menu option to erase the worksheet:

Type E

The typing of the letter E indicates that the user desires to select the Erase option on the menu. The screen now looks like Figure 1–29.

Figure 1–29

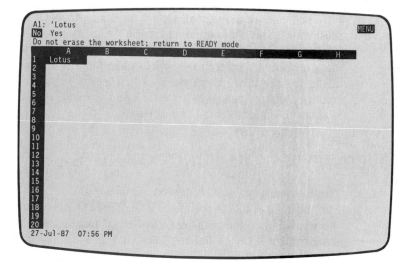

To select the menu option Yes and complete the process for erasing the worksheet:

Type   Y

By typing Y, the user indicates that the worksheet does in fact need to be erased. A blank screen like the one in Figure 1–30 should now appear on the screen.

Figure 1–30

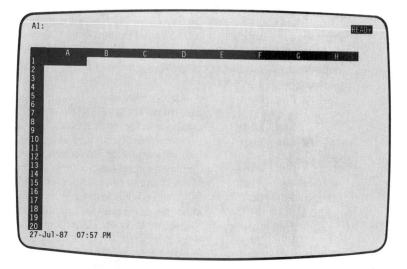

In this text, the alternative method for using the menu structure is utilized in the illustrations. This approach saves time in the creation of worksheets. Initially, it may be advantageous for the user of the text to move the menu pointer to the appropriate menu option and then press the ↵ key. Once the user is comfortable with the way the menus are structured, then the use of first letters for selecting menu options can be employed. After Lotus 1–2–3 is used for a short while, most individuals use the first letter approach for selecting menu options.

■ OVERVIEW OF THE FUNCTION KEYS

The function keys have been "programmed" in Lotus 1–2–3 to perform specific operations. One of these operations is the "GoTo" function, associated with the F5 key, illustrated earlier in this chapter. The "Help" function, located on the F1 key, allows the user to access an on-line reference for 1–2–3 features on the screen. To access the Help menu:

Press   the F1 key

The Help menu appears. To get help on specific topics, choose one of the highlighted menu options listed on the screen (Formula or Number, Label, Command, etc.). Use the arrow keys to move the cursor to the desired option. When the desired option is highlighted, press ↵ . To leave the Help option and return to the spreadsheet currently in use:

Press   the [Esc] key

Pressing the Escape key exits the Help feature.

Many of the function keys will be used in the exercises in subsequent chapters. A brief description of the operations programmed for the function keys follows.

Alt F1:	**Compose**	Used in conjunction with keystrokes to input characters that are not on the standard keyboard
F1:	**Help**	Display Help screens that are available in Lotus 1–2–3
Alt F2:	**Step**	Perform macros one step at a time
F2:	**Edit**	Switch to/from Edit Mode for current entry
F3:	**Name**	Display menu of range names
F4:	**Abs**	Make/Unmake cell address "absolute"
F5:	**GoTo**	Move cell pointer to a particular cell
F6:	**Window**	Move cell pointer when "windows" appear on the screen
F7:	**Query**	Repeat most recent Data Query operation
F8:	**Table**	Repeat most recent Data Table operation
F9:	**Calc**	Recalculate worksheet values
F10:	**Graph**	Draw graph on screen using the most recent graph specifications

SUMMARY

In this chapter, an overview of Lotus 1–2–3 is included. Lotus 1–2–3 is often used for business, government, and personal applications. Microcomputer hardware is required to process 1–2–3. Lotus 1–2–3 can be executed on IBM or IBM compatible PCs and other brands of microcomputers. The actual 1–2–3 software is on a set of diskettes. The software can be loaded into the main memory using the diskettes or it can be read from a hard disk. The key items on the worksheet screen are row numbers, column letters, cells, cell pointer, current cell, cell address, control panel, mode indicator, status indicator, date indicator, and the time indicator. The cell pointer can be moved around the worksheet by using the arrow keys, the [PgDn] and [PgUp] keys, the tab keys and the F5 function key. Lotus 1–2–3 has a set of menus containing various operations that can be applied to a worksheet. There are two ways to use the menu structure in 1–2–3. There are a set of function keys (F1 through F10) that are preprogrammed in Lotus 1–2–3 to perform specific operations such as moving to a specific cell in a worksheet.

KEY CONCEPTS

Cell
Cell Address
Cell Pointer
Column Letters
Command Key
Control Panel
Current Cell
Date Indicator
Function Keys
[GoTo]

Hardware Requirements for 1–2–3
[Help]
Menu Structure
Mode Indicator
Row Numbers
Software Requirements for 1–2–3
Status Indicator
Time Indicator
Worksheet
Worksheet Erase Yes

CHAPTER ONE
EXERCISE 1

INSTRUCTIONS: Answer the following questions in the space provided.

1. Define the following terms:

    a. Row Numbers _____

    _____

    b. Column Letters _____

    _____

    c. Cell _____

    _____

    d. Cell Pointer _____

    _____

    e. Current Cell _____

    _____

    f. Cell Address _____

    _____

    g. Control Panel _____

    _____

    h. Mode Indicator _____

    _____

    i. Status Indicator _____

    _____

    j. Date Indicator _____

    _____

    k. Time Indicator _____

    _____

    l. Worksheet _____

    _____

2. Describe the standard way of using the 1–2–3 menu structure.

    _____

    _____

    _____

    _____

3. Describe the alternative method of using the 1–2–3 menu structure.

_____

_____

_____

_____

4. Describe the purpose of using the function keys F1 through F10.

_____

_____

_____

_____

CHAPTER ONE
EXERCISE 2

INSTRUCTIONS: Identify the circled and enclosed items on the worksheet in Figure 1–31.

Figure 1–31

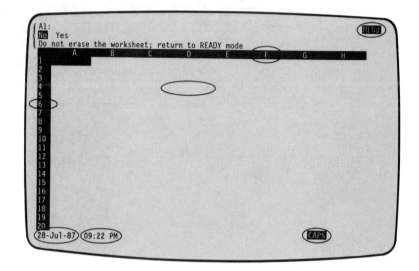

CHAPTER ONE
EXERCISE 3

INSTRUCTIONS: 1. Create the worksheet displayed in Figure 1–32.

Figure 1–32

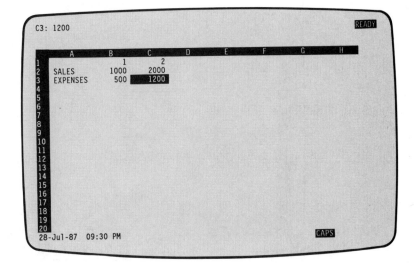

2. Erase the worksheet using the standard method (highlighting the menu option and pressing ↵).

CHAPTER ONE
EXERCISE 4

INSTRUCTIONS: Create the worksheet displayed in Figure 1–33.

Figure 1–33

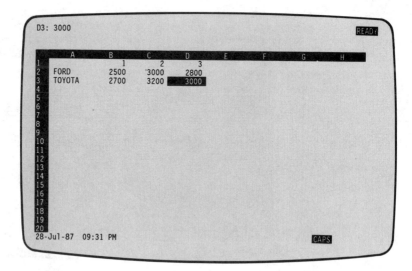

2. Erase the worksheet using the alternate method (pressing the first letter of the menu option name).

CHAPTER TWO

CREATING A SPREADSHEET (WORKSHEET)

OBJECTIVES

In this chapter, the student will learn to:

- Create, print, and save a spreadsheet
- Prevent rounding errors
- Print the cell formulas used to create the spreadsheet
- Use different numeric formats
- Make a backup of the spreadsheet file

CHAPTER OVERVIEW

One of the difficulties the beginning Lotus 1–2–3 user faces when first learning to create a spreadsheet is how to begin! Chapter Two cites an example problem and provides a step-by-step procedure for how to solve the problem with a Lotus 1–2–3 spreadsheet. While guiding the user through the process for building the spreadsheet, the exercise provides information about 1–2–3 capabilities *at the time the user needs them.* After the spreadsheet is created, the user can complete subsequent exercises for printing and storing the spreadsheet on a disk.

Additional exercises address typical problems for the beginning user: how to solve rounding problems, how to print the cell formulas used in the spreadsheet, how to change the numeric display of the spreadsheet, and how to make a backup copy of the spreadsheet file.

EXAMPLE PROBLEM

The spreadsheet in this chapter will project sales for the last three quarters of a year based upon the data from the first quarter. The information from the first quarter and the projections are as follows:

	1st Quarter	Projected Increase Per Quarter
Sales	$60,000	2%
Salaries	35,000	(given below)
Rent	9,000	(constant for all periods)
Telephone	1,000	5%
Office Supplies	750	$50
Miscellaneous	1,000	3%

The salary amounts for the quarters are as follows: $35,000; $35,500; $36,200; $37,000.

To complete the problem cited above, a common procedure for creating a spreadsheet using 1–2–3 will be followed. The procedure is outlined in the following.

Creating Labels for the Spreadsheet
Correcting Errors
Expanding the Width of a Column
Entering Numbers, Formulas, and Copying Information in a Spreadsheet
Selecting a Format for the Data
Inserting Blank Rows for Headings
Entering Headings
Inserting Blank Rows within a Spreadsheet
Entering Underlines and Double Underlines

A printout of the completed spreadsheet is displayed in Figure 2–1.

Figure 2–1

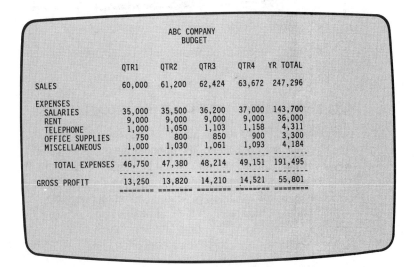

```
                            ABC COMPANY
                              BUDGET


                   QTR1      QTR2      QTR3      QTR4    YR TOTAL

        SALES      60,000    61,200    62,424    63,672  247,296

        EXPENSES
          SALARIES 35,000    35,500    36,200    37,000  143,700
          RENT      9,000     9,000     9,000     9,000   36,000
          TELEPHONE 1,000     1,050     1,103     1,158    4,311
          OFFICE SUPPLIES 750   800       850       900    3,300
          MISCELLANEOUS 1,000  1,030     1,061     1,093    4,184
                    --------  --------  --------  -------- --------
        TOTAL EXPENSES 46,750 47,380    48,214    49,151  191,495
                    --------  --------  --------  -------- --------
        GROSS PROFIT 13,250   13,820    14,210    14,521   55,801
                    ========  ========  ========  ======== ========
```

■ BUILDING THE SPREADSHEET

It is assumed that the microcomputer is turned on and that Lotus 1–2–3 has been loaded. A blank spreadsheet should be displayed on the screen (Figure 2–2).

Figure 2–2

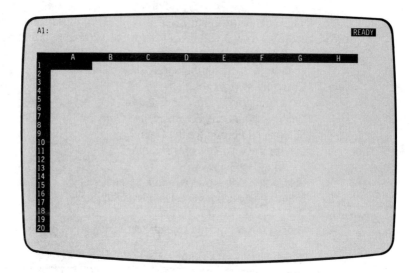

If the screen needs to be erased, refer to the instructions in the previous chapter to clear the screen.

Creating Labels for the Spreadsheet

The term label refers to non-numeric data. Note that even numbers can be made into labels if they are not needed in computations (refer to the section on label prefixes in Chapter Four). Labels will be entered beginning in cell A1 to describe the contents of each row. Rows will be inserted later for the worksheet titles and headings.

To make all of the labels appear in capital letters, make sure that "CAPS" appears at the bottom of the screen. If the Caps Lock key needs to be activated:

      Press   the [Caps Lock] key

"CAPS" should appear at the lower right corner of the screen. All of the alphabetic characters typed will be capital letters. (To turn the CAPS feature off, tap the [Caps Lock] key again to "toggle" the feature off).

The cell pointer should be in cell A1. If it is not, use the arrow keys located to the right of the keyboard to move the cell pointer.

Enter the labels in column A. The first label is SALES. To enter the label SALES in cell A1:

      Type   SALES

At the upper right corner of the screen, the mode indicator message changes from READY to LABEL. When data is first entered, the 1–2–3 program looks at the first character and judges the entry to be either a LABEL or a VALUE. Since the first character of SALES is non-numeric, the entry will be considered a label. Never precede numbers that will be used in computation with spaces or other non-numeric characters, or 1–2–3 will interpret the entry to be a label.

To enter the label SALES:

Press ↵

SALES has been entered in cell A1. The mode indicator changes back to READY.

To input the label EXPENSES in cell A2:

Move the cell pointer to cell A2

Type EXPENSES ↵

To input the label SALARIES in cell A3:

Move the cell pointer to cell A3

To indent the label:

Press the space bar twice

Type SALARIES

Pressing the space bar is an easy way to indent labels. Note that from this point on, the instructions utilize a "short cut" for entering labels. Instead of pressing ↵ , press the down arrow key to enter a label AND move to the next cell.

Press the down arrow key

With one keystroke, the label SALARIES has been entered AND the cell pointer has been moved to the next cell.

The cell pointer should now be in cell A4. To enter the next label:

Press the space bar twice

Type RENT

Press the down arrow key

The cell pointer should now be in cell A5. To enter the next label:

Press	the space bar twice
Type	TELEPHONE
Press	the down arrow key

The cell pointer should now be in cell A6. To enter the next label:

Press	the space bar twice
Type	OFFICE SUPPLIES
Press	the down arrow key

The cell pointer should now be in cell A7. To enter the next label:

Press	the space bar twice
Type	MISCELLANEOUS
Press	the down arrow key

The cell pointer should now be in cell A8. To enter the next label:

Press	the space bar four times
Type	TOTAL EXPENSES
Press	the down arrow key

The cell pointer should now be in cell A9. To enter the next label:

Type	GROSS PROFIT ↵

The down arrow key did not have to be pressed because Gross Profit is the last label on the spreadsheet. The worksheet should look like Figure 2–3. If corrections need to be made, refer to the next exercise to correct any errors.

Figure 2–3

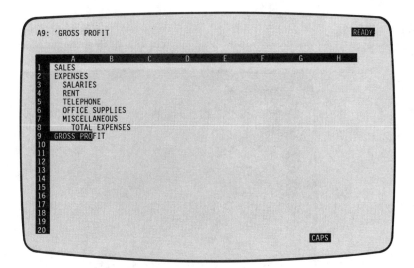

Correcting Errors

If an entry has been misspelled:

Move   the cell pointer to the cell displaying the error

Type   the entry correctly ↵

Refer to Figure 2–4 to see an example. In Figure 2–4, the word EXPENSES in cell A2 is spelled EXPANSES. To correct the error, move the cell pointer to cell A2, type EXPENSES, and press ↵ . The error is replaced with the correction.

Figure 2–4
Part 1

REPLACING AN INCORRECT ENTRY

Move the cell pointer to the cell containing the error and type the desired
entry ...

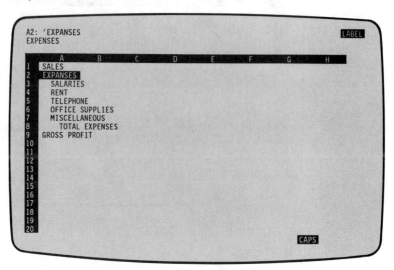

Figure 2–4
Part 2

then press ↵ after typing the correction to replace the previous entry
(EXPANSES is changed to EXPENSES in cell a2).

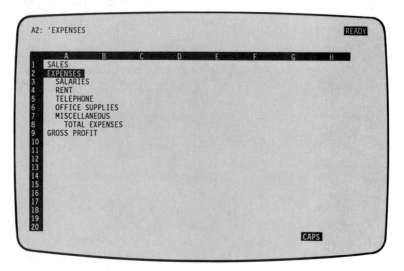

The Escape key (marked [Esc] on the keyboard) can be used to cancel data entered
in the control panel if the ↵ key has not yet been pressed. The Escape key may also
be used to exit from a 1–2–3 menu. An alternative to pressing the Escape key several

times (for example, to exit several levels of menus) is to hold down the [Ctrl] key and tap the [Break] key.

If other errors have been made, clear the screen and begin the exercises again. If necessary, refer to the previous chapter for the instructions to clear a screen. Additional ways to correct errors are discussed in Chapter Four.

Expanding the Width of a Column

Several labels extend into column B. In order to enter data in column B and still see all of the labels in column A, first widen column A. To widen column A:

Move the cell pointer to the longest label in the column

In this example, move to cell A8, which has the indented label TOTAL EXPENSES. Access the Lotus 1–2–3 menu to select the options for expanding a column.

Press	/	(the command key)
Type	W	(for Worksheet)
Type	C	(for Column)
Type	S	(for Set-Width)
Press	the right arrow key until the entire label is highlighted by the cell pointer	

In the control panel, the message "Enter column width (1 .. 240): 18" should be displayed in the control panel (Figure 2–5).

Figure 2–5

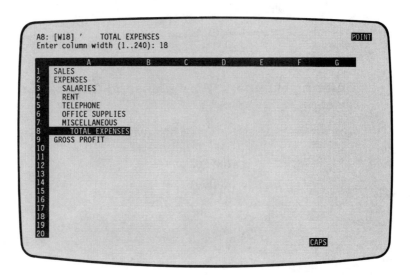

When the entire label is highlighted:

Press ⏎

The column width of column A is now 18 characters (refer to Figure 2–6). Column B has "shifted" to the right and column H has been scrolled off the screen, because column A occupies more screen space. Note that when the prompt "Enter column width (1 .. 240):" appears, the user does not have to highlight the desired width, but can type the desired column width (such as 18) and press ⏎ . The column width can be set from 1 character to 240 characters.

When the cell pointer is in any cell in column A, the control panel will display [W18], indicating that a column width of 18 was set for the column.

Figure 2–6

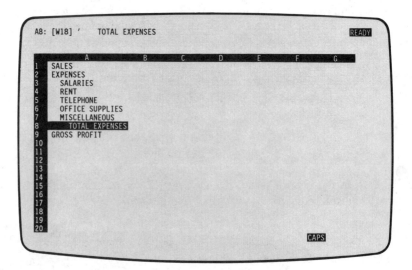

Entering Numbers, Formulas, and Copying Information in a Spreadsheet

To enter the Sales amount for the first quarter:

| **Move** | the cell pointer to cell B1 |
| **Type** | 60000 |

Because 60000 is numeric, it is interpreted by Lotus 1–2–3 as a **value.** The mode indicator at the upper right corner of the screen displays the message VALUE. To enter the number:

Press ↵

The formula for the second quarter of Sales multiplies the Sales amount in the first quarter by 1.02 to show a 2% projected increase. First place the cell pointer in the cell where the formula will be entered.

Move the cell pointer to cell C1

Begin typing the formula:

Type +
Move the cell pointer to cell B1 (Sales)
Type *

The asterisk (*) is the symbol for multiplication.

Type 1.02 ↵

The number 61200 should now appear in cell C1. With cell C1 highlighted, look at the control panel at the upper left corner of the screen. The formula +B1*1.02 should be displayed. This is the formula used to compute the number 61200 (Figure 2–7). A formula can be typed directly into a cell. For example, typing +B1*1.02 at cell C1 and pressing ↵ would obtain the same result.

Note: *See Appendix B for an explanation of the order of precedence for mathematical operators in a formula.*

Figure 2–7

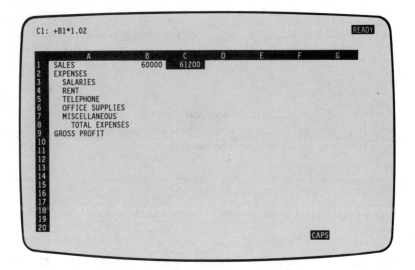

```
C1: +B1*1.02                                                    READY

              A          B        C       D        E       F       G
  1   SALES            60000    61200
  2   EXPENSES
  3      SALARIES
  4      RENT
  5      TELEPHONE
  6      OFFICE SUPPLIES
  7      MISCELLANEOUS
  8         TOTAL EXPENSES
  9   GROSS PROFIT
 10
 11
 12
 13
 14
 15
 16
 17
 18
 19
 20
                                                               CAPS
```

The formulas in Lotus 1–2–3 are based upon **relative cell location.** For example, the formula in cell C1, +B1*1.02, is interpreted by Lotus 1–2–3 as "multiply the cell immediately to the left of the formula location by 1.02." The Sales for Quarters 3 and 4 are also projected to increase the previous quarter (the previous cell) by 2 percent. Therefore, the formula +B1*1.02 can be "copied" to cells D1 and E1 and adjusted to +C1*1.02 and +D1*1.02, respectively.

The cell pointer should be highlighting cell C1.

Press	/	(the command key)
Type	C	(for Copy)

The Copy command consists of two prompts. One prompt requires the user to indicate which cells are to be copied. An easy way to do this is to highlight the cells to copy and press ↵. When the ↵ key is pressed, another prompt requires the user to indicate the area to which the cell or cells will be copied. When the ↵ key is pressed after the second prompt, the Copy procedure is executed.

The first prompt asks for the "range to copy FROM." Make sure that the cell or cells to copy are highlighted. Since C1 is the cell to copy and it is already highlighted:

Press ↵

The second prompt asks for the "range to copy TO."

Move	the cell pointer to cell D1	
Press	.	(the period key)

Notice that "D1" (in the control panel) changes to "D1 . . D1" when the period key is pressed. The period key "anchors" the cell pointer so that more than one cell can be highlighted at a time. In this example, the cell pointer will be "anchored" at cell D1 so that it can be "stretched" to cell E1.

Move   the cell pointer to cell E1 ⏎

The formula in cell C1 has now been copied to cells D1 and E1 (Quarters 3 and 4). Refer to Figure 2–8.

Figure 2–8
Part 1

USING THE COPY COMMAND - RANGE TO COPY FROM

Step 1 of Copy Procedure: Highlight the cell(s) to copy and press ⏎

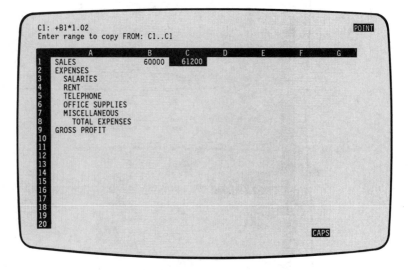

Figure 2–8
Part 2

USING THE COPY PROCEDURE - RANGE TO COPY TO

Step 2 of Copy Procedure: Highlight the first cell to which the cell(s)
                            will be copied

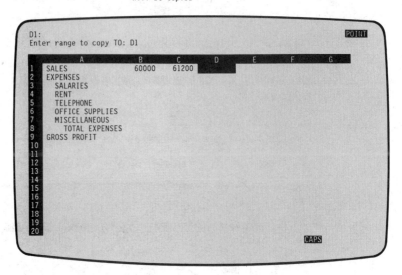

Figure 2–8
Part 3

Step 3 of Copy Procedure: When copying to more than one cell, press the
                           period key to "anchor the **cell pointer**"

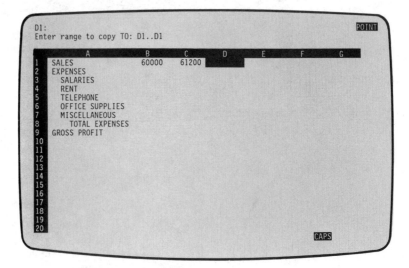

Figure 2–8
Part 4

Step 4 of Copy Procedure: "Stretch" the cell pointer from its anchored
position to the rest of the area to which the
cells will be copied

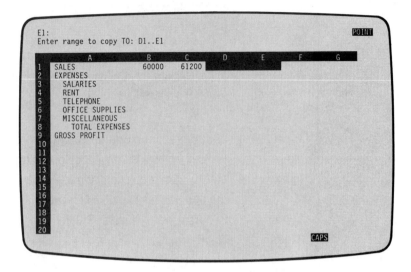

Figure 2–8
Part 5

Step 5 of Copy Procedure: Press ↵ to copy the desired cell(s) and
complete the Copy Procedure

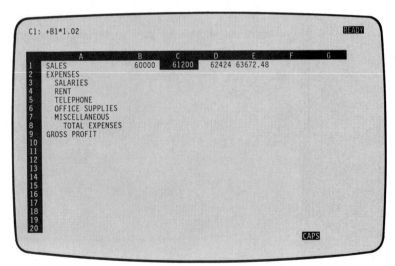

To input the data for Salaries:

Move   the cell pointer to cell B3

Make sure that the cell pointer is in the *third* row.

Type	35000 (first quarter Salaries)
Press	the right arrow key

The cell pointer is in cell C3. Notice that the ↵ key did not have to be pressed. Pressing the right arrow key after typing the value 35000 did two things: entered 35000 in cell B3 and also moved the cell pointer to cell C3.

To enter the salary amounts for Quarters 2, 3, and 4:

Type	35500 (second quarter Salaries)
Move	the cell pointer to cell D3 by pressing the right arrow key
Type	36200 (third quarter Salaries)
Move	the cell pointer to cell E3 by pressing the right arrow key
Type	37000 (fourth quarter Salaries)
Press	↵

Refer to Figure 2–9.

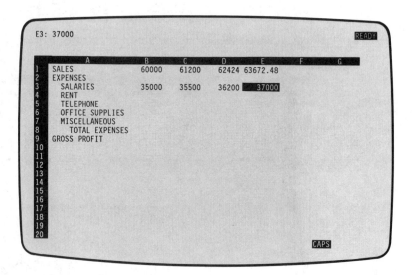

Figure 2–9

To input the data for Rent:

Move	the cell pointer to cell B4
Type	9000 ↵

The Copy command is used to copy 9000 to Quarters 2, 3, and 4. The cell pointer should be in cell B4. To copy the amount:

Press	/	(the command key)
Type	C	(for Copy)

When prompted for the range to copy FROM, note that the cell pointer is highlighting cell B4, which is the cell to copy. To indicate that B4 is the cell to copy:

Press	↵

When prompted for the range to copy TO:

Move	the cell pointer to cell C4
Press	.
Move	the cell pointer to cell E4 ↵

The number 9000 should now be copied to Quarters 2, 3, and 4 (Figure 2–10).

Figure 2–10

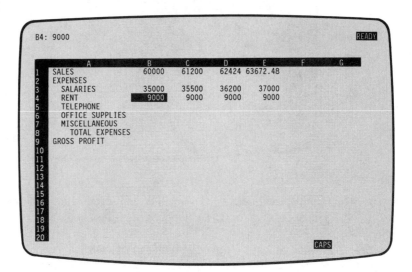

To input the data for Telephone expenses for the first quarter:

Move	the cell pointer to cell B5
Type	1000 ↵

The following formula indicates that Telephone expenses will increase by 5% for the following quarters:

Move	the cell pointer to cell C5
Type	+
Move	the cell pointer to cell B5 (Telephone)
Type	*
Type	1.05 ↵

The number 1050 should appear in cell C5. The formula +B5*1.05 should be displayed in the control panel (refer to Figure 2–11).

Figure 2–11

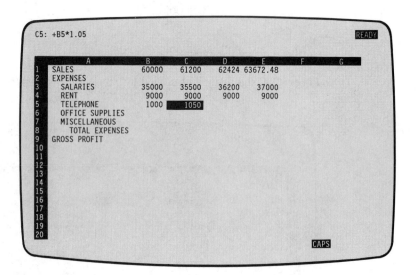

The formula for Quarters 3 and 4 will be completed later in this exercise.

To input the data for Office Supplies expenses for the first quarter:

Move	the cell pointer to cell B6
Type	750 ↵

Office Supplies expenses will increase by $50 for the following quarters. To enter the appropriate formula:

Move	the cell pointer to cell C6
Type	+
Move	the cell pointer to cell B6
Type	+
Type	50 ⏎

The number 800 appears in cell C6. The formula +B6+50 is now displayed in the control panel (refer to Figure 2–12). The formulas for Quarters 3 and 4 are illustrated later in this exercise.

Figure 2–12

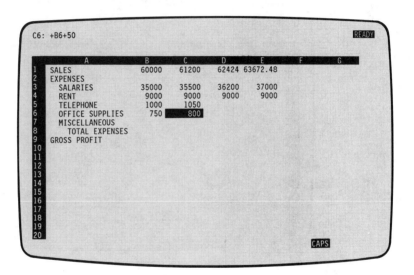

To input the data for Miscellaneous expenses for the first quarter:

Move	the cell pointer to cell B7
Type	1000 ⏎

The following formula indicates that Miscellaneous expenses will increase by 3% for the following quarters. To enter the formula:

Move	the cell pointer to cell C7
Type	+
Move	the cell pointer to cell B7
Type	*
Type	1.03 ↵

The number 1030 now appears in cell C7. The formula +B7*1.03 is displayed in the control panel (refer to Figure 2–13).

Figure 2–13

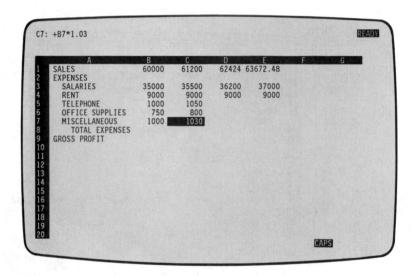

```
C7: +B7*1.03                                                    READY

        A           B        C        D       E       F       G
 1  SALES         60000    61200    62424 63672.48
 2  EXPENSES
 3    SALARIES    35000    35500    36200   37000
 4    RENT         9000     9000     9000    9000
 5    TELEPHONE    1000     1050
 6    OFFICE SUPPLIES 750    800
 7    MISCELLANEOUS 1000    1030
 8        TOTAL EXPENSES
 9  GROSS PROFIT
10
11
12
13
14
15
16
17
18
19
20
                                                          CAPS
```

To copy the formulas for Telephone, Office Supplies, and Miscellaneous expenses to quarters 3 and 4:

Move		the cell pointer to cell C5 (the formula for projecting Telephone expenses)
Press	/	(the command key)
Type	C	(for Copy)

When prompted for the Range to copy FROM:

Move   the cell pointer to cell C7 (the formula for projecting Miscellaneous expenses)

The period key did not have to be pressed because 1–2–3 automatically anchors the cell pointer at its current position when prompting for the "Range to copy FROM." In this example, the period key is anchored at cell C5 and is "stretched" to cell C7.

Press   ↵

When prompted for the range to copy TO:

Move   the cell pointer to cell D5
Press   .

The period key anchors the cursor at cell D5.

Move   the cell pointer to cell E7

The screen currently displays a highlighted rectangle that covers cells D5 through E7.

Press   ↵

The formulas in cells C5 through C7 (to project expenses) have been copied to cells D5 through E7 (refer to Figure 2–14).

Figure 2–14
Part 1

COPYING MULTIPLE FORMULAS TO A RANGE

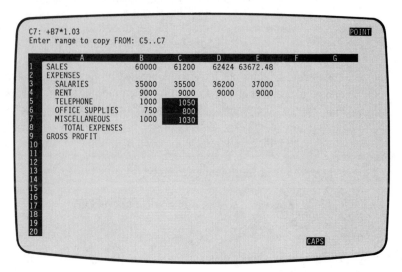

Figure 2–14
Part 2

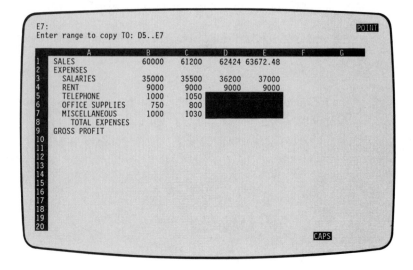

Figure 2–14
Part 3

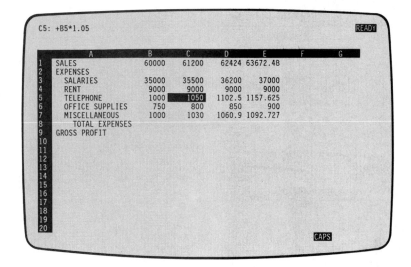

The following instructions total the expenses for the first quarter by using the SUM command. Lotus 1–2–3 has many special functions that are preceded by the "@" character. The general format for the SUM command is:

```
@SUM(first cell..last cell)
```

Note that a range of cells is specified within the set of parentheses.

Move	the cell pointer to cell B8
Type	@SUM(
Move	the cell pointer to cell B3 (the first item in column B to total, which is SALARIES)
Type	.

The period key anchors the cell pointer in cell B3.

Move	the cell pointer to cell B7
Type	) ↵

The number 46750 should appear in cell B8. The formula @SUM(B3..B7) is displayed in the control panel (refer to Figure 2–15).

Figure 2–15

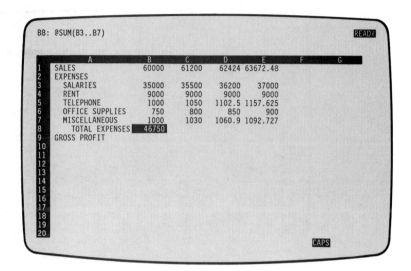

```
B8: @SUM(B3..B7)                                              READY

         A              B        C        D        E       F      G
 1  SALES           60000    61200    62424 63672.48
 2  EXPENSES
 3     SALARIES      35000    35500    36200    37000
 4     RENT           9000     9000     9000     9000
 5     TELEPHONE      1000     1050   1102.5 1157.625
 6     OFFICE SUPPLIES 750      800      850      900
 7     MISCELLANEOUS  1000     1030   1060.9 1092.727
 8        TOTAL EXPENSES 46750
 9  GROSS PROFIT
10
11
12
13
14
15
16
17
18
19
20
                                                             CAPS
```

To compute Gross Profit, create a formula which subtracts Total Expenses from Sales.

Move   the cell pointer to cell B9

Type   +

Move   the cell pointer to cell B1 (Sales)

Type   −

Move   the cell pointer to cell B8 (Total Expenses)

Press   ↵

The number 13250 should appear in B9. The formula +B1–B8 should be displayed in the control panel.

The Copy command is used to copy the formulas for computing the Total Expenses and Gross Profit to the remaining three quarters.

Move   the cell pointer to cell B8 (Total Expenses)

Press   /   (the command key)

Type   C   (for Copy)

When prompted for the Range to copy FROM:

Move   the cell pointer to cell B9 (Gross Profit)

The copy FROM range should highlight cells B8 and B9.

> **Press** ↵

When prompted for the Range to copy TO:

> **Move** the cell pointer to cell C8
> **Press** .
> **Move** the cell pointer to cell E9

A highlighted rectangle covers cells C8 through E9.

> **Press** ↵

Refer to Figure 2–16.

Figure 2–16

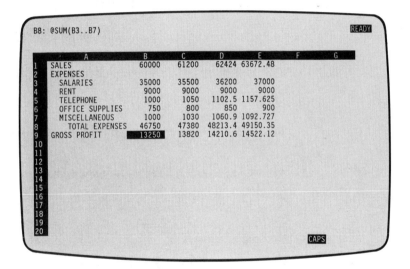

To compute the total for each row:

> **Move** the cell pointer to cell F1
> **Type** @SUM(
> **Move** the cell pointer to cell B1
> **Press** .
> **Move** the cell pointer to cell E1
> **Type**) ↵

The number 247296.4 appears in cell F1. The formula @SUM(B1..E1) appears in the control panel.

To copy the @SUM(B1..E1) formula to the rows below:

Press	/	(the command key)
Type	C	(for Copy)

When prompted for the range to copy FROM:

Press	↵

Since F1 was already highlighted, the cell pointer did not have to be moved.
When prompted for the range to copy TO:

Move	the cell pointer to cell F3
Press	.
Move	the cell pointer to cell F9 ↵

The formula @SUM(B1..E1) has been copied from cells F1 to cells F3 through F9 (refer to Figure 2–17).

Figure 2–17

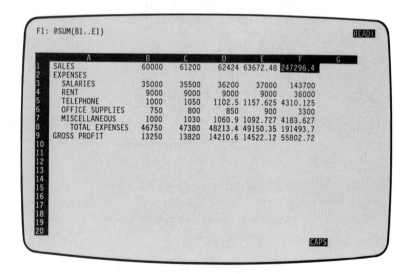

```
F1: @SUM(B1..E1)                                                    READY

          A            B         C         D         E        F         G
 1  SALES            60000     61200     62424  63672.48  247296.4
 2  EXPENSES
 3    SALARIES       35000     35500     36200     37000    143700
 4    RENT            9000      9000      9000      9000     36000
 5    TELEPHONE       1000      1050    1102.5  1157.625  4310.125
 6    OFFICE SUPPLIES  750       800       850       900      3300
 7    MISCELLANEOUS   1000      1030    1060.9  1092.727  4183.627
 8      TOTAL EXPENSES 46750    47380   48213.4  49150.35  191493.7
 9  GROSS PROFIT     13250     13820   14210.6  14522.12  55802.72
10
11
12
13
14
15
16
17
18
19
20
                                                              CAPS
```

Selecting a Format for the Data

To choose a numeric format (commas, dollar signs, the number of decimal places, etc.) for the worksheet:

Press	/	(the command key)
Type	W	(for Worksheet)
Type	G	(for Global)
Type	F	(for Format)
Type	,	(for ,)

Global means that the format chosen will be used as the default; unless another numeric format is specified, commas will be used. The , represents the format chosen, which is the Comma format.

When prompted for the number of decimal places:

| **Type** | 0 ⏎ |

Be sure to type the number "zero" and not the letter "O." The screen should look like Figure 2–18. Notice that rounding errors occur (e.g., Sales of 247,296 minus Total Expenses of 191,494 should equal 55,80<u>2</u> rather than 55,80<u>3</u>). The rounding error occurred because the numbers are *formatted* to *show* 0 decimal places, but the *values* in the cells are not truly *rounded* to 0 decimal places. Rounding errors are resolved later in this chapter.

Figure 2–18

FORMATTING THE WORKSHEET

Using the Format command may cause rounding errors.

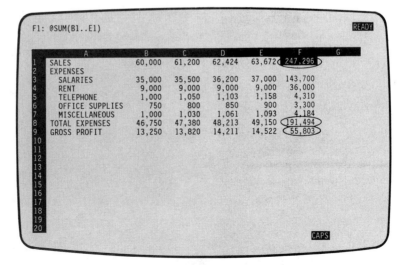

Inserting Blank Rows for Headings

To insert six blank rows at the top of the spreadsheet:

Move		the cell pointer to cell A1
Press	/	(the command key)
Type	W	(for Worksheet)
Type	I	(for Insert)
Type	R	(for Row)

When prompted for the insert range:

Move	the cell pointer to cell A6

The period key did not have to be pressed since the Insert Row feature automatically anchors the cell pointer at its current position. The insert range is from rows A1 through A6, or rows 1 through 6. Note that the entire worksheet does not have to be highlighted. Also note that the cell pointer does not have to be in column A to insert rows; it can be in any column. Column A is preferable, because the labels can be used as a guide to determine where to insert rows.

Press	⏎

Refer to Figure 2–19.

Figure 2–19

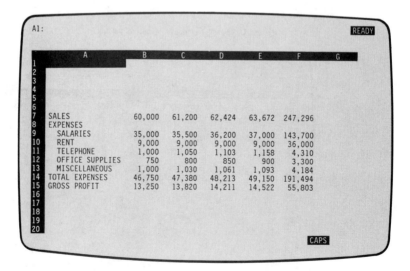

The worksheet formulas and values remain correct and are "adjusted" to the new location. For example, Quarter Two's Sales have been changed from +B1*1.02 to +B7*1.02 in C7.

Entering Headings

When entering headings, the user has to determine where the title of a spreadsheet will be correctly centered. To input the first heading for this example:

Move	the cell pointer to cell C1
Press	the space bar five times
Type	ABC COMPANY ↵

To enter the second heading:

Move	the cell pointer to cell C2
Press	the space bar seven times
Type	BUDGET ↵

To enter the heading for the first quarter:

Move	the cell pointer to cell B5
Type	^QTR1 ↵

The ^ mark causes the labels to be centered within the column; a double quote mark before the heading would cause the labels to be right-justified in the column.

To enter the headings for the last three quarters:

Move	the cell pointer to cell C5
Type	^QTR2

Move	the cell pointer to cell D5
Type	^QTR3

Move	the cell pointer to cell E5
Type	^QTR4

To enter the heading YR TOTAL:

Move   the cell pointer to cell F5
Type   ^YR TOTAL ↵

Refer to Figure 2–20.

Figure 2–20

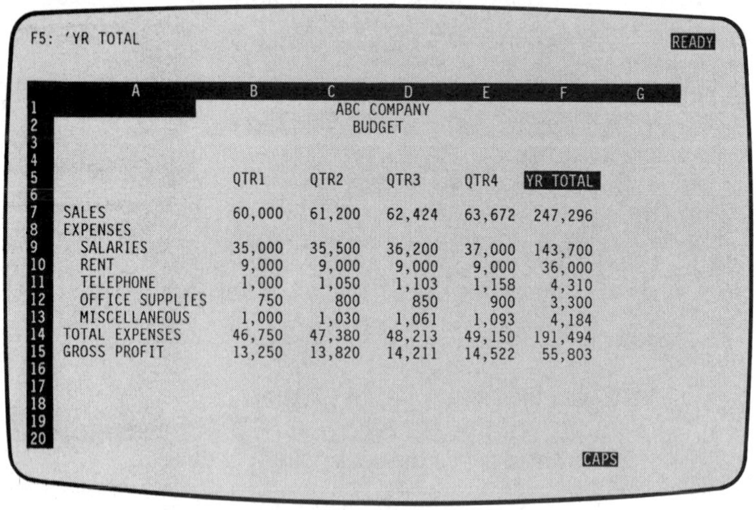

```
F5: 'YR TOTAL                                                          READY

              A           B        C        D        E        F        G
      1                               ABC COMPANY
      2                                 BUDGET
      3
      4
      5                      QTR1     QTR2     QTR3     QTR4   YR TOTAL
      6
      7     SALES          60,000   61,200   62,424   63,672  247,296
      8     EXPENSES
      9        SALARIES    35,000   35,500   36,200   37,000  143,700
     10        RENT         9,000    9,000    9,000    9,000   36,000
     11        TELEPHONE    1,000    1,050    1,103    1,158    4,310
     12        OFFICE SUPPLIES 750     800      850      900    3,300
     13        MISCELLANEOUS 1,000   1,030    1,061    1,093    4,184
     14     TOTAL EXPENSES 46,750   47,380   48,213   49,150  191,494
     15     GROSS PROFIT   13,250   13,820   14,211   14,522   55,803
     16
     17
     18
     19
     20                                                             CAPS
```

Inserting Blank Rows within a Spreadsheet

To insert a blank row between SALES and EXPENSES:

Move   the cell pointer to cell A8 (EXPENSES)
Press   /   (the command key)
Type   W   (for Worksheet)
Type   I   (for Insert)
Type   R   (for Row)

When prompted for the row to insert:

Press   ↵

Since the cell pointer was already highlighting cell A8, pressing the ↵ key at this point caused one row to be inserted at cell A8. The screen now looks like Figure 2–21.

Figure 2–21

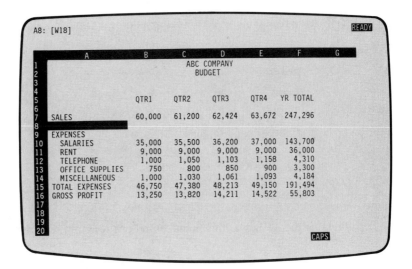

To insert a blank row between MISCELLANEOUS and TOTAL EXPENSES:

Move		the cell pointer to cell A15 (TOTAL EXPENSES)
Press	/	(the command key)
Type	W	(for Worksheet)
Type	I	(for Insert)
Type	R	(for Row)

When prompted for the row to insert:

Press	↵

Pressing the ↵ key at this point causes one row to be inserted at cell A15.
To insert a blank row between TOTAL EXPENSES and GROSS PROFIT:

Move	the cell pointer to cell A17 (GROSS PROFIT)

To insert a blank row when the cell pointer is in another column besides column A:

Move	the cell pointer to cell C17	
Press	/	(the command key)
Type	W	(for Worksheet)
Type	I	(for Insert)
Type	R	(for Row)

When prompted for the row to insert:

Press	↵

Pressing the ↵ key at this point caused one row to be inserted at cell C17 (refer to Figure 2–22).

Figure 2–22

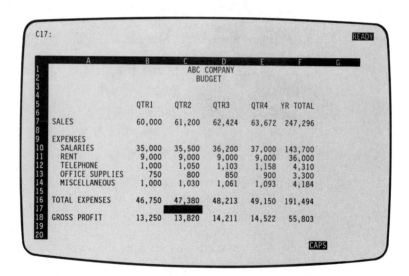

Entering Underlines and Double Underlines

To input subtotal underlines for the expenses:

Move	the cell pointer to cell B15
Press	the space bar one time
Type	– – – – – – – – (eight minus signs or dashes)

By pressing the space bar once and then eight dashes, a subtotal line has been created. The space in front of the dashes is needed so that when this cell is copied to adjacent cells, a space will appear in between the dashes. The space creates the appearance of a column between each column of numbers.

Press ↵

To copy the subtotal underlines to the rest of the current row:

Press / (the command key)
Type C (for Copy)

When prompted for the range to copy FROM:

Press ↵

By pressing ↵, cell B15 is indicated as the cell to copy.
When prompted for the range to copy TO:

Move the cell pointer to cell C15
Press .
Move the cell pointer to cell F15
Press the ↵

Refer to Figure 2–23.

Figure 2–23

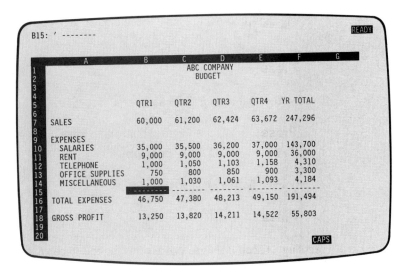

To copy row 15's subtotal underlines to row 17:

    Press   /   (the command key)
    Type   C   (for Copy)

When prompted for the range to copy FROM:

    Move   the cell pointer to cell F15

Cells B15 through F15 should now be highlighted.

    Press   ↵

When prompted for the range to copy TO:

    Move   the cell pointer to cell B17
    Press   ↵

Notice that for a copy of one row or column, it is not necessary to highlight the entire area to which the lines are copied. The method used above is to highlight the cell in which to *begin* copying the cells.

To input the double underlines in cell B19:

    Move   the cell pointer to cell B19
    Press   the space bar one time
    Type   ======== (eight equal signs)

By pressing the space bar one time and the equal sign eight times, a double line was created.

    Press   ↵

To copy the double underlines to the rest of row 19:

    Press   /   (the command key)
    Type   C   (for Copy)

When prompted for the range to copy FROM:

    Press   ↵

By pressing ↵ , cell B19 was indicated as the cell to copy.

When prompted for the range to copy TO:

Move	the cell pointer to cell C19
Press	.
Move	the cell pointer to cell F19
Press	↵

Refer to Figure 2–24.

Figure 2–24

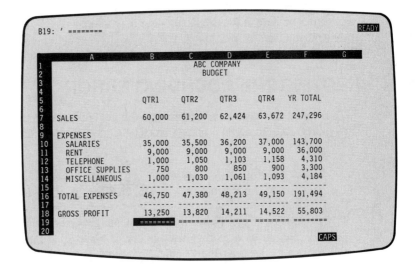

```
B19: '  =========                                           READY

            A        B        C        D        E        F        G
 1                            ABC COMPANY
 2                              BUDGET
 3
 4
 5                   QTR1     QTR2     QTR3     QTR4   YR TOTAL
 6
 7  SALES          60,000   61,200   62,424   63,672  247,296
 8
 9  EXPENSES
10    SALARIES     35,000   35,500   36,200   37,000  143,700
11    RENT          9,000    9,000    9,000    9,000   36,000
12    TELEPHONE     1,000    1,050    1,103    1,158    4,310
13    OFFICE SUPPLIES 750      800      850      900    3,300
14    MISCELLANEOUS 1,000    1,030    1,061    1,093    4,184
15                 --------  -------  -------  -------  -------
16  TOTAL EXPENSES 46,750   47,380   48,213   49,150  191,494
17                 --------  -------  -------  -------  -------
18  GROSS PROFIT   13,250   13,820   14,211   14,522   55,803
19                 ========  =======  =======  =======  =======
20                                                              CAPS
```

■ SAVING AND NAMING THE SPREADSHEET

To save the spreadsheet:

Place	a formatted disk in drive B
Press	the [Home] key

Pressing the [Home] key is an optional step. If the [Home] key is pressed, the cell pointer is saved in cell A1 when the file is saved. When the file is later retrieved from the disk, the cell pointer will appear in cell A1.

Press	/	(the command key)
Type	F	(for File)
Type	S	(for Save)

When prompted for the file name:

Type   BUDGET ↵

File names can be a maximum of eight characters long. Acceptable characters are letters of the alphabet, numbers, and the underline (_) character. (The underline character takes up one character's space; it cannot be used to underline other characters in the file name). Do not include **spaces** or **periods** in the file name. The red light in drive B is briefly illuminated while the file BUDGET is written to the disk in drive B. The file labeled BUDGET on drive B contains the spreadsheet that was created.

Note that 1–2–3 may be set up by the user to save files on a different drive. For example, on hard disk systems, the user may set up 1–2–3 so that the files are saved on drive C (the hard disk).

■ CORRECTING THE ROUNDING ERROR

The worksheet that was just completed did not "foot" or balance correctly. The result in the TOTALS column is shown below:

Sales	$247,296	
−Total Expenses	191,494	
Gross Profit	$ 55,803	(does not foot correctly)

When multiplication, division, or exponents are used in a formula, the @ROUND function can be used to round a number to a specified number of decimal places. Otherwise, Lotus uses the "hidden" decimal places in computation, resulting in rounding errors. The @ROUND function will be explained in more detail later in this chapter. For now, the following steps can be used for rounding the appropriate formulas where necessary in this example.

Note that the user should *immediately* use the @ROUND function when creating formulas rather than going back to edit. This example was done differently to show the results of *not* using the @ROUND function.

The three sets of formulas for Sales, Telephone Expenses, and Miscellaneous Expenses need to be edited to use the @ROUND function because the three lines contain multiplication.

The @ROUND function's format is as follows:

```
@ROUND(formula,number of digits to round to)
```

SALES will be the first formula to be edited. The formula is +B7*1.02 for the SALES projection for the second quarter. To round the Sales projections to 0 decimal places:

Move	the cell pointer to cell C7
Type	@ROUND (
Move	the cell pointer to cell B7
Type	*1.02,0) ↵

The rounded formula @ROUND(B7*1.02,0) is now in cell C7. The formula "B7*1.02" will be rounded to 0 decimal places (refer to Figure 2–25).

Figure 2–25   The formula in cell C7 is rounded to zero decimal places.

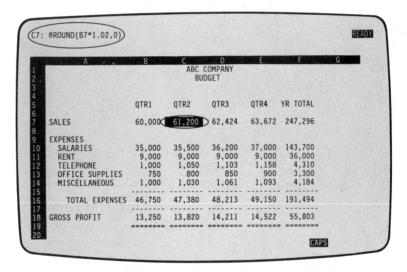

To copy the rounded formula to the rest of the row:

Type	/	(the command key)
Type	C	(for Copy)

When prompted for the range to copy FROM:

Press	↵

By pressing ↵ , C7 was selected as the cell to copy. When prompted for the range to copy TO:

Move	the cell pointer to cell D7
Press	.
Move	the cell pointer to cell E7 ↵

The projections for Sales are now rounded to 0 decimal places.

The second set of formulas to be rounded are for Telephone Expenses. The formula is +B12*1.05 for Telephone Expenses for the second quarter. To round the Telephone Expenses to 0 decimal places:

Move	the cell pointer to cell C12

Rather than retyping the formula, use a shortcut to edit the current formula.

Press	the [Edit] key

The [Edit] key is the name for the [F2] function key when using 1–2–3, as seen on the 1–2–3 keyboard template.

Press	the left arrow key until the cell pointer is under the + sign at the front of the formula—an alternative is to press the [Home] key to move to the beginning of the formula
Type	@ROUND (
Press	the [Del] key one time to delete the + sign
Press	the right arrow key to move the cell pointer to the end of the formula—an alternative is to press the [End] key to move to the end of the formula
Type	,0) ↵

The rounded formula @ROUND (B12*1.05,0) is now in cell C12.

To copy the rounded formula to the rest of the row:

Type	/	(the command key)
Type	C	(for Copy)

When prompted for the range to copy FROM:

Press	↵

By pressing ↵ , cell C12 was selected as the cell to copy.

When prompted for the range to copy TO:

Move	the cell pointer to cell D12
Press	.
Move	the cell pointer to cell E12
Press	⏎

Telephone Expenses are now rounded to 0 decimal places.

The next set of formulas to be rounded are for Miscellaneous Expenses. The formula is +B14*1.03 for Miscellaneous Expenses for the second quarter. To round the Miscellaneous Expenses to 0 decimal places:

Move	the cell pointer to cell C14
Press	the [Edit] key (the [F2] function key)
Press	the [Home] key to move to the beginning of the formula
Type	@ROUND (
Press	the [Del] key one time to delete the + sign
Press	the [End] key to move to the end of a formula
Type	,0) ⏎

The rounded formula @ROUND (B14*1.03,0) is now in cell C14.

To copy the rounded formula to the rest of the row:

Type	/	(the command key)
Type	C	(for Copy)

When prompted for the range to copy FROM:

Press	⏎

By pressing ⏎, cell C14 was selected as the cell to copy.

When prompted for the range to copy TO:

Move	the cell pointer to cell D14
Press	.
Move	the cell pointer to cell E14 ⏎

The projections for Miscellaneous Expenses are rounded to 0 decimal places.

The rounding error in the worksheet has been corrected. The result in the YR TOTAL column is shown below:

Sales	$247,296
–Total Expenses	191,495
Gross Profit	$ 55,801

Refer to Figure 2–26.

Figure 2–26

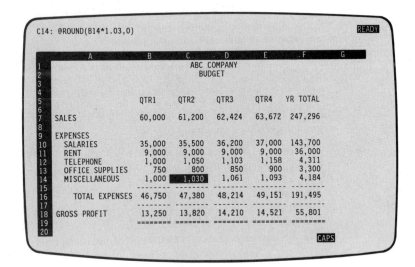

■ PREPARING THE PRINTER AND PRINTING THE SPREADSHEET

The spreadsheet is complete and the rounding errors have been corrected. The following steps outline how to print the results.

Prepare the Printer for Use

If the paper needs to be aligned in the printer, perform the following step before turning on the printer:

Turn the cylinder that moves the paper so the paper perforation is directly above the print head and ribbon

For many printers, the gears can be damaged if the cylinder is manually turned while the motor is running.

Before printing:

Check	to see that the printer is connected to the computer
Turn	on the printer

The printer should now be on. The POWER, READY, and ON LINE lights are illuminated. Note that this example is written for an Epson or Epson-compatible printer; keys on different printers or Epson models may have different names.

Printing the Spreadsheet

To specify the range to print:

Press	/	(the command key)
Type	P	(for Print)
Type	P	(for Printer)
Type	R	(for Range of cells to be printed)

When prompted for the print range:

Move	the cell pointer to cell A1 (if the cell pointer is not already there)
Press	.
Move	the cell pointer to cell F19 ⏎

The entire worksheet is now highlighted. To begin printing the range:

Type	A	(for Align)
Type	G	(for Go)

The printer should begin to print.

Note that the Align command sets a 1–2–3 counter to 0 (top of page) before it begins to print. This command is especially useful when the paper has been readjusted in the printer or the printer has been reloaded.

The printer used in this example does not automatically eject the page when the spreadsheet is printed. To eject the page from the printer using a 1–2–3 command:

Type	P	(for Page)

A page is ejected. For many printers, an additional page needs to be ejected so that the paper remains aligned properly in the printer. To eject a second page:

Type   P   (for Page)

Tear   the perforation to remove the printed page

Reset   the alignment of the paper in the printer, if necessary

To leave the Print menu:

Type   Q   (for Quit)

The printout should appear similar to the printout in Figure 2–27. If the printout is satisfactory, resave the spreadsheet so that the print setting would also be saved with the spreadsheet. To resave the spreadsheet, follow the instructions in the next exercise.

Figure 2–27

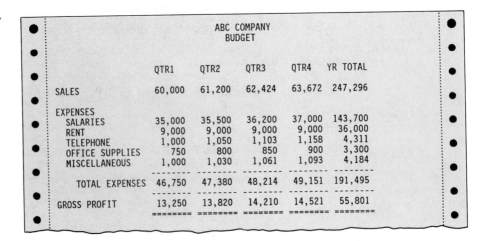

```
                          ABC COMPANY
                            BUDGET

                QTR1      QTR2      QTR3      QTR4    YR TOTAL

SALES           60,000    61,200    62,424    63,672  247,296

EXPENSES
  SALARIES      35,000    35,500    36,200    37,000  143,700
  RENT           9,000     9,000     9,000     9,000   36,000
  TELEPHONE      1,000     1,050     1,103     1,158    4,311
  OFFICE SUPPLIES  750       800       850       900    3,300
  MISCELLANEOUS  1,000     1,030     1,061     1,093    4,184
                -------   -------   -------   -------  -------
  TOTAL EXPENSES 46,750    47,380    48,214    49,151  191,495
                -------   -------   -------   -------  -------
GROSS PROFIT    13,250    13,820    14,210    14,521   55,801
                =======   =======   =======   =======  =======
```

■ SAVING AND REPLACING A SPREADSHEET

The spreadsheet previously created was saved before the rounding errors were edited and before the worksheet was printed. In order to save the changes to the worksheet, it must be saved to the disk again.

To replace the BUDGET spreadsheet file that was previously saved:

Press   the [Home] key

Pressing the [Home] key is optional; doing so will save the cell pointer in the position at the top of the spreadsheet.

Press	/	(the command key)
Type	F	(for File)
Type	S	(for Save)

When prompted for the file name, the name for the file that is currently on the screen should appear. In this example, BUDGET appears. To keep the file name as BUDGET:

Press ⏎

Since the file BUDGET already exists on the disk, a prompt appears requesting whether to cancel the Save command or to replace the BUDGET file with the file version in memory (the file currently being used).

When prompted whether to Cancel or Replace:

Type R (for Replace)

The previously saved version of BUDGET has now been replaced with the updated version that is currently displayed on the screen (refer to Figure 2–28).

Figure 2–28
Part 1

SAVING AND REPLACING A FILE ON A DISK

The first version of BUDGET saved to the file.

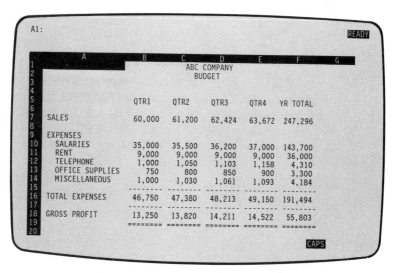

Figure 2–28
Part 2

The version of BUDGET that replaced the old BUDGET file on the disk when the File Save Replace commands were executed.

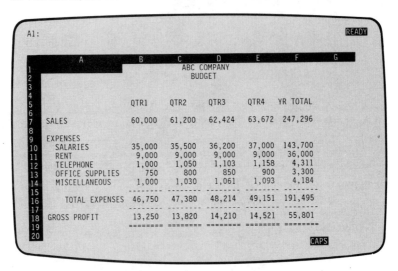

RETRIEVING A SPREADSHEET

First, clear the screen before beginning the exercise. To clear the screen:

Press	/	(the command key)
Type	W	(for Worksheet)
Type	E	(for Erase)
Type	Y	(for Yes)

Clearing the screen is not necessary before retrieving a spreadsheet because the screen will be erased automatically when retrieving a spreadsheet file. Note that Worksheet Erase Yes did **not** erase the file BUDGET from the disk where it was previously saved. Worksheet Erase Yes only erases the spreadsheet from main **memory** so that the screen is cleared. The file BUDGET can still be retrieved from the disk. This action was taken to clarify the steps below.

To retrieve the file BUDGET:

Press	/	(the command key)
Type	F	(for File)
Type	R	(for Retrieve)

When prompted for the file to retrieve:

Type   BUDGET ↵

An alternative to typing the file name is to use the arrow keys to highlight the desired file with the cell pointer in the control panel (since BUDGET is the only file on the disk, it is already highlighted). Once the desired file is highlighted, press ↵ to retrieve the file.

The file BUDGET is visible on the screen. It is now possible to make revisions, reprint it, etc. (Refer to Figure 2–28). Any changes are made *only* to the screen, not to the file on the disk. To save any changes to the file BUDGET, go through the process of saving and replacing a file, as illustrated in the previous section. To save revisions as a completely different file, save the file, but use a different file name.

■ PRINTING THE CELL FORMULAS OF A SPREADSHEET

Sometimes it may be desirable to see the cell formulas which comprise a spreadsheet. To print the cell formulas used to create the spreadsheet BUDGET, follow the steps below. It is assumed that BUDGET is currently in memory and that the Print Range for BUDGET has previously been set.

Press	/	(the command key)
Type	P	(for Print)
Type	P	(for Printer)
Type	O	(for Options)
Type	O	(for Other)
Type	C	(for Cell-Formulas)
Type	Q	(for Quit)
Type	G	(for Go)

Assuming that the print range has been set previously, the printer will begin printing the contents of each cell, line by line.

To eject the printout when it is complete, and also to eject a second page (if necessary) to keep the paper aligned in the printer:

Type	P	(for Page)
Type	P	(for Page)

The printout should look like Figure 2–29.

Figure 2–29
Part 1

```
PRINTING THE CELL FORMULAS IN A WORKSHEET
  C1: '       ABC COMPANY
  C2: '          BUDGET
  B5: ^QTR1
  C5: ^QTR2
  D5: ^QTR3
  E5: ^QTR4
  F5: 'YR TOTAL
  A7: [W18] 'SALES
  B7: 60000
  C7: @ROUND(B7*1.02,0)
  D7: @ROUND(C7*1.02,0)
  E7: @ROUND(D7*1.02,0)
  F7: @SUM(B7..E7)
  A9: [W18] 'EXPENSES
 A10: [W18] '  SALARIES
 B10: 35000
 C10: 35500
 D10: 36200
 E10: 37000
 F10: @SUM(B10..E10)
 A11: [W18] '  RENT
 B11: 9000
 C11: 9000
 D11: 9000
 E11: 9000
 F11: @SUM(B11..E11)
 A12: [W18] '  TELEPHONE
 B12: 1000
 C12: @ROUND(B12*1.05,0)
 D12: @ROUND(C12*1.05,0)
 E12: @ROUND(D12*1.05,0)
 F12: @SUM(B12..E12)
 A13: [W18] '  OFFICE SUPPLIES
 B13: 750
 C13: +B13+50
 D13: +C13+50
 E13: +D13+50
 F13: @SUM(B13..E13)
 A14: [W18] '  MISCELLANEOUS
 B14: 1000
 C14: @ROUND(B14*1.03,0)
 D14: @ROUND(C14*1.03,0)
 E14: @ROUND(D14*1.03,0)
 F14: @SUM(B14..E14)
 B15: ' --------
 C15: ' --------
 D15: ' --------
 E15: ' --------
 F15: ' --------
 A16: [W18] '    TOTAL EXPENSES
 B16: @SUM(B10..B14)
 C16: @SUM(C10..C14)
 D16: @SUM(D10..D14)
 E16: @SUM(E10..E14)
 F16: @SUM(B16..E16)
 B17: ' --------
```

*Figure 2–29
Part 2*

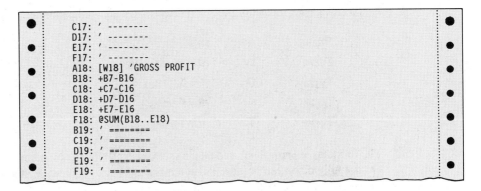

```
C17: ' --------
D17: ' --------
E17: ' --------
F17: ' --------
A18: [W18] 'GROSS PROFIT
B18: +B7-B16
C18: +C7-C16
D18: +D7-D16
E18: +E7-E16
F18: @SUM(B18..E18)
B19: ' ========
C19: ' ========
D19: ' ========
E19: ' ========
F19: ' ========
```

To return the print settings back to their previous setting (i.e., so when Go is selected, the spreadsheet will be printed rather than the cell formulas):

Type	O	(for Options)
Type	O	(for Other)
Type	A	(for As-Displayed)

To leave the current menu:

| **Type** | Q | (for Quit) |

To leave the Print menu:

| **Type** | Q | (for Quit) |

The print settings have now been returned to their previous setting.

■ PRINTING THE CELL FORMULAS OF A SPREADSHEET IN TABULAR FORM

To display cell formulas exactly where they appear on the spreadsheet BUDGET requires changing the format of the spreadsheet. Before changing the format to see cell formulas, make sure the file has been saved to the disk in the desired numeric format. In this way, the "final version" of the spreadsheet is safely saved on the disk and can be retrieved for later use.

To change the format of the spreadsheet to see the cell formulas:

Press	/	(the command key)
Type	W	(for Worksheet)
Type	G	(for Global)
Type	F	(for Format)
Type	T	(for Text)

The formulas are now displayed on the spreadsheet itself. However, many cell formulas are not fully displayed because the column width is not wide enough to accommodate them. For example, column F is not large enough to fully display the @SUM formulas in column F. In row 16, the @SUM command is not displayed fully (refer to Figure 2–30).

Figure 2–30

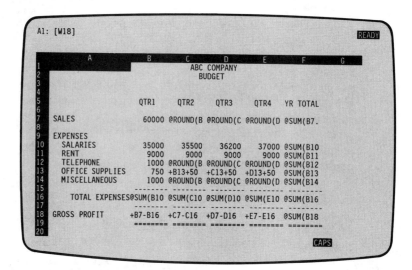

For this example, widen column F in order to view the full formula. The only other formula not fully displayed in columns A through D is the @SUM command in row 16 to compute Total Expenses. For this example, only column F will be altered to fully display the formulas.

To widen column F:

Move		the cell pointer to cell F1 (or any other cell in column F)
Press	/	(the command key)
Type	W	(for Worksheet)
Type	C	(for Column)
Type	S	(for Set-Width)

When prompted for the column width:

Press	the right arrow key until the entire formulas are displayed

In this example, the column width should be 15 characters wide. To accept 15 as the column width:

Press	↵

The entire formula for each cell in column F is now displayed.

Since every column has at least one formula not fully displayed in row 16, it may be desirable to expand more than one column's length at a time. Creating a default column-width is not used at this time; the procedure to do so is to press the command key, **W** for Worksheet, **G** for Global, **C** for Column-Width, and press the right arrow key until all of the formulas in each column are displayed on the screen. The only columns that Worksheet Global Column-Width cannot alter are columns set individually with the Worksheet Column Set-Width command. Columns set with Worksheet Column Set-Width must be individually reset.

To print the cells in tabular form:

Press	/	(the command key)
Type	P	(for Print)
Type	P	(for Printer)
Type	G	(for Go)

The print range did not need to be specified because it was created in an earlier exercise.

To eject the printout and a second page to keep the paper properly aligned in the printer:

Type	P	(for Page)
Type	P	(for Page)

To exit the print menu:

Type   Q   (for Quit)

The printout should look like Figure 2–31.

Figure 2–31

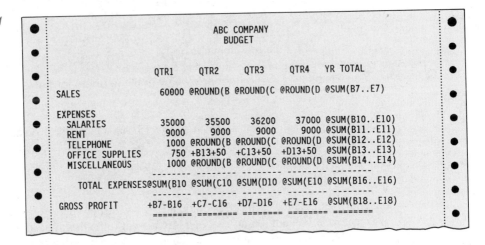

```
                              ABC COMPANY
                                BUDGET


                   QTR1      QTR2      QTR3      QTR4    YR TOTAL

         SALES     60000  @ROUND(B  @ROUND(C  @ROUND(D @SUM(B7..E7)

         EXPENSES
           SALARIES   35000     35500     36200     37000 @SUM(B10..E10)
           RENT        9000      9000      9000      9000 @SUM(B11..E11)
           TELEPHONE   1000  @ROUND(B  @ROUND(C  @ROUND(D @SUM(B12..E12)
           OFFICE SUPPLIES  750 +B13+50   +C13+50   +D13+50 @SUM(B13..E13)
           MISCELLANEOUS  1000 @ROUND(B  @ROUND(C  @ROUND(D @SUM(B14..E14)
                        --------  --------  --------  -------- --------
           TOTAL EXPENSES@SUM(B10 @SUM(C10 @SUM(D10 @SUM(E10 @SUM(B16..E16)
                        --------  --------  --------  -------- --------
         GROSS PROFIT  +B7-B16   +C7-C16   +D7-D16   +E7-E16 @SUM(B18..E18)
                        ========  ========  ========  ======== ========
```

The easiest way to return the BUDGET spreadsheet to the way it originally looked is to simply retrieve the BUDGET spreadsheet that is saved on the disk. However, this exercise will demonstrate how to use 1–2–3 commands to return the spreadsheet to its original format.

To return the format to its original setting:

Press   /   (the command key)

Type   W   (for Worksheet)

Type   G   (for Global)

Type   F   (for Format)

Type   ,   (for ,)

When prompted for the number of decimal places:

Type   0 ↵

Column F needs to be reset so that it once again has a column width of 9. To return column F to its original column width, make sure the cell pointer is within column F.

Type	/	(the command key)
Type	W	(for Worksheet)
Type	C	(for Column)
Type	R	(for Reset-Width)

The spreadsheet default for column widths is returned to the default size of 9 characters. Refer to Figure 2–32.

Figure 2–32

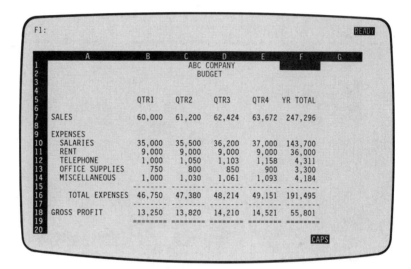

■ PRINTING THE SCREEN DISPLAY

To get a copy of the information currently displayed on the screen, the Lotus 1–2–3 menu is not needed. The keyboard itself has a "Print Screen" function.

Check	to see that the printer is on and the ON LINE light is on
Hold down	either Shift key
Press	the [PrtSc] key

[PrtSc] stands for "Print Screen;" some keyboards have [Print Screen] fully written on the key.

Release	both keys

The printer should start printing a copy of the screen.

To eject the printout and a second page from the printer:

Press   the ON LINE button on the printer
Press   the Form Feed button on the printer
Press   the Form Feed button on the printer again

The printout should now be ejected from the printer. Note that FF stands for "Form Feed" on some printers. The printout should look like Figure 2–33.

Figure 2–33

```
 F1:                                                              READY

              A           B          C        D       E       F       G
         1                       ABC COMPANY
         2                          BUDGET
         3
         4
         5                      QTR1      QTR2     QTR3    QTR4   YR TOTAL
         6
         7  SALES             60,000    61,200   62,424  63,672  247,296
         8
         9  EXPENSES
        10     SALARIES       35,000    35,500   36,200  37,000  143,700
        11     RENT            9,000     9,000    9,000   9,000   36,000
        12     TELEPHONE       1,000     1,050    1,103   1,158    4,311
        13     OFFICE SUPPLIES   750       800      850     900    3,300
        14     MISCELLANEOUS   1,000     1,030    1,061   1,093    4,184
        15                   --------  -------- -------- -------- --------
        16     TOTAL EXPENSES 46,750    47,380   48,214  49,151  191,495
        17                   --------  -------- -------- -------- --------
        18  GROSS PROFIT      13,250    13,820   14,210  14,521   55,801
        19                   ======== ======== ======== ======== ========
        20
                                                                   CAPS
```

The PrintScreen function is *not* a 1–2–3 feature, but it is a feature of the computer. This is why the print menu which features the option "Page" in order to eject pages from the printer did not appear in the control panel.

To prepare the printer for any future printing:

Press   the ON LINE button on the printer

The PrintScreen function prints the entire screen, including column and row headings (e.g., columns headings A, B, C) are visible on the printout. Many times a printer will not be able to print items such as shaded borders or graphics and will substitute other characters.

■ USING OTHER FORMAT SPECIFICATIONS FOR THE SPREADSHEET

When building the spreadsheet BUDGET, the numeric format Worksheet Global Format **, 0** was chosen from the menus to display numbers with commas and no decimal places. The exercises in this section demonstrate how to use some of the available format specifications.

Setting the Entire Spreadsheet with Dollar Signs

It is assumed that the spreadsheet file BUDGET is displayed on the screen. If not, retrieve the file BUDGET before continuing.

To change the numeric format in BUDGET so that dollar signs are added and two decimal places are shown, use the Currency format.

Press	/	(the command key)
Type	W	(for Worksheet)
Type	G	(for Global)
Type	F	(for Format)
Type	C	(for Currency)

When prompted for the number of decimal places:

Press   ↵

By pressing ↵ , the default of two decimal places is accepted. Asterisks fill the majority of the spreadsheet instead of numbers. Due to the addition of a dollar sign, a period, and two decimal places to each cell containing a value or formula, **the columns are no longer wide enough to display many of the cells** in currency format. Sometimes asterisks may appear in only one or two cells in a column rather than throughout the entire worksheet. The entire column needs to be widened in order to see the contents of the cell(s) containing asterisks (refer to Figure 2–34).

Figure 2–34

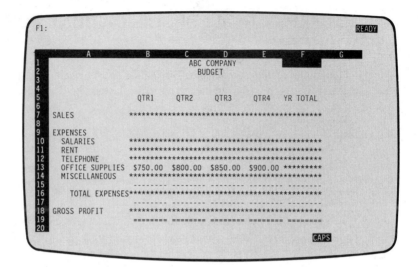

To widen the columns so that the numbers are visible:

Press	/	(the command key)
Type	W	(for Worksheet)
Type	G	(for Global)
Type	C	(for Column-Width)
Press		the right arrow key until the numbers can be seen in their entirety
Press	↵	

The column width should be set to 12 characters. Due to the column width change, column A scrolls off the screen (refer to Figure 2–35).

Figure 2–35

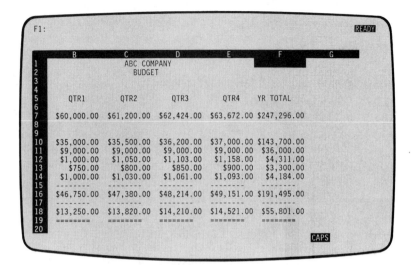

Subtotal and total lines should be set after the format is chosen since, as seen in this example, they may be too short or too long for the final format. When the global column width is set, any columns that have been set individually (using the **W**orksheet **C**olumn Set-Width command) are *not* affected. This is the reason that column A did not change in size.

Using More Than One Numeric Format in a Spreadsheet

In this exercise, the BUDGET spreadsheet is altered so that the top and bottom rows of the spreadsheet display dollar signs.

It is assumed that the original spreadsheet file BUDGET is displayed on the screen. If not, retrieve the file BUDGET before continuing (use the **/ File R**etrieve BUDGET ↵ keystroke sequence).

The BUDGET spreadsheet's format was set by **W**orksheet **G**lobal **F**ormat , 0 which displays all numbers in the spreadsheet with commas and no decimal places. For the majority of the spreadsheet, this format is appropriate. However, another command is needed to change the top and bottom rows of the spreadsheet to show dollar signs.

To change the numeric format of the top row in BUDGET:

Press	/	(the command key)
Type	R	(for Range)
Type	F	(for Format)
Type	C	(for Currency)

When prompted for the number of decimal places:

Type 0 ↵

When prompted for the range to format:

Press [Esc]

The Range Format command automatically "anchors" the cell pointer at its current position with the period key. To release the cell pointer from its anchored position, the Escape key is pressed.

The first range to format is the top row of the BUDGET spreadsheet.

Move the cell pointer to cell B7
Press .
Move the cell pointer to cell F7 ↵

Cells B7 through F7 now have dollar signs.

To change the numeric format of the bottom row in BUDGET:

Move the cell pointer to cell B18

Moving to the first cell of the range to format will eliminate the need to press the Escape key when prompted to highlight the range to format.

Press / (the command key)
Type R (for Range)
Type F (for Format)
Type C (for Currency)

When prompted for the number of decimal places:

Type 0 ↵

When prompted for the range to format:

Move to cell F18 ↵

Since the cell pointer was at cell B18, moving the cell pointer to cell F18 highlighted cells B18 through F18, which now display dollar signs (refer to Figure 2–36).

Figure 2–36

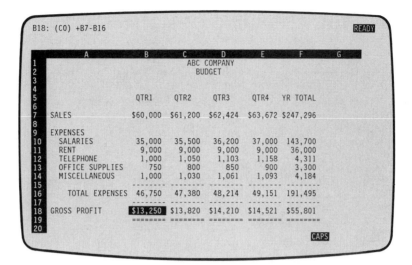

```
B18: (C0) +B7-B16                                                    READY

           A            B        C        D        E        F        G
  1                            ABC COMPANY
  2                              BUDGET
  3
  4
  5                         QTR1     QTR2     QTR3     QTR4   YR TOTAL
  6
  7     SALES           $60,000  $61,200  $62,424  $63,672 $247,296
  8
  9     EXPENSES
 10        SALARIES      35,000   35,500   36,200   37,000  143,700
 11        RENT           9,000    9,000    9,000    9,000   36,000
 12        TELEPHONE      1,000    1,050    1,103    1,158    4,311
 13        OFFICE SUPPLIES  750      800      850      900    3,300
 14        MISCELLANEOUS  1,000    1,030    1,061    1,093    4,184
 15                      -------  -------  -------  -------  -------
 16        TOTAL EXPENSES 46,750   47,380   48,214   49,151  191,495
 17                      -------  -------  -------  -------  -------
 18     GROSS PROFIT    $13,250  $13,820  $14,210  $14,521  $55,801
 19                     =======  =======  =======  =======  =======
 20                                                                 CAPS
```

The dollar signs in the Currency format do not align with each other in a column; the dollar signs are placed flush to the formatted number. If the dollar signs need to be aligned, the Currency format is not the appropriate action to take. Instead, one-character columns must be inserted before each column of values and the dollar sign "$" must be typed manually. The dollar sign must be entered with a label prefix such as the apostrophe (e.g., '$).

Comparing Worksheet Global Format to Range Format

The **Worksheet Global Format** command sequence is used to set the format of how most of the numbers in the spreadsheet are to be displayed. The **Range Format** command sequence is used to set the format of **specified ranges** of numbers in the spreadsheet.

In the BUDGET worksheet, most of the worksheet was set to display commas; therefore, the **Worksheet Global Format** command sequence was used. The **Range Format** could have been used, but the former command sequence is faster. Two specified ranges (the top and bottom row) of the BUDGET command were set to display dollar signs; therefore, the Range Format command sequence was used.

With the cell pointer in cell B18, look at the information in the control panel. "(C0)" is displayed, indicating that the Currency format with **0** decimal places was chosen with **Range Format**. All cells formatted with the **Range Format** command will display a similar message in the control panel when highlighted by the cell pointer (refer to note in Figure 2–36). No format specification appears in the control panel for cells where the **Worksheet Global Format** command is used.

■ USING THE ROUNDING OPTION

As demonstrated in the BUDGET spreadsheet, rounding errors may occur in spreadsheets that have growth rates or percentages. To prevent this problem, use the 1–2–3 @ROUND function whenever a formula includes multiplication, division, or exponents. The format for the @ROUND function is as follows:

```
@ROUND(formula,number of digits to round to)
```

Both the formula and the number of digits to round to must be specified.

In the BUDGET worksheet, the original formula for the fourth quarter of SALES was:

```
+D7*1.02
```

The value of the computation was:

```
63672.48
```

Later, when the Worksheet Global Format Sequence was used to format the numbers to display commas and 0 decimal places, the number was formatted to *appear* as:

```
63,672
```

The number *appeared* as 63,672 but the *number used in computation* was still 63672.48. The use of this number can result in a rounding error.

To truly round the number, use the @ROUND function. The formula above could be written as follows:

```
@ROUND(+D7*1.02,0)
```

A summary of the differences are below:

Formula	Value	Global Format Comma 0 Appears As	Number Used In Computation
+D7*1.02	63672.48	63,672	63672.48
@ROUND(+D7*1.02,0	63672	63,672	63672

The @ROUND function will not work for all situations (e.g., percentages). It may be necessary to "plug a number" to get the desired results.

■ MAKING A BACKUP OF A SPREADSHEET FILE

It is possible to make a copy of a file from one disk to another disk using 1–2–3.

It is assumed that the original BUDGET file is currently in memory and that Drive B is currently being used for save and retrieve operations.

To copy the BUDGET file onto another disk:

Insert		the disk to copy BUDGET onto in drive B
Press	/	(the command key)
Type	F	(for File)
Type	S	(for Save)

When prompted for the file name, the file BUDGET should be displayed.

Press	↵

The file BUDGET is copied from memory onto the disk in drive B. A copy of the file BUDGET now resides on the disk in drive B.

Another way to copy a file and also specify which disk drive on which to save the file is to select **File Save**, press the [Esc] key, and type the desired disk drive and file name. In the example above, after pressing **File Save**, the user could press [Esc] three times and then type B:BUDGET.

To make a backup of more than one file at a time, refer to the Disk Operating System COPY command discussed in the Appendix.

■ PROCESS FOR LEAVING LOTUS 1–2–3

When it is desirable to leave Lotus 1–2–3, perform the following set of operations:

Press	/	(the command key)
Type	Q	(for Quit)
Type	Y	(for Yes)
Type	E	(for Exit)

The user should now be back in DOS with an appropriate prompt on the screen. The type of prompt that appears depends on how the system was initially configured.

SUMMARY

Creating spreadsheets is faster and more effective using a spreadsheet software package such as Lotus 1–2–3. Creating formulas and values that can be copied, inserting and deleting entire rows and columns with menu commands, and saving the file for easy editing are just a few advantages of the Lotus 1–2–3 spreadsheet software package.

KEY CONCEPTS

@ROUND
@SUM
Copy
[Ctrl] [Break]
[Esc]
File Retrieve
File Save
Label
Print Printer Range
Print Printer Align Go
Print Printer Options Other
  As-Displayed

Print Printer Options Other
  Cell-Formulas
[PrtSc]
Range Format Currency
Relative cell location
Value
Worksheet Column Reset-Width
Worksheet Column Set-Width
Worksheet Global Column-Width
Worksheet Global Format ,
Worksheet Insert Row

CHAPTER TWO
EXERCISE 1

INSTRUCTIONS: Circle T if the statement is true and F if the statement is false.

T F 1. One way to erase incorrect data is to move to the incorrect data's cell, retype the data correctly, and press ↵ to enter the correction.

T F 2. The formula SUM(A1 . . A7) will add the data in cells A1 through A7.

T F 3. To round a number to two decimal places, use the **R**ange Format command.

T F 4. The **W**orksheet **E**rase **Y**es command sequence erases the worksheet currently in use from main memory.

T F 5. A print range must be specified before a spreadsheet can be printed.

T F 6. The "@" character must precede special functions such as the SUM and ROUND functions.

T F 7. Lotus 1–2–3 will automatically save changes that are made to a spreadsheet file.

T F 8. To look at a previously saved file, the **F**ile **R**etrieve command is used.

T F 9. "BUDGET 1" is an acceptable file name.

T F 10. The letter "X" is the symbol for multiplication when using Lotus 1–2–3.

CHAPTER TWO
EXERCISE 2

INSTRUCTIONS: Explain a typical situation when the following keystrokes or Lotus 1–2–3 commands are used.

Problem 1:   / File Save

Problem 2:   / Worksheet Insert Row

Problem 3:   +B1*1.09

Problem 4:   / Worksheet Global Column-Width

Problem 5:   / Worksheet Column Set-Width

Problem 6:   / Worksheet Erase Yes

Problem 7:   / Print Printer Range

Problem 8:   / Print Printer Align Go

Problem 9:   [Edit]

Problem 10:   [Shift] + [PrtSc]

Problem 11:   +B7–B6

Problem 12:   @ROUND(+B7*B8,0)

Problem 13:   @SUM(B1..B25)

Problem 14:   Worksheet Global Format , 2

Problem 15:   Range Format Currency, 2

Problem 16:   / File Retrieve

Problem 17:   / Copy

CHAPTER TWO
EXERCISE 3
Correcting a Spreadsheet

INSTRUCTIONS: The following example illustrates a common error.
Follow the instructions below to create the error and answer the
questions below.

Clear the screen (use the **Worksheet Erase Yes** commands).
In cell A1, type 52 and press ⏎ .
In cell A2, type 30 and press ⏎ .
In cell A3, type A1–A2 and press ⏎ .

The screen should appear as follows.

```
A3: ′A1–A2
READY


        A        B        C        D        E        F        G        H
 1      52
 2      30
 3   A1–A2
 4
 5
 6
 7
 8
 9
10
11
12
13
14
15
16
17
18
19
20
                                                                    CAPS
```

1. What caused the error in cell A3?

2. How can the error be corrected?

CHAPTER TWO
EXERCISE 4
Correcting a Spreadsheet

INSTRUCTIONS: The following example illustrates a common error.
Follow the instructions below to create the error and answer the
questions below.

Clear the screen (use the **Worksheet Erase Yes** commands).
In cell A1, type 52 and press ↵.
In cell A2, press the space bar one time. Type 30 and press ↵.
In cell A3, type +A1–A2 and press ↵.

The screen should appear as follows.

```
A3: +A1-A2
READY


         A         B         C         D         E         F         G         H
1             52
2    30
3             52
4
5
6
7
8
9
10
11
12
13
14
15
16
17
18
19
                                                                         CAPS
```

1. What caused the error in computing A1–A2?

2. How can the error be corrected?

CHAPTER TWO
EXERCISE 5
Correcting a Spreadsheet

INSTRUCTIONS: The following example illustrates a common error.
Follow the instructions below to create the error and answer the
questions below.

Clear the screen (use the **Worksheet Erase Yes** commands).
In cell A1, type 52 and press ↵.
In cell A2, type 30 and press ↵.
In cell A3, type +A1 and press ↵. Then type −A2 and press ↵.

The screen should appear as follows.

```
A3: −A2
READY


        A         B         C         D         E         F         G         H
1          52
2          30
3         −30
4
5
6
7
8
9
10
11
12
13
14
15
16
17
18
19
20
                                                                        CAPS
```

1. What caused the error in computing A1−A2?

2. How can the error be corrected?

CHAPTER TWO
EXERCISE 6
Creating a Spreadsheet

INSTRUCTIONS: Create the spreadsheet below. It will be used for exercises in other chapters. The following spreadsheet consists of straight data entry (no formulas). Save the file under the name UNITPROD (for Unit Production). The cell formulas for the worksheet are listed as a reference.

The spreadsheet should appear as follows on the screen.

```
A1: [W21]
READY




            A              B         C            D            E
1                        ABC COMPANY
2
3
4                                  NO. OF     NO. OF
5             UNITS        CODE  UNITS PRODUCED  UNITS SOLD
6
7     REG COLA            REG C     800,000      780,806
8     LOW-CAL COLA        LOW C     750,000      675,123
9     ONE-CAL COLA        ONE C     700,000      650,587
10    REG COLA W/O CAF    REG X     575,000      450,645
11    LOW-CAL W/O CAF     LOW X     550,000      376,589
12    ONE-CAL W/O CAF     ONE X     500,000      488,654
13
14
15
16
17
18
19
20
                                                          CAPS
```

```
B1: [W6] 'ABC COMPANY
C4: [W14] ^NO. OF
B4: [W15] ^NO. OF
A5: [W21] ^UNITS
```

```
B5:  [W6] 'CODE
C5:  [W14] 'UNITS PRODUCED
D5:  [W15] ^UNITS SOLD
A7:  [W21] 'REG COLA
B7:  [W6] 'REG C
C7:  (,0) [W14] 800000
D7:  (,0) [W15] 780806
A8:  [W21] 'LOW-CAL COLA
B8:  [W6] 'LOW C
C8:  (,0) [W14] 750000
D8:  (,0) [W15] 675123
A9:  [W21] 'ONE-CAL COLA
B9:  [W6] 'ONE C
C9:  (,0) [W14] 700000
D9:  (,0) [W15] 650587
A10: [W21] 'REG COLA W/O CAF
B10: [W6] 'REG X
C10: (,0) [W14] 575000
D10: (,0) [W15] 450645
A11: [W21] 'LOW-CAL W/O CAF
B11: [W6] 'LOW X
C11: (,0) [W14] 550000
D11: (,0) [W15] 376589
A12: [W21] 'ONE-CAL W/O CAF
B12: [W6] 'ONE X
C12: (,0) [W14] 500000
D12: (,0) [W15] 488654
```

CHAPTER TWO
EXERCISE 7
Creating a Spreadsheet

INSTRUCTIONS: Create the spreadsheet below. It will be used for an exercise in a later chapter. The following spreadsheet consists of straight data entry except for the SUM formula in cell C15. Save the file under the name SALES. The cell formulas for the worksheet are listed as a reference. Format only cells C8 through C13 and C15.

The spreadsheet should appear as follows on the screen.

```
A1:
READY


            A            B             C            D           E          F
  1                            ABC COMPANY
  2                               SALES
  3
  4
  5
  6          SALESPERSONS       SALES
  7
  8          ALLEN, DARLA       3,678
  9          ALUM, BETH         2,813
 10          JOSEPH, CARLA      6,798
 11          NOTTS, DON         4,378
 12          RANKIN, AL         3,579
 14                            --------
 15          TOTALS            26,228
 16
 17
 18
 19
 20
                                                                        CAPS
```

```
B1:  [W13] '           ABC COMPANY
C2:  [W11] 'SALES
B6:  [W13] 'SALESPERSONS
C6:  [W11] "SALES
B8:  [W13] 'ALLEN, DARLA
```

```
C8:  (,0) [W11] 3678
B9:  [W13] 'ALUM, BETH
C9:  (,0) [W11] 2813
B10: [W13] 'JOSEPH, CARLA
C10: (,0) [W11] 6798
B11: [W13] 'NOTTS, DON
C11: (,0) [W11] 4378
B12: [W13] 'RANKIN, AL
C12: (,0) [W11] 3579
B13: [W13] 'SEBO, JULES
C13: (,0) [W11] 4982
C14: (,0) [W11] '    ---- ----
B15: [W13] 'TOTALS
C15: (,0) [W11] @SUM(C8..C13)
```

CHAPTER TWO
EXERCISE 8
Creating a Spreadsheet

INSTRUCTIONS: Create the spreadsheet below.
REVENUE is 25,000 in YEAR 1 and projected to increase by six percent for years 2 and 3. EXPENSES are 9,500 in YEAR 1 and projected to be twenty-five percent of REVENUE in YEARS 2 and 3. PROFIT BEFORE TAX is REVENUE minus EXPENSES. Save the file under the name PRACTICE. This file will be used in an exercise in a subsequent chapter. The cell formulas for the worksheet are listed as a reference. The spreadsheet should appear as follows on the screen.

```
A1: [W17]
READY


                    A            B         C         D         E         F         G
          1                           PROJECTED PROFITS
          2
          3                         YEAR 1    YEAR 2    YEAR 3    TOTAL
          4
          5    REVENUE              25,000    26,500    28,090    79,590
          6    EXPENSES              9,500     6,625     7,023    23,148
          7    PROFIT BEFORE TAX    15,500    19,875    21,067    56,442
          8
          9
         10
         11
         12
         13
         14
         15
         16
         17
         18
         19
         20                                                                         CAPS



     C1: 'PROJECTED PROFITS
             B3: "YEAR 1
             C3: "YEAR 2
```

```
D3:  "YEAR 3
E3:  "TOTAL
A5:  [W17] 'REVENUE
B5:  25000
C5:  @ROUND(B5*1.06,0)
D5:  @ROUND(C5*1.06,0)
E5:  @SUM(B5..D5)
A6:  [W17] 'EXPENSES
B6:  9500
C6:  @ROUND(0.25*C5,0)
D6:  @ROUND(0.25*D5,0)
E6:  @SUM(B6..D6)
A7:  [W17] 'PROFIT BEFORE TAX
B7:  +B5-B6
C7:  +C5-C6
D7:  +D5-D6
E7:  @SUM(B7..D7)
```

CHAPTER TWO
EXERCISE 9
Editing a Spreadsheet

INSTRUCTIONS: Retrieve the file BUDGET. Edit BUDGET using the instructions below. Use Figure 2–37 as a guide. Note that the file created below will be titled BUDGET2 and will be needed for an exercise in a subsequent chapter.

* Expand the worksheet to include projections through YEAR 10:

Insert six columns (F–K) between QTR4 and YR TOTAL using the Worksheet Insert Column command sequence.
Rename the headings QTR1 through QTR4 with the headings YEAR 1 through YEAR 4 and continue the headings through YEAR 10.
Copy the formulas, subtotal lines, and total lines from YEAR 4 (E7 . . E19) to YEAR 5 through YEAR 10 (F7 . . K19).
The projections will be the same for all ten years.

* Change the sums under YR TOTAL to reflect the additional years:

Change the formula in cell L7 from @SUM(B7..E7) to @SUM(B7..K7).
Copy the formula in cell L7 to cells L10 . . L18.
Replace the result of copying the @SUM formula in cells L15 and L17 (which now display zeroes) with subtotal lines.

* Use the Move command to move the titles ABC COMPANY and BUDGET to column F. The titles will be centered on the new spreadsheet.

* Save the spreadsheet, being sure to name the new spreadsheet BUDGET2. BUDGET and BUDGET2 are two separate files on the disk.

The final result should look like Figure 2–37 (the entire spreadsheet will not be entirely visible on the screen at one time). The cell formulas for the spreadsheet are listed as a reference in Figure 2–38.

Figure 2–37

```
●                                           ABC COMPANY                                    ●
                                             BUDGET

●                                                                                          ●

●          YEAR 1   YEAR 2   YEAR 3   YEAR 4   YEAR 5   YEAR 6   YEAR 7   YEAR 8   YEAR 9   YEAR 10 YR TOTAL   ●

   SALES   60,000   61,200   62,424   63,672   64,945   66,244   67,569   68,920   70,298   71,704  656,976

●  EXPENSES                                                                                 ●
     SALARIES     35,000   35,500   36,200   37,000   37,000   37,000   37,000   37,000   37,000   37,000  365,700
     RENT          9,000    9,000    9,000    9,000    9,000    9,000    9,000    9,000    9,000    9,000   90,000
●    TELEPHONE     1,000    1,050    1,103    1,158    1,216    1,277    1,341    1,408    1,478    1,552   12,583   ●
     OFFICE SUPPLIES 750      800      850      900      950    1,000    1,050    1,100    1,150    1,200    9,750
     MISCELLANEOUS  1,000    1,030    1,061    1,093    1,126    1,160    1,195    1,231    1,268    1,306   11,470
●                ---------------------------------------------------------------------------------------         ●
   TOTAL EXPENSES 46,750   47,380   48,214   49,151   49,292   49,437   49,586   49,739   49,896   50,058  489,503

●                ---------------------------------------------------------------------------------------         ●
   GROSS PROFIT  13,250   13,820   14,210   14,521   15,653   16,807   17,983   19,181   20,402   21,646  167,473
●                =======================================================================================         ●
```

Figure 2–38
Part 1

```
F1:  '       ABC COMPANY
F2:  '          BUDGET
B5:  ^YEAR 1
C5:  ^YEAR 2
D5:  ^YEAR 3
E5:  ^YEAR 4
F5:  ^YEAR 5
G5:  ^YEAR 6
H5:  ^YEAR 7
I5:  ^YEAR 8
J5:  ^YEAR 9
K5:  ^YEAR 10
L5:  'YR TOTAL
A7:  [W18] 'SALES
B7:  60000
C7:  @ROUND(B7*1.02,0)
D7:  @ROUND(C7*1.02,0)
E7:  @ROUND(D7*1.02,0)
F7:  @ROUND(E7*1.02,0)
G7:  @ROUND(F7*1.02,0)
H7:  @ROUND(G7*1.02,0)
I7:  @ROUND(H7*1.02,0)
J7:  @ROUND(I7*1.02,0)
K7:  @ROUND(J7*1.02,0)
L7:  @SUM(B7..K7)
A9:  [W18] 'EXPENSES
A10: [W18] '  SALARIES
B10: 35000
C10: 35500
D10: 36200
E10: 37000
F10: 37000
G10: 37000
H10: 37000
I10: 37000
J10: 37000
K10: 37000
L10: @SUM(B10..K10)
A11: [W18] '   RENT
B11: 9000
C11: 9000
D11: 9000
E11: 9000
F11: 9000
G11: 9000
H11: 9000
I11: 9000
J11: 9000
K11: 9000
L11: @SUM(B11..K11)
A12: [W18] '  TELEPHONE
B12: 1000
C12: @ROUND(B12*1.05,0)
D12: @ROUND(C12*1.05,0)
E12: @ROUND(D12*1.05,0)
F12: @ROUND(E12*1.05,0)
```

Figure 2–38
Part 2

```
G12: @ROUND(F12*1.05,0)
H12: @ROUND(G12*1.05,0)
I12: @ROUND(H12*1.05,0)
J12: @ROUND(I12*1.05,0)
K12: @ROUND(J12*1.05,0)
L12: @SUM(B12..K12)
A13: [W18] '   OFFICE SUPPLIES
B13: 750
C13: +B13+50
D13: +C13+50
E13: +D13+50
F13: +E13+50
G13: +F13+50
H13: +G13+50
I13: +H13+50
J13: +I13+50
K13: +J13+50
L13: @SUM(B13..K13)
A14: [W18] '   MISCELLANEOUS
B14: 1000
C14: @ROUND(B14*1.03,0)
D14: @ROUND(C14*1.03,0)
E14: @ROUND(D14*1.03,0)
F14: @ROUND(E14*1.03,0)
G14: @ROUND(F14*1.03,0)
H14: @ROUND(G14*1.03,0)
I14: @ROUND(H14*1.03,0)
J14: @ROUND(I14*1.03,0)
K14: @ROUND(J14*1.03,0)
L14: @SUM(B14..K14)
B15: ' --------
C15: ' --------
D15: ' --------
E15: ' --------
F15: ' --------
G15: ' --------
H15: ' --------
I15: ' --------
J15: ' --------
K15: ' --------
L15: ' --------
A16: [W18] '    TOTAL EXPENSES
B16: @SUM(B10..B14)
C16: @SUM(C10..C14)
D16: @SUM(D10..D14)
E16: @SUM(E10..E14)
F16: @SUM(F10..F14)
G16: @SUM(G10..G14)
H16: @SUM(H10..H14)
I16: @SUM(I10..I14)
J16: @SUM(J10..J14)
K16: @SUM(K10..K14)
L16: @SUM(B16..K16)
B17: ' --------
C17: ' --------
D17: ' --------
```

Figure 2–38
Part 3

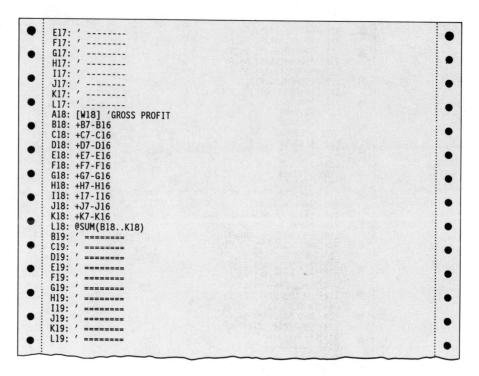

```
E17: ' --------
F17: ' --------
G17: ' --------
H17: ' --------
I17: ' --------
J17: ' --------
K17: ' --------
L17: ' --------
A18: [W18] 'GROSS PROFIT
B18: +B7-B16
C18: +C7-C16
D18: +D7-D16
E18: +E7-E16
F18: +F7-F16
G18: +G7-G16
H18: +H7-H16
I18: +I7-I16
J18: +J7-J16
K18: +K7-K16
L18: @SUM(B18..K18)
B19: ' ========
C19: ' ========
D19: ' ========
E19: ' ========
F19: ' ========
G19: ' ========
H19: ' ========
I19: ' ========
J19: ' ========
K19: ' ========
L19: ' ========
```

CHAPTER THREE

BUILDING AN ANALYSIS MODEL

OBJECTIVES

In this chapter, the student will learn to:

■ Build a spreadsheet for "what-if" analysis

■ CHAPTER OVERVIEW

When the file BUDGET was created in Chapter Two, several formulas were entered with numbers directly within the formula (e.g., the initial Sales formula was +B7*1.02, the Telephone Expenses formula was +B12*1.05).

Suppose that individuals within an organization wished to see how different projections affect a particular formula. For example, someone might wish to see the overall results if Sales were projected to increase by three percent rather than two percent. Perhaps the user wishes to vary the projections for each year (SALES is projected to increase by two percent the first year, by three percent the second year, etc.). The user might also wish to vary the assumptions for other projections in the spreadsheet.

Substituting various values to see the effect on a formula is known as performing a sensitivity analysis, or **"what-if"** analysis. Performing a sensitivity analysis by constantly editing the formulas to enter a new assumption is awkward and time-consuming. If assumptions are listed outside of the formulas in other cells, then they can be changed more visibly and easily.

Chapter Three presents a general approach to building spreadsheets so that assumptions can be changed quickly and easily. Because the worksheet recalculates with every new change, the user can see the true power of the "what-if" capability of 1–2–3. This exercise also uses the @ROUND function to avoid rounding errors. Chapter Three reinforces and enhances the concepts learned in Chapter Two.

A printout of the completed worksheet is displayed in Figure 3–1.

Figure 3–1

```
                             ABC COMPANY
                               BUDGET


                  QTR1      QTR2      QTR3      QTR4    YR TOTAL

   SALES          60,000    61,200    62,424    63,672   247,296

   EXPENSES
     SALARIES     35,000    35,500    36,200    37,000   143,700
     RENT          9,000     9,000     9,000     9,000    36,000
     TELEPHONE     1,000     1,050     1,103     1,158     4,311
     OFFICE SUPPLIES  750      800       850       900     3,300
     MISCELLANEOUS  1,000     1,030     1,061     1,093     4,184
                  --------  --------  --------  --------  --------
     TOTAL EXPENSES 46,750   47,380    48,214    49,151   191,495
                  --------  --------  --------  --------  --------
   GROSS PROFIT   13,250    13,820    14,210    14,521    55,801
                  ========  ========  ========  ========  ========

   ASSUMPTIONS

   SALES RATE                  1.02      1.02      1.02
   TELEPHONE EXP               1.05      1.05      1.05
   OFFICE SUPPLIES EXP        50.00     50.00     50.00
   MISCELLANEOUS EXP           1.03      1.03      1.03
```

■ CLEARING THE SCREEN

To erase the screen before beginning the spreadsheet, complete the steps below:

Press	/	(the command key)
Type	W	(for Worksheet)
Type	E	(for Erase)
Type	Y	(for Yes)

The screen is now clear and ready for the preparation of a new worksheet.

■ CREATING LABELS FOR THE WORKSHEET

To make all of the labels appear in capital letters, make sure that "CAPS" appears at the bottom of the screen. If the Caps Lock key needs to be activated:

Press	the [Caps Lock] key

"CAPS" now appears at the lower right corner of the screen.

The cell pointer should be in cell A1. If it is not, use the arrow keys located to the right of the keyboard to move the cell pointer.

The first step is to enter the labels in column A. The first label is SALES. To enter the label SALES in cell A1:

Type	SALES ↵

To input the label EXPENSES in cell A2:

Move	the cell pointer to cell A2
Type	EXPENSES ↵

To input the label SALARIES in cell A3:

Move	the cell pointer to cell A3

To indent the label:

Press	the space bar twice
Type	SALARIES

Pressing the space bar is an easy way to indent labels. Note that from this point on, the instructions utilize a "short cut" to entering labels. Instead of pressing ↵ , press the down arrow key to enter a label AND move to the next cell.

Press	the down arrow key

The cell pointer is in cell A4. To enter the next label:

Press	the space bar twice
Type	RENT
Press	the down arrow key

The cell pointer is in cell A5. To enter the next label:

Press	the space bar twice
Type	TELEPHONE
Press	the down arrow key

The cell pointer is in cell A6. To enter the next label:

Press	the space bar twice
Type	OFFICE SUPPLIES
Press	the down arrow key

The cell pointer is in cell A7. To enter the next label:

Press	the space bar twice
Type	MISCELLANEOUS
Press	the down arrow key

The cell pointer is in cell A8. To enter the next label:

Press	the space bar four times
Type	TOTAL EXPENSES
Press	the down arrow key

The cell pointer is in cell A9. To enter the next label:

Type	GROSS PROFIT ↵

The down arrow key did not have to be pressed since Gross Profit is the last label on the spreadsheet. The worksheet should look like Figure 3–2.

Figure 3–2

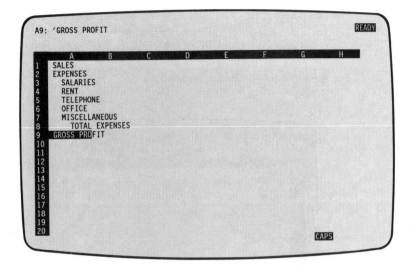

```
A9: 'GROSS PROFIT                                              READY
        A        B        C        D        E        F        G        H
1   SALES
2   EXPENSES
3      SALARIES
4      RENT
5      TELEPHONE
6      OFFICE
7      MISCELLANEOUS
8         TOTAL EXPENSES
9   GROSS PROFIT
10
11
12
13
14
15
16
17
18
19
20                                                                CAPS
```

■ ENTERING THE DESCRIPTIONS FOR THE ASSUMPTIONS BELOW THE SPREADSHEET

To enter the labels for the assumptions:

Move	the cell pointer to cell A12
Type	ASSUMPTIONS
Press	the down arrow key *twice*

The cell pointer is in cell A14. To enter the next label:

Type	SALES RATE
Press	the down arrow key

The cell pointer is in cell A15. To enter the next label:

Type	TELEPHONE EXP
Press	the down arrow key

The cell pointer is in cell A16. To enter the next label:

Type	OFFICE SUPPLIES EXP
Press	the down arrow key

The cell pointer is in cell A17. To enter the next label:

Type   MISCELLANEOUS EXP ↵

The screen should look like Figure 3–3.

Figure 3–3

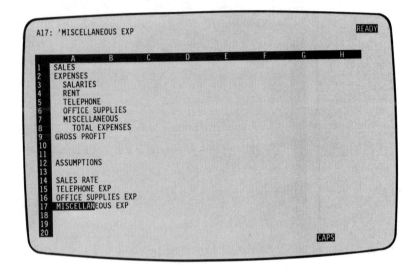

◼ WIDENING A COLUMN TO SEE THE LABELS

To widen column A:

Move   the cell pointer to the longest label in the column

In this example, A16 should be highlighted since it has the longest label (OFFICE SUPPLIES EXP.).

Press   /   (the command key)

Type   W   (for Worksheet)

Type   C   (for Column)

Type   S   (for Set-Width)

Press   the right arrow key until the entire label is highlighted

In the control panel, the following message is displayed:

```
Enter column width (1..240): 19
```

Press ↵

The column width of column A is now 19 characters. Column B "shifts" to the right and columns G and H scroll out of sight. The screen should resemble Figure 3–4.

Figure 3–4

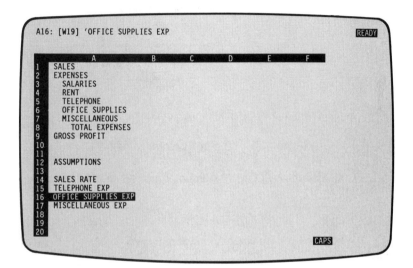

■ ENTERING THE ASSUMPTIONS

To input the assumed sales rate:

Move the cell pointer to cell C14
Type 1.02
Press the down arrow key

The sales rate is not placed in column B because the rate is not needed for the first quarter.

The cell pointer is in cell C15. To input the Telephone expense rate:

Type 1.05
Press the down arrow key

The cell pointer is in cell C16. To input the Office Supplies expense rate:

Type   50
Press   the down arrow key

The cell pointer is in cell C17. To input the Miscellaneous expense rate:

Type   1.03 ↵

To copy the expense rates to the last three quarters:

Move   the cell pointer to cell C14
Press   /   (the command key)
Type   C   (for Copy)

When prompted to enter the range to copy FROM:

Move   the cell pointer to cell C17

Cells C14 through C17 (the assumptions) are highlighted as the cells to copy.

Press   ↵

When prompted to enter the range to copy TO:

Move   the cell pointer to cell D14
Press   .
Move   the cell pointer to cell E17
Press   ↵

Now that the assumptions have been entered, the rest of the spreadsheet will be built. The formulas will be constructed so that they are dependent upon the assumptions. If the assumptions are changed, the worksheet will be recalculated according to the changes. At this point, the screen should resemble Figure 3–5.

Figure 3–5

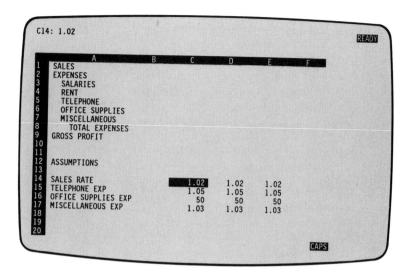

ENTERING NUMBERS AND FORMULAS, AND COPYING FORMULAS TO THE REST OF THE SPREADSHEET

To enter the Sales amount for the first quarter:

Move	the cell pointer to cell B1
Type	60000 ↵

The first formula in this worksheet will multiply the Sales amount by the amount listed in the assumptions below the worksheet. To enter the formula:

Move	the cell pointer to cell C1
Type	@ROUND (
Move	the cell pointer to cell B1 (Sales)
Type	* (the symbol for multiplication)
Move	the cell pointer to cell C14 (Sales Rate)
Type	,0) ↵

The number 61200 appears in cell C1. With cell C1 highlighted, look at the control panel at the upper left corner of the screen. The formula @ROUND (B1*C14,0) is displayed, which was the formula used to compute the number 61200. Since C14 is an assumption listed below the spreadsheet, the Sales Rate can easily be changed so that the formula placed in cell C1 is recalculated.

The cell pointer is highlighting cell C1. To copy the formula for projecting Sales to cells D1 and E1 (for Quarters 3 and 4):

Press / (the command key)

Type C (for Copy)

When prompted to enter the range to copy FROM:

Press ↵

(The cell pointer was already highlighting C1, which is the cell to copy). When prompted to enter the range to copy TO:

Move the cell pointer to cell D1

Press .

Move the cell pointer to cell E1 ↵

The screen should resemble Figure 3–6.

Figure 3–6

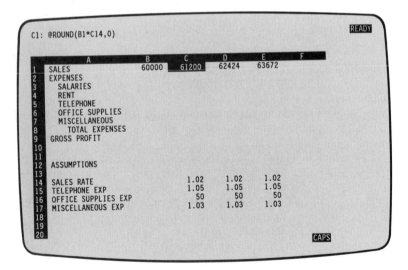

To input the data for Salaries:

Move the cell pointer to cell B3

Make sure the cell pointer is in the *third* row.

Type	35000 (first quarter Salaries)
Move	the cell pointer to cell C3
Type	35500 (second quarter Salaries)
Move	the cell pointer to cell D3
Type	36200 (third quarter Salaries)
Move	the cell pointer to cell E3
Type	37000 (fourth quarter Salaries) ↵

The screen should resemble Figure 3–7.

Figure 3–7

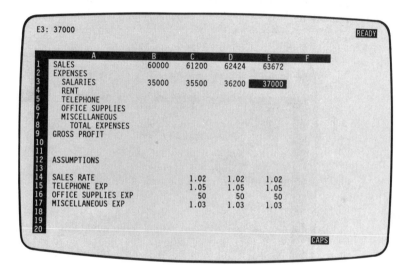

To input the data for Rent:

| Move | the cell pointer to cell B4 |
| Type | 9000 ↵ |

The cell pointer is in cell B4. To copy 9000 to Quarters 2, 3, and 4:

| Press | / | (the command key) |
| Type | C | (for Copy) |

When prompted to enter the range to copy FROM:

Press ↵

The cell pointer was already highlighting cell B4. When prompted to enter the range to copy TO:

Move the cell pointer to cell C4
Press .
Move the cell pointer to cell E4 ↵

The number 9000 is copied to Quarters 2, 3, and 4. The screen should look like Figure 3–8.

Figure 3–8

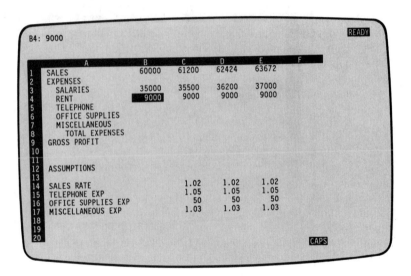

To input the data for Telephone expenses for the first quarter:

Move the cell pointer to cell B5
Type 1000 ↵

The following formula will indicate that Telephone expenses will increase by 5% for the following quarters:

Move	the cell pointer to cell C5
Type	@ROUND (
Move	the cell pointer to cell B5
Type	*
Move	the cell pointer to cell C15
Type	,0) ↵

The number 1050 appears in cell C5. The formula @ROUND (B5*C15,0) is displayed in the control panel. The formula for Quarters 3 and 4 will be copied later in this exercise.

To input the data for Office Supplies expenses for the first quarter:

Move	the cell pointer to cell B6
Type	750 ↵

The following formula indicates that Office Supplies expenses will increase by $50 for the following quarters. Because the only operation performed within the formula is addition, the ROUND function is not needed to prevent rounding errors. To enter the formula:

Move	the cell pointer to cell C6
Type	+
Move	the cell pointer to cell B6
Type	+
Move	the cell pointer to cell C16 ↵

The number 800 appears in cell C6. The formula +B6+C16 is displayed in the control panel. The formula for Quarters 3 and 4 will be copied later in this exercise.

To input the data for Miscellaneous expenses for the first quarter:

Move	the cell pointer to cell B7
Type	1000 ↵

The following formula will indicate that Miscellaneous expenses will increase by 3% for the following quarters. To enter the formula:

Move	the cell pointer to cell C7
Type	@ROUND (
Move	the cell pointer to cell B7
Type	*
Move	the cell pointer to cell C17
Type	,0) ↵

The number 1030 appears in cell C7. The formula @ROUND (B7*C17,0) is displayed in the control panel. The screen should look like Figure 3–9.

Figure 3–9

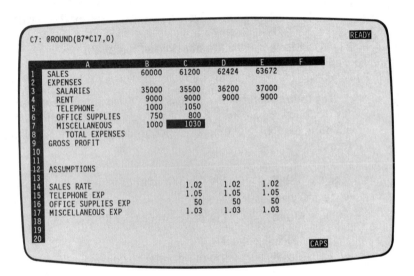

To copy the formulas for the projected expenses to quarters 3 and 4:

Move	the cell pointer to cell C5 (the formula for projecting Telephone expenses)	
Press	/	(the command key)
Type	C	(for Copy)

When prompted to enter the range to copy FROM:

Move   the cell pointer to cell C7 (the formula for projecting Miscellaneous expenses)

Press   ↵

When prompted to enter the range to copy TO:

Move   the cell pointer to cell D5

Press   .

The period key will anchor the cursor at cell D5.

Move   the cell pointer to cell E7

Cells D5 through E7 are highlighted.

Press   ↵

The formulas in cells C5 through C7 (to project Telephone, Office Supplies and Miscellaneous Expenses) are now copied to cells D5 through E7. The screen should resemble Figure 3–10.

Figure 3–10

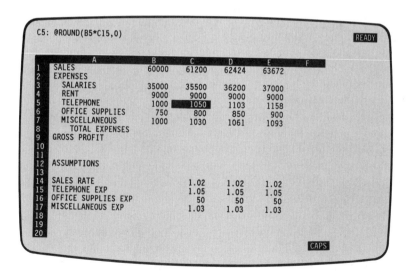

```
C5:  @ROUND(B5*C15,0)                                              READY

              A              B         C         D         E        F
 1   SALES               60000     61200     62424     63672
 2   EXPENSES
 3     SALARIES          35000     35500     36200     37000
 4     RENT               9000      9000      9000      9000
 5     TELEPHONE          1000      1050      1103      1158
 6     OFFICE SUPPLIES     750       800       850       900
 7     MISCELLANEOUS      1000      1030      1061      1093
 8       TOTAL EXPENSES
 9   GROSS PROFIT
10
11
12   ASSUMPTIONS
13
14   SALES RATE                     1.02      1.02      1.02
15   TELEPHONE EXP                  1.05      1.05      1.05
16   OFFICE SUPPLIES EXP              50        50        50
17   MISCELLANEOUS EXP              1.03      1.03      1.03
18
19
20
                                                          CAPS
```

The following instructions total the expenses for the first quarter by using the 1–2–3 SUM command:

Move	the cell pointer to cell B8
Type	@SUM(
Move	the cell pointer to cell B3 (the first item in column B to total, which is SALARIES)
Type	.
Move	the cell pointer to cell B7
Type	) ↵

The number 46750 appears. The formula @SUM(B3..B7) is displayed in the control panel.

To compute Gross Profit:

Move	the cell pointer to cell B9
Type	+
Move	the cell pointer to cell B1 (Sales)
Type	−
Move	the cell pointer to cell B8 (Total Expenses) ↵

The number 13250 appears. The formula +B1−B8 is displayed in the control panel.

In the following instructions, the Copy command will be used to copy the formulas for computing the Total Expenses and Gross Profit to the remaining three quarters.

Move	the cell pointer to cell B8 (Total Expenses)	
Press	/	(the command key)
Type	C	(for Copy)

When prompted to enter the range to copy FROM:

Move	the cell pointer to cell B9 (Gross Profit)

Cells B8 and B9 are highlighted.

Press	↵

When prompted to enter the Range to copy TO:

Move	the cell pointer to cell C8
Press	.
Move	the cell pointer to cell E9

Cells C8 through E9 are highlighted.

Press	↵

The screen should resemble Figure 3–11.

Figure 3–11

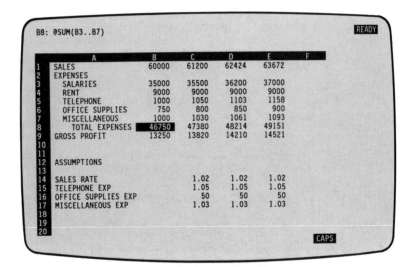

Computing Totals

To compute the total of each row:

Move	the cell pointer to cell F1
Type	@SUM(
Move	the cell pointer to cell B1
Press	.
Move	the cell pointer to cell E1
Type	) ↵

The number 247296 appears in cell F1. The formula @SUM(B1..E1) appears in the control panel.

To copy the @SUM(B1..E1) formula to the rows below:

Press	/	(the command key)
Type	C	(for Copy)

When prompted to enter the range to copy FROM:

Press	↵

Cell F1 (the SUM formula) is now designated as the range to copy. When prompted to enter the range to copy TO:

Move	the cell pointer to cell F3
Press	.
Move	the cell pointer to cell F9 ↵

The formula @SUM(B1..E1) is now copied from cell F1 to cells F3 through F9. The screen should look like Figure 3–12.

Figure 3–12

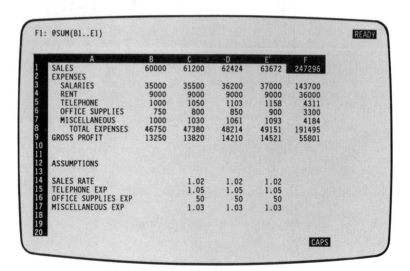

CHOOSING A FORMAT FOR THE DATA IN THE WORKSHEET

To choose a format (commas, dollar signs, the number of decimal places, etc.,) for the worksheet:

Press	/	(the command key)
Type	W	(for Worksheet)
Type	G	(for Global)
Type	F	(for Format)
Type	,	(for ,)

The , menu option represents the comma format. When prompted to enter the number of decimal places:

Type	0 ↵

Most of the assumptions need to display two decimal places. The screen should resemble Figure 3–13.

Figure 3–13

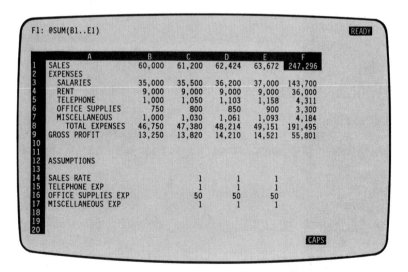

```
F1: @SUM(B1..E1)                                               READY

              A         B         C         D         E         F
 1  SALES          60,000    61,200    62,424    63,672   247,296
 2  EXPENSES
 3     SALARIES    35,000    35,500    36,200    37,000   143,700
 4     RENT         9,000     9,000     9,000     9,000    36,000
 5     TELEPHONE    1,000     1,050     1,103     1,158     4,311
 6     OFFICE SUPPLIES 750      800       850       900     3,300
 7     MISCELLANEOUS 1,000     1,030     1,061     1,093     4,184
 8       TOTAL EXPENSES 46,750 47,380   48,214    49,151   191,495
 9  GROSS PROFIT   13,250    13,820    14,210    14,521    55,801
10
11
12  ASSUMPTIONS
13
14  SALES RATE                        1         1         1
15  TELEPHONE EXP                     1         1         1
16  OFFICE SUPPLIES EXP              50        50        50
17  MISCELLANEOUS EXP                 1         1         1
18
19
20                                                          CAPS
```

The steps in the following section will format the assumptions appropriately.

■ FORMATTING THE ASSUMPTIONS TO TWO DECIMAL PLACES

To format the assumptions to two decimal places:

Move		the cell pointer to cell C14
Press	/	(the command key)
Type	R	(for Range)
Type	F	(for Format)
Type	F	(for Fixed)

When prompted to enter the number of decimal places:

Press ↵

Since the default setting for decimal places is 2, pressing ↵ accepts the default. When prompted to enter the range to format:

Move the cell pointer to cell E17

Cells C14 through E17 are highlighted.

Press ↵

The screen should resemble Figure 3–14.

Figure 3–14

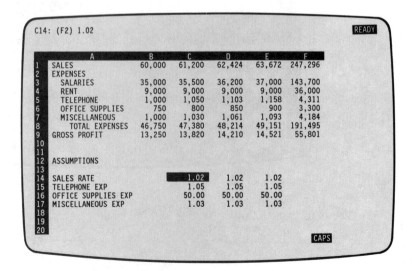

```
C14: (F2) 1.02                                                    READY

             A            B        C        D        E        F
 1   SALES              60,000   61,200   62,424   63,672  247,296
 2   EXPENSES
 3     SALARIES         35,000   35,500   36,200   37,000  143,700
 4     RENT              9,000    9,000    9,000    9,000   36,000
 5     TELEPHONE         1,000    1,050    1,103    1,158    4,311
 6     OFFICE SUPPLIES     750      800      850      900    3,300
 7     MISCELLANEOUS     1,000    1,030    1,061    1,093    4,184
 8       TOTAL EXPENSES 46,750   47,380   48,214   49,151  191,495
 9   GROSS PROFIT       13,250   13,820   14,210   14,521   55,801
10
11
12   ASSUMPTIONS
13
14   SALES RATE                   1.02     1.02     1.02
15   TELEPHONE EXP                1.05     1.05     1.05
16   OFFICE SUPPLIES EXP         50.00    50.00    50.00
17   MISCELLANEOUS EXP            1.03     1.03     1.03
18
19
20                                                         CAPS
```

◼ INSERTING BLANK ROWS FOR HEADINGS

To insert six blank rows at the top of the spreadsheet:

Move	the cell pointer to cell A1	
Press	/	
Type	W	(for Worksheet)
Type	I	(for Insert)
Type	R	(for Row)

When prompted to enter the row insert range:

Move	the cell pointer to cell A6
Press	⏎

The screen should resemble Figure 3–15.

Figure 3–15

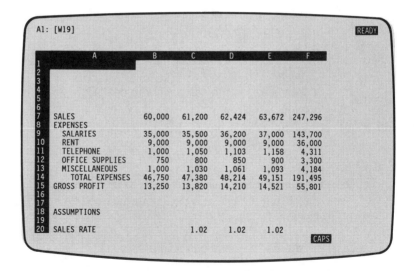

■ ENTERING HEADINGS

Lotus does not have a function that centers headings above an entire worksheet. The user must rely on his/her own judgment, often entering spaces before the heading to center it as accurately as possible. To input the first heading for this example:

Move	the cell pointer to cell C1
Press	the space bar five times
Type	ABC COMPANY ↵

To input the second heading:

Move	the cell pointer to cell C2
Press	the space bar seven times
Type	BUDGET ↵

To input the headings for all four quarters:

Move	the cell pointer to cell B5
Type	^QTR1
Move	the cell pointer to cell C5
Type	^QTR2
Move	the cell pointer to cell D5
Type	^QTR3
Move	the cell pointer to cell E5
Type	^QTR4 ↵

Recall that the ^ mark causes the labels to be centered within the column; a double quote mark before the heading would cause the labels to be right-justified in the column.

To input the heading YR TOTAL:

Move	the cell pointer to cell F5
Type	^YR TOTAL ↵

YR TOTAL is entered with the ^ symbol to be consistent, even though it is too long to be centered in the current column's width. Refer to Figure 3–16.

Figure 3–16

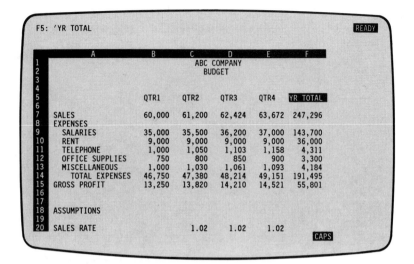

■ INSERTING BLANK ROWS WITHIN THE SPREADSHEET

To insert a blank row between SALES and EXPENSES:

Move		the cell pointer to cell A8 (EXPENSES)
Press	/	(the command key)
Type	W	(for Worksheet)
Type	I	(for Insert)
Type	R	(for Row)

When prompted to enter the row insert range:

Press	↵

Since the cell pointer was already highlighting cell A8, pressing the ↵ key at this point caused one row to be inserted at cell A8. The screen should resemble Figure 3–17.

Figure 3–17

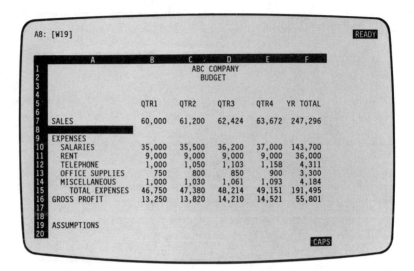

To insert a blank row between MISCELLANEOUS and TOTAL EXPENSES:

Move		the cell pointer to cell A15 (TOTAL EXPENSES)
Press	/	(the command key)
Type	W	(for Worksheet)
Type	I	(for Insert)
Type	R	(for Row)

When prompted to enter the row insert range:

Press	↵

Pressing ↵ at this point caused one row to be inserted at cell A15.

To insert a blank row between TOTAL EXPENSES and GROSS PROFIT:

Move		the cell pointer to cell A17 (GROSS PROFIT)
Press	/	(the command key)
Type	W	(for Worksheet)
Type	I	(for Insert)
Type	R	(for Row)

When prompted to enter the row insert range:

Press ⏎

Pressing ⏎ caused a row to be inserted at cell A17. The screen should resemble Figure 3–18.

Figure 3–18

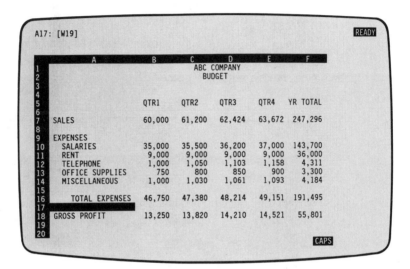

```
A17: [W19]                                                          READY

          A          B       C       D       E       F
 1                        ABC COMPANY
 2                          BUDGET
 3
 4
 5                       QTR1    QTR2    QTR3    QTR4   YR TOTAL
 6
 7  SALES              60,000  61,200  62,424  63,672  247,296
 8
 9  EXPENSES
10    SALARIES         35,000  35,500  36,200  37,000  143,700
11    RENT              9,000   9,000   9,000   9,000   36,000
12    TELEPHONE         1,000   1,050   1,103   1,158    4,311
13    OFFICE SUPPLIES     750     800     850     900    3,300
14    MISCELLANEOUS     1,000   1,030   1,061   1,093    4,184
15
16      TOTAL EXPENSES 46,750  47,380  48,214  49,151  191,495
17
18  GROSS PROFIT       13,250  13,820  14,210  14,521   55,801
19
20                                                            CAPS
```

■ ENTERING SUBTOTAL AND TOTAL LINES

To input subtotal lines for the expenses:

Move the cell pointer to cell B15

Press the space bar one time

Type – – – – – – – –

By pressing the space bar once and then eight dashes, a subtotal line is created.

Press ⏎

To copy the subtotal line to the rest of the current row:

Press / (the command key)

Type C (for Copy)

When prompted to enter the range to copy FROM:

Press ↵

Cell B15 was indicated as the cell to copy. When prompted to enter the range to copy TO:

Move the cell pointer to cell C15
Press .
Move the cell pointer to cell F15 ↵

The screen should resemble Figure 3–19.

Figure 3–19

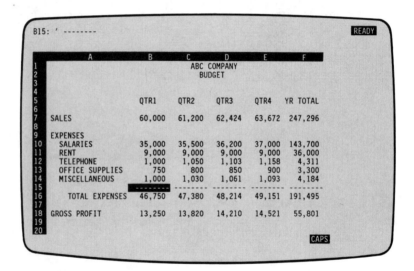

To copy row 15's subtotal lines to row 17:

Press / (the command key)
Type C (for Copy)

When prompted to enter the range to copy FROM:

Move the cell pointer to cell F15

Cells B15 through F15 are highlighted.

Press ⏎

When prompted to enter the range to copy TO:

Move the cell pointer to cell B17 ⏎

When copying multiple data in a row or a column, it is not necessary to highlight the entire area to which the lines were copied; it is only necessary to highlight the first cell to *begin* copying the cells.

To input total lines in cell B19:

Press the space bar one time

Type ========

By pressing the space bar one time and the equal sign eight times, a double line is created.

Press ⏎

To copy the double line to the rest of row 19:

Press / (the command key)

Type C (for Copy)

When prompted to enter the range to copy FROM:

Press ⏎

Cell B19 is the cell to copy. When prompted to enter the range to copy TO:

Move the cell pointer to cell C19

Press .

Move the cell pointer to cell F19 ⏎

The screen should resemble Figure 3–20.

Figure 3–20

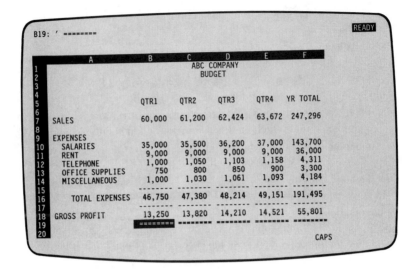

SAVING AND NAMING THE SPREADSHEET

To save the spreadsheet:

Press	the [Home] key	
Place	a formatted disk in drive B	
Press	/	(the command key)
Type	F	(for File)
Type	S	(for Save)

When prompted to enter the file name:

Type	BUDGET1 ↵

The red light goes on in drive B briefly while the file BUDGET is written to the disk in drive B. The file labeled BUDGET1 on drive B contains the spreadsheet that was created and saved.

■ USING THE ASSUMPTIONS FOR "WHAT-IF" ANALYSIS

To enter a different sales rate:

Move   the cell pointer to cell C23

Type   1.03

The worksheet will be recalculated using 1.03 as the sales rate for the second quarter. Since the formulas in the spreadsheet are dependent upon the assumptions, changing any assumption causes the spreadsheet to be recalculated accordingly. The screen should resemble Figure 3–21.

Figure 3–21

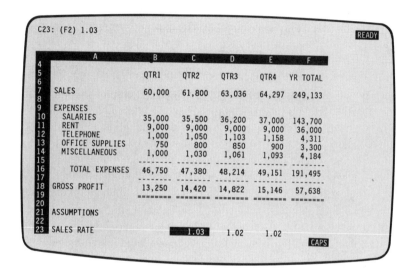

SUMMARY

An analysis model can be created by using dependent formulas that rely upon assumptions listed elsewhere on the spreadsheet. The user can change assumptions and recalculate the worksheet, perhaps printing out the results of each assumption or creating graphs depicting the results. An analysis model more completely exemplifies the "what-if" capability of 1–2–3.

KEY CONCEPTS

What-if analysis

CHAPTER THREE
EXERCISE 1

INSTRUCTIONS: Circle T if the statement is true and F if the statement is false.

T   F   1. Dependent formulas use numbers located elsewhere in a worksheet to perform calculations.

T   F   2. If the number in cell B1 is changed in a worksheet, the cell entry containing the formula +B1–260 will change when the worksheet is recalculated.

T   F   3. The cell entry 260–10 is an example of a dependent formula.

T   F   4. When assumptions in a worksheet are changed, the results can be printed without permanently saving the changes to the file.

T   F   5. Assumptions do not have to be printed if they are not included in the highlighted print range.

CHAPTER THREE
EXERCISE 2
Creating Dependent Formulas

INSTRUCTIONS: Follow the instructions below to practice creating dependent formulas.

Clear the screen (/ **W**orksheet **E**rase **Y**es).
Enter REVENUE in cell A1.
Enter 25000 in cell B1.
Enter ASSUMED REV RATE in cell A3.
Widen column A to 17 characters (/ **W**orksheet **C**olumn
Set-Width 17)
Enter 1.06 in cell C3.
Enter 1.07 in cell D3.

The screen should appear as follows.

```
A1: [W17] 'REVENUE
READY
```

	A	B	C	D	E	F	G
1	REVENUE	25,000					
2							
3	ASSUMED REV RATE		1.06	1.07			
4							
5							
6							

Enter dependent formulas in cells C1 and D1 as follows:

The formula in cell C1 should multiply the contents of cell B1 and C3.
The formula in cell D1 should multiply the contents of cell C1 and D3.
When the assumptions are changed, the results in cells C1 and D1
should also change. To serve as a guide, a printout of the cell formulas
in tabular form as well as a listing of cell formulas are included.

The worksheet should appear as follows.

```
A1: [W17] 'REVENUE
READY
```

	A	B	C	D	E	F	G
1	REVENUE	25,000	26,500	28,355			
2							
3	ASSUMED REV RATE		1.06	1.07			
4							
5							
6							

A printout of the formulas in tabular form appears as follows.

```
 A1: (T) [W17] 'REVENUE
READY
```

	A	B	C	D
1	REVENUE		25000 @ROUND(B1*C3,0)	@ROUND(C1*D3,0)
2				
3	ASSUMED REV RATE		1.06	1.07
4				
5				
6				

A line-by-line listing of cell formulas is as follows.

```
A1: [W17] 'REVENUE
B1: 25000
C1: @ROUND(B1*C3,0)
D1: @ROUND(C1*D3,0)
A3: [W17] 'ASSUMED REV RATE
C3: (F2) 1.06
D3: (F2) 1.07
```

CHAPTER THREE
EXERCISE 3
Creating Dependent Formulas

INSTRUCTIONS: Follow the instructions below to practice creating dependent formulas.

Retrieve the file PRACTICE, which was created in an assignment at the end of Chapter Two.
Alter the formulas for REVENUE and EXPENSES for years 2 and 3 so that they depend upon the ASSUMPTIONS line in rows 11 and 12.
When the ASSUMPTIONS are changed in rows 11 and 12, the formulas within the worksheet should show the results of the changes. Save the file as PRAC1. The cell formulas for the worksheet are included to serve as a guide.

A1: [W17]
READY

	A	B	C	D	E	F	G
1			PROJECTED PROFITS				
2							
3			YEAR 1	YEAR 2	YEAR 3	TOTAL	
4							
5	REVENUE		25,000	26,500	28,090	79,590	
6	EXPENSES		9,500	6,625	7,023	23,148	
7	PROFIT BEFORE TAX		15,500	19,875	21,067	56,442	
8							
9	ASSUMPTIONS						
10							
11	REV RATE			1.06	1.06		
12	EXP RATE			0.25	0.25		
13							

The cell formulas for Assignment 3 are listed below.

```
C1:  'PROJECTED PROFITS
B3:  "YEAR 1
C3:  "YEAR 2
D3:  "YEAR 3
E3:  "TOTAL
A5:  [W17] 'REVENUE
B5:  25000
C5:  @ROUND(B5*C11,0)
D5:  @ROUND(C5*D11,0)
```

```
E5:  @SUM(B5..D5)
A6:  [W17] 'EXPENSES
B6:  9500
C6:  @ROUND(C12*C5,0)
D6:  @ROUND(D12*D5,0)
E6:  @SUM(B6..D6)
A7:  [W17] 'PROFIT BEFORE TAX
B7:  +B5-B6
C7:  +C5-C6
D7:  +D5-D6
E7:  @SUM(B7..D7)
A9:  [W17] 'ASSUMPTIONS
A11: [W17] 'REV RATE
C11: (F2) 1.06
D11: (F2) 1.06
A12: [W17] 'EXP RATE
C12: (F2) 0.25
D12: (F2) 0.25
```

CHAPTER FOUR

USEFUL LOTUS COMMANDS

Chapter Overview
Using the Num Lock Key
    The Standard Method
    Using the Short Cut
Keeping a Cell Address Constant in a Formula
Using the Percent Format
Freezing Titles
Creating Windows
Checking the Status of the Worksheet
Inserting Columns and Rows
Deleting Columns and Rows
Hiding Columns from View
Creating Page Breaks
Suppressing Zeros in a Worksheet
Controlling the Recalculation of a Spreadsheet
Erasing Cells
Copying Cells
    Copying from One Cell to Another Cell
    Copying from One Cell to Many Cells
    Copying Many Cells to Another Location on the Worksheet
Moving Cells
    Moving One Cell to Another Cell
    Moving Many Cells to Another Location on the Worksheet
Useful File Commands
    File List
    File Erase
    File Directory
Using the System Command

Correcting Errors/Editing the Worksheet
    Typing Over an Erroneous Entry
    Editing an Entry Using the [Edit] Key
    Erasing an Entry
Using Label Prefixes
Summary

OBJECTIVES

In this chapter, the student will learn to:

- Use the Num Lock key
- Keep a cell address constant in a formula
- Use the Percent format
- Freeze titles on the screen
- Create windows
- Check the status of the worksheet
- Insert columns and rows (a review exercise)
- Delete columns and rows
- Hide columns from view
- Create page breaks
- Suppress zeros in a worksheet
- Control the recalculation of a spreadsheet
- Erase cells
- Copy cells (a review exercise)
- Move cells
- Use additional File menu options
- Use the System command
- Correct errors/edit the worksheet
- Use label prefixes

■ CHAPTER OVERVIEW

Chapters Two and Three provided general procedures for building spreadsheets. Chapter Four describes a variety of Lotus 1–2–3 commands that are often indispensable when creating and editing spreadsheets. For example, one exercise demonstrates how to use the Worksheet Titles command so that column headings and row labels do not scroll out of sight on the screen when the user moves the cell pointer around on a large spreadsheet. Some exercises introduce 1–2–3 commands not covered before in this book; other exercises provide a thorough review of commonly used commands such as the Copy command.

Before starting the exercises, make sure the screen is clear:

Press	/	(to bring up the 1–2–3 menu)
Type	W	(for the Worksheet menu option)
Type	E	(for the Erase menu option)
Type	Y	(for the Yes menu option)

◼ USING THE NUM LOCK KEY

On many keyboards, the arrow keys that are used to move around on an electronic spreadsheet are located on the numeric keypad, or ten key. This placement can be awkward when the user wishes to use the ten key to enter numbers quickly. The exercises below show three different way to use the numeric/directional keypad. If the user has a separate numeric keypad from the directional keypad, he/she may still wish to go through this exercise.

The Standard Method

To enter a column of numbers using the [Num Lock] key:

Move	the cell pointer to cell A1
Press	the [Num Lock] key

Pressing the [Num Lock] key causes NUM to appear at the lower right corner of the screen. The numbers on the numeric/directional keypad are now activated rather than the arrows. If NUM does not appear on the screen, tap the [Num Lock] key again. The [Num Lock] key causes the NUM function to turn either off or on; for this reason, be sure to *tap* this key rather than hold it down.

Using the numeric keypad, input the following:

Type	456 ↵
Press	the [Num Lock] key (to turn it off)
Move	the cell pointer to cell A2
Press	the [Num Lock] key (to turn it on)
Type	234 ↵
Press	the [Num Lock] key (to turn it off)
Move	the cell pointer to cell A3

Pressing the [Num Lock] key again deactivates "NUM" and reactivates the arrow keys. This method is tedious; it requires the user to tap the [Num Lock] key every time the user wishes to move to another place on the worksheet.

Using the Short Cut

To use the faster method of entering a series of numbers:

Move	the cell pointer to cell B1
Press	the [Num Lock] key

NUM should appear at the lower right corner of the screen.
Using the numeric keypad, input the following:

Type	789

Instead of pressing [Num Lock] in order to use the arrow keys:

Hold down	the shift key and **tap** the down arrow key
Release	the shift key
Type	123
Hold down	the shift key and **tap** the down arrow key
Release	the shift key

The cell pointer should now be in cell B3. It is not necessary to keep turning [Num Lock] on and off with this method. Because the shift key is easier to reach on the keyboard, this method is faster than the standard method. (There are two shift keys on the keyboard; either shift key can be used).

Press	the [Num Lock] key (to turn it off)

The "short cut" also works in reverse fashion. It is possible to use the numeric keypad without ever using the [Num Lock] function. When [Num Lock] is not in use, hold down either shift key and type numbers using the numeric keypad. While the shift key is depressed, the numbers on the ten key are activated. To use the arrow keys, simply release the shift key that had been depressed.

As a result of the above exercise, the screen should look like Figure 4–1.

Figure 4–1

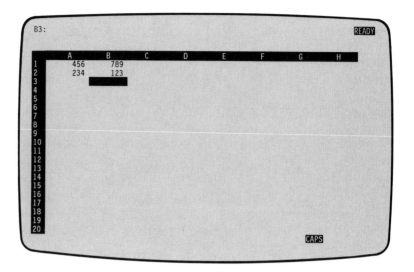

▓ KEEPING A CELL ADDRESS CONSTANT IN A FORMULA

Use the file SALES in this exercise. SALES was created in an assignment at the end of Chapter Two. To retrieve the file SALES:

Press	/	(the command key)
Type	F	(for File)
Type	R	(for Retrieve)

When prompted for the file name:

Move	the cell pointer to the word SALES ↵

To enter a formula that will compute the percentage of sales for each salesperson:

Move	the cell pointer to cell D8
Type	+
Move	the cell pointer to cell C8
Type	/ (for division)
Move	the cell pointer to cell C15 ↵

Cell D8 should now display the following number: 0.140231.

To copy the formula for the rest of the salespersons:

Press   /   (the command key)

Type   C   (for Copy)

When prompted for the range to copy FROM:

Press   ↵

Since the cell pointer was highlighting cell D8, D8 is now designated as the range to copy.

When prompted for the range to copy TO:

Move   the cell pointer to cell D9

Type   .

Move   the cell pointer to cell D13 ↵

ERR ("Error") will appear in cells D9 through D13. The screen should look like Figure 4–2.

Figure 4–2

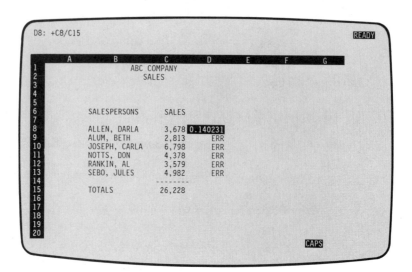

To see why the formula +C8/C15, when copied, did not compute the expected amount:

Move   the cell pointer to cell D9

Look in the control panel to see the formula in cell D9. The formula that was *intended* to be copied was +C9/C15. However, when the formula was copied, it became +C9/C**16**. The same results occurred for the formulas in cells D10 through D13 (+C10/C**17**, +C11/C**18**, etc.). Formulas are based upon **relative location** in Lotus. Lotus interprets the formula that was copied not as **C8/C15** but as "divide the number one cell to the left by the number to the left and *seven rows down*." The problem occurs when the formula is copied; cell C15 is not ". . . to the left and seven rows down" for cells D9 through D13. Furthermore, since the cells C16, C17, etc. are blank and a number cannot be divided by zero, the ERR message appears.

To solve the problem encountered above, keep cell C15 (the address for total sales) *constant* in the formula, even when the formula is copied to other cells. Lotus refers to constant cells as being **absolute.**

To enter a formula that will compute the percentage of sales for each salesperson and keep the total sales constant:

Move	the cell pointer to cell D8
Type	+
Move	the cell pointer to cell C8
Type	/ (for division)
Move	the cell pointer to cell C15
Press	the [Abs] key (the [F4] function key)
Press	↵

Look at the formula for cell D8 in the control panel. It should appear as **+C8/$C$15.** The dollar signs in front of the C and in front of the 15 indicate that both the column (C) and the row (15) will remain constant, or absolute, when copied. Cell D8 should now display the following number: 0.140231.

Note that $C$15 can be typed directly into the cell without having to use the [Abs] key. In Release 2 and later releases of Lotus 1–2–3, the user can simply type **+C8/C15** and press the [F4] key. When the [F4] key is depressed, C15 changes to $C$15.

The [Abs] key actually has four "cycles" or ways of changing a cell. In this example, pressing the [Abs] key four times would yield the following four options: $C$15, C$15, $C15, and C15. $C$15 holds both the column and the row absolute, C$15 only holds the row absolute, $C15 only holds the column absolute, and C15 is not absolute at all. Be sure the desired result of $C$15 has been selected.

To copy the formula for the rest of the salespersons:

Press	/	(the command key)
Type	C	(for Copy)

When prompted for the range to copy FROM:

Press ↵

Since the cell pointer was highlighting cell D8, D8 is now designated as the range to copy.

When prompted for the range to copy TO:

Move the cell pointer to cell D9
Type .
Move the cell pointer to cell D13 ↵

The correct computation will occur. The screen should look like Figure 4–3.

Figure 4–3

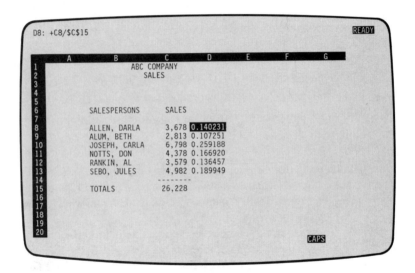

To see how the formula +C8/$C$15 was copied:

Move the cell pointer to cell D9

The formula +C9/$C$15 should be visible in the control panel; $C$15 is held constant. If desired, move to cells D10 through D13 to see that $C$15 was held constant in these cells also.

To add a column heading to column D:

Move	the cell pointer to cell D6
Type	"% SALES ↵

The heading % SALES should be right justified in cell D6.
To place a subtotal line in cell D14:

Move	the cell pointer to cell D14
Press	the space bar
Type	– – – – – – – – (eight minus signs)
Press	↵

To sum up the percentages in cell D15:

Move	the cell pointer to cell D15
Type	@SUM(D8..D13) ↵

The number 1 appears. In the following exercise, the numbers in column D will be formatted with percent signs.

■ USING THE PERCENT FORMAT

Assuming that the previous exercise has just been completed, the data in column D will now be formatted so that percent signs and two decimal places are displayed.
To format the numbers in column D:

Press	/	(the command key)
Type	R	(for Range)
Type	F	(for Format)
Type	P	(for Percent)

To accept the default of two decimal places:

Press	↵

When prompted for the range to format:

Move	the cell pointer to cell D8

The range to format should be cells D15 . . D8. If it is not, press the [Esc] key to release the anchor and set the range to D15 . . D8 (or D8 . . D15). Note that the range D15 . . D8 is equivalent to D8 . . D15 and that the range can be set either way. When the range is correct:

Press   ↵

The percentages now use the Percent format, which multiplies the data by 100, displays the desired number of decimal places, and attaches the % symbol to the end of the data. Note that percentages do not always add up to 100 percent, but may add up to 99 or 101 percent. Using the @ROUND function for percentages (e.g., @ROUND(+C8/$C$15,2)), may not solve the problem. It may also be necessary to "plug" or to alter a formula (e.g., subtract .01 from one of the data items) to achieve the desired results.

The screen should look like Figure 4–4.

Figure 4–4

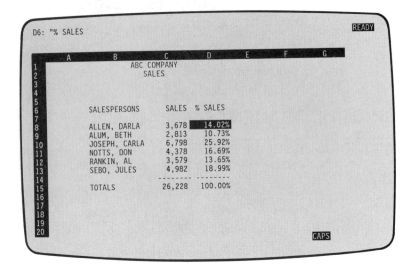

To erase the worksheet:

Press	/	(the command key)
Type	W	(for Worksheet)
Type	E	(for Erase)
Type	Y	(for Yes)

■ FREEZING TITLES

When working on a large spreadsheet and moving the cell pointer to a distant row or column, headings and descriptions may "scroll" off the screen. When this happens, it is difficult to see exactly where data is to be input. The following example will demonstrate how such a problem may occur, and how to solve the problem by freezing titles on the screen.

The file BUDGET2 was created in an assignment at the end of Chapter Two. To retrieve the file BUDGET2 for use in the following exercise:

Press	/	(the command key)
Type	F	(for File)
Type	R	(for Retrieve)

When prompted for the file to retrieve:

Move	the cell pointer to BUDGET2 ↵

To move to a "distant" cell location:

Move	the cell pointer to cell H25 (in this example, use the right and down arrow keys and *not* the [GOTO] key to move to H25)

Note that it is difficult to tell what the numbers represent because neither the column titles in row 5 nor the descriptive labels in column A are displayed on the screen as guides. The screen should look like Figure 4–5.

Figure 4–5

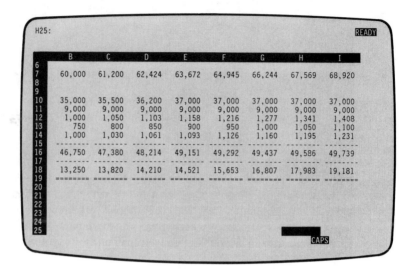

To position the cell pointer so that the appropriate headings and descriptive labels are visible on the screen:

> **Press**   the [Home] key
>
> **Move**   the cell pointer to cell B6

Before using the menu to freeze the titles, the cell pointer must already be in the correct position, as described below:

- The column(s) the user wishes to keep displayed on the screen must be directly to the left of the cell pointer (in this example, column A will remain frozen on the screen, because the cell pointer is in column B).
- The row(s) the user wishes to keep displayed on the screen must be directly above the cell pointer (in this example, rows 1 through 5 will remain frozen on the screen, because the cell pointer is in row 6).

To access the menu commands to freeze the titles and descriptive labels:

> **Press**   /   (the command key)
>
> **Type**   W   (for Worksheet)
>
> **Type**   T   (for Titles)
>
> **Move**   the cell pointer to the Vertical menu option (do NOT press **V** for Vertical)

The description "Freeze all columns to the left of the cell pointer" under the Vertical option explains how to freeze vertical titles. A similar description is displayed when the Horizontal option is highlighted. See Figure 4–6.

Figure 4–6

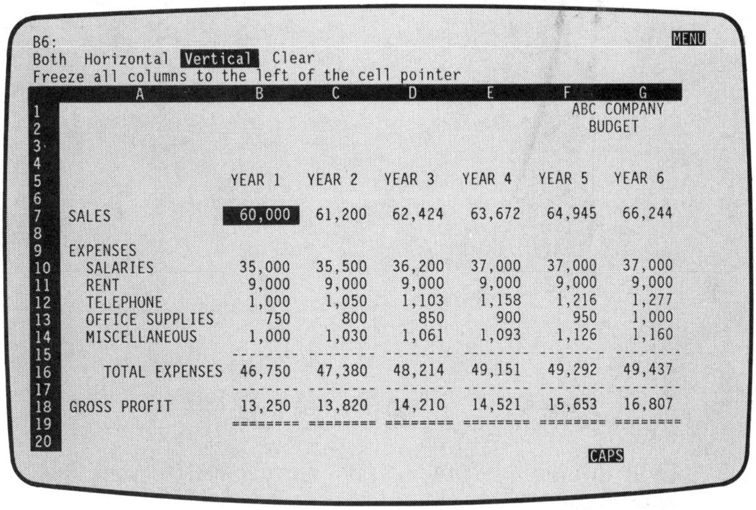

```
B6:                                                                    MENU
Both  Horizontal  Vertical  Clear
Freeze all columns to the left of the cell pointer
            A           B        C        D        E        F        G
 1                                                                ABC COMPANY
 2                                                                   BUDGET
 3
 4
 5                       YEAR 1   YEAR 2   YEAR 3   YEAR 4   YEAR 5   YEAR 6
 6
 7  SALES               60,000   61,200   62,424   63,672   64,945   66,244
 8
 9  EXPENSES
10    SALARIES          35,000   35,500   36,200   37,000   37,000   37,000
11    RENT               9,000    9,000    9,000    9,000    9,000    9,000
12    TELEPHONE          1,000    1,050    1,103    1,158    1,216    1,277
13    OFFICE SUPPLIES      750      800      850      900      950    1,000
14    MISCELLANEOUS      1,000    1,030    1,061    1,093    1,126    1,160
15                     --------  -------  -------  -------  -------  -------
16    TOTAL EXPENSES    46,750   47,380   48,214   49,151   49,292   49,437
17                     --------  -------  -------  -------  -------  -------
18  GROSS PROFIT        13,250   13,820   14,210   14,521   15,653   16,807
19                     ========  =======  =======  =======  =======  =======
20
                                                                        CAPS
```

Type   B   (for Both columns and rows)

Note that the user can choose to freeze only the columns or only the rows. Both rows and columns are frozen in this example.

To see the results of freezing the screen:

Move   the cell pointer to cell H25 (use the right and down arrow keys to move to this position)

Note that even though the cell pointer has been moved to a "distant" area of the spreadsheet, rows 1 through 6 and column A remain frozen on the screen. By using this option, it is possible to see the descriptions and understand the content of the spreadsheet. For example, H18 contains the contents of Gross Profit for Year 7. The screen should look like Figure 4–7.

Figure 4–7

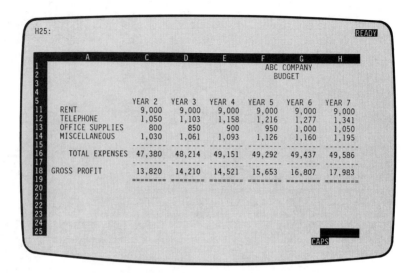

Press   the [Home] key

Note that the cell pointer cannot move to cell A1 since the titles are frozen but goes only to cell B6.

To cancel the frozen title settings:

Press	/	(the command key)
Type	W	(for Worksheet)
Type	T	(for Titles)
Type	C	(for Clear)
Press	the [Home] key	

The cell pointer can now be moved to the "true" home position.

■ CREATING WINDOWS

Lotus 1–2–3 allows the user to view two different areas of the spreadsheet on the screen by using the Windows command. If necessary, retrieve the BUDGET2 file for use in the following exercise.

When creating windows, the cell pointer must be in the desired position before the menus are accessed. To position the cell pointer so that the windows will be divided at this position:

Move   the cell pointer to cell D7

To access the menu commands to create the window:

Press	/	(for command)
Type	W	(for Worksheet)
Type	W	(for Window)
Type	V	(for Vertical)

Two windows are visible on the screen. Note that Lotus 1–2–3 allows the user to make either horizontal or vertical windows. The screen should look like Figure 4–8.

Figure 4–8

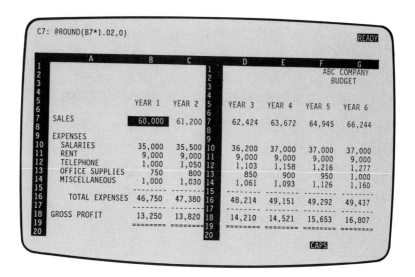

To move around in the left window:

Move   the cell pointer to cell B7

Notice that the cell pointer can be moved anywhere in the spreadsheet.

To move to the right window:

Press	the [Window] key (the F6 function key)
Move	the cell pointer to cell L7 (Year Total for SALES)

To move back to the left window:

Press	the [Window] key (the F6 function key)
Move	the cell pointer to cell B7 (if the cell pointer is not already there)
Type	65000 ↵

By using windows, the user is able to see the effect of changing Sales on another area of the worksheet. In this example, the user can see the amount of the Year Total for Sales updated when Sales is changed.

Using windows is also helpful when copying or moving data from one part of the worksheet to another. The worksheet should look like Figure 4–9.

Figure 4–9

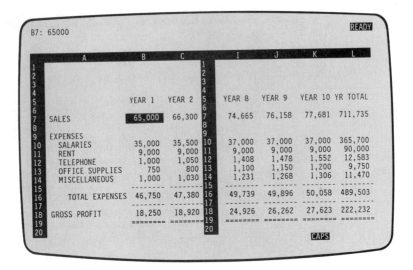

To clear the window setting:

Press	/	(the command key)
Type	W	(for Worksheet)
Type	W	(for Windows)
Type	C	(for Clear)

The window settings are now erased.

■ CHECKING THE STATUS OF THE WORKSHEET

If necessary, retrieve the BUDGET2 file for use in the following exercise.
To look at the Status (settings) of the worksheet:

Press	/	(the command key)
Type	W	(for Worksheet)
Type	S	(for Status)

Various settings are displayed. Release 2 and later releases have a status screen that takes up an entire screen. The displayed settings indicate available memory as well as the settings for recalculation, format, label prefixes, column widths, and protected cells for the current file (in this example, the BUDGET2 file). Release 2 and later releases contain additional information, such as whether a math co-processor is used, how many iterations are used to recalculate the worksheet, whether circular references exist, and whether zero suppression is being used. The screen should look like Figure 4–10. The available memory feature depends upon the amount of memory in the system being used.

Figure 4–10

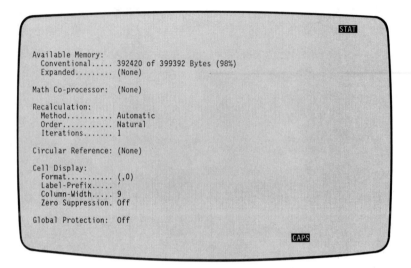

```
                                                                      STAT
    Available Memory:
      Conventional..... 392420 of 399392 Bytes (98%)
      Expanded......... (None)

    Math Co-processor:  (None)

    Recalculation:
      Method.......... Automatic
      Order........... Natural
      Iterations...... 1

    Circular Reference: (None)

    Cell Display:
      Format.......... (,0)
      Label-Prefix..... '
      Column-Width..... 9
      Zero Suppression. Off

    Global Protection:  Off

                                                                      CAPS
```

To exit from the status screen:

    Press   [Esc]   (the Escape key)

■ INSERTING COLUMNS AND ROWS

For this exercise, retrieve the original BUDGET2 file. It is not necessary to save the results of the previous exercise in a file.

To insert 2 columns between the headings YEAR 1 and YEAR 2:

Move		the cell pointer to cell C1 (or any other cell in column C)
Press	/	(the command key)
Type	W	(for Worksheet)
Type	I	(for Insert)
Type	C	(for Column)

When prompted for the columns to insert:

Move		the cell pointer to cell D1 (or any other cell in column D)
Press	↵	

The screen should look like Figure 4–11. In the following exercise, two columns will be deleted.

Figure 4–11

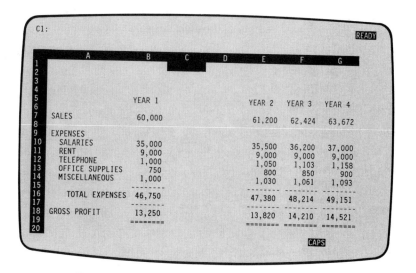

```
C1:                                                              READY

        A          B      C      D       E        F        G
 1
 2
 3
 4
 5
 6                      YEAR 1             YEAR 2   YEAR 3   YEAR 4
 7  SALES             60,000             61,200   62,424   63,672
 8
 9  EXPENSES
10    SALARIES        35,000             35,500   36,200   37,000
11    RENT             9,000              9,000    9,000    9,000
12    TELEPHONE        1,000              1,050    1,103    1,158
13    OFFICE SUPPLIES    750                800      850      900
14    MISCELLANEOUS    1,000              1,030    1,061    1,093
15                   --------           -------- -------- --------
16    TOTAL EXPENSES  46,750             47,380   48,214   49,151
17                   --------           -------- -------- --------
18  GROSS PROFIT      13,250             13,820   14,210   14,521
19                   ========           ======== ======== ========
20
                                                              CAPS
```

The process for inserting rows was discussed in Chapter Two.

■ DELETING COLUMNS AND ROWS

Assuming that the previous exercise on inserting two blank columns has been completed, the two blank columns will now be deleted.

To delete columns C and D:

> **Move**   the cell pointer to cell C1 (if it is not already there)

(The cell pointer can be moved to any other cell in column C to achieve the same results).

> **Press**   /   (the command key)
> **Type**   W   (for Worksheet)
> **Type**   D   (for Delete)
> **Type**   C   (for Column)

When prompted for the range to delete:

> **Move**   the cell pointer to cell D1 (or any other cell in column D)
> **Press**   ↵

The two blank columns have now been deleted. The screen should look like Figure 4–12.

Figure 4–12

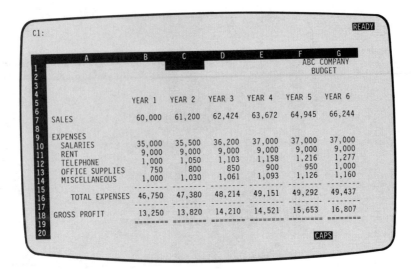

The process for deleting rows is exactly the same except Row is selected instead of Column after Delete is chosen.

■ HIDING COLUMNS FROM VIEW

Retrieve the BUDGET2 file for use in the following exercise.

Worksheet Column Hide is available in Release 2 and later releases of Lotus 1–2–3. This feature allows certain columns to be hidden from view, either on the screen or when printing a worksheet.

To hide column E:

Press	/	(the command key)
Type	W	(for Worksheet)
Type	C	(for Column)
Type	H	(for Hide)

When prompted for the column(s) to hide:

Move	the cell pointer to cell E1 (or any other cell in column E)

Note that the cell pointer could be in any cell in column E.

Press	↵

Column E is no longer visible on the screen. The screen should look like Figure 4–13.

Figure 4–13   Columns can be hidden from view using with the Worksheet Column Hide command sequence.

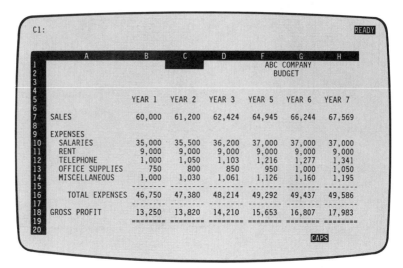

To make column E visible on the screen again:

Press	/	(the command key)
Type	W	(for Worksheet)
Type	C	(for Column)
Type	D	(for Display)

All columns which had been hidden will now be visible (in this example, only column E was hidden). An asterisk appears beside each column that is hidden (in this example, only column E should have an asterisk).

When prompted for the column to unhide:

| **Move** | the cell pointer to cell E1 (or any other cell in column E) |

The screen should look like Figure 4–14.

Figure 4–14

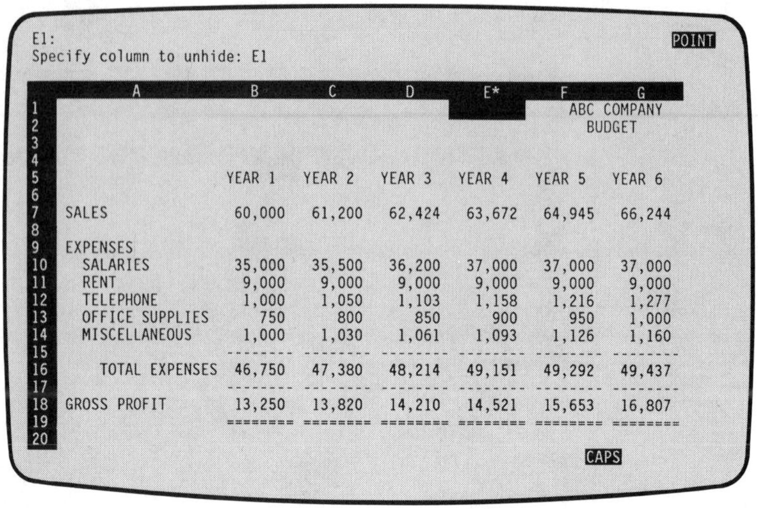

```
E1:                                                      POINT
Specify column to unhide: E1

          A         B        C        D       E*      F        G
 1                                                   ABC COMPANY
 2                                                      BUDGET
 3
 4
 5                  YEAR 1   YEAR 2   YEAR 3   YEAR 4  YEAR 5   YEAR 6
 6
 7    SALES         60,000   61,200   62,424   63,672  64,945   66,244
 8
 9    EXPENSES
10      SALARIES    35,000   35,500   36,200   37,000  37,000   37,000
11      RENT         9,000    9,000    9,000    9,000   9,000    9,000
12      TELEPHONE    1,000    1,050    1,103    1,158   1,216    1,277
13      OFFICE SUPPLIES 750     800      850      900     950    1,000
14      MISCELLANEOUS 1,000    1,030    1,061    1,093   1,126    1,160
15                  -------  -------  -------  ------- -------  -------
16    TOTAL EXPENSES 46,750  47,380   48,214   49,151  49,292   49,437
17                  -------  -------  -------  ------- -------  -------
18    GROSS PROFIT  13,250   13,820   14,210   14,521  15,653   16,807
19                  =======  =======  =======  ======= =======  =======
20                                                               CAPS
```

Press ↵

Column E is visible again.

Individual cells can be hidden using the **R**ange **F**ormat **H**idden command sequence.

■ CREATING PAGE BREAKS

When printing a spreadsheet in Lotus 1–2–3, Lotus prints as much as it can on a single page based upon the page length. The following rows are printed on the next page. Sometimes, the user may wish to specify where he/she wants page breaks to occur. The page break feature is available in Release 2 and later releases of Lotus 1–2–3.

If necessary, retrieve the BUDGET2 file for use in the following exercise. To set a print range:

Press	/	(the command key)
Type	P	(for Print)
Type	P	(for Printer)
Type	R	(for Range)

When prompted for the range to print:

Press	[Home] (if the cell pointer is not already in cell A1)
Type	.
Move	the cell pointer to cell G19

Cells A1 .. G19 (the descriptions and data for YEAR 1 through YEAR 6) are now highlighted.

Press	↵	
Type	Q	(for Quit)

To insert a page break at cell A12:

Move	the cell pointer to cell A12	
Press	/	(the command key)
Type	W	(for Worksheet)
Type	P	(for Page)
Move	the cell pointer to cell A12	

Note that two colons (::) now appear in cell A12. The data that was previously in rows 12 through to the end of the worksheet has been moved down one row. If the print range for BUDGET2 is printed, the data in row 13 (Telephone Expenses) would be printed at the top of the second page. Note that |:: (the pipe symbol and two colons) appear in the control panel as the contents of A12. The symbols |:: can be manually typed on the spreadsheet where a page break is desired. However, no data should be contained in the row with the designation for the page break. Note that the page break symbol can be erased just as though it were a typical data entry—one option is the **Range Erase** command sequence. The **Worksheet Delete Row** command sequence may be preferable since a row was added to accommodate the page break symbol.

To print the spreadsheet:

Press	/	(the command key)
Type	P for Print	
Type	P for Printer	
Type	A for Align	
Type	G for Go	

After printing:

Type   P for Page (twice) (if necessary, to eject the paper from the printer)

Type   Q for Quit

Assuming that the printing was performed on 8 1/2" by 11" paper and the print is in 10 pitch (10 characters per inch), the printout should look like the printout in Figure 4–15.

Figure 4–15
Part 1

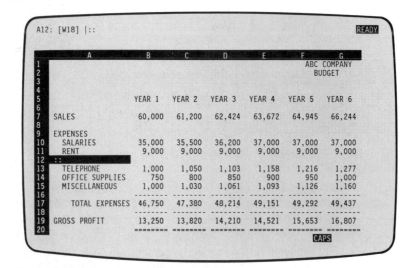

Figure 4–15
Part 2

Page 1 of the printout stops at the point of the page break.

```
                                                         ABC COMPANY
                                                           BUDGET

              YEAR 1   YEAR 2   YEAR 3   YEAR 4   YEAR 5   YEAR 6
   SALES      60,000   61,200   62,424   63,672   64,945   66,244

   EXPENSES
    SALARIES  35,000   35,500   36,200   37,000   37,000   37,000
    RENT       9,000    9,000    9,000    9,000    9,000    9,000
```

Figure 4–15
Part 3

The line following the page break to appears at the top of the following page.

```
   TELEPHONE        1,000    1,050    1,103    1,158    1,216    1,277
   OFFICE SUPPLIES    750      800      850      900      950    1,000
   MISCELLANEOUS    1,000    1,030    1,061    1,093    1,126    1,160
                   -------- -------- -------- -------- -------- --------
   TOTAL EXPENSES  46,750   47,380   48,214   49,151   49,292   49,437
                   -------- -------- -------- -------- -------- --------
   GROSS PROFIT    13,250   13,820   14,210   14,521   15,653   16,807
                   ======== ======== ======== ======== ======== ========
```

■ SUPPRESSING ZEROS IN A WORKSHEET

The zero suppression feature in Lotus 1–2–3 suppresses the display of all zeros in a worksheet. This feature places a blank in place of a cell entry of zero whether the cell entry consists of the number zero or a cell formula that currently results in zero. This feature is available in Release 2 and later releases of Lotus 1–2–3.

To perform this exercise, retrieve the original file BUDGET2.

For the purposes of this example, a zero will be placed in YEAR 1 of Sales. All of the projections for Sales in the following years are based upon this number and therefore will also display zeros.

Move	the cell pointer to cell B7
Type	0 ↵

The row containing the Sales data now consists of zeros. The screen should look like Figure 4–16.

Figure 4–16

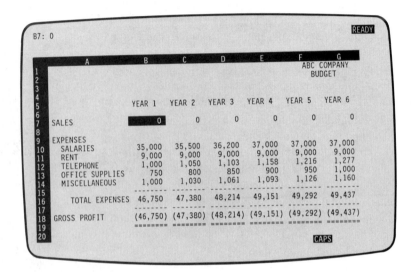

The Worksheet Global Zero menu option allows the user to suppress zeros from being displayed. To suppress the zeros in the file BUDGET2:

Press	/	(the command key)
Type	W	(for Worksheet)
Type	G	(for Global)
Type	Z	(for Zero)
Type	Y	(for Yes)
Move	the cell pointer to cell C7	

The zeros are now suppressed. The screen should look like Figure 4–17.

It is possible to accidentally write over the cells that are being suppressed. One solution is to use the **G**lobal **P**rotection or **R**ange **P**rotect menu options to protect the cells from being changed. Notice that when the cell pointer is located in a cell that has zero suppression, the formula will appear in the control panel. In Figure 4–17, cell C7 is "blank" (the zero is suppressed from view) and the control panel shows the formula that is located in cell C7.

Figure 4–17

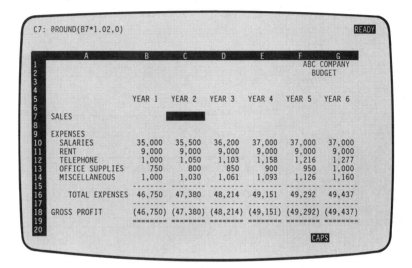

To allow the zeros to be visible on the screen:

Press	/	(the command key)
Type	W	(for Worksheet)
Type	G	(for Global)
Type	Z	(for Zero)
Type	N	(for No)

The zeros should now be visible again. The screen should look like Figure 4–18.

Figure 4–18

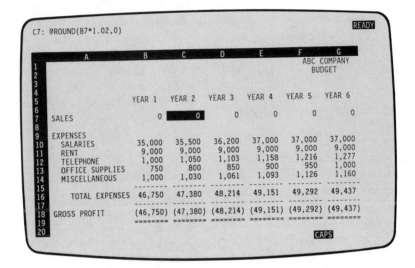

CONTROLLING THE RECALCULATION OF A SPREADSHEET

Retrieve the file BUDGET2 for this exercise.

To change a cell on the worksheet:

Move	the cell pointer to cell B7
Type	70000 ↵

The worksheet is recalculated with the new entry $70,000 for YEAR 1 of Sales. The initial settings for recalculation are Automatic and Natural; the worksheet recalculates automatically and in natural order every time an item is changed. Sometimes when new data is input, it may take several seconds or even minutes for the worksheet to recalculate. One solution is to set the Recalculation option to Manual.

To control the recalculation in a worksheet:

Press	/	(the command key)
Type	W	(for Worksheet)
Type	G	(for Global)
Type	R	(for Recalculation)
Type	M	(for Manual)

The recalculation options are described below.

- *Natural* causes the worksheet to recalculate a formula only if the formula(s) it depends on have already been calculated.
- *Columnwise* causes the worksheet to recalculate in columnwise order.
- *Rowwise* causes the worksheet to recalculate in rowwise order.
- *Automatic* causes the worksheet to recalculate every time the worksheet data is changed.
- *Manual* causes the worksheet to recalculate only by pressing the [Calc] key (the F9 function key).
- *Iteration* causes the worksheet to recalculate a designated number of times, or iterations.

To change the sales in cell B7 again:

Type   80000 ⏎

Note that the number 80000 was entered instantly; however, the worksheet was not recalculated. Note also that the word CALC appears at the bottom right corner of the screen. The screen should look like Figure 4–19.

Figure 4–19
Part 1

Worksheets can be recalculated automatically upon each new change to the worksheet...

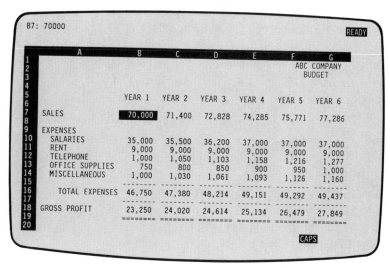

Figure 4–19
Part 2

or they can be set to recalculate manually (Worksheet Global Recalculation
Manual).

To recalculate the worksheet:

Press   the [Calc] key (the [F9] function key)

The worksheet has now recalculated. If another number is changed at this point, CALC
reappears on the screen. Multiple entries can be made without the worksheet
recalculating after each new entry. The [Calc] key would have to be pressed again
before the worksheet would recalculate. The screen should look like Figure 4–20.

Figure 4–20

Press the [Calc] key to recalculate the entire worksheet.

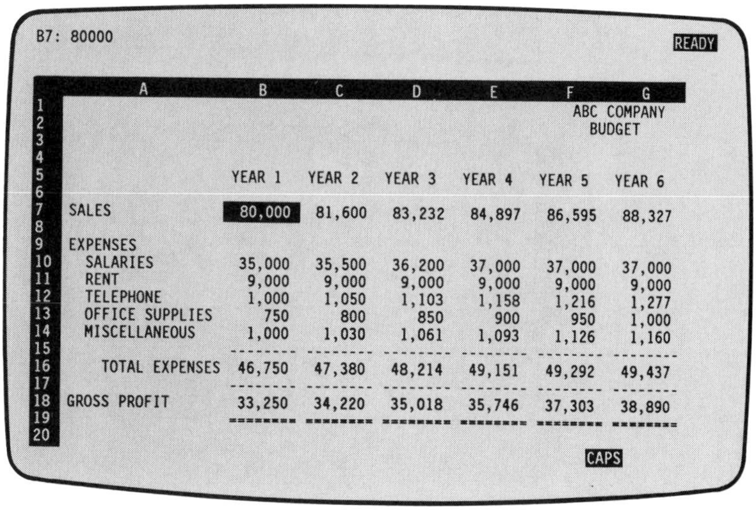

```
B7: 80000                                                              READY

            A           B       C       D       E       F       G
  1                                                         ABC COMPANY
  2                                                            BUDGET
  3
  4
  5                     YEAR 1  YEAR 2  YEAR 3  YEAR 4  YEAR 5  YEAR 6
  6
  7   SALES            80,000  81,600  83,232  84,897  86,595  88,327
  8
  9   EXPENSES
 10     SALARIES       35,000  35,500  36,200  37,000  37,000  37,000
 11     RENT            9,000   9,000   9,000   9,000   9,000   9,000
 12     TELEPHONE       1,000   1,050   1,103   1,158   1,216   1,277
 13     OFFICE SUPPLIES   750     800     850     900     950   1,000
 14     MISCELLANEOUS   1,000   1,030   1,061   1,093   1,126   1,160
 15                    -------  ------  ------  ------  ------  ------
 16     TOTAL EXPENSES 46,750  47,380  48,214  49,151  49,292  49,437
 17                    -------  ------  ------  ------  ------  ------
 18   GROSS PROFIT     33,250  34,220  35,018  35,746  37,303  38,890
 19                    =======  ======  ======  ======  ======  ======
 20
                                                                   CAPS
```

To cause the worksheet to recalculate automatically again:

Press	/	(the command key)
Type	W	(for Worksheet)
Type	G	(for Global)
Type	R	(for Recalculation)
Type	A	(for Automatic)

The worksheet will now recalculate automatically and in natural order every time a cell is changed.

■ ERASING CELLS

Retrieve the file BUDGET2 for this exercise.
To erase the label ABC COMPANY in cell F1:

Move		the cell pointer to cell F1
Press	/	(the command key)
Type	R	(for Range)
Type	E	(for Erase)
Press	↵	

Cell B4 is now erased. The screen should look like Figure 4–21.

Figure 4–21
Part 1

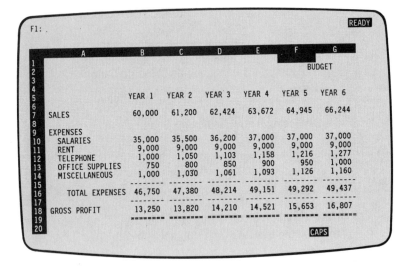

◼ COPYING CELLS

The following exercises serve as a review for how the Copy command works.

Copying from One Cell to Another Cell

To clear the screen from any previous exercise:

Press	/	(the command key)
Type	W	(for Worksheet)
Type	E	(for Erase)
Type	Y	(for Yes)

To enter the data to copy in cell A1:

Type	100 ⏎

100 is now entered in cell A1.

To copy the contents of cell A1 to cell B1, first make sure that the cell pointer is already highlighting the cell to copy from (cell A1). This will make it easier to use the Copy command.

Press	/	(the command key)
Type	C	(for Copy)

When prompted for the range to copy FROM:

Press	⏎

The cell to copy (cell A1) was already highlighted, so only ⏎ had to be pressed.

When prompted for the range to copy TO:

Move	the cell pointer to cell B1 ⏎

The screen should look like Figure 4–22.

Figure 4–22

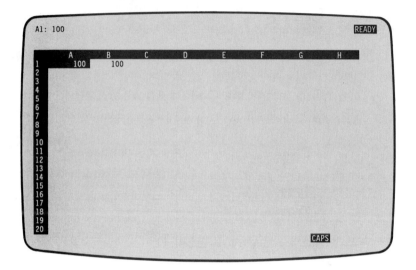

Copying from One Cell to Many Cells

To copy the contents of cell A1 to cells A2 through F2, first make sure the cursor is already highlighting the cell to copy (cell A1).

Press	/	(the command key)
Type	C	(for Copy)

When prompted for the range to copy FROM:

Press ↵

By pressing ↵ , the currently highlighted cell (cell A1) was selected as the cell to copy. When prompted for the range to copy TO:

Move	the cell pointer to cell A2
Press	.

The period key will anchor the cell pointer at its present position.

Move	the cell pointer to cell F2 ↵

The contents of cell A1 have now been copied to cells A2 through F2. The screen should look like Figure 4–23.

Figure 4–23

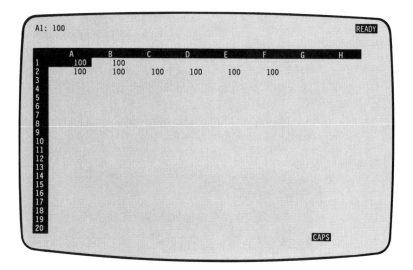

Copying Many Cells to Another Location on the Worksheet

To copy cells A2 through F2 to cells A7 through F7:

Move   the cell pointer to cell A2

Before accessing the menu to use the Copy command, place the cell pointer in the leftmost cell of the range of cells to be copied. In this way, the cell pointer is already in the correct starting position when the prompt "Range to copy FROM:" appears on the screen.

Press   /   (the command key)
Type   C   (for Copy)

When prompted for the range to copy FROM:

Move   the cell pointer to cell F2

Cells A2 through F2 are now highlighted as the cells to copy.

Press   ↵

When prompted for the range to copy TO:

Move   the cell pointer to cell A7

Press   .

Move   the cell pointer to cell F7 ↵

The contents of cells A2 through F2 have now been copied to cells A7 through F7. The screen should look like Figure 4–24.

Figure 4–24

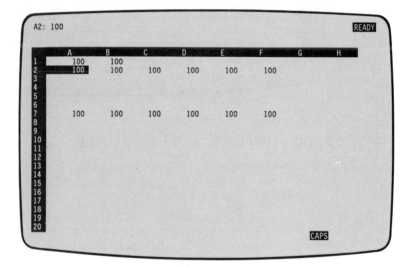

Note the following shortcut; when prompted for the range to copy to, the user could have highlighted cell A7 and pressed [RETURN]. When copying a single column or row, only the first cell in which to begin copying the column or row has to be indicated.

If the cell pointer is anchored at the wrong cell, tap the [Esc] key to release the anchor and move the cell pointer to the desired cell. If needed, press the period key to anchor the cell pointer at the new position.

■ MOVING CELLS

The following exercises use the Move command. This exercise is written with the assumption that the previous exercise has been completed.

Moving One Cell to Another Cell

To move the contents of cell A1 to cell H1:

Move   the cell pointer to cell A1

When the cell pointer is already highlighting the cell to move, it will be easier to use the Move command.

Press   /   (the command key)
Type   M   (for Move)

When prompted for the range to move FROM:

Press   ↵

The cell to move (cell A1) was already highlighted, so only ↵ had to be pressed. When prompted for the range to move TO:

Move   the cell pointer to cell H1 ↵

The screen should look like Figure 4–25.

Figure 4–25

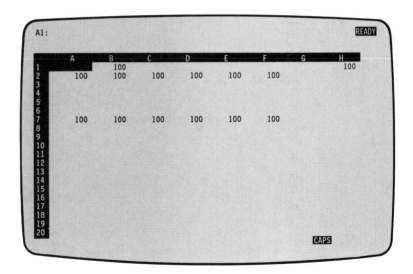

Moving Many Cells to Another Location on the Worksheet

To move cells A2 through F2 to cells A14 through F14:

Move   the cell pointer to cell A2
Press   /   (the command key)
Type   M   (for Move)

When prompted for the range to move FROM:

Move   the cell pointer to cell F2

Cells A2 through F2 are now highlighted as the cells to move.

Press   ↵

When prompted for the range to move TO:

Move   the cell pointer to cell A14 ↵

The contents of cells A2 through A7 have now been moved to cells A14 through F14. The screen should look like Figure 4–26.

Figure 4–26

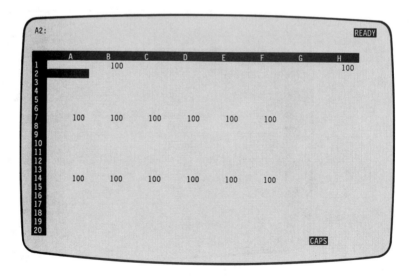

■ USEFUL FILE COMMANDS

File commands affect files that are saved on the disk. The following exercises illustrate how to list and erase files. An additional exercise shows how to change the drive designation or path that Lotus uses as a guide to retrieve and save files.

File List

The File List command sequence lists the files on the data disk. To list the worksheet files:

Press	/	(the command key)
Type	F	(for File)
Type	L	(for List)

When prompted for the type of file to list:

Type	W	(for Worksheet)

Note four options—Worksheet, Print, Graph, or Other.

- *Worksheet* allows you to see worksheet files (created using the File Save command sequence).
- *Print* lists print files (created using the Print File command sequence and printing a range to a file)
- *Graph* lists graph files (created using the Graph Save command sequence in order to print a graph from the graph settings in the current file)
- *Other* (available in Release 2 of Lotus 1–2–3) lists all files on the disk, including those that were not created with Lotus 1–2–3.

The screen should look like Figure 4–27. The screen may not display exactly the same files. For example, the user may have Release 1A of Lotus.

Figure 4–27

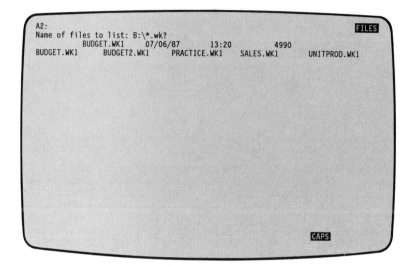

To return to the worksheet mode:

Press ↵

File Erase

The File Erase command sequence erases files on the data disk. To erase a worksheet file on a disk:

Press / (the command key)
Type F (for File)
Type E (for Erase)

Four types of files are listed on the menu—Worksheet, Print, Graph, or Other. When prompted for the type of file to erase:

Type W (for Worksheet)

The screen should look like Figure 4–28.

Figure 4–28

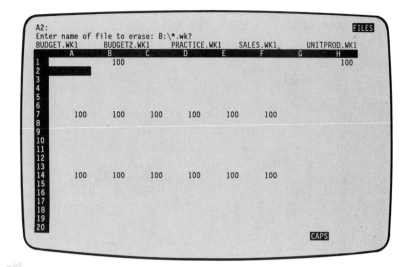

```
A2:                                                              FILES
Enter name of file to erase: B:\*.wk?
BUDGET.WK1      BUDGET2.WK1      PRACTICE.WK1     SALES.WK1      UNITPROD.WK1
          A         B         C         D         E         F         G         H
 1                 100                                                          100
 2
 3
 4
 5
 6
 7        100       100       100       100       100       100
 8
 9
10
11
12
13
14        100       100       100       100       100       100
15
16
17
18
19
20
                                                          CAPS
```

To erase a file, the user could highlight the file to erase and press ⏎ (do *not* do so at this time). To escape from this process and not erase a file:

Press	the [Esc] key until all the menus disappear from the control panel

File Directory

The File Directory command changes the drive specification from which files are retrieved and saved. To change from drive B to drive A, for example:

Press	/	(the command key)
Type	F	(for File)
Type	D	(for Directory)

The screen should look like Figure 4–29.

Figure 4–29

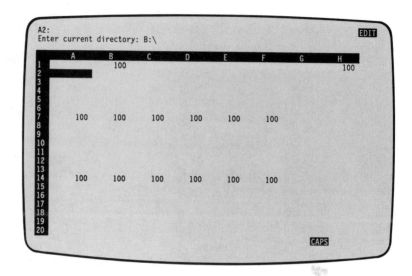

The current directory (where data files are being retrieved and saved) should be displayed. If currently saving all of data on drive B, the following directory setting is obtained B:\ .

To change the directory to drive A, for example, the user could type A:\ and press ↵ to save or retrieve files from drive A (do *not* do so at this time). To avoid changing the directory from its present setting:

Press   the [Esc] key until all menus disappear from the control panel

Note: To permanently change the directory, access *W*orksheet *G*lobal *D*efault *D*irectory. Change the directory here to the desired drive or path, press ↵ , select *U*pdate to permanently save the change, and choose *Q*uit to exit the menu.

■ USING THE SYSTEM COMMAND

The System command is available in Release 2 of Lotus 1–2–3.
To access the System command:

Press   /   (the command key)
Type   S   (for System)

Lotus is still in memory, but the cursor is blinking at the DOS prompt. The screen should look like Figure 4–30.

Figure 4–30

The System command temporarily returns to DOS

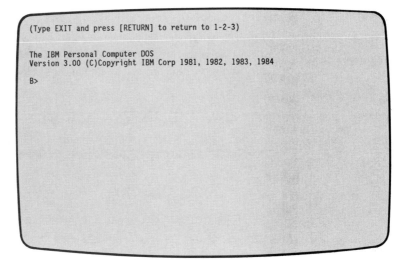

```
(Type EXIT and press [RETURN] to return to 1-2-3)

The IBM Personal Computer DOS
Version 3.00 (C)Copyright IBM Corp 1981, 1982, 1983, 1984

B>
```

At this point, the user can perform DOS commands or possibly even enter another software program (if there is enough memory to do so).

To return to Lotus 1–2–3:

Type   exit (or EXIT) ⏎

The cell pointer returns to the same worksheet that was in use before the System menu option was accessed.

■ CORRECTING ERRORS/EDITING THE WORKSHEET

There are various ways to correct errors on a worksheet. Three commonly used methods are illustrated below.

Typing Over an Erroneous Entry

Clear the screen using the Worksheet Erase Yes menu options.

In cell A1:

Type   100 ↵

To change the entry to 1000:

Type   1000 ↵

To replace an item that is incorrect, make sure the cell pointer is highlighting the incorrect cell entry and retype the entry. The screen should look like Figure 4–31.

*Figure 4–31
Part 1*

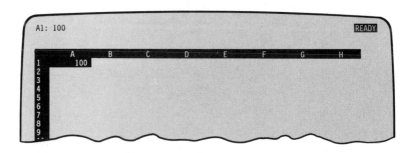

*Figure 4–31
Part 2*

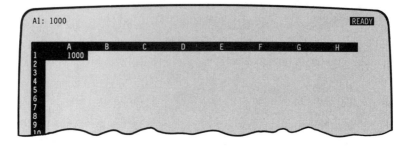

Editing an Entry using the [Edit] Key

To change the cell entry in cell A1 from 1000 to 1000*1.03:

Move   the cell pointer to cell A1 (if necessary)
Press   the [Edit] key (the [F2] key)

The entry is displayed in the control panel and a blinking cursor appears at the end of the entry. EDIT appears as the mode indicator at the upper right corner of the screen, indicating that EDIT mode has been activated. The screen should look like Figure 4–32.

Figure 4-32

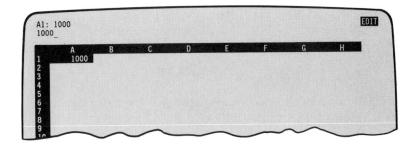

To add to the end of the existing entry:

Type   *1.03 ↵

The entry in cell A1 has now been changed from 1000 to 1000*1.03. The screen should look like Figure 4-33.

Figure 4-33

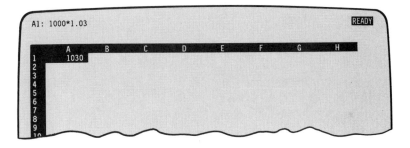

When EDIT mode is activated, the left and right arrow keys as well as the [Home] and [End] keys can be used to move to the middle of an entry.

Clear the screen using the **W**orksheet **E**rase **Y**es menu options.

Move   the cell pointer to cell C3
Type   ABC COMPANY ↵

To change the entry to THE ABC MANUFACTURING COMPANY, INC.:

Press   the [Edit] key
Press   the [Home] key

The cursor is now underlining the apostrophe, which is the default label prefix. The [Home] key places the cursor at the first position of the cell entry.

Move	the cursor to the letter A in ABC (use the right arrow key)
Type	THE
Press	the space bar

When additional text is typed, the remaining text "moves over" so that the new text is inserted. To insert MANUFACTURING:

Move	the cursor to the space after ABC (use the right arrow key)
Press	the space bar
Type	MANUFACTURING

To move quickly to the end of the line, the [End] key will be used so that , INC. can be added:

Press	the [End] key
Type	, INC.

Since the entry is completely edited:

Press	↵

The screen should look like Figure 4–34.

Figure 4–34

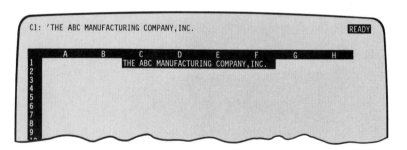

```
C1:  'THE ABC MANUFACTURING COMPANY,INC.                              READY

         A       B       C       D       E       F       G       H
    1                    THE ABC MANUFACTURING COMPANY,INC.
    2
    3
    4
    5
    6
    7
    8
    9
```

When in EDIT mode, additional text can be typed and the remaining text is "moved over," as illustrated in the example above.

In Release 2 and later releases of Lotus 1–2–3, the [Ins] or Insert key can be pressed to activate Overstrike (OVR will appear on the screen). If the Overstrike function is activated, the new text will overstrike or type over the existing test. For example, to replace the letters ABC with XYZ:

Move	the cell pointer to cell C1 (if necessary)
Press	the [Edit] key
Press	the left arrow key to move to the letter A in ABC (or use the [Home] key and the right arrow key to achieve the same result)
Press	the [Ins] key

OVR appears at the bottom right corner of the screen.

Type	XYZ ↵

The letters ABC have now been replaced with the letters XYZ. The screen should look like Figure 4–35.

Figure 4–35

```
C1: 'THE XYZ MANUFACTURING COMPANY,INC.                          READY

          A        B        C        D        E        F        G        H
  1                         THE XYZ MANUFACTURING COMPANY,INC.
  2
  3
  4
  5
  6
  7
  8
  9
```

Erasing an Entry

The following exercise reviews the **Range Erase** command covered in the section titled "Erasing Cells" discussed earlier in this chapter. To erase an entry completely:

Move		the cell pointer to cell C1 (if necessary)
Press	/	(the command key)
Type	R	(for Range)
Type	E	(for Erase)
Press	↵	

The entry THE XYZ MANUFACTURING COMPANY, INC. has now been erased. The screen should look like Figure 4–36.

Figure 4–36

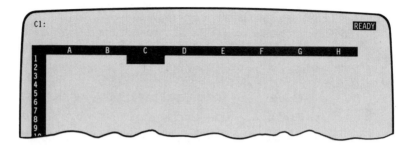

Spaces (made with the space bar) should NEVER be used to "erase" a cell as the spaces will be considered a label by Lotus. Since labels have a value of zero, this entry may cause serious problems with spreadsheet calculations (for example, averages will count labels in the range as zero).

Additional ways to edit a spreadsheet were covered in the following sections in this chapter:

> Inserting Columns and Rows
> Deleting Columns and Rows
> Copying Cells
> Moving Cells

■ USING LABEL PREFIXES

The use of the caret (the ∧ symbol) to center labels and the double-quote (the " symbol) to right-justify labels were first mentioned in Chapter Two. The caret and the double-quote are **label prefixes.** 1–2–3 has four label prefixes that affect the appearance of labels on the screen. In this section, the label prefixes will be discussed and demonstrated. Before starting the following exercise, erase the screen using the **W**orksheet **E**rase **Y**es command sequence.

The apostrophe (the ' symbol located on the double-quote key) is the default label prefix in 1–2–3. When a non-numeric character is the first character of an entry, 1–2–3 automatically places an apostrophe as the prefix to the label. The entry then appears at the left of the cell in which it is input. Input the following label in cell A1:

> **Type**   USA ⏎

Look in the control panel. Notice that an apostrophe appears in the control panel before USA. In the worksheet, notice that USA appears on the left side of column A. Because the user did not specify a label prefix, the apostrophe was used. Refer to Figure 4–37.

Figure 4–37

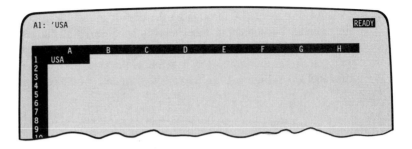

Erase the screen using the **Worksheet Erase Yes** command sequence. In cell A1, manually input the apostrophe before entering USA:

Type   'USA ↵

Again, USA appears at the left side of the cell. The apostrophe only appears before USA in the control panel when cell A1 is highlighted.

The caret symbol causes a label to appear in the center of a cell. The caret must be typed as the first character of the entry. To center a label:

Move   the cell pointer to cell A2
Type   ^USA ↵

USA appears in the center of the cell. The caret only appears before USA in the control panel when cell A2 is highlighted. If a label is the same length or longer than the cell in which it is entered, the column will have to be made wider in order to display the label as centered.

The double-quote symbol causes a label to appear at the right side of the cell. The double-quote must be typed as the first character of the entry. To right justify a label:

Move   the cell pointer to cell A3
Type   "USA ↵

USA appears to the right of the cell. The double-quote only appears before USA in the control panel when cell A3 is highlighted.

The backward slash (the \ symbol) causes a label to repeat the characters entered after the backward slash. To cause the label USA to be repeated in a cell:

Move   the cell pointer to cell A4
Type   \USA ↵

Cell A4 displays USA throughout the cell. If the width of column A is shortened or lengthened, the repeating label adjusts accordingly. This label prefix is useful for subtotal and total lines. For example, entering \‑ will cause repeating dashes to appear in a cell. Refer to Figure 4–38 to see how the label prefixes altered the appearance of the label USA. Figure 4–39 displays the contents of the cells for each of the entries.

Figure 4–38

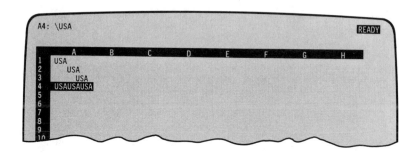

Figure 4–39

Note that label prefixes are to be used only for *labels*. If ^123 is entered in a cell, for example, 123 is centered as a label in a cell and cannot be used in computation.

SUMMARY

Lotus 1–2–3 has various menu options and features that allow the user to control how data is entered and viewed. Useful Lotus commands allow the user to work more efficiently and effectively when creating, editing, and/or analyzing spreadsheets.

KEY CONCEPTS

[Abs]
Absolute cell reference
[Calc]
Copy
[Edit]
File Directory
File Erase
File List
[Ins] Move
Label prefix
[Num Lock]
Range Erase
Range Format Percent

Relative cell reference
System
[Window]
Worksheet Column Hide
Worksheet Delete Column
Worksheet Global Recalculation
   Manual
Worksheet Global Zero Yes
Worksheet Insert Row
Worksheet Page
Worksheet Status
Worksheet Titles
Worksheet Window

CHAPTER FOUR
EXERCISE 1

INSTRUCTIONS: Circle T if the statement is true and F if the statement is false.

T   F   1. An absolute cell reference means that the reference is kept constant, even when copied.

T   F   2. The [Edit] key allows the user to correct a cell entry without having to retype the entire entry.

T   F   3. Worksheet Titles allows the user to center titles on a spreadsheet.

T   F   4. Worksheet Window allows the user to view two different areas of a spreadsheet at the same time.

T   F   5. Worksheet Page creates a page break in a spreadsheet.

T   F   6. If column D is hidden on a worksheet using Worksheet Column Hide, column D will not appear if the worksheet is printed.

T   F   7. Worksheet Global Recalculation Manual is activated so that data can be entered without the worksheet recalculating after each new entry.

T   F   8. Changing the File Directory changes the drive designation or path to which Lotus saves and retrieves files.

T   F   9. File Erase erases a file from memory.

T   F   10. The System command permanently returns the user to DOS.

CHAPTER FOUR
EXERCISE 2

INSTRUCTIONS: Explain a typical situation when the following keystrokes or Lotus 1–2–3 commands are used.

Problem 1:	[Num Lock]
Problem 2:	[Abs]
Problem 3:	Range Format %
Problem 4:	Worksheet Titles
Problem 5:	Worksheet Windows
Problem 6:	[Window]
Problem 7:	Worksheet Insert Row
Problem 8:	Worksheet Delete Column
Problem 9:	Worksheet Column Hide
Problem 10:	Worksheet Page
Problem 11:	Worksheet Global Recalculation Manual
Problem 12:	[Calc]
Problem 13:	Worksheet Global Zero Yes
Problem 14:	Range Erase
Problem 15:	File List
Problem 16:	File Erase
Problem 17:	File Directory
Problem 18:	System
Problem 19:	[Edit]
Problem 20:	[Ins] in EDIT mode

CHAPTER FOUR
EXERCISE 3
Making a Cell Entry Absolute

INSTRUCTIONS: The following example illustrates a common error. Follow the instructions below to create the error and answer the question below.

Clear the screen (use the **Worksheet Erase Yes** commands).
In cell A1, type REVENUE and press ↵.
In cell A2, type ASSUMED REV RATE and press ↵.
Widen column A to 16 characters.
In cell B1, type 10000 and press ↵.
In cell B2, type 1.15 and press ↵.
In cell C1, type +B1*B2 and press ↵.
Copy the formula in cell C1 to cells D1 and E1.

The screen should look like Figure 4–40.

Figure 4–40

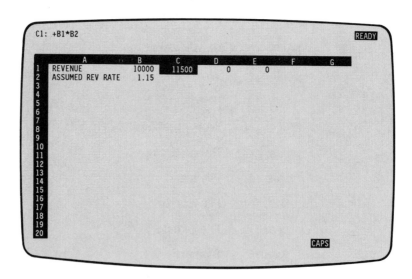

1. How can the formula in cell C1 be changed so that the formulas in cells D1 and E1 also refer to cell B2 for the projected revenue rate?

CHAPTER FOUR
EXERCISE 4
Hiding a Column

INSTRUCTIONS: Follow the instructions below.

Retrieve the file BUDGET that was created in Chapter Two.
Hide columns B and F.
Print the spreadsheet. The printout should look like Figure 4–41.

Figure 4–41

```
                    ABC COMPANY
                      BUDGET


                   QTR2     QTR3     QTR4

    SALES          61,200   62,424   63,672

    EXPENSES
       SALARIES    35,500   36,200   37,000
       RENT         9,000    9,000    9,000
       TELEPHONE    1,050    1,103    1,158
       OFFICE SUPPLIES  800     850      900
       MISCELLANEOUS   1,030   1,061    1,093
                   --------  --------  --------
       TOTAL EXPENSES 47,380  48,214   49,151
                   --------  --------  --------
    GROSS PROFIT    13,820   14,210   14,521
                   ========  ========  ========
```

CHAPTER FOUR
EXERCISE 5
Entering Page Breaks in a Spreadsheet

INSTRUCTIONS: Follow the instructions below.

Retrieve the file BUDGET that was created in Chapter Two.
Create a page break after the subtotal line for TOTAL EXPENSES.
Print the spreadsheet. The printout should look like Figure 4–42.

*Figure 4–42
Part 1*

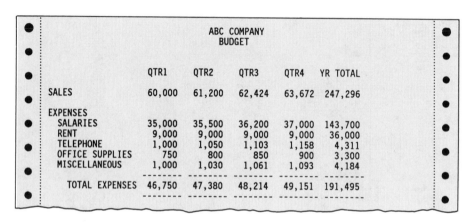

```
                              ABC COMPANY
                                BUDGET


                     QTR1      QTR2      QTR3      QTR4    YR TOTAL

        SALES        60,000    61,200    62,424    63,672  247,296

        EXPENSES
          SALARIES   35,000    35,500    36,200    37,000  143,700
          RENT        9,000     9,000     9,000     9,000   36,000
          TELEPHONE   1,000     1,050     1,103     1,158    4,311
          OFFICE SUPPLIES 750     800       850       900    3,300
          MISCELLANEOUS 1,000   1,030     1,061     1,093    4,184
                     --------  --------  --------  --------  --------
        TOTAL EXPENSES 46,750  47,380    48,214    49,151  191,495
                     --------  --------  --------  --------  --------
```

*Figure 4–42
Part 2*

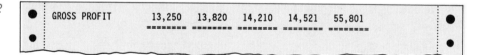

```
        GROSS PROFIT   13,250    13,820    14,210    14,521    55,801
                     ========  ========  ========  ========  ========
```

CHAPTER FIVE

CREATING AND USING A TEMPLATE

OBJECTIVES

In this chapter, the student will learn to:

■ Create and use a template

■ CHAPTER OVERVIEW

In Lotus 1–2–3, a **template** is the term used to describe a spreadsheet that can be used to create a series of other spreadsheets. A template usually consists of the general format (headings, labels, numeric format) and formulas that will be common to all of the spreadsheets. When data is input into the template, the spreadsheet formulas calculate accordingly. The new data is then saved under a different file name. The template can save the user hours of time and effort in recreating the same basic spreadsheet.

The template that will be created in this chapter will be used to compute the salaries for employees in various divisions of the ABC Company example used earlier. Since each division will be on a separate spreadsheet, a template is built so that each division can be created using the division template. When the template is complete, it should look like Figure 5–1.

Figure 5–1

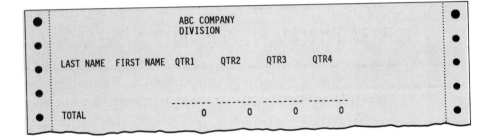

■ CREATING A TEMPLATE

There are three steps for creating the template:

1. Create the spreadsheet title, column headings, and labels.

2. Enter subtotal lines, total lines, and formulas.

3. Set the numeric format for the spreadsheet.

It is also useful to name areas of the spreadsheet with range names where appropriate. The use of range names is explained in Chapter Six.

Creating the Spreadsheet Title, Column Headings, and Labels

If necessary, clear the screen using the **Worksheet Erase Yes** menu options.

To enter the titles for the template:

Press	the [Caps Lock] key (if CAPS is not already on)
Move	the cell pointer to cell C1
Press	the space bar three times
Type	ABC COMPANY ↵
Move	the cell pointer to cell C2
Press	the space bar three times
Type	DIVISION ↵
Move	the cell pointer to cell A5
Type	LAST NAME ↵

To widen column A:

Press	/	(the command key)
Type	W	(for Worksheet)
Type	C	(for Column)
Type	S	(for Set-Width)

When prompted for the column width:

Type	11 ↵

To enter the next heading:

Move	the cell pointer to cell B5
Type	FIRST NAME ↵

To widen column B:

Press	/	(the command key)
Type	W	(for Worksheet)
Type	C	(for Column)
Type	S	(for Set-Width)

When prompted for the column width:

Type	10 ↵

To enter labels in cells C5 through F5, respectively:

Move	the cell pointer to cell C5
Type	^QTR1
Move	the cell pointer to cell D5
Type	^QTR2
Move	the cell pointer to cell E5
Type	^QTR3
Move	the cell pointer to cell F5
Type	^QTR4 ↵

To enter the label TOTAL:

Move	the cell pointer to cell A10
Type	TOTAL ↵

The screen should look like Figure 5–2.

Figure 5–2

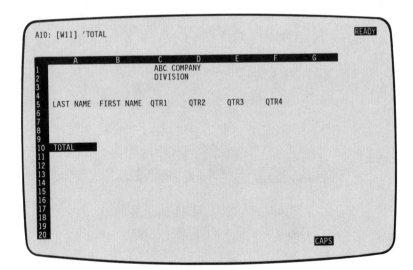

Entering Subtotal Lines, Total Lines, and Formulas

To enter subtotal lines:

Move	the cell pointer to cell C9
Press	the space bar one time
Type	— — — — — — — — (eight dashes)
Press	↵

To copy the subtotal line to the rest of the row:

Press	/	(the command key)
Type	C	(for Copy)

When prompted for the range to copy FROM:

Press	↵

C9 (the cell containing the subtotal line) is the selection for the range to copy. When prompted for the range to copy TO:

Move	the cell pointer to cell D9
Type	.
Move	the cell pointer to cell F9 ↵

To enter the formula to add up the salaries:

Move	the cell pointer to cell C10
Type	@SUM (
Move	the cell pointer to cell C5
Press	.
Move	the cell pointer to cell C9
Type	) ↵

A 0 (zero) should appear in the cell since the template does not contain any numbers to add. Including the rows above and below where data will be input in the @SUM formula allows the @SUM command to adjust correctly in the event that rows of data are inserted or deleted when data is used on the template. Since the rows are not numeric, their "values" are assumed to be zero and therefore will not cause the results of using the @SUM formula to be incorrect.

To copy the formula to the rest of the row:

Press	/	(the command key)
Type	C	(for Copy)

When prompted for the range to copy FROM:

Press	⏎

Cell C10 (the @ SUM formula) is the selection for the cell to copy. When prompted for the range to copy TO:

Move	the cell pointer to cell D10
Press	.
Move	the cell pointer to cell F10 ⏎

Setting the Numeric Format for the Worksheet

To set the global format:

Press	/	(the command key)
Type	W	(for Worksheet)
Type	G	(for Global)
Type	F	(for Format)
Type	,	(the Comma)
Type	0	(zero) ⏎

When numbers are entered on the template, the numbers will be formatted with commas and no decimal places. The template worksheet is now complete. The screen should look like Figure 5–3.

Figure 5–3

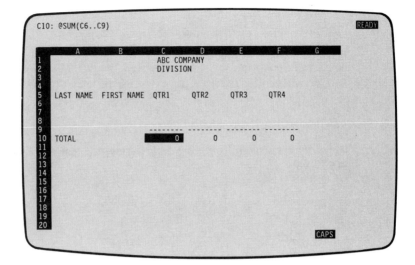

Saving the Template on a File

To save the file:

Press	the [Home] key	
Press	/	(the command key)
Type	F	(for File)
Type	S	(for Save)

When prompted for the file name:

Type	DIVTEMP ↵

The worksheet has now been saved and can be used as a template for the various division worksheets.

An alternative way to create the template would be to create the first detail spreadsheet. After creating the file and making sure that all of the formulas and other elements of the worksheet are correct, save the file. Then erase the data for all lines that will be different for the other detail worksheets and save the **shell** as the template. In this example, the names and the title would be erased. This method may be preferable in some cases because it would be easier to check the appearance and accuracy of the worksheet, especially if it is large and complex.

To erase the screen before going on to the next exercise, erase the template from the screen using the Worksheet Erase Yes command sequence.

■ USING A TEMPLATE

The purpose of having a template is to use it as a shell for other spreadsheets. In this exercise, the template DIVTEMP (Division Template) that was created in the previous exercise will be used to create the spreadsheet file DIV1 (Division 1).

Retrieve the Template

To use the template for inserting data, retrieve the template. To retrieve the template DIVTEMP:

Press	/	(the command key)
Type	F	(for File)
Type	R	(for Retrieve)

When prompted for the file to retrieve:

Type	DIVTEMP ↵

DIVTEMP should be visible on the screen after it is retrieved from the disk.

Enter Data into the Template

To enter the appropriate division number in the title:

Move	the cell pointer to cell C2
Press	the [Edit] key (the [F2] function key)
Press	the space bar
Type	1 ↵

To enter the data for Division 1:

Move	the cell pointer to cell A7

Using the printscreen of the completed worksheet for Division 1 as a reference (displayed in Figure 5–4), type the names and the salary information for each quarter in rows 7 and 8 in columns A through F. The TOTAL row will compute the totals as the relevant data for each quarter is being input.

Figure 5–4

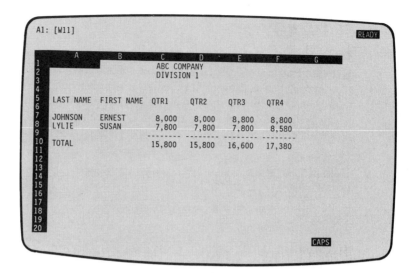

A1: [W11]   READY

	A	B	C	D	E	F	G
1			ABC COMPANY				
2			DIVISION 1				
3							
4							
5	LAST NAME	FIRST NAME	QTR1	QTR2	QTR3	QTR4	
6							
7	JOHNSON	ERNEST	8,000	8,000	8,800	8,800	
8	LYLIE	SUSAN	7,800	7,800	7,800	8,580	
9							
10	TOTAL		15,800	15,800	16,600	17,380	
11							
12							
13							
14							
15							
16							
17							
18							
19							
20							

CAPS

Saving the Worksheet Under Another Name

To save the worksheet as DIV1:

Press	the [Home] key	
Press	/	(the command key)
Type	F	(for File)
Type	S	(for Save)

When prompted for the file name, be SURE to give the file a new name. Otherwise, the file DIVTEMP will be replaced with DIV1's information. To name the new file:

| **Type** | DIV1 ↵ (for Division 1) |

Two files exist. DIVTEMP is the template, which can be used for more detail spreadsheets. DIV1 contains the data for Division 1. When DIVTEMP is in **memory,** it can be altered and saved under a different file name; the file DIVTEMP on the **disk** is not altered *unless* a **File Save** command is executed and the original file DIVTEMP is replaced. Since it is very easy to accidentally save over a template, it is wise to keep a copy of the template file handy as a backup.

SUMMARY

A template is a shell document that can be used to create multiple spreadsheets that have the same basic format. The template contains the features that will be common to all of the detail spreadsheets. For example, titles, descriptions, formulas, and even print settings may be created in the template. When data is entered into the template, the results are saved under a separate name so that the template may be used to create additional detail spreadsheets.

KEY CONCEPTS

Template
Shell
Spreadsheet in memory
Spreadsheet on disk

CHAPTER FIVE
EXERCISE 1

INSTRUCTIONS: Circle T if the statement is true and F if the statement is false.

T   **F**   1. In Lotus 1–2–3, a template file must be combined with another file containing data to generate a new spreadsheet.

T   **F**   2. A template is a good way to keep detail spreadsheets standardized.

T   **F**   3. When data is added to a template in memory, it is automatically added to the template file on the disk.

T   **F**   4. A template can be used to create multiple files.

T   **F**   5. When adding data to a template in order to create a new spreadsheet, save the spreadsheet under a new name rather than the template name so that the template file will not be altered.

CHAPTER FIVE
EXERCISE 2
Creating a Template

INSTRUCTIONS: Following the instructions below to create a template from an existing detail spreadsheet.

Retrieve the file DIV1.
Erase the number 1 from the title DIVISION 1.
Erase the data for Name, First Name, and all four quarters for Ernest Johnson and Susan Lylie.
Save the file as DIVTEMP2. The file DIVTEMP2 should be identical to the file DIVTEMP that was created in this chapter. The screen should look like Figure 5–5.

Figure 5–5

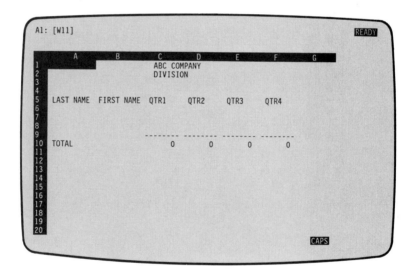

CHAPTER SIX

COMBINING INFORMATION BETWEEN SPREADSHEETS

OBJECTIVES

In this chapter, the student will learn to:

■ Consolidate information from a detail spreadsheet into a summary spreadsheet
■ Consolidate information from several detail spreadsheets into a summary spreadsheet
■ Use the Range Value command sequence for consolidating worksheets

■ CHAPTER OVERVIEW

Sometimes it is necessary to move data from a detail spreadsheet to a summary spreadsheet. **Detail spreadsheets** may contain a considerable amount of information about a particular topic. For example, a company can have detail spreadsheets that contain information about the budgets for each department. A **summary spreadsheet** summarizes information contained in detail spreadsheets. When the totals or "bottom line" items for each department budget are brought into a summary spreadsheet, a manager can more effectively assess the overall picture.

In Chapter Five, the file entitled DIV1 was created from a template and used to record the salaries for Division 1. In this chapter, Division 1 will be used as a detail spreadsheet. In Chapter Two, the file BUDGET was created and contained a line for SALARIES data. In this chapter, BUDGET will be used as a summary spreadsheet. Using the **File Combine** feature, the totals from the salaries in DIV1 and additional spreadsheets are brought into the BUDGET file. The summary spreadsheet BUDGET is displayed in Figure 6–1.

Figure 6–1

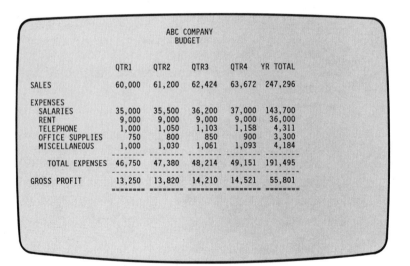

```
                              ABC COMPANY
                                BUDGET

                        QTR1    QTR2    QTR3    QTR4   YR TOTAL

        SALES          60,000  61,200  62,424  63,672  247,296

        EXPENSES
          SALARIES     35,000  35,500  36,200  37,000  143,700
          RENT          9,000   9,000   9,000   9,000   36,000
          TELEPHONE     1,000   1,050   1,103   1,158    4,311
          OFFICE SUPPLIES  750     800     850     900    3,300
          MISCELLANEOUS  1,000   1,030   1,061   1,093    4,184
                       -------- ------- ------- ------- --------
          TOTAL EXPENSES 46,750  47,380  48,214  49,151  191,495
                       -------- ------- ------- ------- --------
        GROSS PROFIT    13,250  13,820  14,210  14,521   55,801
                       ======== ======= ======= ======= ========
```

■ CONSOLIDATING INFORMATION FROM A DETAIL SPREADSHEET INTO A SUMMARY SPREADSHEET

In the following exercise, a name will be assigned to the cells on the spreadsheet containing the totals in the file DIV1. The data from those cells will then be consolidated into the summary spreadsheet BUDGET.

Define a Named Range in the Detail Spreadsheet

Retrieve the file DIV1, which is displayed in Figure 6–2.

Figure 6–2

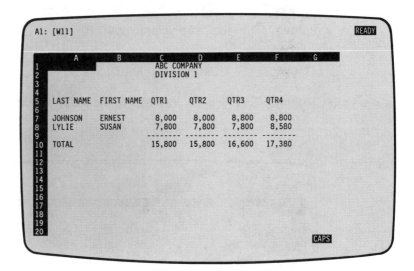

```
A1: [W11]                                                    READY

          A         B         C         D         E         F         G
  1                           ABC COMPANY
  2                           DIVISION 1
  3
  4
  5   LAST NAME FIRST NAME  QTR1      QTR2      QTR3      QTR4
  6
  7   JOHNSON   ERNEST      8,000     8,000     8,800     8,800
  8   LYLIE     SUSAN       7,800     7,800     7,800     8,580
  9                        --------  --------  --------  --------
 10   TOTAL                 15,800    15,800    16,600    17,380
 11
 12
 13
 14
 15
 16
 17
 18
 19
 20                                                              CAPS
```

To bring a specific area of one worksheet into another worksheet, the user must indicate which areas are to be used. The most common procedure is to give the range a **range name** using the **R**ange **N**ame sequence. A **range** refers to a single cell or an adjacent group of cells within a spreadsheet. Range commands only affect the spreadsheet area specified by the user (recall the use of **R**ange **E**rase and **R**ange **F**ormat in previous chapters). The name TOTAL will be assigned to the range of cells on the TOTAL line in DIV1. The following exercise will illustrate how to bring the TOTAL line from the file DIV1 into the file BUDGET. To set up the range name TOTAL:

Press	/	(the command key)
Type	R	(for Range)
Type	N	(for Name)
Type	C	(for Create)

When prompted for the range name:

| **Type** | ⸱TOTAL ↵ |

Range names can contain up to 15 characters. The name of a range is up to the discretion of the user; ideally, the range name is a description of the data in the range. When prompted for the range to be assigned to the name TOTAL:

Press	[Esc] (the Escape key) to release the "anchor"
Move	the cell pointer to cell C10
Type	.
Move	the cell pointer to F10

Cells C10 through F10 should be highlighted. The screen should look like Figure 6–3.

Figure 6–3

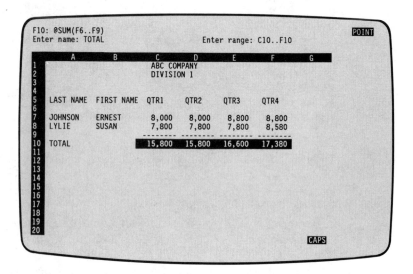

Press ↵

The range name TOTAL has now been given to the range of cells C10 through F10.

Saving and Replacing the Worksheet to Keep the Named Range

To save the worksheet with the named range:

Press	[Home]	(if not already at cell A1)
Press	/	(the command key)
Type	F	(for File)
Type	S	(for Save)

When prompted for the file name, DIV1 will appear since the file has been saved previously. To keep the file name DIV1:

Press	⏎

When prompted whether to Cancel or Replace:

Type	R	(for Replace)

The file DIV1 now contains the range name TOTAL.

Preparing the Summary Worksheet

The TOTAL range from DIV1 will be brought into the BUDGET file. In this exercise, the SALARIES data in BUDGET will be erased. For the purposes of this exercise, the BUDGET file will be acting as a summary worksheet so the DIV1 data can be brought into a blank area.

First, retrieve the spreadsheet BUDGET.

To delete the SALARIES line in BUDGET:

Move	the cell pointer to cell B10	
Press	/	(the Command key)
Type	R	(for Range)
Type	E	(for Erase)
Move	the cell pointer to cell E10 ⏎	

The screen should look like Figure 6–4.

Figure 6–4

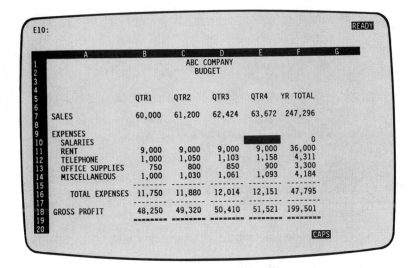

Moving the Detail Worksheet Data to the Summary Worksheet

The cell pointer must be placed on the summary spreadsheet in the proper cell so that the data from the detail spreadsheet will be placed in the proper cell. To position the cell pointer where the detail spreadsheet data is to be placed in the summary spreadsheet:

Move	the cell pointer to cell B10 (if necessary)

The TOTAL line from the file DIV1 will be placed in the spreadsheet beginning at cell B10 (the first quarter for SALARIES).

To move the data in the range TOTAL from the detail spreadsheet DIV1 to the summary spreadsheet BUDGET:

Press	/	(the command key)
Type	F	(for File)
Type	C	(for Combine)
Type	A	(for Add)
Type	N	(for Named/Specified-Range)

When prompted for the range name:

Type	TOTAL ↵

The word TOTAL must be typed exactly as it was specified in the file DIV1. However, Lotus 1–2–3 is not "case sensitive" with range names; for example, "Total" or "total" is also acceptable. Release 2 and later releases of Lotus 1–2–3 contain the menu option Named/Specified-Range. The Specified-Range portion of the Named/Specified-Range option means that the user may specify either a named range or the exact range in the file that he/she wishes to pull into the current spreadsheet. In this exercise, either the named range TOTAL or the specified range C10 . . F10 can be specified. C10 . . F10 is the set of cells in the range named TOTAL that exists in the DIV1 file.

When prompted for the file to combine, the worksheet files on the currently used directory appear in the control panel (the cell pointer can be moved to highlight any file name currently displayed in the control panel):

Type   DIV1 ⏎

An alternative to typing the file name DIV1 would be to move the cell pointer to the file name DIV1 and press ⏎ .

The summary spreadsheet BUDGET now contains the data from the TOTAL line in DIV1 on its SALARIES line, and the spreadsheet has recalculated accordingly. The SALARIES line data from DIV1 now exists in both DIV1 and on the summary spreadsheet. The screen should look like Figure 6–5.

Figure 6–5

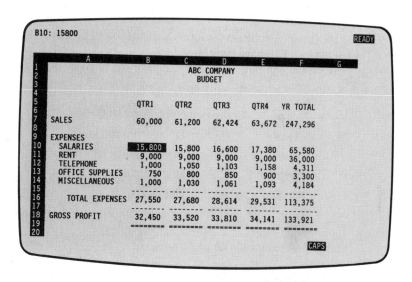

Only numbers, not formulas or labels, are added when using the **F**ile **C**ombine **A**dd *command sequence*. (Use the **F**ile **C**ombine **C**opy command to bring in labels and formulas; the data brought in *replaces* any existing data on a spreadsheet). The File Combine Add sequence cannot add numbers to an area where formulas exist on the current worksheet. A formula will override a number coming into the spreadsheet.

To see an example of how **F**ile **C**ombine **A**dd cannot add numbers to formulas, first erase cells B10 through E10 by following the directions below. (Do *not* save the result of the previous exercise. The original file BUDGET will be used in the next exercise).

Move		the cell pointer to cell B10
Press	/	(the command key)
Type	R	(for Range)
Type	E	(for Erase)

When prompted for the range to erase:

Move	the cell pointer to cell E10

Make sure that cells B10 through E10 are highlighted.

Press	↵

Cell F10, which contains the formula @SUM(B10..F10), displays a zero since cells B10 through E10 have been erased.

Move the cell pointer to cell C10. For the puposes of this illustration, the range TOTAL from DIV1 will be added beginning in cell C10.

Move		the cell pointer to cell C10
Press	/	(the command key)
Type	F	(for File)
Type	C	(for Combine)
Type	A	(for Add)
Type	N	(for Named/Specified-Range)

When prompted for the range name:

Type	TOTAL ↵

When prompted for the file name:

Type	DIV1 ↵

The result is that the first number from TOTAL will be added to cell C10, the second number from TOTAL will be added to cell D10, and the third number will be added to cell E10. The fourth number, however, will not be added to cell F10 because F10 contains a formula.

Move   the cell pointer to cell F10

Instead of the number 17,380 from DIV1 being brought into the spreadsheet in cell F10, the number 48,200 will appear. The number 48,200 is a result of the formula @SUM(B10..E10) in cell F10, which "overrides" the number 17,380 from being brought into the cell. See Figure 6–6.

Figure 6–6

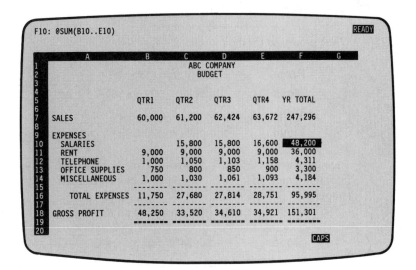

F10: @SUM(B10..E10)   READY

```
             A            B       C       D       E        F        G
                                  ABC COMPANY
                                    BUDGET

                           QTR1    QTR2    QTR3    QTR4   YR TOTAL
     SALES               60,000  61,200  62,424  63,672  247,296

     EXPENSES
       SALARIES                   15,800  15,800  16,600   48,200
       RENT               9,000    9,000   9,000   9,000   36,000
       TELEPHONE          1,000    1,050   1,103   1,158    4,311
       OFFICE SUPPLIES      750      800     850     900    3,300
       MISCELLANEOUS      1,000    1,030   1,061   1,093    4,184

       TOTAL EXPENSES    11,750   27,680  27,814  28,751   95,995

     GROSS PROFIT        48,250   33,520  34,610  34,921  151,301
```

                                                                   CAPS

■ CONSOLIDATING INFORMATION FROM SEVERAL DETAIL SPREADSHEETS INTO A SUMMARY SPREADSHEET

In this exercise, the template DIVTEMP will be altered to include the range name TOTAL. If the template contains the range name, it is not necessary to add the range name to all future spreadsheets made from the template. A second file (DIV2) will be created using the template DIVTEMP so that the range TOTAL from both DIV1 and DIV2 can be consolidated into the summary file BUDGET.

Altering the Template

Retrieve the file DIVTEMP.

To set up the range name TOTAL on the template:

Press	/	(the command key)
Type	R	(for Range)
Type	N	(for Name)
Type	C	(for Create)

When prompted for the range name:

Type	TOTAL ⏎

When prompted for the range:

Press	[Esc] (the Escape key)
Move	the cell pointer to cell C10
Type	.
Move	the cell pointer to F10 ⏎

The range name TOTAL is now part of this template and all future spreadsheets made from this template. It is a useful idea to include all range names when first creating the template.

To make the inserting of the title more efficient:

Move	the cell pointer to cell C2
Press	the [Edit] key (the [F2] function key)
Press	the space bar
Press	⏎

The space after the word DIVISION on the spreadsheet prevents the user from having to add a space when putting in each division number.

When a file is saved, the cell pointer is saved in the position it is at when the **File Save** command sequence is executed. The next time the file is retrieved, the cell pointer appears in the same position it was in when the file was last saved. In this exercise, the cell pointer will be saved in cell C2 so that it is already highlighting the word DIVISION. To save the cell pointer in cell C2:

Press	/	(the command key)
Type	F	(for File)
Type	S	(for Save)

When prompted for the file to save:

Press	⏎

When prompted whether to Cancel or Replace:

Type	R	(for Replace)

The cell pointer is now saved in cell C2. When the template is retrieved, the cell pointer will already be highlighting C2, the title that needs to be edited for every DIVISION spreadsheet created from the template.

Another way to alter the template would be to delete all data from DIV1 and also to delete the number 1 from the title DIVISION 1, saving the result as DIVTEMP.

Retrieving the Template and Entering Data

In this exercise, the revised template DIVTEMP (Division Template) is used to build a second detail worksheet named DIV2 (Division 2).

Retrieve the template file DIVTEMP, if necessary.

To enter the division number:

Press	the [Edit] key (the [F2] function key)
Type	2 ⏎

The cell pointer appears in cell C2 since the cell pointer was saved in this position. It is not necessary to press the space bar before typing the division number since a space was added in the template.

To enter the data for Division 2:

Move	the cell pointer to cell A7

Using the printscreen of the completed worksheet for Division 2 as a reference (see Figure 6–7), type the names and the salary information for each quarter in rows 7 and 8 in columns A through F.

Figure 6–7

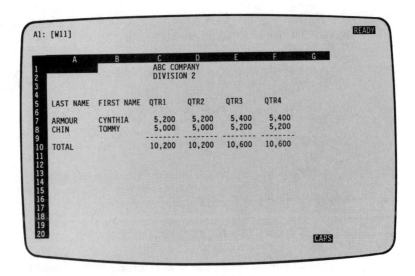

Saving the Worksheet Under Another Name

To save the worksheet as DIV2:

Press	the [Home] key (if the cell pointer is not already there)	
Press	/	(the command key)
Type	F	(for File)
Type	S	(for Save)

When prompted for the file name:

Type   DIV2 ⏎

Since the range TOTAL was entered in the template in the section titled "Altering the Template," the range already exists. To make sure that the range already exists, use the **R**ange **N**ame **C**reate command sequence. When prompted to enter the range name, highlight TOTAL (if necessary) and press ⏎ . The range for TOTAL (cells C10 through F10) should be highlighted. Press the ⏎ key to return to the READY mode.

Preparing the Summary Worksheet

In this exercise, the SALARIES data in the BUDGET file will again be erased. The BUDGET file will serve as a summary worksheet into which the TOTAL ranges for DIV1 and DIV2 will be added together.

First, retrieve the spreadsheet BUDGET.

To erase the SALARIES line in BUDGET:

Move	the cell pointer to cell B10	
Press	/	(the command key)
Type	R	(for Range)
Type	E	(for Erase)
Move	the cell pointer to cell E10 ↵	

The screen should look like Figure 6–8.

Figure 6–8

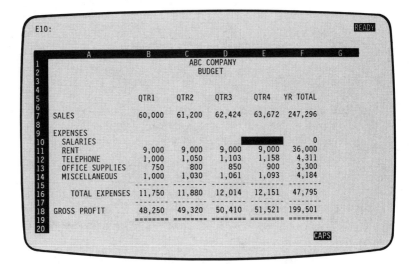

Moving the Detail Worksheet Data to the Summary Worksheet

The cell pointer must be placed in the summary spreadsheet correctly so that the data will be added at the correct place in the spreadsheet. To position the cell pointer correctly:

Move   the cell pointer to cell B10

The TOTAL range from the file DIV1 will be brought in beginning at cell B10 (the first quarter for SALARIES).

To move the salaries data in the range TOTAL from the detail spreadsheet DIV1 to the summary spreadsheet BUDGET:

Press	/	(the command key)
Type	F	(for File)
Type	C	(for Combine)
Type	A	(for Add)
Type	N	(for Named/Specified-Range)

When prompted for the range name:

Type   TOTAL ↵

When prompted for the file to combine:

Type   DIV1 ↵

The summary spreadsheet BUDGET now contains the data from the TOTAL line in DIV1 on its SALARIES line, and the spreadsheet has recalculated accordingly. The screen should look like Figure 6–9.

Figure 6–9

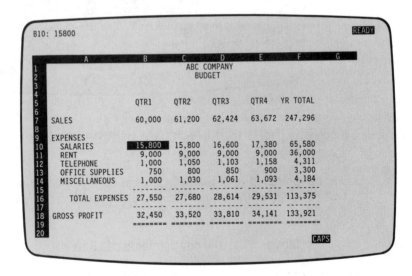

To add the salary data from DIV2 to the salary data from DIV1:

Move the cell pointer to cell B10 (if it is not already there)

The TOTAL line from the file DIV2 will now be added beginning at cell B10 (the first quarter for SALARIES) and then added to the data already moved (added) from the file DIV1.

To move (add) the salaries data in the range TOTAL from the detail spreadsheet DIV2 to the summary spreadsheet BUDGET:

Press	/	(the command key)
Type	F	(for File)
Type	C	(for Combine)
Type	A	(for Add)
Type	N	(for Named/Specified-Range)

When prompted for the range name:

Type TOTAL ↵

When prompted for the file to combine:

Type DIV2 ↵

The summary spreadsheet BUDGET now contains the TOTAL line data from both DIV1 and DIV2 on its SALARIES line, and the spreadsheet has recalculated other cells appropriately. The screen should look like Figure 6–10.

Figure 6–10

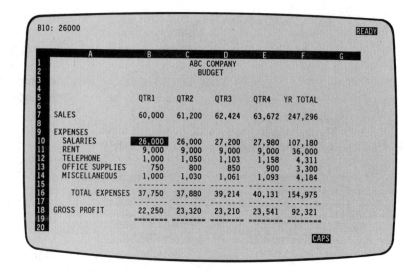

```
B10: 26000                                                    READY

         A          B        C        D       E      F       G
 1                          ABC COMPANY
 2                            BUDGET
 3
 4
 5                  QTR1    QTR2    QTR3    QTR4  YR TOTAL
 6
 7    SALES        60,000  61,200  62,424  63,672  247,296
 8
 9    EXPENSES
10      SALARIES   26,000  26,000  27,200  27,980  107,180
11      RENT        9,000   9,000   9,000   9,000   36,000
12      TELEPHONE   1,000   1,050   1,103   1,158    4,311
13      OFFICE SUPPLIES 750   800     850     900    3,300
14      MISCELLANEOUS 1,000 1,030   1,061   1,093    4,184
15                 -------- -------- -------- -------- --------
16    TOTAL EXPENSES 37,750 37,880  39,214  40,131  154,975
17                 -------- -------- -------- -------- --------
18    GROSS PROFIT  22,250  23,320  23,210  23,541   92,321
19                 ======== ======== ======== ======== ========
20
                                                          CAPS
```

Do *not* save the results of this exercise, as the original file BUDGET will be used for later exercises.

USING THE RANGE VALUE COMMAND FOR CONSOLIDATING WORKSHEETS

The **Range Value** menu option is available in Release 2 and later releases of Lotus 1–2–3. (For the corresponding method available in Release 1A of Lotus, see the note at the end of this exercise).

Sometimes it is necessary to add numbers from File A to a row or column of numbers in File B that have been created with formulas. When the **File Combine Add** command sequence is used, Lotus will not add the File A numbers to File B if the cells in File B contain formulas. To solve this problem, change the cells in File B so that they only contain the numbers (the results of the calculated formulas) and not the formulas. This can be accomplished using the Range Value command sequence.

Retrieve the file BUDGET for the following exercise.

Move   the cell pointer to cell C14

Look at the control panel. Note that cell C14 contains the formula @ROUND(B14*1.03,0). D14 and E14 contain similar formulas. In order to use the File Combine Add function to add data to the MISCELLANEOUS line, cells C14 through E14 need to be changed so that only numbers exist in the cell.

To change the formulas in cells C14 through E14 to values (rather than the results of formulas):

Move		the cell pointer to cell C14 (if necessary)
Press	/	(the command key)
Type	R	(for Range)
Type	V	(for Value)

When prompted for the range to copy FROM:

Move   the cell pointer to cell E14

Cells C14 through E14 should be highlighted.

Press   ↵

When prompted for the range to copy TO:

Type   .
Move   the cell pointer to cell E14

Cells C14 through E14 should be highlighted. In this example, the values (the results of the calculated formulas) of cells C14 through E14 will be copied over the formulas themselves. In other instances, it may be appropriate to copy the values to another part of the worksheet (leaving the formulas intact in their original position).

Press   ↵

With the cursor in cell C14, look at the control panel. 1030 (the actual value of cell C14) is displayed in the control panel. The formula no longer exists in the cell. If the user desires to keep the original file with the formulas intact, he/she could save the spreadsheet in memory (the spreadsheet with values only) under a different name.

To see the contents of cells D14 and E14:

Move   the cell pointer to cell D14
Move   the cell pointer to cell E14

Numbers exist in cells D14 and E14 rather than formulas.

If a File Combine Add is performed to the MISCELLANEOUS line in the BUDGET spreadsheet, there will be no problem adding the numbers from the incoming file to the BUDGET spreadsheet. This is because the MISCELLANEOUS line now consists of numbers, not formulas.

If using Release 1A, note that the File Xtract Values command allows the user to copy a range of cells (or an entire worksheet) into a new file that consists only of the values.

To change only a few cells, the following method can be used in all releases of Lotus 1–2–3. If the cell pointer is on a cell containing a formula, pressing the [Edit] (F2) key and then the [Calc] (F9) key causes the cell to display the value of the calculation in the control panel. Pressing ↵ replaces the cell formula with the value. The disadvantage of using this method is that it works for only one cell at a time.

SUMMARY

The File Combine Add feature allows the user to bring data from one or more files into a summary spreadsheet. Range names can be assigned so that only the specified ranges are pulled into the summary spreadsheet. There can be multiple range names in a spreadsheet. Only one range can be brought in at a time, although the range can consist of multiple lines of data. Only one named range and one file can be combined at a time.

An efficient way to standardize range names for all detail spreadsheets is to create them in a template. The template can then be used to create all of the detail spreadsheets.

The File Combine Add feature will not bring data into an area that consists of formulas. The Range Value command can change formulas into values so that the File Combine Add feature can be used.

KEY CONCEPTS

Detail spreadsheet

File Combine Add

File Combine Copy

File Xtract Value

Named/Specified Range

Range

Range name

Range Name Create

Range Value

Summary spreadsheet

CHAPTER SIX
EXERCISE 1

INSTRUCTIONS: Circle T if the statement is true and F if the statement is false.

T   F   1. The range name for a line of data must be taken from a label already existing on the spreadsheet.

T   F   2. A template is a good way to keep range names standardized.

T   F   3. A detail spreadsheet is used for summarizing data from several spreadsheets.

T   F   4. File **C**ombine **C**opy is used to add numbers together from various spreadsheets.

T   F   5. If desired, the exact range location rather than range names can be specified when using the **N**amed/**S**pecified-Range command to combine data.

T   F   6. File **C**ombine **A**dd can add numbers to existing numbers and formulas.

T   F   7. The **R**ange **V**alue command can change values into formulas.

T   F   8. The File **X**tract command can be used to create a spreadsheet containing values from a spreadsheet containing formulas.

T   F   9. File **C**ombine **C**opy can copy formulas from one spreadsheet to another spreadsheet.

T   F   10. When files are combined, the original detail spreadsheet and summary spreadsheet are automatically changed.

CHAPTER SIX
EXERCISE 2
Creating a Detail Spreadsheet

INSTRUCTIONS: Follow the instructions below to create a spreadsheet from an existing template.

Using the template DIVTEMP, create a spreadsheet for Division 3 as seen in Figure 6–11. The cell formulas for the worksheet appear in Figure 6–12 as a guide. Note that a row will need to be inserted to accommodate three lines of data. Save the file as DIV3.

Figure 6–11

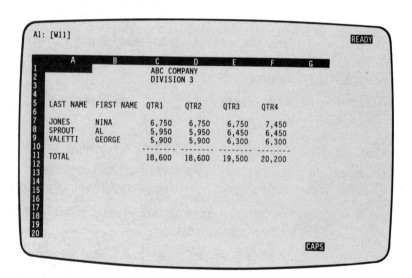

```
A1: [W11]                                                              READY

          A         B         C         D         E         F      G
 1                            ABC COMPANY
 2                            DIVISION 3
 3
 4
 5   LAST NAME  FIRST NAME  QTR1      QTR2      QTR3      QTR4
 6
 7   JONES      NINA        6,750     6,750     6,750     7,450
 8   SPROUT     AL          5,950     5,950     6,450     6,450
 9   VALETTI    GEORGE      5,900     5,900     6,300     6,300
10                         --------  --------  --------  --------
11   TOTAL                  18,600    18,600    19,500    20,200
12
13
14
15
16
17
18
19
20
                                                               CAPS
```

Figure 6–12

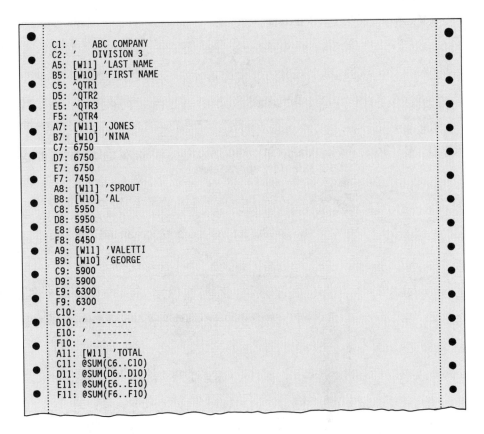

```
C1:  '    ABC COMPANY
C2:  '    DIVISION 3
A5:  [W11] 'LAST NAME
B5:  [W10] 'FIRST NAME
C5:  ^QTR1
D5:  ^QTR2
E5:  ^QTR3
F5:  ^QTR4
A7:  [W11] 'JONES
B7:  [W10] 'NINA
C7:  6750
D7:  6750
E7:  6750
F7:  7450
A8:  [W11] 'SPROUT
B8:  [W10] 'AL
C8:  5950
D8:  5950
E8:  6450
F8:  6450
A9:  [W11] 'VALETTI
B9:  [W10] 'GEORGE
C9:  5900
D9:  5900
E9:  6300
F9:  6300
C10: ' --------
D10: ' --------
E10: ' --------
F10: ' --------
A11: [W11] 'TOTAL
C11: @SUM(C6..C10)
D11: @SUM(D6..D10)
E11: @SUM(E6..E10)
F11: @SUM(F6..F10)
```

CHAPTER SIX
EXERCISE 3
Combining a Detail Spreadsheet
with a Summary Spreadsheet

INSTRUCTIONS: Follow the instructions below to combine data from a detail spreadsheet with a summary spreadsheet.

Erase the SALARIES row in BUDGET. Bring the TOTAL row from Division 3 to the BUDGET spreadsheet using **F**ile **C**ombine **A**dd. The output should appear like the printscreen in Figure 6–13.

Figure 6–13

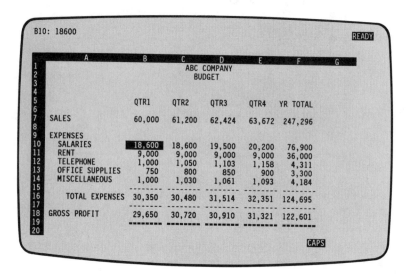

```
B10: 18600                                                            READY

        A           B         C         D         E         F       G
1                             ABC COMPANY
2                               BUDGET
3
4
5                     QTR1      QTR2      QTR3      QTR4    YR TOTAL
6
7    SALES          60,000    61,200    62,424    63,672   247,296
8
9    EXPENSES
10     SALARIES     18,600    18,600    19,500    20,200    76,900
11     RENT          9,000     9,000     9,000     9,000    36,000
12     TELEPHONE     1,000     1,050     1,103     1,158     4,311
13     OFFICE SUPPLIES  750      800       850       900     3,300
14     MISCELLANEOUS 1,000     1,030     1,061     1,093     4,184
15                   -------   -------   -------   -------   -------
16     TOTAL EXPENSES 30,350   30,480    31,514    32,351   124,695
17                   -------   -------   -------   -------   -------
18   GROSS PROFIT    29,650    30,720    30,910    31,321   122,601
19                   =======   =======   =======   =======   =======
20
                                                              CAPS
```

CHAPTER SIX
EXERCISE 4
Combining Multiple Detail Spreadsheets
into a Summary Spreadsheet

INSTRUCTIONS: Follow the instructions below to combine multiple detail spreadsheets into a summary spreadsheet.

Erase the SALARIES row in BUDGET. Combine the salary data from Divisions 1, 2, and 3 into BUDGET. The output should appear like the printscreen in Figure 6–14.

Figure 6–14

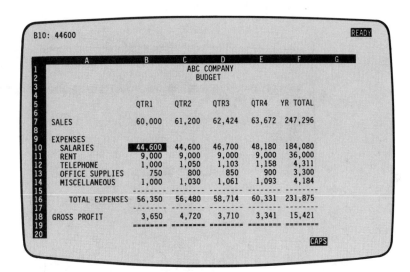

```
B10: 44600                                                          READY

             A          B        C        D        E        F       G
 1                              ABC COMPANY
 2                                BUDGET
 3
 4
 5                     QTR1     QTR2     QTR3     QTR4   YR TOTAL
 6
 7   SALES            60,000   61,200   62,424   63,672  247,296
 8
 9   EXPENSES
10     SALARIES       44,600   44,600   46,700   48,180  184,080
11     RENT            9,000    9,000    9,000    9,000   36,000
12     TELEPHONE       1,000    1,050    1,103    1,158    4,311
13     OFFICE SUPPLIES   750      800      850      900    3,300
14     MISCELLANEOUS   1,000    1,030    1,061    1,093    4,184
15                   -------- -------- -------- -------- --------
16     TOTAL EXPENSES 56,350   56,480   58,714   60,331  231,875
17                   -------- -------- -------- -------- --------
18   GROSS PROFIT      3,650    4,720    3,710    3,341   15,421
19                   ======== ======== ======== ======== ========
20                                                          CAPS
```

CHAPTER SIX
EXERCISE 5
Correcting a Spreadsheet

INSTRUCTIONS: Follow the instructions below to combine multiple detail spreadsheets into a summary spreadsheet. Then answer the questions below.

Erase the screen.
In cell A1, type 0.
In cell B1, type +A1*1.02.
Copy the formula in cell B1 to cells C1 and D1.

The screen should look like Figure 6–15. Use the cell formulas in Figure 6–16 as a guide.

Figure 6–15

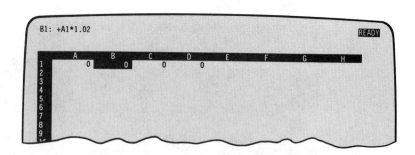

Figure 6–16

Place the cell pointer in cell A1.
Bring the TOTAL data from DIV1 into the existing blank spreadsheet.
See Figure 6–17.

*Figure 6–17
Part 1*

The file DIV1.

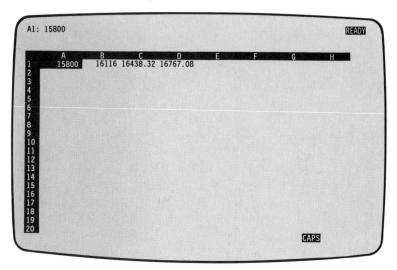

*Figure 6–17
Part 2*

The results of using **File Combine Add** to consolidate the range TOTAL from the file DIV1 into the current spreadsheet.

Make sure that the numbers from DIV1 are not altered when the **File Combine Add** command is executed. The solution should look like Figure 6–18.

Figure 6–18

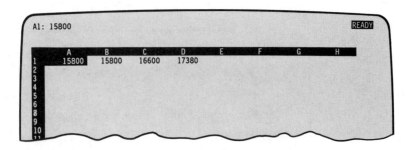

1. Why didn't the numbers from DIV1 appear correctly in the current spreadsheet?

2. How can the problem be solved?

CHAPTER SIX
EXERCISE 6
Using the Range Value Commands

INSTRUCTIONS: Follow the instructions below to use the **R**ange **V**alue command sequence.

Retrieve the file BUDGET.
Use the **R**ange **V**alue command to change the SALARIES line (range B10 . . E10) for BUDGET from formulas to values.
Use the **F**ile **C**ombine **A**dd command sequence to add the TOTAL line from DIV1 to existing values in BUDGET. The output should look like Figure 6–19. Note that the numbers for GROSS PROFIT are displayed within parentheses when the worksheet recalculated because they are negative values.

Figure 6–19

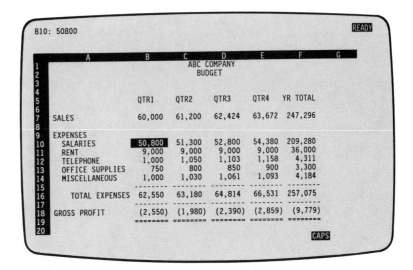

	A	B	C	D	E	F	G
				ABC COMPANY			
				BUDGET			
5		QTR1	QTR2	QTR3	QTR4	YR TOTAL	
7	SALES	60,000	61,200	62,424	63,672	247,296	
9	EXPENSES						
10	SALARIES	50,800	51,300	52,800	54,380	209,280	
11	RENT	9,000	9,000	9,000	9,000	36,000	
12	TELEPHONE	1,000	1,050	1,103	1,158	4,311	
13	OFFICE SUPPLIES	750	800	850	900	3,300	
14	MISCELLANEOUS	1,000	1,030	1,061	1,093	4,184	
16	TOTAL EXPENSES	62,550	63,180	64,814	66,531	257,075	
18	GROSS PROFIT	(2,550)	(1,980)	(2,390)	(2,859)	(9,779)	

B10: 50800   READY

CAPS

CHAPTER SEVEN

INTRODUCTION TO MACROS

OBJECTIVES

In this chapter, the student will learn to:

- Use a standard procedure for creating a macro
- Create and execute a macro
- Create a print macro

◼ CHAPTER OVERVIEW

A **macro** is a set of written instructions representing keystrokes in Lotus 1–2–3. The macro keystrokes represent the keystrokes exactly as they are typed when selecting from the various worksheet menus, entering data, or moving the cell pointer.

Macros are especially useful when performing detailed, repetitive routines. A macro can be written so that it consolidates different worksheets, performs a special edit routine, or even prints reports or graphs. Advanced uses of macros can involve using macro command words that allow macros to perform loops, subroutines, "if" statements, and many other features common to programming languages. A macro enables users with little training in using 1–2–3 to do intricate spreadsheet analysis.

■ PROCESS FOR CREATING A MACRO

Before starting the exercises, read through the basic steps to get an overview of the procedure to follow for creating a macro. The steps for writing a macro are as follows:

1. Create a macro by first *practicing the procedure* that the macro is to perform; manually press the keystrokes necessary to execute the macro.

2. While going through the macro steps, *record every keystroke* exactly as it is typed.

3. After practicing the macro manually, *record the keystrokes on the spreadsheet* that are needed to execute the macro. The macro keystrokes should be entered on the spreadsheet for which the macro will be used. The instructions should be near the spreadsheet, but not so close that they are distracting.

   The macro instructions must be in the proper order and must be contained in only one column. Begin each of the macro instructions with a label prefix such as the apostrophe (the ' symbol is located on the double quote key). This will prevent the macro from executing some commands as they are being entered (for example, typing / to bring up the command menu). Using the apostrophe will also allow 1–2–3 to accept all macro instructions when they contain a combination of numeric and alphabetic characters.

   Up to 240 characters for macro steps can be entered on a single line. 240 characters is the limit for the number of characters that can be entered in a single cell. Usually macro steps are broken into smaller segments per line so that the macro can be easily read and edited. Since a macro is read from top to bottom in sequential order, the author can choose when to begin a new line of instructions.

   Be sure to refer to the 1–2–3 manual for the proper way to record keystrokes. For example, type a **tilde** (the ~ symbol) to represent pressing the ↵ key.

4. After typing the complete macro, *name the macro as a named range*. The **macro range name** must begin with a backward slash (the \ symbol) and have only one letter following the slash.

   Example: \M

Only the first line of the macro is needed for the range name; however, the entire macro can be specified for the range. The macro will stop executing when it reads a blank cell in the column containing the macro.

5. Before running and testing the macro, *save the macro with the worksheet*. In this way, if the macro does not run properly, it will be possible to retrieve the worksheet as it was before any changes were made by the macro.

6. *Execute the macro* by pressing the [**Alt**] key and then the letter that was selected for the range name. For example, if the range name used for the macro is \M, hold down the [Alt] key and press the letter M to begin running the macro. In Release 2 and later releases of 1–2–3, the [Alt] key is referred to as the **MACRO** key.

7. The macro should perform automatically. If it does not, the macro instructions are incorrect and it is necessary to *edit and revise the macro*. It may be necessary to press the [Esc] key to exit a macro that has stopped because it encountered an error. Another way to stop a macro once it has begun execution is to hold down the [**Ctrl**] key and to press the [**Break**] key (the keys are held down simultaneously). The [Break] key is located on the [Scroll Lock] key.

   After determining the error, *retrieve* the worksheet with the macro. Edit the macro on the retrieved worksheet and then *save* and replace it before testing the macro again. If the original worksheet and macro are not retrieved from the disk after it has incorrectly run, the worksheet will contain unwanted changes that may have been made to the worksheet during the macro execution.

8. After a macro has executed correctly, it is wise to *document (write an explanation of what the macro instructions do)* in a column to the right of the macro steps and then write the macro's name either above or to the left of the macro steps. The **documentation** process is optional. However, a written explanation of a macro's purpose will prove valuable to a user who did not create the macro but needs to know what the macro does without having to spend extra time analyzing or executing the macro. Documentation is also useful for the macro's author, saving time from having to decipher the macro at a later date when the macro may need to be altered or used in another file.

■ CREATING AND EXECUTING A MACRO

In this section, an example problem is specified and a macro is created. After creating the macro, the macro is executed.

An Example Problem

In the following exercise, a simple macro will be written to automate keystrokes used in Chapter Six to combine files. The macro will automatically erase the salaries data in the summary file BUDGET and bring the named range TOTAL from DIV1 into the salaries line. Figure 7–1 displays a printout of the spreadsheet with the completed macro as it appears before the macro is executed and a printout of the spreadsheet after the macro is executed.

Figure 7–1
Part 1
The macro is written on the BUDGET spreadsheet.

```
                            ABC COMPANY
                              BUDGET


                    QTR1      QTR2      QTR3      QTR4    YR TOTAL

        SALES      60,000    61,200    62,424    63,672   247,296

        EXPENSES
          SALARIES 35,000    35,500    36,200    37,000   143,700
          RENT      9,000     9,000     9,000     9,000    36,000
          TELEPHONE 1,000     1,050     1,103     1,158     4,311
          OFFICE SUPPLIES 750   800       850       900     3,300
          MISCELLANEOUS 1,000  1,030     1,061     1,093     4,184
                    --------  --------  --------  --------  --------
           TOTAL EXPENSES 46,750  47,380  48,214  49,151   191,495
                    --------  --------  --------  --------  --------
        GROSS PROFIT 13,250   13,820    14,210    14,521    55,801
                    ========  ========  ========  ========  ========


        ********************************************************************


        \P           /reB10.E10~          ERASE THE RANGE B10..E10
                     {goto}B10~           MOVE TO CELL B10
                     /fcanTOTAL~          COMBINE THE NAMED RANGE TOTAL
                     DIV1~                FROM THE FILE DIV1
                     {goto}A1~            MOVE TO CELL A1
```

Figure 7–1
Part 2
When the macro is executed, the SALARIES line is erased and data from the
file DIV1 is added to the SALARIES line of the BUDGET spreadsheet.

```
                            ABC COMPANY
                              BUDGET


                    QTR1      QTR2      QTR3      QTR4    YR TOTAL

        SALES      60,000    61,200    62,424    63,672   247,296

        EXPENSES
          SALARIES 15,800    15,800    16,600    17,380    65,580
          RENT      9,000     9,000     9,000     9,000    36,000
          TELEPHONE 1,000     1,050     1,103     1,158     4,311
          OFFICE SUPPLIES 750   800       850       900     3,300
          MISCELLANEOUS 1,000  1,030     1,061     1,093     4,184
                    --------  --------  --------  --------  --------
           TOTAL EXPENSES 27,550  27,680  28,614  29,531   113,375
                    --------  --------  --------  --------  --------
        GROSS PROFIT 32,450   33,520    33,810    34,141   133,921
                    ========  ========  ========  ========  ========


        ********************************************************************


        \P           /reB10.E10~          ERASE THE RANGE B10..E10
                     {goto}B10~           MOVE TO CELL B10
                     /fcanTOTAL~          COMBINE THE NAMED RANGE TOTAL
                     DIV1~                FROM THE FILE DIV1
                     {goto}A1~            MOVE TO CELL A1
```

Retrieve the file BUDGET for use in this exercise using the File **Retrieve** command sequence.

In this example, the macro will be separated from the worksheet by asterisks. This step is optional.

To place a series of asterisks beneath the spreadsheet:

Move	the cell pointer to cell A21
Type	\ * ↵

Cell A21 should now be filled with asterisks. The backward slash is a label prefix that repeats any character(s) following it.

To copy the asterisks to the rest of the row:

Press	/	(the command key)
Type	C	(for Copy)

When prompted for the range to copy from, make sure that the cell pointer is highlighting A21:

Press	↵

When prompted for the range to copy to:

Move	the cell pointer to cell B21
Press	. (the period key)
Move	the cell pointer to cell F21 ↵

Cells A21 through F21 should now be filled with asterisks.

Manually Practicing the Macro Keystrokes and Recording Every Keystroke on Paper

For the purposes of this exercise, it will be assumed that the macro has been practiced manually and that the keystrokes have been written on paper (the macro keystrokes were performed manually in an exercise in Chapter Six).

Entering the Keystrokes in the Appropriate Spreadsheet File

To begin entering the instructions for the macro in the BUDGET file, make sure that the cell pointer is in cell B24. When entering the instructions, type an apostrophe (the apostrophe is located on the double quote key) before each instruction. To enter the first macro instruction:

Move	the cell pointer to cell B24
Type	'/reB10.E10~ ↵

This line records pressing the command key, choosing **Range Erase** from the menu, typing B10.E10 when prompted for the range to erase, and pressing ↵ to complete the procedure. The line must begin with an apostrophe to enter the keystrokes as a label. Notice that the command letters for Range Erase were written in lowercase letters and that the range B10.E10 was in uppercase letters. This procedure is optional, but many macro authors use this convention so that the macro can be read more easily; the uppercase characters represent what the user input, such as cell addresses, range names, or file names. Lotus 1–2–3 range specifications require only one period, so the range B10 . . E10 was entered as B10.E10.

When entering macro keystrokes, be sure to use the apostrophe that is located on the double quote key. Also make sure that the **tilde** (the ~ symbol) is the symbol that is used to represent pressing the ↵ key.

To enter the second macro instruction:

Move	the cell pointer to cell B25
Type	'{goto}B10~ ↵

This line records pressing the GOTO key (the [F5] function key), typing B10 when prompted for the address to go to, and pressing ↵.

Be sure to use the brace symbols (the { } symbols) rather than the parentheses or bracket symbols (the ( ) and [ ] symbols). Also be sure not to insert spaces where they are not listed above (a common error is to insert a space between GO and TO in the {GOTO} command.

The '{goto}B10~ command could be written as follows: '{down 9}{right} to move the cell pointer from cell A1 to cell B10. However, if the cell pointer was not in cell A1 when the macro was executed, the macro would not go to cell B10—it would go down 9 cells and 1 to the right and execute the macro at the wrong position. The GOTO key prevents this problem because the cell pointer is specifically sent to cell B10. For the same reason, the range TOTAL and the file name DIV1 will be specifically typed into the macro rather than using the pointer movement keys to highlight the range name and file name.

To enter the remaining macro instructions:

Move	the cell pointer to cell B26
Type	'/fcanTOTAL~ ↵
Move	the cell pointer to cell B27
Type	'DIV1~ ↵
Move	the cell pointer to cell B28
Type	'{goto}A1~ ↵

These lines invoke the **File Combine Add Named/Specified-Range** menu sequence, specify TOTAL for the named range and DIV1 as the file to combine. The last line of the macro returns the cell pointer to cell A1. The convention of using lowercase letters for macro commands and uppercase letters for the data specified by the user is used throughout the entire macro. The last line ('{goto}A1~) is optional; it was entered so that the cell pointer will go to cell A1 when the macro is through executing. This command can also be written as {home}. If the cell pointer is *not* in cell A1 after the macro is executed, the user will know that the macro has not executed correctly. When all of the steps are entered, the screen should look like Figure 7–2.

Since Lotus 1–2–3 reads the contents of the column containing the macro and stops only when it encounters a blank cell, it is up to the author to decide where to divide up the macro steps. Up to 240 characters can be entered into a single cell. Ideally, macro steps are broken up into brief statements as illustrated above so they will be logically divided, easy to understand, and easy to document.

Figure 7–2

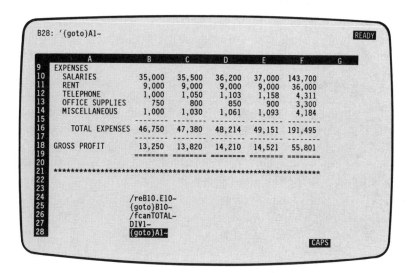

Naming the Macro as a Named Range

To name the macro:

Move		the cell pointer to cell B24
Press	/	(the command key)
Type	R	(for Range)
Type	N	(for Name)
Type	C	(for Create)

When prompted for the range name:

Type	\P ↵

Macro range names must begin with a backward slash and one letter of the alphabet. The only exception to this rule is for automatically executing macros that are always named \0 (zero). When prompted for the range, make sure that cell B24 (the first line of the macro ('/reB10.E10~) is highlighted:

Press	↵

The macro is now named \P. The macro range is the first line of the macro. The macro will read each line in column B where the macro instructions were entered and will stop when it reads a blank cell in the column (in this example, cell B29). The macro range could include all of the macro instructions, but the first instruction in the macro must always be the first cell specified at the top of the range.

Saving the File Containing the Macro Keystrokes

Save the macro with the worksheet *before* executing, or testing, the macro. If the macro contains an error and cannot execute properly, it will be possible to retrieve the file and correct the macro error. In this way, the file will be protected from being altered incorrectly when using a macro that is not working properly.

To save the cell pointer in cell A1 (optional):

Press	the [Home] key

Use the **File Save** command sequence to save the file as BUDGET3.

Executing the Macro

To execute the macro:

Press   the [Alt] key

While holding down the [Alt] key:

Type   P

Release both keys. The macro will now execute. Because the range name given the macro is \P, pressing the **[Alt]** key and the letter P executes the macro. The backward slash can be thought of as corresponding to the [Alt] key. The [Alt] key is also referred to as the **MACRO** key.

If the macro has executed correctly, the screen should look like Figure 7–3. Check the SALARIES line to see if the amounts from the named range TOTAL were brought into the spreadsheet.

Figure 7–3

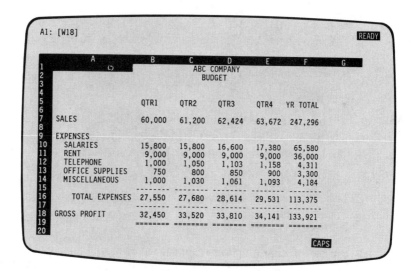

Editing and Correcting a Macro

If the macro stops and "beeps," look carefully at the screen to determine at what point the macro seemed to have trouble executing. To exit the macro error and stop the macro, press the **[Ctrl]** and **[Break]** keys simultaneously. Depending upon the macro, the [Esc] key may need to be pressed after pressing [Ctrl] [Break]. (The [Break] key is located on the [Scroll Lock] key). Move to the area where the macro instructions are written to see if the error can be determined.

Compare keystrokes with the macro keystrokes in Figure 7–2. Typical errors are as follows:

- macro steps were preceded with the incorrect apostrophe (use the apostrophe on the double quote key)
- another character was entered instead of the tilde or a tilde was omitted in an instruction
- parentheses (the ( ) symbols) or brackets (the [ ] symbols) were entered instead of braces (the { } symbols)
- the backward slash (the \ symbol) was used instead of the forward slash (the / symbol) to represent the command key. (recall that the backward slash is a repeating prefix that repeats any characters behind it)
- a space was inserted in an inappropriate place
- the uppercase letter O was typed instead of a zero; the lowercase letter l was typed instead of the number one

If the macro doesn't execute at all or attempts to enter a label and stops, two typical errors are as follows:

- the forward slash was used for the range name instead of the backward slash (use **Range Name Create** to see if the range was named /P instead of \P) or no range name was given to the macro
- the range name was correct but the first line of the macro is not a macro step (for example, if the top line of the macro is a blank line, the macro will never execute

Once the error is determined, **retrieve** the file BUDGET3 and correct the incorrect macro step(s). Then **save** the file before trying to execute the macro again. If the original file is not retrieved, the results of the incorrect macro will remain on the spreadsheet.

Do not save the results of executing the macro, as the original BUDGET3 file will be used in the next exercise.

Documenting the Macro

Documentation is optional, but can save valuable time later when a user is trying to edit or execute the macro. The documentation in this example explains every line of the macro. Sometimes it is more appropriate to document a macro by writing a paragraph to explain a macro's overall purpose and then writing additional paragraphs to explain sections of the macro. Refer to Chapter Eleven for instructions on how to write a paragraph on a spreadsheet.

To enter corresponding explanations of the macro commands in column A to document what the macro does, retrieve the file BUDGET3 using the **File Retrieve** command sequence.

To create a title for the macro (an optional step):

Move   the cell pointer to cell A24

Type   '\P ↵

Creating a title is optional because it is not necessary to make the macro execute; however, the macro title is useful as documentation. A common convention is to put the macro name in the column to the left of the macro keystrokes. In this way, if several macros are on a single spreadsheet, the names will be clearly visible in the column to the left of the multiple macros. Be sure to precede the \P with an apostrophe or the repeating prefix \ will cause the cell to be filled with P's.

To document the macro steps:

Move   the cell pointer to cell D24

Refer to Figure 7–4 to enter the documentation for the macro beginning in cell D24.

Figure 7–4

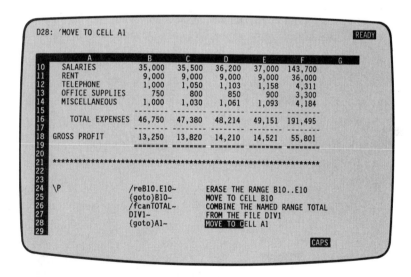

After entering the documentation:

Press   the [Home] key

Save the BUDGET3 file using the **File Save** and **Replace** command sequence.

CREATING A PRINT MACRO

Macro steps can be written to print a spreadsheet. In this exercise, macro steps will be written to print the spreadsheet in the file BUDGET3 after the the File Combine procedure in Macro P has been executed. The macro steps could be written as a separate macro in the file BUDGET3 and given a macro name other than Macro P. In this example, the macro steps will simply be added to the end of Macro P. When Macro P is executed again, the macro will continue to execute the newly added steps and print the spreadsheet because the macro will continue to execute until it reads a blank cell.

First, execute Macro P again in order to make sure the macro steps work correctly. To execute Macro P:

Press   the [Alt] (MACRO) key

While holding down the [Alt] key:

Press   P

Release both keys. The macro should execute.

To add the new steps to Macro P to print the spreadsheet, manually practice the macro and record the steps on paper so they can later be entered on the spreadsheet and added to Macro P.

Press	/	(the command key)
Type	P	(for Print)
Type	P	(for Printer)
Type	R	(for Range)

On a sheet of paper, write **/ppr** to record the keystrokes typed thus far. When prompted for the range to print (if the range is already set, press [Esc] so that only A1 is listed in the control panel):

Press	.
Move	the cell pointer to cell F19

The entire spreadsheet should be highlighted. To accept cells A1 . . F19 as the range to print:

Press   ↵

To record the macro steps, note that the keys pressed for the range name were
.{DOWN 18}{RIGHT 5}~ (press the period key, move the cursor down 18 and to the
right 5). Record the keystrokes as **A1.F19~** so that the keystrokes are easier to
understand. Compare the commands below:

> **/pprA1.F19~**
> **/ppr.{down 18}{right 5}~**

The first command is easier to understand. The range **A1.F19** in the first command is
written in uppercase letters to distinguish it from the commands **/ppr**; using lowercase
letters is optional.

Note: *In Lotus 1–2–3 releases before Release 2, {down 3} has to be
entered as {down}{down}{down}.*

To print the spreadsheet, make sure the printer is on and that the paper is aligned
properly.

Type	A	(for Align)
Type	G	(for Go)

When the printer has finished printing the worksheet:

Type	P	(for Page) twice

This procedure is used to eject pages from continuous forms so that the printout can be
removed. If a sheet feeder is being used, pressing the P for Page is not necessary.

To leave the print menu:

Type	Q	(for Quit)

The printout should look like Figure 7–5.

Figure 7–5

```
                    ABC COMPANY
                      BUDGET

              QTR1     QTR2     QTR3     QTR4    YR TOTAL

  SALES       60,000   61,200   62,424   63,672  247,296

  EXPENSES
    SALARIES  15,800   15,800   16,600   17,380   65,580
    RENT       9,000    9,000    9,000    9,000   36,000
    TELEPHONE  1,000    1,050    1,103    1,158    4,311
    OFFICE SUPPLIES 750    800      850      900    3,300
    MISCELLANEOUS 1,000  1,030    1,061    1,093    4,184
              --------  --------  --------  --------  --------
    TOTAL EXPENSES 27,550 27,680  28,614   29,531  113,375
              --------  --------  --------  --------  --------
  GROSS PROFIT 32,450   33,520   33,810   34,141  133,921
              ========  ========  ========  ========  ========
```

Add the keystrokes **agppq** to the sheet of paper used for recording the macro keystrokes. The paper should now have the following instructions:

/pprA1.F19~agppq

To make sure the keystrokes work exactly as written, execute the macro manually once again by following the macro keystrokes:

Type   /pprA1.F19 ↵

The steps for entering the print menu and specifying A1 . . F19 as the print range have now been entered. Note that the tilde symbol ~ represented pressing ↵ and that the ↵ key must be pressed rather than actually typing the tilde.

Type   ag

The printer prints out the spreadsheet. After the printing is completed:

Type   ppq

Two pages are ejected from the printer (the "pp" represents **P**age **P**age) and the print menu disappears from the screen (the "Q" represents Quit).

Now that the steps have been manually practiced, retrieve the original file and add the steps to Macro P. To retrieve the file BUDGET3, execute the **F**ile **R**etrieve command sequence. To move to the last line of the macro:

Move   the cell pointer to cell B28

The step {**GOTO**}**A1~** will not be needed at this point since it was only inserted to move the cell pointer to cell A1 when the macro completed execution. To erase cell B28 and its documentation in D28:

Press	/	(the command key)
Type	R	(for Range)
Type	E	(for Erase)

When prompted for the range to erase:

Move   the cell pointer to cell D28

Cells B28 . . D28 should now be highlighted.

Press   ⏎

In cell B28, type the following macro keystrokes. Be sure to precede the keystrokes with an apostrophe.

Type	'/pprA1.F19~ ⏎
Move	the cell pointer to cell B29
Type	'agppq ⏎

The apostrophe is not needed in front of all macro lines because some lines happen to be labels due to the content of the macro line (if a macro line begins with a non-numeric character, Lotus 1–2–3 automatically inserts an apostrophe and recognizes the line as a label). To save time, instead of trying to decide which lines need apostrophes and which lines don't, add an apostrophe at the front of each line when entering the line.

The last line of the macro will return the cell pointer to cell A1.

Move	the cell pointer to cell B30
Type	'{goto}A1~ ⏎

The screen should look like Figure 7–6.

Figure 7–6

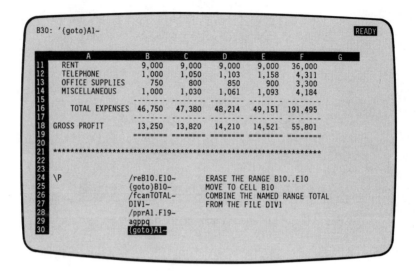

Press the [Home] key

Save the file BUDGET3 using the **F**ile **S**ave and **R**eplace command sequence so that the new macro steps are saved to the disk.

To execute the macro, first make sure that the printer is on and that the paper is aligned properly.

Press the [Alt] (MACRO) key

While holding down the [Alt] key:

Type P

Release both keys. The macro will execute by combining the range TOTAL from DIV1 into BUDGET3 and printing the spreadsheet. The printout should look exactly like the printout when the macro was practiced (see Figure 7–5). A print macro can be quite intricate and may even change additional print settings such as the margins (through the **P**rint **P**rinter **O**ptions **M**argins command sequence).

To add the documentation to BUDGET3 for the additional changes, retrieve the original file BUDGET3 with the **F**ile **R**etrieve command sequence.

Move the cell pointer to cell D28

Use Figure 7–7 as a guide to type in the documentation for cells D28, D29, and D30.

Figure 7–7

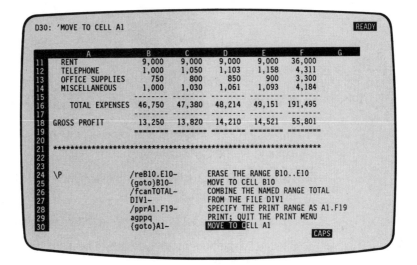

After entering the documentation:

Press   the [Home] key

Save the file BUDGET3 using the **F**ile **S**ave and **R**eplace command sequence.

SUMMARY

A macro is a way to automate Lotus 1–2–3 keystrokes. Macros are an efficient way to automate repetitive procedures. Macros are also useful for users who do not know Lotus 1–2–3 well, but can execute macros to print reports, etc. Macros can be as simple or as complex as the author desires. Advanced macro techniques allow the user to use command words for macros that can perform special functions such as prompting the user for input or even generating a custom menu.

KEY CONCEPTS

[Alt]
[Ctrl] [Break]
Documentation
Macro
MACRO key
Macro range names
Tilde

CHAPTER SEVEN
EXERCISE 1

INSTRUCTIONS: Circle T if the statement is true and F if the statement is false.

T   F   1. The range name for a macro must be taken from a label already existing on the spreadsheet.

T   F   2. The range name for a macro must begin with a forward slash and a letter of the alphabet.

T   F   3. A macro is a way to automate a repetitive procedure.

T   F   4. Certain keystrokes in a macro must be enclosed in braces (the { and } characters).

T   F   5. In a macro, the tilde (the ~ symbol) represents pressing the forward slash (the command key /).

T   F   6. To execute the macro named \Z, the user must hold down the [Ctrl] key and tap the letter Z.

T   F   7. A named range for a macro must contain the first macro step as the first line in the range.

T   F   8. When entering data on a spreadsheet manually, the tilde can be used instead of pressing ⏎.

T   F   9. Either apostrophe (the ' or the ') can be used to preface a macro step.

T   F   10. Documentation should be included in a macro.

CHAPTER SEVEN
EXERCISE 2
Creating a Macro

INSTRUCTIONS: Retrieve the file BUDGET3. Edit the exiting macro by inserting rows and adding instructions in the middle of the macro to combine DIV1, DIV2, and DIV3 into the BUDGET spreadsheet, then print the spreadsheet. (The files DIV1, DIV2, and DIV3 were created in Chapter Six). Document the new instructions. Delete the macro name \P (use the **R**ange **N**ame **D**elete command sequence) and name the macro \A. Save the file as BUDMAC. The macro should look like Figure 7–8. After the macro executes, the spreadsheet printout should look like Figure 7–9. Do not save the results of the macro execution in BUDMAC.

Figure 7–8

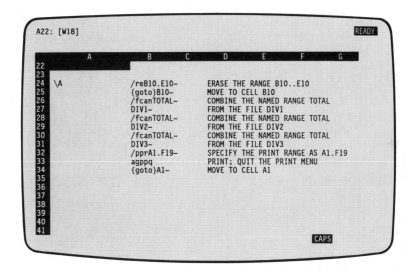

```
A22: [W18]                                                               READY

              A            B          C        D         E        F        G
22
23
24    \A                /reB10.E10~        ERASE THE RANGE B10..E10
25                      {goto}B10~         MOVE TO CELL B10
26                      /fcanTOTAL~        COMBINE THE NAMED RANGE TOTAL
27                      DIV1~              FROM THE FILE DIV1
28                      /fcanTOTAL~        COMBINE THE NAMED RANGE TOTAL
29                      DIV2~              FROM THE FILE DIV2
30                      /fcanTOTAL~        COMBINE THE NAMED RANGE TOTAL
31                      DIV3~              FROM THE FILE DIV3
32                      /pprA1.F19~        SPECIFY THE PRINT RANGE AS A1.F19
33                      agppq              PRINT; QUIT THE PRINT MENU
34                      {goto}A1~          MOVE TO CELL A1
35
36
37
38
39
40
41                                                                        CAPS
```

Figure 7–9

```
                              ABC COMPANY
                                BUDGET


                 QTR1      QTR2      QTR3      QTR4    YR TOTAL

SALES           60,000    61,200    62,424    63,672   247,296

EXPENSES
  SALARIES      44,600    44,600    46,700    48,180   184,080
  RENT           9,000     9,000     9,000     9,000    36,000
  TELEPHONE      1,000     1,050     1,103     1,158     4,311
  OFFICE SUPPLIES  750       800       850       900     3,300
  MISCELLANEOUS  1,000     1,030     1,061     1,093     4,184
                -------   -------   -------   -------   -------
  TOTAL EXPENSES 56,350    56,480    58,714    60,331   231,875
                -------   -------   -------   -------   -------
GROSS PROFIT     3,650     4,720     3,710     3,341    15,421
                =======   =======   =======   =======   =======
```

CHAPTER SEVEN
EXERCISE 3
Creating a Print Macro

INSTRUCTIONS: Retrieve the file BUDMAC. Move the macro keystrokes for printing the macro \A in BUDMAC (written for Assignment 2) so that the keystrokes are a separate macro from macro \A. Name the print macro \B. Save the file as BUDMAC1. The macros should look like the macros in Figure 7–10. Execute macro A. The screen should look like Figure 7–11. Execute macro B. After the macro executes, the spreadsheet printout should look like Figure 7–12.

Figure 7–10

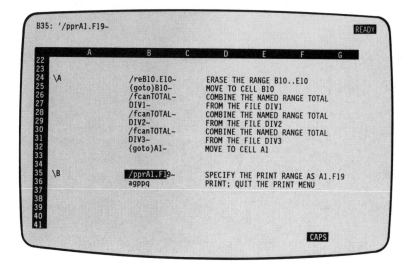

```
B35: '/pprA1.F19~                                                    READY

             A          B          C       D         E        F        G
22
23
24   \A                 /reB10.E10~           ERASE THE RANGE B10..E10
25                      (goto)B10~            MOVE TO CELL B10
26                      /fcanTOTAL~           COMBINE THE NAMED RANGE TOTAL
27                      DIV1~                  FROM THE FILE DIV1
28                      /fcanTOTAL~            COMBINE THE NAMED RANGE TOTAL
29                      DIV2~                  FROM THE FILE DIV2
30                      /fcanTOTAL~            COMBINE THE NAMED RANGE TOTAL
31                      DIV3~                  FROM THE FILE DIV3
32                      (goto)A1~              MOVE TO CELL A1
33
34
35   \B                 /pprA1.F19~           SPECIFY THE PRINT RANGE AS A1.F19
36                      agppq                  PRINT; QUIT THE PRINT MENU
37
38
39
40
41
                                                                     CAPS
```

Figure 7–11

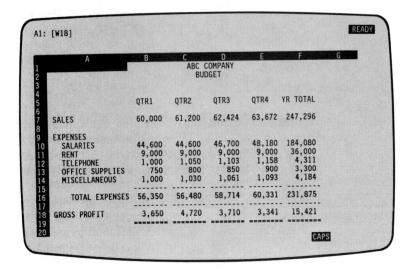

Figure 7–12

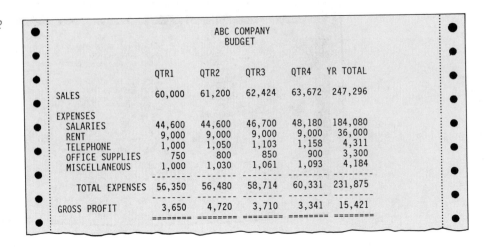

CHAPTER EIGHT

SPECIAL FUNCTIONS IN LOTUS 1–2–3

OBJECTIVES

In this chapter, the student will learn to:

- Use the data (statistical) analysis functions @SUM, @COUNT, @AVG, @MIN, @MAX, @VAR, @STD
- Use the financial analysis functions @IRR, @NPV, @FV, @PV, @PMT, @SLN, @DDB, @SYD, @CTERM, @RATE, @TERM
- Use the date and time functions @DATE, @DAY, @MONTH, @YEAR, @TODAY, @NOW, @DATEVALUE, @TIME, @HOUR, @MINUTE, @SECOND, @TIMEVALUE
- Use the conditional function @IF
- Use the database statistical functions @DSUM, @DCOUNT, @DAVG, @DMIN, @DMAX, @DVAR, @DSTD

■ CHAPTER OVERVIEW

Lotus 1–2–3 has a number of special functions available. For example, suppose an individual wished to compute the monthly payment for a 30-year, $100,000 bank loan at 11% interest. 1–2–3 has a @PMT function that allows the user to compute the payment. The @SUM function and @ROUND function are the only functions which have been discussed in earlier chapters. In this chapter, functions for data (statistical) analysis, financial analysis, the date and time, testing conditions, and database statistical analysis are discussed.

■ DATA ANALYSIS FUNCTIONS

Lotus 1–2–3 has several data analysis functions. A description of each function is listed below.

@SUM	Compute the sum of a list of cells
@COUNT	Compute the number of items in a list of cells
@AVG	Compute the arithmetic mean for a list of cells
@MIN	Identify the minimum value for a list of cells

@MAX	Identify the maximum value for a list of cells
@VAR	Compute the variance for a list of cells
@STD	Compute the standard deviation for a list of cells

The general format for the data analysis functions is as follows:

```
@function name(first cell..last cell)
```

For example, to compute the sum of the numbers in cells A1 through G1 in a worksheet, the formula @SUM(A1..G1) is used. The function name should be used exactly as it is listed above (e.g., the function for averaging numbers is written as AVG).

Using the Data Analysis Functions

In this section, the worksheet displayed in Figure 8–1 will be created. Each of the data analysis functions are in this worksheet.

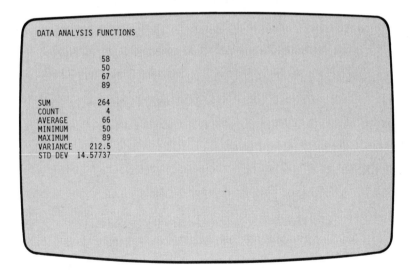

```
DATA ANALYSIS FUNCTIONS

                58
                50
                67
                89

SUM            264
COUNT            4
AVERAGE         66
MINIMUM         50
MAXIMUM         89
VARIANCE      212.5
STD DEV    14.57737
```

Creating a Title and Labels

If necessary, clear the screen by using the **Worksheet Erase Yes** command sequence. To enter the title in cell A1:

Type   DATA ANALYSIS FUNCTIONS ⏎

To enter the labels:

Move	the cell pointer to cell A9
Type	SUM
Move	the cell pointer to cell A10
Type	COUNT
Move	the cell pointer to cell A11
Type	AVERAGE
Move	the cell pointer to cell A12
Type	MINIMUM
Move	the cell pointer to cell A13
Type	MAXIMUM
Move	the cell pointer to cell A14
Type	VARIANCE
Move	the cell pointer to cell A15
Type	STD DEV

Entering the Numbers to be used in Computations

To enter the numbers to be used with the data analysis functions:

Move	the cell pointer to cell B4
Type	58
Move	the cell pointer to cell B5
Type	50
Move	the cell pointer to cell B6
Type	67
Move	the cell pointer to cell B7
Type	89 ⏎

Sum

To compute the sum of the four numbers in cells B4 through B7 using the @SUM function:

Move	the cell pointer to cell B9
Type	@SUM(
Move	the cell pointer to cell B4
Press	.
Move	the cell pointer to cell B7
Type	)

The formula @SUM(B4..B7) should now appear in the control panel.

Press	↵

The formula was entered into cell B9; the result is 264.

When using the @SUM formula in spreadsheets, the user may wish to include the cell immediately above and below the range of numbers actually being added. For example, the formula @SUM(B3..B8) could be used instead of @SUM(B4..B7) to total the numbers in this exercise. If a row is inserted (or deleted) at the top or bottom of the range to add (or delete) a number, the @SUM command will adjust correctly to the change. If a label such as a subtotal line is included in the range, it will not be a problem because Lotus 1–2–3 considers labels to have a value of 0. For the purposes of this example, this technique was not used.

Rather than moving the cell pointer to the cells to be used in computation, the user has the option to type the formula @SUM(B4.B7) directly in cell B9 and press ↵ to get the same result. The advantage of highlighting the numbers to be used in the formula is that the user will be less likely to make errors and enter the wrong cells. When entering the remaining data analysis functions, the formula will be typed directly into the cell.

Count

To count the items in cells B4 through B7 using the @COUNT function:

Move	the cell pointer to cell B10
Type	@COUNT(B4.B7)

Note that only one period can be typed within the formula. Typing @COUNT(B4.B7) produces the same result as typing @COUNT(B4..B7).

> **Press** ↵

The formula @COUNT(B4..B7) appears in the control panel. The number 4 appears in cell B10.

Average

To compute the average of the numbers in cells B4 through B7 using the @AVG function:

> **Move**   the cell pointer to cell B11
>
> **Type**   @AVG(B4.B7) ↵

The formula @AVG(B4..B7) appears in the control panel. The number 66 appears in cell B11.

Minimum

To determine the smallest value of the items in cells B4 through B7 using the @MIN function:

> **Move**   the cell pointer to cell B12
>
> **Type**   @MIN(B4.B7) ↵

The formula @MIN(B4..B7) appears in the control panel. The number 50 appears in cell B12.

Maximum

To determine the largest value of the items in cells B4 through B7 using the @MAX function:

> **Move**   the cell pointer to cell B13
>
> **Type**   @MAX(B4.B7) ↵

The formula @MAX(B4..B7) appears in the control panel. The number 89 appears in cell B13.

Variance

To determine the variance of the numbers in cells B4 through B7 using the @VAR function:

Move   the cell pointer to cell B14

Type   @VAR(B4.B7) ↵

The formula @VAR(B4..B7) appears in the control panel. The number 212.5 appears in cell B14.

Standard Deviation

To determine the standard deviation of the numbers in cells B4 through B7 using the @STD function:

Move   the cell pointer to cell B15

Type   @STD(B4.B7) ↵

The formula @STD(B4..B7) appears in the control panel. The number 14.57737 appears in cell B15. The screen should look like Figure 8–2. A screen displaying the cell formulas appears in Figure 8–3.

Figure 8–2

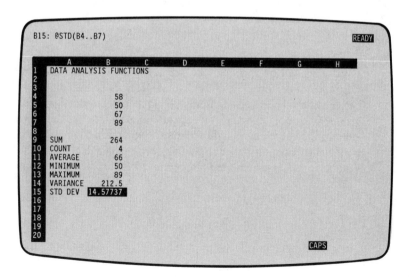

Figure 8–3

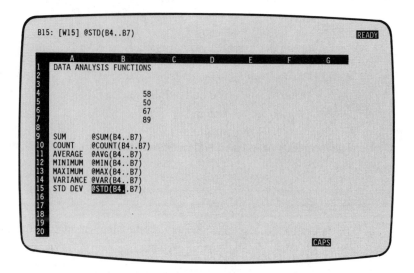

When using the data analysis functions, it is important to note that labels have a value of zero and can distort the desired computations. In the following exercise, one of the numbers in the range B4 .. B7 will be "erased" by pressing the space bar. The results are then discussed.

Move	the cell pointer to cell B6
Press	the space bar
Press	↵

Although cell B6 appears to be blank, it actually contains a label. In the control panel, an apostrophe appears. Whenever a label is typed, the default label prefix is the apostrophe. The cell is not really blank; it contains a cell whose value is counted as the value 0 in computations. The computations include the number zero. For example, the minimum value computed by the @MIN function is zero. The count computed by the @COUNT function still counts four items since the @COUNT function counts both numeric and non-numeric items. Refer to Figure 8–4 to see how the label distorts the results of the computations.

Figure 8–4   A label counts as the value 0 in computations.

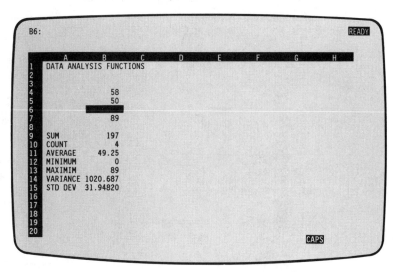

To truly erase cell B6, use the Range Erase command sequence.

> **Press**   /   (the command key)
> **Type**   R   (for Range)
> **Type**   E   (for Erase)

When prompted for the range to erase, make sure the cell pointer is highlighting cell B6:

> **Press**   ↵

Notice that the formulas have adjusted and are accurately computing the desired results. Refer to Figure 8–5.

Figure 8–5   A blank cell will not count as any value in computations.

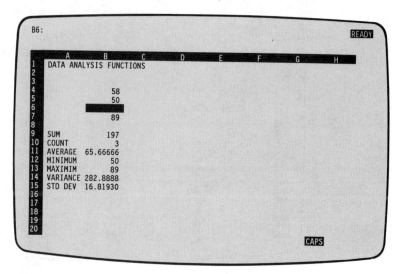

```
B6:                                                          READY

         A     B        C      D      E      F      G      H
1  DATA ANALYSIS FUNCTIONS
2
3
4            58
5            50
6
7            89
8
9  SUM       197
10 COUNT       3
11 AVERAGE 65.66666
12 MINIMUM    50
13 MAXIMIM    89
14 VARIANCE 282.8888
15 STD DEV 16.81930
16
17
18
19
20
                                                         CAPS
```

It is not necessary to save the results of this exercise. Clear the screen using the Worksheet Erase Yes command sequence.

■ FINANCIAL ANALYSIS FUNCTIONS

The financial functions available in Lotus, Release 1A are as follows:

@IRR	Internal rate of return
@NPV	Net present value
@FV	Future value
@PV	Present value
@PMT	Payment

Additional financial functions available in later releases are as follows:

@SLN	Straight-line depreciation
@DDB	Double-declining balance method for depreciation
@SYD	Sum-of-the-years'-digits method for depreciation
@CTERM	Number of compounding periods taken for the value of a number to increase to a specified future value

@TERM Number of specified payment periods needed in the term of an ordinary annuity to accumulate a future value earning a specified periodic interest rate

@RATE Periodic interest necessary for the value of a number to increase to a specified future value

The format for each financial analysis function varies and is discussed with each individual function.

Internal Rate of Return

The @IRR function computes the internal rate of return for a series of cash flows that occur at regular periodic intervals. The user must supply the cash flows and a guess rate for the internal rate of return. The format of the @IRR function is as follows:

```
@IRR(rate,range of cash flows)
```

Two sets of information are needed in the formula—the guess rate and the cash flows. Sets of information needed for a function to compute accurately are referred to as **arguments.** Arguments must be entered in the correct order and must be separated by a comma. Note that no space should be entered after the comma that separates the two arguments in the @IRR function.

In this exercise, suppose that an investment is being considered that requires a cash investment of $2,100 the first year and the anticipated cash flows in years 2 through 5 are respectively $1,300, $700, $500, and $300.

First, erase the screen (if necessary).

To enter the initial investment:

 Press the [Home] key (if necessary)

 Type –2100

The negative number indicates the initial cash investment made by the investor.

To enter the range of anticipated cash flows:

Move	the cell pointer to cell A2
Type	1300
Move	the cell pointer to cell A3
Type	700
Move	the cell pointer to cell A4
Type	500
Move	the cell pointer to cell A5
Type	300 ↵

To enter a guess at the internal rate of return:

Move	the cell pointer to cell A8
Type	.18

To find the internal rate of return of the given data:

Move	the cell pointer to cell A11
Type	@IRR(A8,A1..A5)

The first argument in the @IRR formula identifies A8 as the guess rate of 18 percent. The second argument identifies A1 .. A5 as the cash flows beginning with the initial investment of $2,100 and ending with the cash flow in year 5 of $300.

To enter the formula in cell A11:

Press	↵

The formula appears in the control panel. The result .168348 or about 16.83 percent is displayed. The screen should look like Figure 8–6.

Figure 8–6

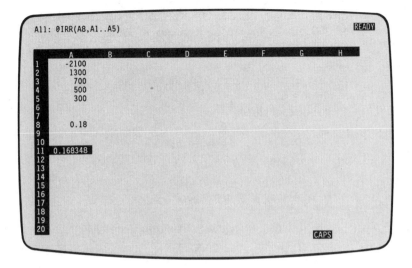

If desired, the results could be formatted with a percent sign and two decimal places by using the **Range Format Percent** command sequence.

Note that the guess rate could have been entered directly into the formula as @IRR(.18,A1..A5). The advantage of the guess rate being entered outside of the formula is that it can be changed more readily. The cash flows, however, must be entered as a range that is located elsewhere on the worksheet. A single-cell item, however, can be either entered directly into the formula or referenced with a cell address (e.g., .18 or A8 was acceptable in the @IRR formula in the previous exercise).

ERR may appear as a result of using the @IRR function if convergence to within .0000001 does not occur within 20 iterations. For example, if the internal rate of return is .32 and the user entered a guess rate of .1, ERR (error) will occur. When the user changes the guess rate to .12, the internal rate of return at .32 will appear, replacing ERR.

The arguments for 1–2–3 functions may be placed anywhere on the worksheet. In this example and all following examples, the placement on the spreadsheet of the arguments and the formulas is arbitrary.

Net Present Value

The net present value computes the present value for a set of cash flows using a specified discount rate. The first cash flow is assumed to be made at the end of the first year. The format of the NPV function is as follows:

```
@NPV(rate,range of cells)
```

In this exercise, consider an investment project that requires the investor to invest $2,000 initially and receive payments of $900, $850, $600, $350, $200, and $50 at the end of the first through the sixth years. Assume that 10% is an appropriate discount rate.

First, erase the screen from the previous exercise. It is not necessary to save the results in a file.

To enter the discount rate:

Press	the [Home] key (if necessary)
Type	.1 ↵

To enter the initial investment:

Move	the cell pointer to cell A3
Type	−2000 ↵

To enter the payments:

Move	the cell pointer to cell B1
Type	900
Move	the cell pointer to cell B2
Type	850
Move	the cell pointer to cell B3
Type	600
Move	the cell pointer to cell B4
Type	350
Move	the cell pointer to cell B5
Type	200
Move	the cell pointer to cell B6
Type	50 ↵

To compute the net present value of the cash flows and add it to the initial investment of $2,000 (in cell A3):

Move	the cell pointer to cell C1
Type	@NPV(A1,B1..B6)+A3

The first argument identifies A1 as the discount rate of 10 percent. The second argument identifies B1 . . B5 as the cash flows beginning with the first year of $900 and ending with the last year at $50. Note that A3 (the initial investment) must be added to the net present value of the cash flows because. If it is included in the formula, it will be discounted.

To enter the formula in cell C1:

Press ↵

The formula appears in the control panel. The result 362.9127 or $362.91 is displayed. The screen should look like Figure 8–7.

Figure 8–7

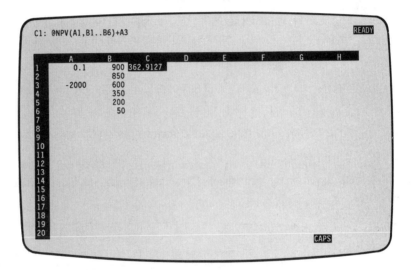

If desired, the results could be formatted with a dollar sign and two decimal places by using the **R**ange **F**ormat **C**urrency command sequence.

Future Value

The present value function computes the future value of an annuity given the payment per period, an interest rate per period, and the number of periods. The general format of the FV function is as follows:

```
@FV(payment, interest rate, term)
```

In this exercise, the future value of an annuity is computed. The payment is $1,500, the interest rate is 13%, and the term is 10 years.

First, erase the screen from the previous exercise. It is not necessary to save the previous exercise in a file.

In the previous exercises in this chapter, single-cell items used in the financial analysis functions were not placed directly into the formula, but were referenced by cell address. In this example, all three arguments are single-cell items. Instead of entering a formula in a format such as the following—@FV(C1,C2,C3)—all of the arguments in this formula can be placed directly into the formula—@FV(1500,.13,10).

To find the future value of the given data:

Press   the [Home] key (if necessary)

Type   @FV(1500,.13,10)

The first argument specifies the payment per period as $1,500. The second argument specifies the interest rate as 13 percent. The third argument specifies the term as 10 years. To enter the formula:

Press   ↵

Note: *There are no spaces between the commas and the arguments.*

The formula appears in the control panel. The result 27629.62 or $27,629.62 is displayed on the worksheet. The screen should look like Figure 8–8.

Figure 8–8

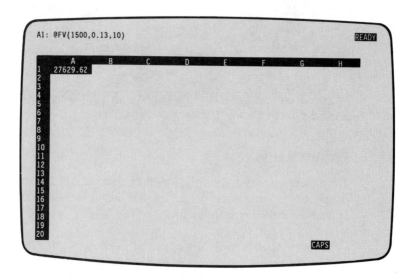

If desired, the results could be formatted with a dollar sign and two decimal places by using the **Range** **Format** Currency command sequence.

Present Value

The present value function computes the present value of an annuity given a payment per period, interest rate per period, and the number of time periods. The general format of the PV function is as follows:

```
@PV(payment, rate, number of periods)
```

In this exercise, determine the present value of an annuity where payments are $1,500, the interest rate is 13%, and the term is 10 years.

First, erase the screen from the previous exercise if necessary. To find the present value of the given data:

Press   the [Home] key (if necessary)

Type   @PV(1500,.13,10)

The first argument identifies the payment of $1,500. The second argument identifies the interest rate of 13 percent. The third argument identifies the term as 10 years.

To enter the formula:

Press   ↵

The formula appears in the control panel. The result is 8139.365 or $8,139.37. The screen should look like Figure 8–9.

Figure 8–9

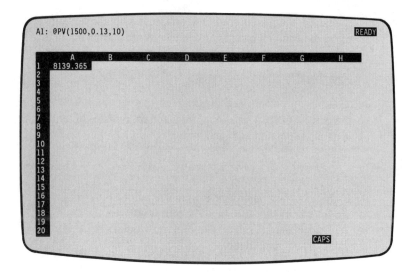

If desired, the results could be formatted with a dollar sign and two decimal places by using the **Range Format Currency** command sequence.

Payment

A payment per period can be computed given the principal amount, the interest rate per period and the number of periods. The general format for the PMT function is as follows:

```
@PMT(principal, interest rate, term)
```

Suppose the principal of a loan is $1,200, the interest rate is 15% and the number of time periods is 10 years.

First, erase the screen from the previous exercise if necessary. To determine the payment per period of the given data:

Press	the [Home] key (if necessary)
Type	@PMT(1200,.15,10)

The first argument identifies the principal of $1,200. The second argument identifies the interest rate of 15 percent. The third argument identifies the term as 10 years. To enter the formula:

Press   ↵

The formula appears in the control panel. The result is 239.1024 or $239.10. The screen should look like Figure 8–10.

Figure 8–10

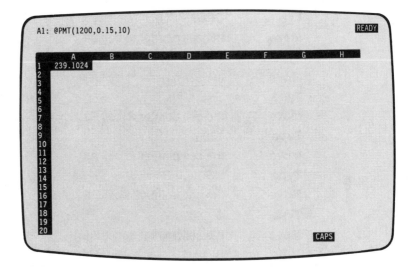

If desired, the results could be formatted with a dollar sign and two decimal places by using the **R**ange **F**ormat **C**urrency command sequence.

Straight-Line Depreciation

The straight-line depreciation of an asset can be computed for one period given the cost, salvage value, and estimated useful life of the asset. The general format for the @SLN function is as follows:

@SLN(cost,salvage value,estimated useful life)

In this exercise, the straight-line depreciation will be determined for equipment that was purchased for $13,000. The estimated useful life of the equipment is 6 years and the salvage value is estimated at $1,000.

First, erase the screen from the previous screen. It is not necessary to save the previous exercise in a file.

To insert labels and example data that will be used for the following exercises on the three Lotus 1–2–3 depreciation functions:

Press	the [Home] key (if necessary)
Type	COST
Move	the cell pointer to cell B1
Type	13000
Move	the cell pointer to cell A2
Type	SAL. VAL.
Move	the cell pointer to cell B2
Type	1000
Move	the cell pointer to cell A3
Type	USE. LIFE
Move	the cell pointer to cell B3
Type	6
Move	the cell pointer to cell A5
Type	SLN
Move	the cell pointer to cell A6
Type	DDB
Move	the cell pointer to cell A7
Type	SYD ↵

To determine the straight-line depreciation for the following data:

Move	the cell pointer to cell B5
Type	@SLN(B1,B2,B3)

The first argument identifies B1 as the cell containing the cost of $13,000. The second argument identifies B2 as the cell containing the salvage value of $1,000. The third argument identifies B3 as the cell containing the useful life of 6 years. The formula @SLN(13000,1000,6) could have been entered as an alternative to using cell addresses for the various arguments.

To enter the formula:

Press	↵

The formula appears in the control panel. The result 2000 or $2,000 is displayed on the worksheet. The screen should look like Figure 8–11.

Figure 8–11

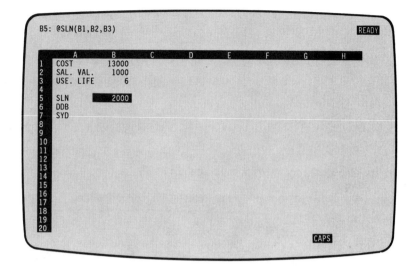

If desired, the results could be formatted with a dollar sign and two decimal places by using the **R**ange **F**ormat **C**urrency command sequence.

Double-Declining Balance Depreciation

This exercise is written with the assumption that the results of the previous exercise are still displayed on the screen.

The depreciation of an asset using the double- declining balance method can be computed for a specified period given the cost, salvage value, estimated useful life, and the desired time period. The general format for the @DDB function is as follows:

```
@DDB(cost,salvage value,estimated useful life,period)
```

In this exercise, use the data given in the previous exercise to compute the depreciation for the equipment for the first year using the double-declining balance method.

To document that the depreciation will be computed only for year 1 in this example (an optional step):

| **Move** | the cell pointer to cell C6 |
| **Type** | YEAR 1 |

To compute the depreciation using the double-declining balance method:

| **Move** | the cell pointer to cell B6 |
| **Type** | @DDB(B1,B2,B3,1) |

The first argument identifies B1 as the cell containing the cost at $13,000. The second argument identifies B2 as the cell containing the salvage value at $1,000. The third argument identifies B3 as the cell containing the useful life of the equipment at 6 years. The fourth argument indicates that this computation represents the depreciation for year 1.

To enter the formula:

Press ↵

The formula appears in the control panel. The result 4333.333 or $4,333.33 is displayed. The screen should look like Figure 8–12.

Figure 8–12

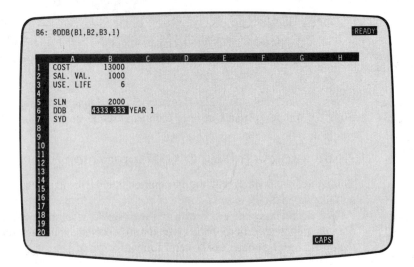

If desired, the results could be formatted with a dollar sign and two decimal places by using the **R**ange **F**ormat **C**urrency command sequence.

Sum-of-the-Years'-Digits Depreciation

This exercise is written with the assumption that the results of the previous exercise are still displayed on the screen.

The depreciation of an asset using the sum-of-the-years'-digits method can be computed for a specified period given the cost, salvage value, estimated useful life, and the desired time period. The general format for the @SYD function is as follows:

```
@SYD(cost,salvage value,estimated useful life,period)
```

In this exercise, the data given in the previous exercise will be used to compute the depreciation for the equipment for the third year using the sum-of-the-years'-digits method.

To indicate that the depreciation will be computed only for year 3 in this example:

Move	the cell pointer to cell C7
Type	YEAR 3

To compute the depreciation using the sum-of-the-years'-digits method:

Move	the cell pointer to cell B7
Type	@SYD(B1,B2,B3,3)

The first argument identifies B1 as the cell containing the cost at $13,000. The second argument identifies B2 as the cell containing the salvage value at $1,000. The third argument identifies B3 as the cell containing the useful life of 6 years. The fourth argument indicates that this computation is for year 3.

To enter the formula:

Press

The formula appears in the control panel. The result 2285.714 or $2,285.71 is displayed on the worksheet. The screen should look like Figure 8–13.

Figure 8–13

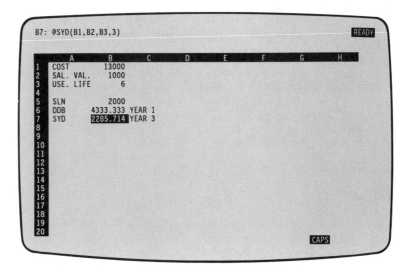

If desired, the results could be formatted with a dollar sign and two decimal places by using the **Range Format Currency** command sequence.

Cterm

@CTERM calculates the number of compounding periods for an investment with a specified initial value to increase to a future value. A fixed interest rate per compounding period is used. The general format for the CTERM function is as follows:

```
@CTERM(periodic interest rate,future value,present value)
```

In this exercise, assume that $4,500 was deposited in an account that pays an annual interest rate of 6%, compounded monthly. The @CTERM function can be used to determine how long it will take to have $20,000 in the account.

First, erase the screen from the results of the previous exercise. It is not necessary to save the results in a file.

Using the given data:

> **Press**   the [Home] key (if necessary)
>
> **Type**   @CTERM(.06/12,20000,4500)

The first argument identifies the periodic interest rate compounded monthly as .06/12. The second argument identifies the future value at $20,000. The third argument identifies the present value of $4,500.

To enter the formula:

> **Press**   ↵

The answer is 299.0761 (represented in months), or about 25 years. The screen should look like Figure 8–14.

Figure 8–14

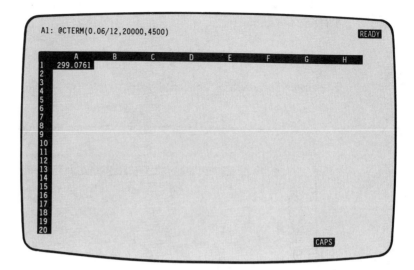

If desired, the number 299.0761 can be divided by 12. This process displays the number 24.92301, which represents about 25 years.

Term

@TERM calculates the number of payment periods in a term of an ordinary annuity necessary to accumulate a future value earning a periodic interest rate. Each payment is equal to the given payment amount in the formula. The general format for the @TERM function is as follows:

@TERM(payment,periodic interest rate,future value)

In this exercise, assume that $4,500 has been deposited at the end of each year into an account that pays an interest rate of 6%, compounded annually. The @TERM function will be used to determine how long it will take to have $20,000 in the account.

First, erase the screen from the previous exercise. It is not necessary to save the results of the previous exercise.

Using the given data:

Press	the [Home] key (if necessary)
Type	@TERM(4500,.06,20000)

The first argument identifies $4,500 as the payment amount. The second argument identifies .06 as the periodic interest rate. The third argument represents $20,000 as the future value.

To enter the formula:

Press   ↵

The answer is 4.056859, or about 4 years. The screen should look like Figure 8–15.

Figure 8–15

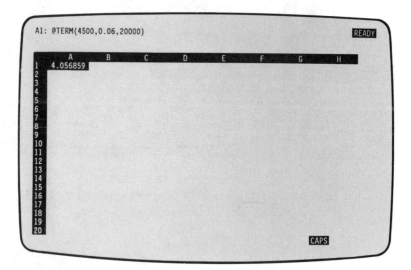

```
A1:  @TERM(4500,0.06,20000)                                         READY

         A         B         C         D         E         F         G         H
1     4.056859
2
3
4
5
6
7
8
9
10
11
12
13
14
15
16
17
18
19
20
                                                                        CAPS
```

If desired, the number 4.056859 can be formatted to 0 decimal places using the **Range Format Fixed** command sequence in order to display the number 4, which represents 4 years.

Rate

@RATE calculates the periodic interest rate necessary for a specific initial value to increase to a specified future value over the number of compounding periods in the term. If the investment is compounded monthly, multiply the @RATE by 12 to compute the annual rate. The general format for the @RATE function is as follows:

@RATE(future value,present value,term)

Suppose $4,500 has been invested in a bond which matures in 14 years to $20,000. Interest is compounded monthly in this example. Use the @RATE function to determine the periodic interest rate.

First, erase the screen from the previous exercise. It is not necessary to save the results of the previous exercise.

Using the given data:

Press   the [Home] key (if necessary)

Type   @RATE(20000,4500,14*12)

The first argument identifies $20,000 as the future value. The second argument identifies $4,500 as the present value. The third argument identifies 14*12 (interest is compounded monthly) as the term.

To enter the formula:

Press   ↵

The answer is 0.008918. Multiplied by 12, the annual rate is 0.107021 or about 10.7%. The screen should look like Figure 8–16.

Figure 8–16

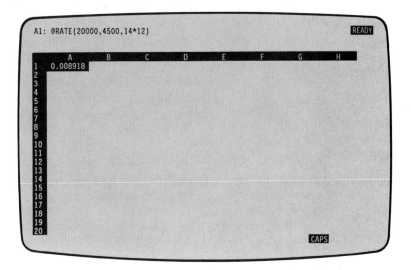

If desired, format the rate using the **R**ange **F**ormat **P**ercent command sequence.

■ DATE AND TIME FUNCTIONS

There are several date and time functions available in Lotus 1–2–3. The date functions are listed below:

@DATE(year,month,day)	Number of days since 12/31/1899
@DAY(date)	Day number
@MONTH(date)	Month number
@YEAR(date)	Year number
@TODAY	Today's date number (in Release 1A)
@NOW	Today's date and time
@DATEVALUE(string)	Number of days since 12/31/1899

The @NOW and @DATEVALUE functions are available in Release 2 and later releases of Lotus 1–2–3. The @NOW function replaces the @TODAY function in Release 1A.

The time functions listed below are available in Release 2 and later releases of Lotus 1–2–3:

@TIME(hr,min,sec)	Numeric value for time
@HOUR(time number)	Hour number
@MINUTE(time number)	Minute number
@SECOND(time number)	Second number
@TIMEVALUE(string)	Numeric value for time

Date

First, erase the screen. It is not necessary to save the results of the previous exercise.

To enter the date June 24, 1987 with the @DATE function in cell A1:

Press	the [Home] key (if necessary)
Type	@DATE(87,6,24)
Press	⏎

The number 31952 appears in cell A1. This number indicates that 31,952 days have passed since December 31 of 1899. In order to see the desired date, format this cell using the following instructions.

To bring up the menu with date format options:

Press	/	(the command key)
Type	R	(for Range)
Type	F	(for Format)
Type	D	(for Date)

Five different options for ways to display the date appear on the menu. The sixth option for displaying the time is discussed later in this chapter. The screen should look like Figure 8–17.

Figure 8–17

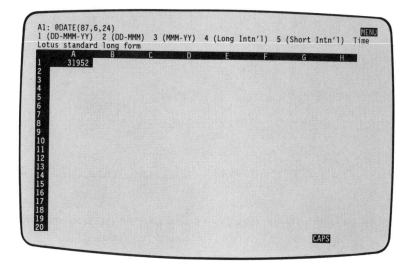

Depending upon which option is chosen, the date in cell A1 can be displayed in one of the following five formats:

24-Jun-87
24-Jun
Jun-87
06/24/87
06/24

There are other formats for options 4 and 5 that can be accessed through the **W**orksheet **G**lobal **D**efault **O**ther **I**nternational **D**ate command sequence.

To choose option 4 from the Data Format menu:

Type   4

When prompted for the range to format:

Press   ↵

The date format 06/24/87 is now displayed. The screen should look like Figure 8–18.

Figure 8–18

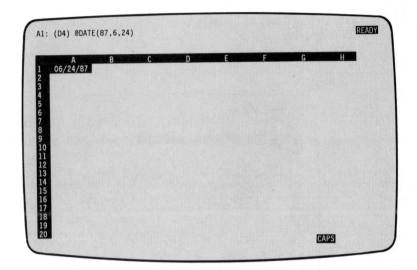

A cell can be formatted using the **R**ange **F**ormat **D**ate sequence either before or after the desired date function is entered in the worksheet.

Now

Clear the screen from the previous exercise. It is not necessary to save the results of the previous exercise.

The @NOW function returns the **system** date and time. The computer system determines the current system date and time. The date and time can be determined by an internal clock that resides inside the computer, or it can be determined by the user inputting the date and time when prompted at the beginning of a work session when the machine is turned on. The @NOW function's counterpart in Release 1A is the @TODAY function, which can return only the date.

To receive the current date (again, the current date is determined by whatever date is currently assigned to the computer system):

> **Press**   the [Home] key (if necessary)
>
> **Type**   @NOW ⏎

The number in the cell indicates the number of days that have passed since December 31, 1899 to the present system date. For example, if the current system date is September 14, 1987, typing @NOW will cause the number 32034.62 to appear, indicating that 32,034 days have passed since December 31 of 1899. (The decimal values refer to the time of day and will be discussed later in this section). The integer portion of the number returned by @NOW is the same as typing @DATE(87,9,14). In order to see the desired date, format this cell using the **Format Date** command sequence.

To choose a date format:

Press	/	(the command key)
Type	R	(for Range)
Type	F	(for Format)
Type	D	(for Date)

To choose option 1 from the **Date** menu:

| **Type** | 1 |

When prompted for the range to format:

| **Press** | ↵ |

Notice that the cell is filled with asterisks. The column is not wide enough to display the date with the chosen data format. To widen the column:

Press	/	(the command key)
Type	W	(for Worksheet)
Type	C	(for Column)
Type	S	(for Set-Width)

When prompted for the column width:

| **Press** | the right arrow key |

Notice that a column width of 10 is sufficient to display the date. To accept 10 as the column width:

| **Press** | ↵ |

The current system date is displayed. If the date is August 4, 1989, for example, the date is displayed as 08/04/89.

To erase the screen before proceeding with the next exercise, use the **Worksheet Erase Yes** command sequence.

The @NOW feature can be formatted to display either the date or the time. To format @NOW to display the current time:

Move	the cell pointer to cell A1 (if necessary)	
Type	@NOW ↵	
Press	/	(the command key)
Type	R	(for Range)
Type	F	(for Format)
Type	D	(for Date)
Type	T	(for Time)

There are 4 options for the time. The screen should look like the first illustration in Figure 8–19.

Figure 8–19
Part 1

There are four options to display the time.

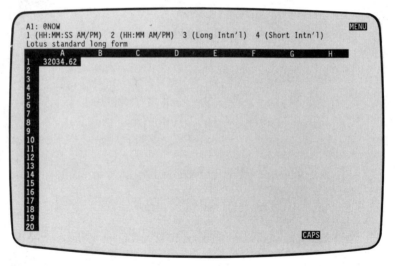

Figure 8–19
Part 2

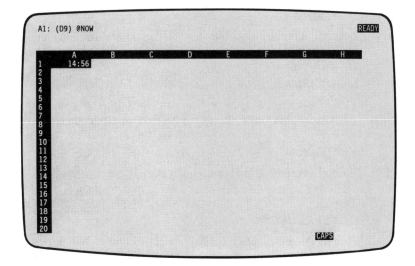

To choose number 4 of the time options:

Type   4 ↵

When prompted for the range to format:

Press   ↵

The time should be returned in hours and minutes in military time; for example, if the system time is 2:56 P.M., the time would be returned as 14:56. Other options will display seconds also, as illustrated later in this chapter. Refer to Figure 8–19. All four options for displaying the time 2:56 P.M. are displayed below:

    02:56:55 PM
    02:56 PM
    14:56:55
    14:56

Additional Date and Time Options

The @DATE, @NOW, and @TIME are the three date and time functions that are most often used. Additional date and time options are available. Information about these options is listed below as a reference and not as a written exercise.

DAY(date)

This function displays the day of the month for a given date. For example, if @DAY(@DATE(86,8,4)) is entered on a worksheet, the display will be 4.

MONTH(date)

This function displays the month for a given date. For example, if @MONTH(@DATE(86,8,4)) is entered on a worksheet, the display will be 8.

YEAR(date)

This function displays the year for a given date. For example, if @YEAR(@DATE(86,8,4)) is entered on a worksheet, the display will be 86.

DATEVALUE(string)

This function is available in Release 2 of Lotus 1–2–3. It returns the number of days that have elapsed since December 31, 1899, just as the @DATE function does. However, a single string can be entered for the argument in the parentheses.

The date string used in the @DATEVALUE function must be in one of the Lotus date formats. For example, any of the following strings are acceptable:

```
@DATEVALUE("15-Jun-87")-@DATEVALUE("31-Aug-85")
@DATEVALUE("15-Jun")-@DATEVALUE("31-Aug")
@DATEVALUE(B3)-@DATEVALUE(B4)
```

The second @DATEVALUE example listed above will yield a different answer from the first example because the differing years (1985 and 1987) are not included in the string.

The third @DATEVALUE example demonstrates that cell addresses were used. This format is correct only if a date in the correct format is located in the designated cell.

TIME(hour,minute,second)

This function is used to produce the serial number for a time of day, ranging from 0 to 0.99999. 0 designates midnight, and 0.99999 designates the time right before midnight.

For example, if @TIME(19,10,59) is entered in a cell, the numeric designation is 0.799293. @TIME(19,10,59) is 7:10:59 P.M., which is about 80% of the amount of time in a day.

HOUR(time serial number)

This function will produce the hour for a given serial number. For example, @HOUR(0.799293) = 19.

MINUTE (time serial number)

This function produces the minute for a given serial number, It is very similar to the @HOUR function. For example, @MINUTE (0.799293) = 10.

SECOND *(time serial number)*

This function produces the second for a given serial number. It is similar to the @HOUR and @MINUTE functions. For example, @SECOND (0.799293) = 59.

TIMEVALUE *(string)*

@TIMEVALUE produces the same output as @TIME, except that it can accept a single string as input. The time string must be in one of the four Lotus time formats; it must also be entered within double quotes. For example, @TIMEVALUE ("07:10:59 PM") will return the number 0.799293, which is the time value of @TIME(19,10,59).

■ CONDITIONAL FUNCTIONS

The @IF function can be used to create formulas that return an answer dependent upon a test, or condition. The @IF statement and various ways that it can be used are illustrated in this section.

IF

The @IF function permits the user to test a condition and select one of two options depending on the result of the test. The general format of the @IF function is as follows:

```
@IF(test,result if the test is true,result if the test is false)
```

In this exercise, suppose the income before tax of a company is entered in cell A1 at $250,000. Assume a tax rate of 46% that is placed in A2. For this exercise, an @IF statement is created that tests any amount entered in cell A1 to see if the income is greater than zero. If the income is greater than zero, the income amount is multiplied by the tax rate .46 (stored in cell A2) to determine the tax amount. If the income is not greater than zero, the amount entered for taxes is the number zero.

First, erase the screen. It is not necessary to save the results of the previous exercise. To enter the data upon which to perform the test:

Press	the [Home] key (if necessary)
Type	250000 ⏎
Move	the cell pointer to cell A2
Type	.46 ⏎

To enter the @IF statement that will test whether the amount entered in cell A1 is greater than zero:

Move   the cell pointer to cell A3

Type   @IF(A1>0,A1*A2,0)

The first argument, A1>0, is the test. This test determines whether the amount in cell A1 is greater than 0. The second argument, A1*A2, is the formula that will be computed if the test is true and cell A1 is greater than zero. The third argument, 0, returns the value 0 if the test is false and cell A1 is not greater than 0.

To enter the If function:

Press   ⏎

The formula appears in the control panel. The number 115000 appears in cell A3. Since the test was true, the formula A1*A2 (in this case, 250000*.46) was computed. The screen should look like Figure 8–20.

Figure 8–20

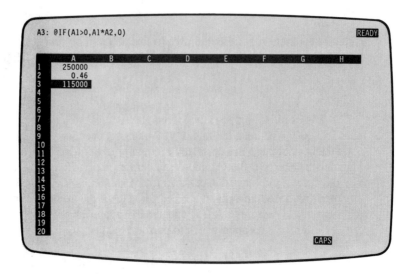

To test the "false" return in the @IF statement:

Move   the cell pointer to cell A1

Type   −250000

The number in cell A3 changes to 0, returning the answer for the test being false (A1 is not greater than 0).

The remainder of this section illustrates various applications of the @IF statement for the user's reference; there are no exercises to complete.

Logical Operators

Logical operators combine the numbers within conditional statements or formulas. The logical operators for simple logical statements are as follows:

> =
> <
> <=
> >
> >=

In order to indicate that two values are not equal, the following operator is used:

> <>

Logical Operators for Compound Statements

Logical operators can be used to combine multiple conditions. The #AND#, #OR#, and #NOT# logical operators for Lotus 1–2–3 are now discussed.

#AND#

#AND# can be used to combine multiple statements. For example, @IF(A5=0#AND#B5=0,Z5,C5) tests two conditions. More than one #AND# may be used in a formula. When the #AND# statement is used to link multiple conditions, *all* conditions must be true before the true result (Z5) can be executed.

#OR#

#OR# can be used to test if one argument *or* the other is true. For example, @IF(A5=0#OR#B5=0,Z5,C5) would result in the *true* result (Z5) if *either* A5=0 or B5=0. When the #OR# statement is used to link multiple conditions, *all* conditions must be false before the false result (C5) can be executed.

#NOT#

#NOT# can be used to indicate that a condition is not true. For example, @IF(#NOT#A5=0#OR#B5=0,Z5,C5) tests whether A5 is *not* equal to zero or if B5=0. Unlike the logical operators #OR# and #AND#, the #NOT# logical operator is used *before* a condition.

@Na

@NA can be used in an @IF statement if the desired answer is "not available." Using @NA returns "NA" in a cell as the result. For example, if the @IF statement @IF(B1>B2,3,@NA) finds that B1 is not greater than B2, the answer placed in the cell containing the @IF statement would be NA.

Nested IF

One @IF function may be nested inside another, as illustrated by the following example:

```
@IF(B1=25,B2*B1,@IF(B1=35,B3*B1,@IF(B1=45,B4*B1,0)))
```

The @IF function is read from left to right. The first two @IF functions have @IF functions for the false response. The parentheses used to end the @IF functions are at the end of the formula.

■ DATABASE STATISTICAL FUNCTIONS

Lotus has a number of database statistical functions that are very similar to the functions used for data analysis. A **database** is a collection of related information, or records. With the database statistical functions, the user can select specified items in a database range. For example, the user may have a database of all employees located in California, but wishes to count only the number of employees from Los Angeles. @COUNT can count all employees in the database; @DCOUNT uses criteria specified by the user and can count only the employees from Los Angeles. The database statistical functions are specifically designed for use in a database. The "D" in front of each function indicates that it is a database function. (The database capabilities of 1–2–3 will be discussed in more detail in Chapter Ten.)

A list of the database functions and a brief explanation of each function are provided below:

@DSUM	Computes the sum of selected items in a range
@DCOUNT	Determines the number of selected items in a range
@DAVG	Computes the arithmetic mean of selected items in a range
@DMIN	Determines the minimum value of selected items in a range
@DMAX	Determine the maximum value for selected items in a range
@DSTD	Compute the standard deviation of selected items in a range
@DVAR	Computes the variance of selected items in a range

General Rules for Using the Database Statistical Functions

Each function is implemented by using the following format:

```
@function name (input range, field location, criterion range)
```

The input range is the database area which encompasses the field titles and the records. The criterion range specifies the field title(s) and criterion desired.

The field location is used to indicate which column should be used for the calculations. When choosing the column, begin counting with the number zero. Therefore, if the third column in a database is the desired field location, it is referred to as number *two* in the function.

Using the Database Statistical Functions

Create a small file for use in this exercise. Place the headings NAME, SALARY, and ST in cells A1 . . C1, respectively. In cells A2 . . A5, place the names, BROWN, JONES, SMITH, and WHITE (Do NOT leave row 2 blank). In cells B2 . . B5, place the salaries 32000, 28000, 40000, and 25000. Change column B's width to 7 using the **Worksheet Column Set-Width** command sequence. In cells C2 . . C5, place the states TX, LA, TX, and LA. Use the **Worksheet Global Format , 0** command sequence to display the numbers with commas and 0 decimal places. Save the file under the name SALS. Refer to Figure 8–21 as a guide when creating this file.

Figure 8–21
Part 1

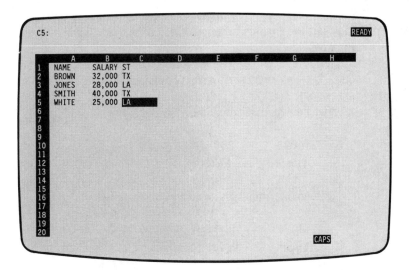

Figure 8–21
Part 2

```
A1: 'NAME
B1: [W7] 'SALARY
C1: 'ST
A2: 'BROWN
B2: [W7] 32000
C2: 'TX
A3: 'JONES
B3: [W7] 28000
C3: 'LA
A4: 'SMITH
B4: [W7] 40000
C4: 'TX
A5: 'WHITE
B5: [W7] 25000
C5: 'LA
```

In this exercise, the @DCOUNT function will be used to count the number of employees earning over $30,000 that are in the SALS database. To specify the criterion range:

Move	the cell pointer to cell F17
Type	SALARY (exactly as it is typed in cell B1)
Move	the cell pointer to cell F18
Type	+B2>30000 ↵

The number 1 will appear in cell F18. The first salary (whether B2 is greater than 30000) was tested and found to be true, resulting in the number 1. (If the test was false, a 0 (zero) would appear). The response of 0 or 1 is not a significant part of the @DCOUNT process; the formula is important, however, for it specifies the desired criteria and indicates the first record upon which to perform the test. See the first illustration in Figure 8–22.

(If desired, cell F18 may be formatted to show the formula rather than the number one. Use the **Range** Format Text command sequence and widen the column to show the entire formula).

To document the formula (an optional step):

Move	the cursor to cell A17
Type	EMPLOYEES EARNING OVER $30,000 ↵

To count the employees who make over $30,000:

Move	the cell pointer to cell A18
Type	@DCOUNT(A1..C5,1,F17..F18)

The information before the first comma in the formula (A1 .. C5) indicates the input range, or records, including the column titles.

The information after the first command in the formula (1) indicates the column in which the tested data is located in the database; in this instance, the data is in the SALARY column. *Note that it is necessary to count the columns from left to right beginning with the number 0; SALARY is therefore in column 1, not column 2.*

The information after the second comma in the formula (F17 . . F18) indicates the area in which the criterion is located.

Press   ⏎

The number 2 appears in cell A18 because there are 2 employees that earn over $30,000. The screen should look like the second illustration in Figure 8–22.

Figure 8–22
Part 1

Cells F17 and F18 define the criterion for the @DCOUNT formula.

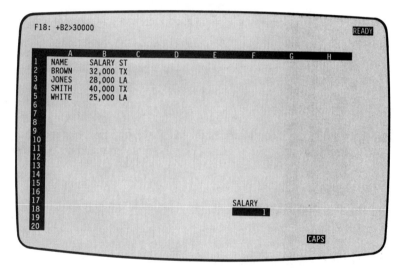

Figure 8–22
Part 2

The @DCOUNT formula in cell A18 specifies the database area, the column containing the specified data in the criterion range, and the location of the criterion range.

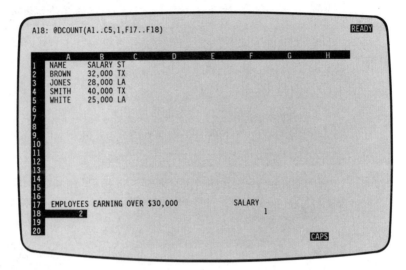

Because of the file SAL's small size, the user could easily have computed the number of employees who earn over $30,000 by simply looking at the file. However, when used for a file containing hundreds or even thousands of records, the database statistical functions are quite useful. The other database statistical functions work in a similar manner.

■ OTHER FUNCTIONS

There are a number of other functions available in Lotus 1–2–3 that are not covered in this book. They are as follows:

> Mathematical functions
> Logical functions*
> Special functions**
> String functions

* the @IF function is the only logical function that is included in this chapter.

** the @NA function is the only special function that is included in this chapter.

SUMMARY

Lotus 1–2–3 has many functions that can perform standard calculations. There are several different categories of functions: Mathematical, Special, Date and Time, Financial, Data (Statistical) Analysis, String, Logical, and Database Statistical functions. The functions discussed in this chapter were the Data (Statistical) Analysis, Financial, Date and Time, and Database Statistical functions.

KEY CONCEPTS

@AVG	@MAX
@COUNT	@MONTH
@CTERM	@NA
Database	@NOW
@DATE	@NPV
@DATEVALUE	@PMT
@DAVG	@PV
@DAY	@RATE
@DCOUNT	@SECOND
@DDB	@SLN
@DMIN	@STD
@DMAX	@SUM
@DSTD	@SYD
@DSUM	@TERM
@DVAR	@TIME
@FV	@TIMEVALUE
@HOUR	@TODAY
@IF	@VAR
@IRR	@YEAR
@MIN	Argument
@MINUTE	Logical operators

CHAPTER EIGHT
EXERCISE 1

INSTRUCTIONS: Circle T if the statement is true and F if the statement is false.

T   F   1. @MIN determines the minute for a given serial number.

T   F   2. Multiple items in a range may be listed individually (e.g., the syntax in the formula @COUNT(B1,B3,B4) is correct).

T   F   3. Arguments within an @ function may be placed in any order desired by the user.

T   F   4. Extra spaces are not acceptable within @ functions.

T   F   5. A label has a value of 0 and will be counted as such if included in a range for an @ function.

T   F   6. It is possible to alter an @ function with arithmetic operations to get the desired result (e.g., the formula @PMT(B1,B2/12,B3*12) is syntactically correct).

T   F   7. If a worksheet file containing the @NOW function (formatted to show the date) is retrieved from a file and actively recalculates, the @NOW function will display the *current* system date.

T   F   8. A single-cell item in an argument may not be entered directly into the formula (e.g., the formula @NPV(A1,B1..B6) cannot be entered as @NPV(.1,B1..B6).

T   F   9. More than one @ function may be used in a formula.

T   F   10. The @IF statement allows the user to test one or more conditions in a worksheet and provide appropriate responses for either a true result or a false result.

CHAPTER EIGHT
EXERCISE 2
Using the Data Analysis Functions

INSTRUCTIONS: Use the Data Analysis Functions available in Lotus 1–2–3 to perform calculations upon the numbers 111, 125, 116, 130, and 127. The screen should look like Figure 8–23. Use Figure 8–24 as a guide for the cell formulas, if necessary.

Figure 8–23

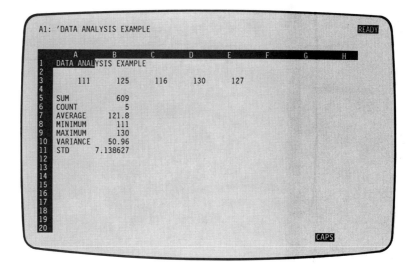

```
A1:  'DATA ANALYSIS EXAMPLE                                              READY

        A          B          C          D          E        F       G       H
 1   DATA ANALYSIS EXAMPLE
 2
 3       111        125       116        130        127
 4
 5   SUM          609
 6   COUNT          5
 7   AVERAGE     121.8
 8   MINIMUM      111
 9   MAXIMUM      130
10   VARIANCE    50.96
11   STD       7.138627
12
13
14
15
16
17
18
19
20
                                                                        CAPS
```

Figure 8–24

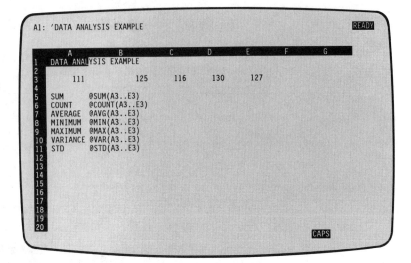

CHAPTER EIGHT
EXERCISE 3
Using the Financial Analysis Functions

INSTRUCTIONS: Use the Financial Analysis Functions available in Lotus 1–2–3 to solve the following exercises. Each exercise provides the correct answer.

1. Compute the internal rate of return for the following cash flow stream using .15 as the guess rate:
   −1000, −500, 900, 800, 700, 600, 400, 200, 100

2. Compute the net present value for the following cash flow stream using .10 as the discount rate:
   −1500, 900, 800, 700, 600, 400, 200, 100

3. Compute the future value if the payment per period is 500, the interest rate is 10%, and the term is 15 years.

4. Compute the present value using the arguments previously given in problem number 3.

5. Compute the payment amount for a 100,000 loan that has an interest rate of 10% and is to be paid on an annual basis for a period of 12 years.

6. Compute the *monthly* payment amount assuming all arguments in problem 5 stay the same except the time period is 30 years.

Complete the following exercises if using Release 2 or a later release of Lotus 1–2–3.

7. Compute the straight-line depreciation for an office machine having an initial cost of $13,000, an estimated useful life of 8 years, and a salvage value of $200.

8. Using the data given in problem 7, compute the depreciation of the office machine for the sixth year using the double-declining balance method.

9. Using the data given in problem 7, compute the depreciation of the office machine for the sixth year using the sum-of-the-years'-digits method.

10. Suppose $10,000 has been invested in an account that pays an annual interest rate of 10%, compounded monthly. Determine how long it will take to get $30,000 in the account.

11. Suppose that $5,000 is deposited at the end of each year into a bank account. If 8% interest is earned per year, compute how long it will take to earn $20,000.

12. Suppose $15,000 has been invested in a bond which matures in 9 years to 25,000. Interest is compounded monthly. Determine the monthly interest rate.

CHAPTER EIGHT
EXERCISE 4
Using the @Date Function

INSTRUCTIONS: Using the @DATE function format, enter the date January 19, 1989 into cell A1.
Format the date using option 1 from the Date format menu.
Notice that the cell fills with asterisks; widen column A appropriately.
When finished, the screen should look like Figure 8–25.

Figure 8–25

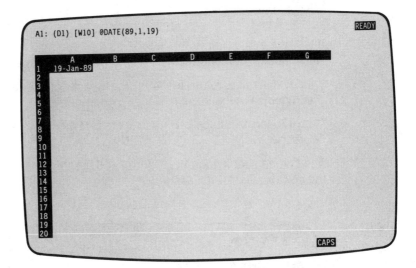

CHAPTER EIGHT
EXERCISE 5
Using the @IF Function

INSTRUCTIONS: Use the @IF Functions available in Lotus 1–2–3 to solve the following exercise.

On a blank spreadsheet, enter the numbers 20, 30, and 50 in cells A1, A2, and A3, respectively.

In cell B1, design an @IF statement that can test whether the number to the left of the formula (cell A1) is within the range 30 through 40, inclusive (use the logical operator #AND#).

If the test is true, return the letter T as the response. Input the letter T within quotes in the formula since it is non-numeric.

If the test is false, return the letter F as the response. Input the letter F within quotes in the formula since it is non-numeric.

Copy the formula to cells B2 and B3 to test the numbers in cells A2 and A3, respectively.

The screen should look like Figure 8–26. Use Figure 8–27 as a guide for the cell formulas, if necessary.

Figure 8–26

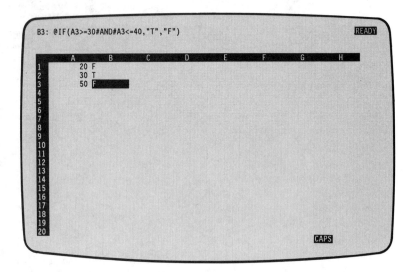

Figure 8–27

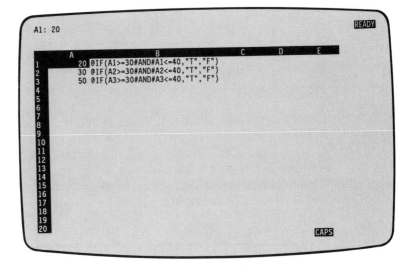

CHAPTER EIGHT
EXERCISE 6
Using the @DCOUNT Function

INSTRUCTIONS: Retrieve the original file SALS for use in this exercise.

Use the @DCOUNT function in cell E18 to determine the number of people from Texas in the database. When finished, the screen should look like Figure 8–28. Note that the criterion may be specified as either +C2="TX" or TX in cell A16.

Figure 8–28

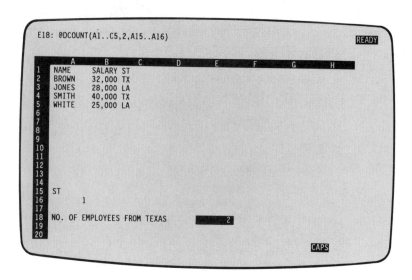

CHAPTER NINE

CREATING AND PRINTING A GRAPH

OBJECTIVES

In this chapter, the student will learn to:

- Create a Graph
- Print a Graph
- Create Various Types of Graphs
- Use additional graph commands

■ CHAPTER OVERVIEW

If a spreadsheet contains a large amount of data, it can be very difficult to detect trends and see relationships between various numbers. A graph depicting key elements of a spreadsheet can facilitate more accurate spreadsheet analysis. Graphs can be easily created in Lotus 1–2–3 by using data that is entered on a spreadsheet. The graphic image can be viewed on the screen and may also be printed.

■ LOADING THE SPREADSHEET FILE

The first graph that will be created in this chapter is based upon data in the file BUDGET that was created in Chapter Two. Retrieve the file BUDGET:

Press	/	(the command key)
Type	F	(for File)
Type	R	(for Retrieve)

When prompted for the file name:

Type	BUDGET ↵

The file BUDGET should now be visible on the screen (Figure 9–1).

Figure 9–1

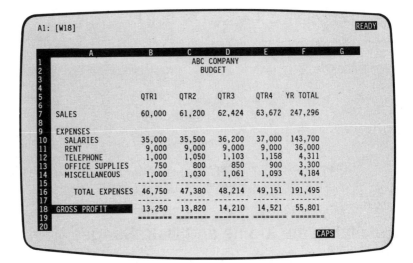

■ CREATING A GRAPH

It is now assumed that the file BUDGET has been read from the disk and is currently on the screen. The graph to be created will be a bar graph. The bars will represent the SALES, TOTAL EXPENSES, and GROSS PROFIT for the four quarters in BUDGET. When the graph is completed, it will look like Figure 9–2.

Figure 9–2

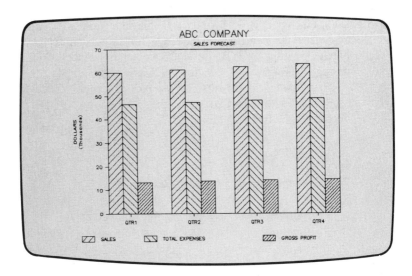

Specifying the Type of Graph

To specify the type of graph to create:

Press	/	(the command key)
Type	G	(for Graph)
Type	T	(for Type)
Type	B	(for Bar)

The previous menu reappears. The other types of graphs available are illustrated in exercises later in this chapter.

■ Specifying the X-axis and Data Ranges

To specify the labels that will be on the X-axis:

Type	X

When prompted for the X-axis range:

Move	the cell pointer to cell B5
Press	.
Move	the cell pointer to cell E5 ⏎

Do not include YR TOTAL data. If this data was accidentally highlighted, choose **X** again from the menu to reset the range. If necessary, press the Escape key to cancel the previous setting. Cells B5 through E5 contain the labels QTR1 through QTR4. QTR1 through QTR4 are the labels for the X-axis of the graph.

To indicate the data to display, use the menu variables A through F. In this exercise, use variable A through C to specify the data for Sales, Total Expenses, and Gross Profit. To specify the first data range:

Type	A

When prompted to enter the first data range:

Move	the cell pointer to cell B7
Press	.
Move	the cell pointer to cell E7 ⏎

Cells B7 through E7 contain the data for SALES. The data for Sales for all four quarters will be the first data range displayed on the graph.

To specify the second data range:

Type   B

When prompted to enter the second data range:

Move   the cell pointer to cell B16
Press   .
Move   the cell pointer to cell E16 ↵

Cells B16 through E16 contain the data for TOTAL EXPENSES. The data for Total Expenses will be the second data range displayed on the graph.

To specify the third data range:

Type   C

When prompted to enter the third data range:

Move   the cell pointer to cell B18
Press   .
Move   the cell pointer to cell E18 ↵

The data for GROSS PROFIT for all four quarters will be the third data range displayed on the graph.

Viewing the Graph

To view the graph:

Type   V   (for View)

The graph should look like Figure 9–3. If the screen does not display a graph, it may be that the computer being used does not have a graphics card. If this is the case, a graph cannot be seen on the screen, but it can still be created and printed. Complete this exercise in order to obtain a printout.

Figure 9–3
Part 1

The X range highlights the data used for the X axis labels in bar graphs.

```
E5: ^QTR4                                                          POINT
Enter X axis range: B5..E5

          A          B        C        D        E        F        G
                               ABC COMPANY
  1                               BUDGET
  2
  3
  4
  5                    QTR1     QTR2     QTR3     QTR4   YR TOTAL
  6
  7   SALES          60,000   61,200   62,424   63,672  247,296
  8
  9   EXPENSES
 10     SALARIES     35,000   35,500   36,200   37,000  143,700
 11     RENT          9,000    9,000    9,000    9,000   36,000
 12     TELEPHONE     1,000    1,050    1,103    1,158    4,311
 13     OFFICE SUPPLIES  750      800      850      900    3,300
 14     MISCELLANEOUS 1,000    1,030    1,061    1,093    4,184
 15                  -------  -------  -------  -------  -------
 16     TOTAL EXPENSES 46,750 47,380   48,214   49,151  191,495
 17                  -------  -------  -------  -------  -------
 18   GROSS PROFIT   13,250   13,820   14,210   14,521   55,801
 19                  =======  =======  =======  =======  =======
 20                                                        CAPS
```

Figure 9–3
Part 2

The A range highlights the data used for the first data range in the graph.

```
E7: @ROUND(D7*1.02,0)                                             POINT
Enter first data range: B7..E7

          A          B        C        D        E        F        G
                               ABC COMPANY
  1                               BUDGET
  2
  3
  4
  5                    QTR1     QTR2     QTR3     QTR4   YR TOTAL
  6
  7   SALES          60,000   61,200   62,424   63,672  247,296
  8
  9   EXPENSES
 10     SALARIES     35,000   35,500   36,200   37,000  143,700
 11     RENT          9,000    9,000    9,000    9,000   36,000
 12     TELEPHONE     1,000    1,050    1,103    1,158    4,311
 13     OFFICE SUPPLIES  750      800      850      900    3,300
 14     MISCELLANEOUS 1,000    1,030    1,061    1,093    4,184
 15                  -------  -------  -------  -------  -------
 16     TOTAL EXPENSES 46,750 47,380   48,214   49,151  191,495
 17                  -------  -------  -------  -------  -------
 18   GROSS PROFIT   13,250   13,820   14,210   14,521   55,801
 19                  =======  =======  =======  =======  =======
 20                                                        CAPS
```

Figure 9–3
Part 3

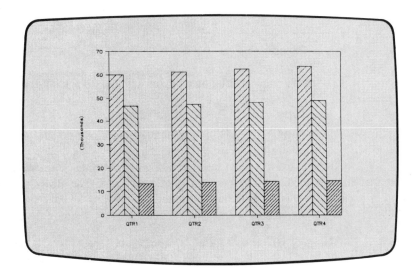

To return to the worksheet after viewing the graph:

Press   ↵

The basics of the graph have been created. The rest of the exercise adds the titles, legends, and other features necessary to complete the graph.

If a color monitor is being used, the following menu options will display the graph in color. To display a color graph:

Type	O	(for Options)
Type	C	(for Color)
Type	Q	(for Quit)

To view the color graph:

Type	V	(for View)

The graph is displayed in solid color bars. If the monitor is not a color monitor, the graph will be displayed as solid bars in varying shades of the monitor's primary color (e.g., green or amber). Note that the color graph is not an appropriate setting if the graph is to be printed on a one-color printer because all bars will appear in just one color. The colors on the screen are *not* indicative of the color the graph will be when it is printed with a color printer or plotter. The colors on the printed graph depend solely upon the *printer's* available ink or pen colors.

To return to the worksheet after viewing the color graph:

Press ↵

To set the graph to print on a printer with only black ink (i.e., not a color plotter):

| **Type** | O | (for Options) |
| **Type** | B | (for B&W—Black and White) |

If the graph remained set as a color graph, a printer with only a black ribbon would have printed out a graph with solid black bars. The B&W setting sets cross-hatch patterns to distinguish the bars from each other.

Entering the Titles for the Graph

To enter the first title:

| **Type** | T | (for Titles) |
| **Type** | F | (for First) |

When prompted to enter the top line of the graph title:

Type ABC COMPANY ↵

To enter the second title:

| **Type** | T | (for Titles) |
| **Type** | S | (for Second) |

When prompted to enter the second line of the graph title:

Type SALES FORECAST ↵

To enter a title for the Y-axis:

| **Type** | T | (for Titles) |
| **Type** | Y | (for Y-Axis) |

When prompted to enter the Y-axis title:

Type DOLLARS ↵

To return to the previous menu:

Type   Q   (for Quit)

To view the graph with titles:

Type   V   (for View)

The graph should look like Figure 9–4.

Figure 9–4

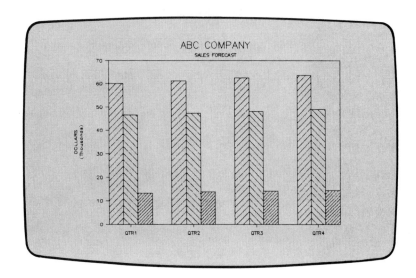

To return to the graph menu after viewing the graph:

Press   ⏎

Specifying the Legends

To enter the legend for the first data range (SALES, which was highlighted as data range A earlier in this exercise):

Type   O   (for Options)
Type   L   (for Legend)
Type   A

When prompted to enter the legend for range A:

    Type   SALES ⏎

To enter the legend for the second data range (placed in data range B earlier in this exercise):

    Type   L   (for Legend)
    Type   B

When prompted for the legend for range B:

    Type   TOTAL EXPENSES ⏎

To enter the legend for the third data range (placed in data range C earlier in this exercise):

    Type   L   (for Legend)
    Type   C

When prompted for the legend for range C:

    Type   GROSS PROFIT ⏎

To leave the Option menu:

    Type   Q   (for Quit)

To view the graph with titles and legends:

    Type   V   (for View)

The screen should look like Figure 9–5.

Figure 9–5

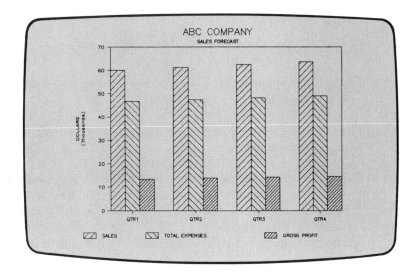

To return to the worksheet:

Press　　⏎

Naming and Saving the Graph

To name the graph:

Type　　N　　(for Name)
Type　　C　　(for Create)

When prompted for the graph name:

Type　　BUDBAR ⏎

Naming a graph in a worksheet is especially important if more than one graph will be created from a worksheet. Lotus 1–2–3 can only remember the settings for one graph unless names are assigned to each graph. When a particular graph setting is needed, **Graph Name U**se will display all graph names so that the desired graph can be viewed and edited, if necessary.

To save a picture of the graph for printing:

Type　　S　　(for Save)

When prompted for the graph file name:

Type   BUDBAR ↵

A file entitled BUDBAR is now saved to a disk. This file contains only a *picture* of the graph that can be used to print the graph. The file BUDBAR does not end with the extension .WK1 because it is not a worksheet file. BUDBAR is listed on the disk as BUDBAR.PIC (it is possible to see the file listing for graph files using the **File List Graph** command sequence).

Name Create BUDBAR assigned the name BUDBAR to the graph settings *in the worksheet*. The file BUDBAR created with the Save command in the Graph menu is a separate file containing only the picture of the graph, *not* the graph settings. The graph settings are a part of the worksheet BUDGET. The settings sheet and the .PIC file do not have to have the same name. If BUDBAR.PIC does not print the desired graph, the user must retrieve the file BUDGET and correct the settings sheet; if the settings sheet has the same name as the graph file, it will be easier to find and edit. Then the file BUDBAR.PIC would have to be saved again and replaced so that it would show the changes made the next time it is printed. Refer to Figure 9–6.

Figure 9–6
Part 1

Graph **Name Create** assigns a name to the graph settings for a graph. (**File Save** will permanently save the graph settings).

```
A1: [W18]                                                    EDIT
Enter graph name: BUDBAR

        A           B        C        D        E        F        G
 1                          ABC COMPANY
 2                            BUDGET
 3
 4
 5                    QTR1     QTR2     QTR3     QTR4   YR TOTAL
 6
 7   SALES          60,000   61,200   62,424   63,672  247,296
 8
 9   EXPENSES
10     SALARIES     35,000   35,500   36,200   37,000  143,700
11     RENT          9,000    9,000    9,000    9,000   36,000
12     TELEPHONE     1,000    1,050    1,103    1,158    4,311
13     OFFICE SUPPLIES 750      800      850      900    3,300
14     MISCELLANEOUS 1,000    1,030    1,061    1,093    4,184
15                  -------- -------- -------- -------- --------
16     TOTAL EXPENSES 46,750  47,380   48,214   49,151  191,495
17                  -------- -------- -------- -------- --------
18   GROSS PROFIT   13,250   13,820   14,210   14,521   55,801
19                  ======== ======== ======== ======== ========
20
                                                          CAPS
```

Figure 9–6
Part 2

Graph **Save** saves the graph in a .PIC file for later printing.

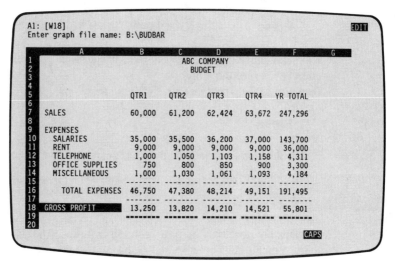

```
A1: [W18]                                                        EDIT
Enter graph file name: B:\BUDBAR
          A              B        C        D        E        F        G
 1                           ABC COMPANY
 2                             BUDGET
 3
 4
 5                         QTR1     QTR2     QTR3     QTR4   YR TOTAL
 6
 7   SALES                60,000   61,200   62,424   63,672  247,296
 8
 9   EXPENSES
10     SALARIES           35,000   35,500   36,200   37,000  143,700
11     RENT                9,000    9,000    9,000    9,000   36,000
12     TELEPHONE           1,000    1,050    1,103    1,158    4,311
13     OFFICE SUPPLIES       750      800      850      900    3,300
14     MISCELLANEOUS       1,000    1,030    1,061    1,093    4,184
15                        --------  --------  --------  --------  --------
16     TOTAL EXPENSES     46,750   47,380   48,214   49,151  191,495
17                        --------  --------  --------  --------  --------
18   GROSS PROFIT         13,250   13,820   14,210   14,521   55,801
19                        ========  ========  ========  ========  ========
20                                                                 CAPS
```

As explained above, the graph file BUDBAR.PIC contains a picture of the graph to be printed. However, the settings used to make the graph should also be saved with the worksheet file BUDGET.WK1 in the event that changes will be made later. For this reason, the next step is to save and replace the BUDGET.WK1 file so that the file will include the graph settings.

To exit the graph menu:

Type   Q   (for Quit)

To save the graph settings with the spreadsheet BUDGET:

Press   /   (the command key)

Type   F   (for File)

Type   S   (for Save)

When prompted for the file name:

Press   ⏎

By pressing ⏎, the file name BUDGET is kept. In response to the prompt to either Cancel or **R**eplace the file:

Type   R   (for Replace)

Before printing the graph, view it once more:

Press   the [Graph] key (the [F10] function key)

When a menu does not appear in the control panel, press the [Graph] key (the F10 function key) to see the graph.

To return to the worksheet after viewing the graph:

Press   ⏎

Follow the instructions in the next section to print the graph.

■ PRINTING A GRAPH

Three steps are necessary to print a graph in Lotus. The user must enter the Lotus PrintGraph menu, select the desired graph, and send the graphic image to the printer.

Entering the Lotus PrintGraph Menu

To print the graph, the PrintGraph option must be accessed. In order to reach this option, it is necessary to leave the Lotus 1–2–3 spreadsheet menu.

To leave the current Lotus menu:

Press	/	(the command key)
Type	Q	(for Quit)
Type	Y	(for Yes)

The Lotus Access System Menu should appear on the screen (refer to Figure 9–7). If the Access Menu does not appear, insert the Lotus PrintGraph disk in drive A and type LOTUS ⏎ .

Figure 9–7   The Lotus Access Menu

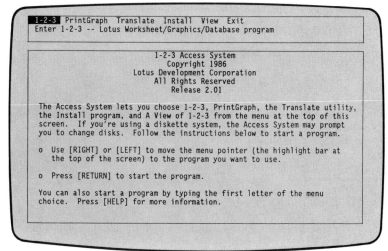

```
1-2-3  PrintGraph  Translate  Install  View  Exit
Enter 1-2-3 -- Lotus Worksheet/Graphics/Database program

                     1-2-3 Access System
                       Copyright 1986
                 Lotus Development Corporation
                      All Rights Reserved
                         Release 2.01

    The Access System lets you choose 1-2-3, PrintGraph, the Translate utility,
    the Install program, and A View of 1-2-3 from the menu at the top of this
    screen.  If you're using a diskette system, the Access System may prompt
    you to change disks.  Follow the instructions below to start a program.

    o  Use [RIGHT] or [LEFT] to move the menu pointer (the highlight bar at
       the top of the screen) to the program you want to use.

    o  Press [RETURN] to start the program.

    You can also start a program by typing the first letter of the menu
    choice.  Press [HELP] for more information.
```

With the Lotus Access System Menu on the screen:

Type   P   (for PrintGraph)

If Lotus 1–2–3 is being used in drive A, a prompt will appear on the screen to remove the Lotus 1–2–3 System disk and insert the Lotus 1–2–3 PrintGraph disk in drive A. When ⏎ is pressed, the PrintGraph program will be loaded. (Another way to load the PrintGraph program from the DOS prompt A> is to insert the Lotus PrintGraph disk in drive A and type PGRAPH ⏎). If a hard disk contains the Lotus programs being used but the PrintGraph menu does not appear, it may be that the PrintGraph programs are not on the hard disk. Refer to Figure 9–8 to see the PrintGraph screen. The PrintGraph screen currently displays the primary PrintGraph menu. The screen also displays the default settings for graphs to be printed, such as the graph's size, the graph's directory (indicates what disk drive the graph file is located on), and the printer to use. All of the settings may be changed, if desired.

Figure 9–8   The Lotus PrintGraph Menu

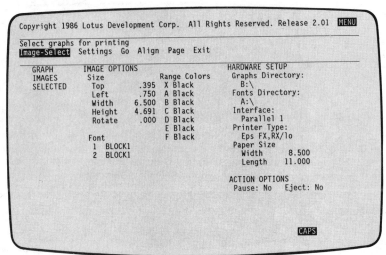

Copyright 1986 Lotus Development Corp. All Rights Reserved. Release 2.01 MENU

Select graphs for printing
Image-Select Settings Go Align Page Exit

GRAPH	IMAGE OPTIONS			HARDWARE SETUP
IMAGES	Size		Range Colors	Graphs Directory:
SELECTED	Top	.395	X Black	B:\
	Left	.750	A Black	Fonts Directory:
	Width	6.500	B Black	A:\
	Height	4.691	C Black	Interface:
	Rotate	.000	D Black	Parallel 1
			E Black	Printer Type:
			F Black	Eps FX,RX/lo
	Font			Paper Size
	1 BLOCK1			Width 8.500
	2 BLOCK1			Length 11.000
				ACTION OPTIONS
				Pause: No Eject: No

CAPS

Selecting the Graph to Be Printed and Previewing the Graph

To select the graph to print:

Type   I   (for Image-Select)

A screen displaying all of the graphs on the data diskette should appear. Only one graph file has been created (BUDBAR.PIC), so only one graph file should be listed (refer to Figure 9–9).

Figure 9–9

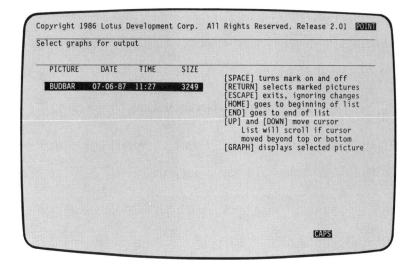

```
Copyright 1986 Lotus Development Corp.  All Rights Reserved. Release 2.01  POINT

Select graphs for output


   PICTURE    DATE     TIME     SIZE
                                        [SPACE] turns mark on and off
   BUDBAR   07-06-87  11:27     3249    [RETURN] selects marked pictures
                                        [ESCAPE] exits, ignoring changes
                                        [HOME] goes to beginning of list
                                        [END] goes to end of list
                                        [UP] and [DOWN] move cursor
                                           List will scroll if cursor
                                           moved beyond top or bottom
                                        [GRAPH] displays selected picture




                                                                    CAPS
```

To print the BUDBAR graph, make sure the graph name is highlighted. The name should be highlighted since only one graph file is listed.

Press   the space bar

A pound (#) sign should appear in front of the word BUDBAR. The # sign marks BUDBAR as a graph to be printed. If there were several graph files listed, the user could select a particular graph to print by moving the cell pointer to the name using the arrow keys. Pressing the space bar causes a # sign to appear in front of the graph name and marks it to be printed. If desired, multiple graphs can be selected for printing by marking the graphs to print with the # sign. Refer to Figure 9–10.

Figure 9–10   The # sign indicates that a graph has been selected for printing.

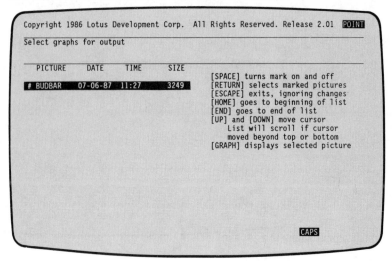

```
Copyright 1986 Lotus Development Corp.  All Rights Reserved. Release 2.01 POINT

Select graphs for output
───────────────────────────────────────────────────────────────────────────
    PICTURE     DATE      TIME      SIZE
                                              [SPACE] turns mark on and off
  # BUDBAR    07-06-87   11:27     3249       [RETURN] selects marked pictures
                                              [ESCAPE] exits, ignoring changes
                                              [HOME] goes to beginning of list
                                              [END] goes to end of list
                                              [UP] and [DOWN] move cursor
                                                  List will scroll if cursor
                                                  moved beyond top or bottom
                                              [GRAPH] displays selected picture




                                                              CAPS
```

To remove the # sign, press the space bar again. The # sign will disappear and the graph in question will not be printed. Note that the space bar is used to *place* and to *remove* the # sign from graph names. Make sure that the # sign is in front of BUDBAR before continuing with this exercise.

The following step is optional. To preview the graph before printing it:

Press   the [Graph] key (the [F10] function key)

The graph, as it will be printed, appears on the screen. If the bars are solid colors, the graph will only print correctly on a color plotter. There will be more detail on the printed graph than there is on the screen. Refer to Figure 9–11. Note that a graph's appearance may differ slightly when viewed from within the PrintGraph menu, as compared to within the 1–2–3 menu when the graph was created using the spreadsheet settings. Even the scale may be different.

Figure 9–11

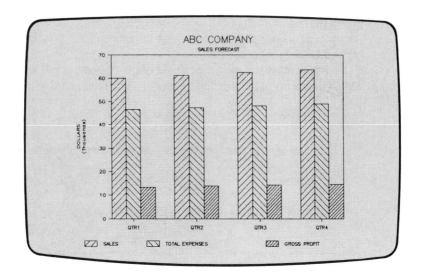

After viewing the graph:

Press ⏎

Notice that BUDBAR is now listed under "Graph Images Selected."

Printing the Graph

To prepare the printer for operation:

Check	to see that the printer is connected to the computer
Align	the paper, if necessary
Turn	on the printer, if it is off

To print the graph:

Type	A	(for Align)
Type	G	(for Go)

The system will load the fonts and then start generating the printed graph. This can be a slow process; do not disturb or interrupt the computer.

WAIT will appear in the top right corner of the screen. Even if the printer stops, do not assume the graph is finished until WAIT is replaced by MENU. Expect the graph to take about 2 minutes to print. This may seem like a long time, but it is much faster than manually producing the graph. The amount of time a graph takes to print depends upon the quality of the draft (a low or high density) and the type of printer used. Low density drafts are rough drafts; high density graphs are better-quality graphs that typically take longer to print.

If it is necessary to eject the printed graph when the graph has finished printing (and MENU appears in the top right corner of the screen):

Type   P   (for Page)

To eject a second page so that the paper can be easily removed from the printer:

Type   P   (for Page)

The graph should appear as follows (refer to Figure 9–12).

Figure 9–12

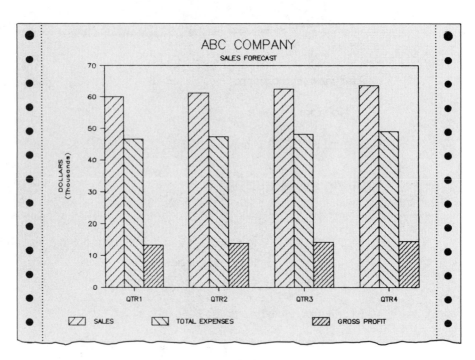

Exiting the PrintGraph Menu and Returning to Spreadsheet Mode

To exit the PrintGraph menu:

Type	E	(for Exit)
Type	Y	(for Yes)

The Lotus Access System Menu will appear. If using Lotus 1–2–3 in drive A, replace the PrintGraph diskette with the Lotus System diskette in drive A. If the Access Menu does not appear, make sure the System diskette is in drive A and type LOTUS ↵.

To return to the Lotus spreadsheet area:

Type	1	(for 1–2–3)

A blank worksheet should appear on the screen.

■ CREATING VARIOUS TYPES OF GRAPHS

In the previous exercise, a bar graph was created. Lotus has four other types of graphs that can be created: Line, XY, Stacked-Bar, and Pie graphs. The file BUDGET will be the first file used to create some of the different types of graphs. To retrieve BUDGET:

Press	/	(the command key)
Type	F	(for File)
Type	R	(for Retrieve)

When prompted for the file name:

Move	the cell pointer to the word BUDGET ↵

Creating a Bar Graph

The directions for creating the data specifications for a graph and how to create a bar graph are written in the previous section entitled "Creating a Graph," so they are not duplicated here.

Creating a Line Graph

The file BUDGET is used in this exercise. The graph settings saved under BUDBAR contain graph settings for SALES, TOTAL EXPENSES, and GROSS PROFIT. Because the graph settings are already set, they can be used to display the same data as a line graph. Only the graph type has to be changed. The newly designated graph will be given a graph name.

To create a line graph:

Press	/	(the command key)
Type	G	(for Graph)
Type	T	(for Type)
Type	L	(for Line)

To view the graph:

Type	V	(for View)

The lines on the screen may appear more "jagged" than on the printout. Refer to the printed graph displayed in Figure 9–13.

Figure 9–13

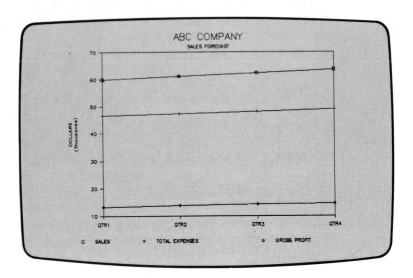

To return to the worksheet:

Press	⏎

The graph settings were set in an earlier exercise; therefore, specifications such as data ranges, titles, and legends do not have to be set again.

To name the graph:

Type	N	(for Name)
Type	C	(for Create)

When prompted for the graph name:

Type	BUDLINE ↵

To save the graph:

Type	S	(for Save)

When prompted for the graph file name:

Type	BUDLINE ↵

The graph has now been saved to a graph file so that it can later be printed, if necessary.

To leave the graph menu:

Type	Q	(for Quit)

To save the line graph specifications with the worksheet BUDGET:

Press	/	(the command key)
Type	F	(for File)
Type	S	(for Save)

The word BUDGET should appear. To replace the current version of BUDGET:

Press	↵

When prompted to either Cancel or **R**eplace:

Type	R	(for Replace)

The data specifications and name for the line graph are now saved with the worksheet.

Creating a Pie Graph

The file BUDGET is also used in this exercise. The graph settings saved under BUDBAR contain graph settings for SALES, TOTAL EXPENSES, and GROSS PROFIT. Because the graph settings are already set, they can be used to display the same data as a pie graph. Only the graph type has to be changed. The newly designated graph will be given a graph name.

To create a pie graph:

Press	/	(the command key)
Type	G	(for Graph)
Type	T	(for Type)
Type	P	(for Pie)

To view the graph:

Type	V	(for View)

Notice that the pie graph can only display the values of one data range—A. The pie graph for BUDGET displays the contents for range A. The pie will appear more oval than round on a curved screen. It will appear round on the final printout. Refer to the printed graph displayed in Figure 9–14.

Figure 9–14

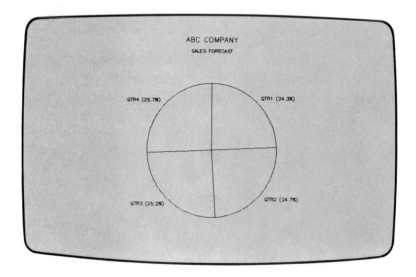

To return to the worksheet:

Press   ↵

The graph settings were set in an earlier exercise; therefore, specifications such as data ranges, titles, and legends do not have to be set again.

To name the graph:

Type	N	(for Name)
Type	C	(for Create)

When prompted for the graph name:

Type   BUDPIE ↵

To save the graph:

Type   S   (for Save)

When prompted for the graph file name:

Type   BUDPIE ↵

The graph has now been saved to a graph file so that it can later be printed, if necessary.

To leave the graph menu:

Type   Q   (for Quit)

To save the pie graph specifications with the worksheet BUDGET:

Press	/	(the command key)
Type	F	(for File)
Type	S	(for Save)

The word BUDGET should appear. To replace the current version of BUDGET:

Press   ↵

When prompted to either Cancel or **R**eplace:

Type   R   (for Replace)

The data specifications and name for the pie graph are now saved with the worksheet.

Creating a Stacked-Bar Graph

The file BUDGET is again used in this exercise. The graph settings saved under BUDBAR contain graph settings for SALES, TOTAL EXPENSES, and GROSS PROFIT. Because the graph settings are already set, they can be used to display the same data as a stacked-bar graph. Only the graph type has to be changed. The newly designated graph will be given a graph name.

To create a stacked-bar graph:

Press	/	(the command key)
Type	G	(for Graph)
Type	T	(for Type)
Type	S	(for Stacked-Bar)

To view the graph:

Type	V	(for View)

Refer to Figure 9–15.

Figure 9–15

The data options and legends need to be altered so that the stacked-bar graph more accurately depicts the data on the worksheet.

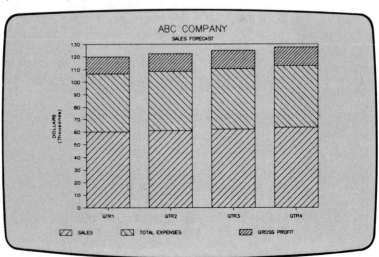

To return to the worksheet:

Press	↵

The graph settings were completed in an earlier exercise; therefore, specifications such as data ranges, titles, and legends are already set. The settings are not appropriate, however, for a stacked-bar graph (it appears that GROSS PROFIT, TOTAL EXPENSES, AND SALES are stacked in a single bar). The data options and legends need to be altered so the stacked-bar graph more accurately depicts the data on the BUDGET worksheet.

To reset data ranges:

Type	R	(for Reset)

When prompted for the ranges to reset:

Type	A
Type	C

To leave the Reset menu:

Type	Q	(for Quit)

To reset range A:

Type	A

When prompted for the first data range:

Move	the cell pointer to cell B18
Press	.
Move	the cell pointer to cell E18 ⏎

Variable A now contains the data for GROSS PROFIT.

Before the changes were made, data ranges A, B, and C represented SALES, TOTAL EXPENSES, and GROSS PROFIT, respectively. The three data ranges added together were not appropriate on a stacked-bar graph. The data was rearranged as follows: data range A was changed to the data for GROSS PROFIT, data range B was left as TOTAL EXPENSES, data range C was cancelled. In this way the stacked-bar stacks ranges A and B (GROSS PROFIT and TOTAL EXPENSES), which adds up to total SALES.

To change the legends:

Type	O	(for Options)
Type	L	(for Legend)
Type	A	

The current legend is SALES. To replace the legend for range A:

Press   the [Esc] key

Type   GROSS PROFIT ⏎

To reset the legend for range C:

Type   L   (for Legend)

Type   C

Press   the [Esc] key ⏎

The Escape key was pressed to cancel the C range.
To return to the previous graph menu:

Type   Q   (for Quit)

To view the graph:

Type   V   (for View)

Note that the data ranges are now appropriate. Data range A (Gross Profit) and data range B (Total Expenses) are stacked and result in a pictorial addition and representation of Sales. A third data range is not needed. Refer to Figure 9–16.

Figure 9–16

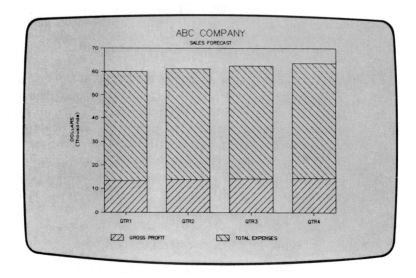

When through viewing the graph:

Press   ↵

To name the graph:

Type   N   (for Name)
Type   C   (for Create)

When prompted for the graph name:

Type   BUDSTBAR ↵

To save the graph:

Type   S   (for Save)

When prompted for the graph file name:

Type   BUDSTBAR ↵

The graph has now been saved to a graph file so that it can later be printed, if necessary.
To leave the graph menu:

Type   Q   (for Quit)

To save the stacked-bar graph specifications with the worksheet BUDGET:

Press   /   (the command key)
Type   F   (for File)
Type   S   (for Save)

The word BUDGET should appear. To replace the current version of BUDGET:

Press   ↵

When prompted to either Cancel or **R**eplace:

Type   R   (for Replace)

The data specifications and name for the stacked-bar graph are now saved with the worksheet.

Creating an XY Graph

XY graphs are basically line graphs that use numeric values for both the X-axis and the Y-axis. To designate an XY graph, retrieve the file UNITPROD (Unit Production) for use in this exercise. Creating the file UNITPROD was listed as an exercise at the end of Chapter Two. Since the file has no graph settings, all graph settings will be created in this exercise.

To designate the graph type:

Press	/	(the command key)
Type	G	(for Graph)
Type	T	(for Type)

When prompted for the graph type:

Type	X	(for XY)

To designate the data for the X-axis:

Type	X

When prompted for the X range:

Move	the cell pointer to cell C7
Press	.
Move	the cell pointer to cell C12 ↵

To designate the data for the Y-axis:

Type	A

When prompted to enter the A range:

Move	the cell pointer to cell D7
Press	.
Move	the cell pointer to cell D12 ↵

An option that would clarify the data points is **Data-Labels**, which can place data labels above each data point:

Type	O	(for Options)
Type	D	(for Data-Labels)
Type	A	
Move	the cell pointer to cell B7	
Press	.	
Move	the cell pointer to cell B12 ⌐	
Type	A	(for Above)

To exit the current menu:

Type	Q	(for Quit)

To enter the first title:

Type	T	(for Titles)
Type	F	(for First)

When prompted to enter the top line of the graph title:

Type	ABC COMPANY ⌐

To enter an X-Axis title:

Type	T	(for Titles)
Type	X	(for X-Axis)

When prompted for the title:

Press	the space bar nine times
Type	UNITS PRODUCED ⌐

Pressing the space bar nine times centers the X-axis title with the "(Thousands)" indicator placed at the X-axis by Lotus 1–2–3.

To enter a Y-Axis title:

Type	T	(for Titles)
Type	Y	(for Y-Axis)

When prompted for the title:

Type   UNITS SOLD ⏎

To exit the current menu:

Type   Q   (for Quit)

To view the graph:

Type   V   (for View)

The graph should look like Figure 9–17. Note that the graph on the screen display and the printed graph may look slightly different since the scale on the printout may vary from the scale on the screen display. For example, the screen's Y axis scale is in increments of 100 (300 . . . 400 . . . 800) while the printout's Y axis scale is in increments of 50 (350 . . . 400 . . . 800). The X axis also has different increments in the screen display and the printed display.

Figure 9–17

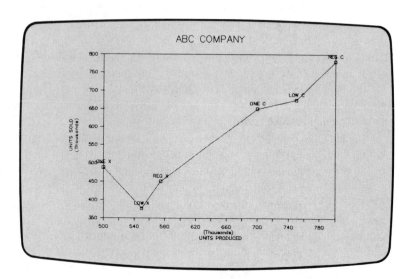

To return to the worksheet after viewing the graph:

Press   ⏎

To exit the current menu:

Type   Q   (for Quit)

The graph settings in this exercise are not saved for later use.

Special Uses for Pie Graphs

A common use for a pie graph is illustrated in the following exercise. If the file UNITPROD is not already in main memory, retrieve the file UNITPROD. To ensure that no previous graph settings will interfere with completing the following exercise, reset any graph settings that may have been created:

Press   /   (the command key)
Type   G   (for Graph)
Type   R   (for Reset)
Type   G   (for Graph)

To designate the graph type:

Type   T   (for Type)
Type   P   (for Pie)

To enter the top line of the graph title:

Type   O   (for Options)
Type   T   (for Titles)
Type   F   (for First)

When prompted for the title:

Type   ABC COMPANY ⏎

To enter a second title:

Type   T   (for Titles)
Type   S   (for Second)

When prompted for the title:

Type   UNITS SOLD ⏎

To exit the current menu:

Type   Q   (for Quit)

To designate the X-Axis labels:

Type   X

When prompted for the data labels:

Move   the cell pointer to cell B7
Press   .
Move   the cell pointer to cell B12 ⏎

To designate the data for the pie graph:

Type   A

When prompted for the data range:

Move   the cell pointer to cell D7
Press   .
Move   the cell pointer to cell D12 ⏎

To view the graph:

Type   V   (for View)

Compare the screen output with Figure 9–18. Note that in some cases data labels are not completely displayed or "wrap around" on the screen, but may print out correctly. If the printout prints incorrectly, the text in the data labels may need to be reduced.

Figure 9–18

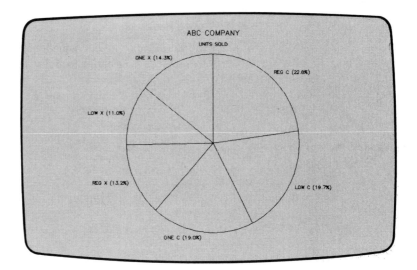

To return to the worksheet after viewing the graph:

Press ↵

To exit the menu:

Type Q (for Quit)

The graph settings in this exercise are not saved for later use.

■ OTHER GRAPH COMMANDS

A summary of commonly used graph commands are included for the user's reference. Tasks such as viewing a particular graph, deleting graph settings, erasing all graphs in a worksheet, erasing graph files, and removing the scale indicator from a graph are discussed.

Viewing the Current Graph

Retrieve the file BUDGET for this exercise. It is assumed that the previous exercises on graphs have been completed. As seen in an earlier exercise, the primary way to view the most current graph in a worksheet is as follows:

Press	/	(the command key)
Type	G	(for Graph)
Type	V	(for View)

The most current graph appears.
To return to the worksheet after viewing the graph:

Press	↵

To exit the current menu:

Type	Q	(for Quit)

Another way to view a graph is to use the [Graph] key (the F10 function key) as follows:

Press	the [Graph] key (the F10 function key)

To return to the worksheet after viewing the graph:

Press	↵

Note that the [Graph] key works only when a menu is not in use.

Selecting the Graph to View

In order to assign two or more graphs to a worksheet, each graph must be named and saved with the worksheet, just as BUDBAR and BUDLINE were two of the graphs named in the BUDGET file.
To choose the graph to view:

Press	/	(the command key)
Type	G	(for Graph)
Type	N	(for Name)
Type	U	(for Use)

At this point, all of the graph names are listed.

Move   the cell pointer to the graph to view

In this example, highlight the name BUDBAR. When BUDBAR is highlighted:

Press   ↵

The graph will appear on the screen (refer to Figure 9–19).

Figure 9–19

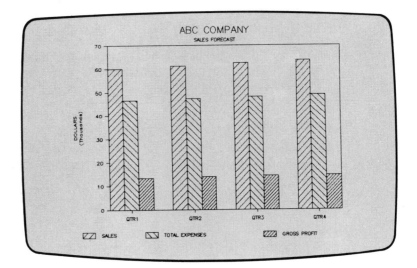

To return to the worksheet after viewing the graph:

Press   ↵

To exit the current menu:

Type   Q   (for Quit)

Note: The following steps give further information about graphs and are not a part of the exercise. If the exercises are completed, graphs that were created earlier may be erased. This will not cause a problem because the graphs are not used again in this book.

Deleting Graph Settings

To erase a named graph that was designated in a worksheet:

Press	/	(the command key)
Type	G	(for Graph)
Type	N	(for Name)
Type	D	(for Delete)

When prompted for the graph to delete:

Move	the cursor to the name of the graph to erase (in this case, BUDLINE)
Press	↵

To exit the menu:

Type	Q	(for Quit)

To permanently delete the graph setting, the BUDGET file would have to be saved and replaced.

Erasing All Graphs in a Worksheet

To erase all graph settings in a worksheet:

Press	/	(the command key)
Type	G	(for Graph)
Type	R	(for Reset)
Type	G	(for Graph)

All graph settings in the file would be erased except for graph settings saved with the Graph Name Create command. To permanently erase the graph settings, the BUDGET file would have to be saved and replaced.

To erase graph names and their assigned settings:

Type	N	(for Name)
Type	R	(for Reset)

To exit the menu:

Type   Q   (for Quit)

To permanently erase the graph settings, the BUDGET file must be saved and replaced.

Erasing Graph Files from the Disk

Even if the BUDGET worksheet file was erased from the disk, any files saved as graph files would remain on the disk. To list graph files on the disk:

Press	/	(the command key)
Type	F	(for File)
Type	L	(for List)
Type	G	(for Graph)

If there are any graph files on the data disks, they will be listed at this point. If there are not, a message will indicate that no graph files are on the disk. Refer to Figure 9–20. To return to the worksheet screen:

Press   ↵

Figure 9–20

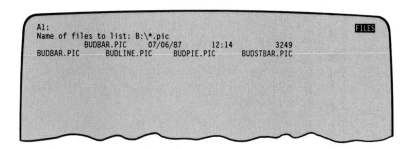

```
A1:                                                                    FILES
Name of files to list: B:\*.pic
            BUDBAR.PIC     07/06/87     12:14        3249
  BUDBAR.PIC      BUDLINE.PIC      BUDPIE.PIC     BUDSTBAR.PIC
```

To erase a graph file:

Press	/	(the command key)
Type	F	(for File)
Type	E	(for Erase)
Type	G	(for Graph)

A list of the graph files appears.

Move	the cell pointer to the graph file to erase (BUDLINE in this case)
Press	⏎

Menu choices of No and Yes appear. To erase the graph file:

Type	Y	(for Yes)

The graph file has been erased from the disk. In order to check if the file has been erased, list the graph files. Refer to the steps in this exercise to list the graph files.

Removing the Scale Indicator from a Graph

The **Graph Options Scale** (Y-Scale or X-Scale) **Indicator** menu option can remove the scale indicator from a graph.

Retrieve the file BUDGET for use in this exercise.

To pick a graph for use:

Press	/	(the command key)
Type	G	(for Graph)
Type	N	(for Name)
Type	U	(for Use)

When prompted for the graph to use:

Move	the cell pointer to BUDBAR ⏎

On the Y scale the word (Thousands) is displayed as the scale indicator. Refer to Figure 9–21.

To return to the worksheet:

Press	⏎

Figure 9–21

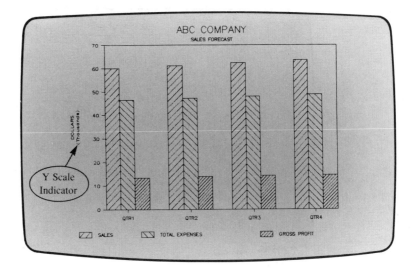

To remove the indicator from the Y Scale, select the following menu options:

Type	O	(for Options)
Type	S	(for Scale)
Type	Y	(for Y-Scale)
Type	I	(for Indicator)
Type	N	(for No)

To exit current menus and view the graph:

Type	Q	(for Quit) *twice*
Type	V	(for View)

The indicator is no longer displayed with the graph. Refer to Figure 9–22.
To return to the worksheet after viewing the graph:

Press	↵

Figure 9–22

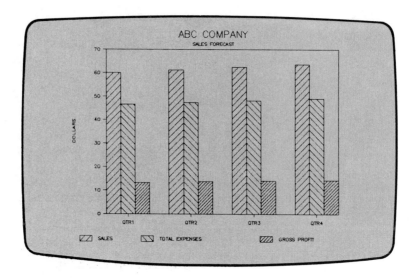

To exit from the menu:

Type   Q   (for Quit)

Printing a Full-Page Graph

To print a full-page graph rather than a half-page graph, choose Settings Image Size Full when using the PrintGraph menu. Select **Q**uit three times to return to the main graph menu. The graph will be printed sideways on a full page. Note that options listed in the Settings menu can affect the appearance of the printed graph.

SUMMARY

Software packages such as 1–2–3 allow the user to integrate graphics with spreadsheets. Creating graphics using spreadsheet data is easy to do, because the data to be graphed does not have to be entered a second time. In fact, if the data on a spreadsheet is changed and the spreadsheet is recalculated, the graph reflects the changes in the data the next time the graph is viewed. Graphic representations of data on a spreadsheet allow the user to use graphs as an aid not only in analyzing spreadsheet data, but in presenting the data to others.

KEY CONCEPTS

A-Range
B-Range
Bar graph
C-Range
D-Range
E-Range
Erasing graphs
F-Range
Graph
Image-Select
Legends
Line graph
Naming a graph

Pie graph
Print-Graph
Saving a graph
Scale indicator
Stacked Bar graph
Titles
Type of graph
Viewing a graph
X-Axis
X-Range
XY graph
Y-Axis

CHAPTER NINE
EXERCISE 1

INSTRUCTIONS: Circle T if the statement is true and F if the statement is false.

T   F   1. A Lotus 1–2–3 graph can contain up to six different data ranges.

T   F   2. To change a bar graph into a line graph, change the **Graph Type** from **Bar** to **Line**.

T   F   3. If numbers are changed on the spreadsheet, the graph will reflect the changes when the graph is viewed again on the screen.

T   F   4. If numbers are changed on the spreadsheet, the changes will be automatically reflected on any graph file that was created from the worksheet previously.

T   F   5. It is possible to create three completely different graphs with data from one worksheet.

T   F   6. If **File Save** is not executed after a graph is made, the graph settings will not be saved.

T   F   7. If a computer is not configured to show graphics on the screen, it is not possible to create and print a Lotus 1–2–3 graph.

T   F   8. A color graph on the screen displays the colors in which the graph will be printed on a color printer or plotter.

T   F   9. A pie graph displays the data in data range A.

T   F   10. An XY graph is different from other Lotus graphs because it graphs data for the X-range.

CHAPTER NINE
EXERCISE 2

INSTRUCTIONS: Explain a typical situation when the following keystrokes or Lotus 1–2–3 commands are used.

Problem 1:	/ **G**raph **A**
Problem 2:	/ **G**raph **N**ame **U**se
Problem 3:	/ **G**raph **V**iew
Problem 4:	/ **G**raph **N**ame **C**reate
Problem 5:	/ **G**raph **O**ptions Legends
Problem 6:	/ **G**raph **O**ptions Titles
Problem 7:	/ **G**raph **O**ptions **D**ata-Labels
Problem 8:	/ **I**mage-Select
Problem 9:	/ **G**raph **T**ype Pie
Problem 10:	**P**rintGraph

CHAPTER NINE
EXERCISE 3
Correcting a Graph

INSTRUCTIONS: The following example illustrates a common error. Follow the instructions below to create the error and answer the questions below.

Clear the screen (use the **Worksheet Erase Y**es command sequence).
In cell A1, type 52 and press ↵.
In cell A2, type 30 and press ↵.
In cell A3, type 48 and press ↵.
Press / Graph A.
Highlight cells A1 through A2 and press ↵.
View the graph.

The screen should appear as follows.

Figure 9–23

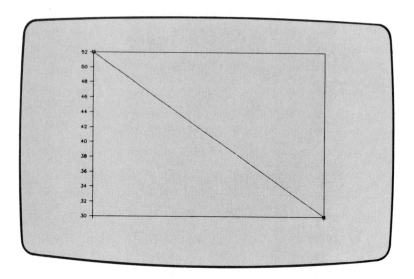

1. How can the graph be changed so that cells A1 through *A3* are graphed as seen in Figure 9–24?

Figure 9–24

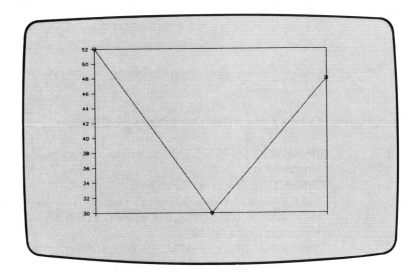

CHAPTER NINE
EXERCISE 4
Creating a Graph

INSTRUCTIONS: Create a graph using the following instructions.

Retrieve the file PRACTICE that was created as an exercise in Chapter Two.
Create a bar graph for REVENUE.
Set the X axis as Year 1 through Year 3, the graph legend as REVENUE and the graph title as ABC COMPANY.
Name the graph GRAPH1.
Save the graph as GRAPH1 for later printing.
Save and replace the file PRACTICE.

When viewed, the graph should appear similar to Figure 9–25 with one difference. The increments for the Y scale on the screen are in fives (0 . . . 5 . . . 30) while the increments for the printout are in twos (0 . . . 2 . . . 30).

Figure 9–25

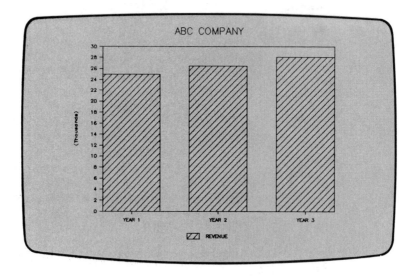

CHAPTER NINE
EXERCISE 5
Printing a Graph

INSTRUCTIONS: Print a graph using the following instructions.

Print the graph GRAPH1 that was created in Exercise 4.

The printout of the graph should appear as seen in Figure 9–25.

CHAPTER NINE
EXERCISE 6
Creating a Graph

INSTRUCTIONS: Create a graph using the following instructions.

Retrieve the file PRACTICE.
Change cell B5 (the first year of REVENUE) from 25000 to 30000.
View the graph (a graph should be visible since graph settings for
GRAPH1 were created in Exercise 5.
Name the graph GRAPH2.
Save the graph as GRAPH2 for later printing.
Do *not* save and replace the file PRACTICE.

Change cell B5 (the first year of REVENUE) from 30000 to 40000.
View the graph.
Name the graph GRAPH3.
Save the graph as GRAPH3 for later printing.
Do *not* save and replace the file PRACTICE.

Note that GRAPH2 and GRAPH3's printouts have different increments
on the Y-axis scale from the screen version of the graph.

These graphs will serve as snapshots of a "what-if" change made to the
spreadsheet where the "what-if" data is not permanently part of the
spreadsheet file. When viewed, GRAPH2 and GRAPH3 should appear
as seen in Figure 9–26.

Figure 9–26
Part 1

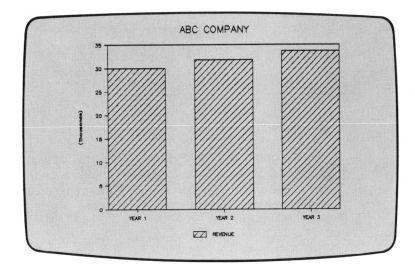

Figure 9–26
Part 2

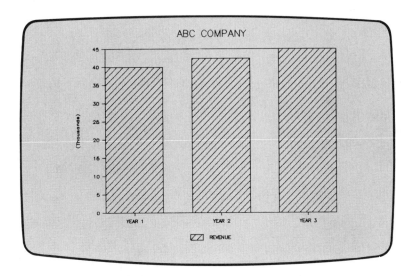

CHAPTER NINE
EXERCISE 7
Printing a Graph

INSTRUCTIONS: Print a graph using the following instructions.

Print the graph files GRAPH2 and GRAPH3 that were created in Exercise 6. When viewed, the graphs should appear as seen in Figure 9–26. The increments in the Y-axis scale on the screen will differ slightly from the increments on the printout.

CHAPTER NINE
EXERCISE 8
Editing a Graph

INSTRUCTIONS: Print a graph using the following instructions.

Retrieve the file PRACTICE. Edit the graph GRAPH1 so that GRAPH1 is a line graph.

Save and replace the file PRACTICE.

Print the file GRAPH1 as a line graph.

The printed graph should appear as seen in Figure 9–27.

Figure 9–27

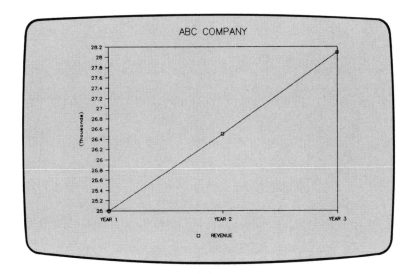

CHAPTER TEN

OVERVIEW OF DATABASE CAPABILITIES

Chapter Overview
Some Basic Definitions
Sorting
    Sorting by a Primary Key
        Specifying the Data Range
        Specifying the Primary Key
        Sorting the Data
    Sorting by a Primary and Secondary Key
        Specifying the Data Range
        Specifying the Primary Key
        Specifying the Secondary Key
        Sorting the Data
Querying
    Querying with a Simple Criteria
        Placing the Criterion on the Spreadsheet
        Placing the Output Range on the Spreadsheet
        Specifying the Input Range through the Menu
        Specifying the Criterion Range through the Menu
        Specifying the Output Range through the Menu
        Performing a Find
        Extracting (Copying) the Desired Fields to the Output Range
    Querying with Multiple Conditions Using #AND#
    Querying with Multiple Conditions Using #OR# and Using the Query (F7) Key
    Querying with Multiple Criteria
Useful Data Query Options
    Using the Query Unique Command
    Using the Query Delete Command
Creating a Frequency Distribution
Graphing a Distribution
Summary
Key Concepts
Exercises

OBJECTIVES

In this chapter, the student will learn to:

- Identify basic database terms
- Sort data on a spreadsheet
- Query for desired data on a spreadsheet
- Use additional Data Query options
- Use the Data Distribution command

■ CHAPTER OVERVIEW

Lotus 1–2–3 can perform **database** capabilities such as sorting data and querying on data in a spreadsheet. Suppose that the information for all employees of a company is entered into a single spreadsheet. To sort the names by division, the user can use the **Data Sort** command sequence. To generate a report listing all employees who had been with the company for over 10 years, the user can use the **Data Query** command sequence. However, 1–2–3 cannot perform database capabilities as extensively as a database management system like dBASE III PLUS,[1] R:BASE System V,[2] or Paradox Release 2.0.[3] This chapter discusses the database capabilities of 1–2–3.

■ BASIC DEFINITIONS

Some of the basic terms used in database management are **field, record, file,** and **key.**

A **field** is a collection of characters that are grouped together. In 1–2–3, each field is contained in a separate column within the database, or file. An example would be a person's last name. A **field title** is the term used to describe each field. For example, the title LAST NAME might be the field title for the field in which a person's last name is listed. In 1–2–3, each field title is listed in the column containing the field and is located in the cell *immediately* above the first listed field.

A **record** is a group of data fields that are combined in some logical pattern. For example, the personnel record for individuals in a company might include the individual's social security number, last name, first name, middle initial, department in which the individual works, etc. In 1–2–3, each record is listed as a separate row.

A **file** is a group of records that are combined together. For example, the personnel file would include all of the personnel records.

---

1. dBASE III PLUS is a registered trademark of Ashton-Tate; Culver City, California.
2. R:BASE System V is a registered trademark of Microrim, Inc.; Bellevue, Washington.
3. Paradox Release 2.0 is a registered trademark of Ansa Software, a Borland Company; Belmont, California.

A **key** is a specific field that can be used for distinguishing between records. For example, the social security number of employees is a unique number for individuals and can be used as a key for the personnel file.

■ SORTING

Sometimes the Lotus 1–2–3 user may need to sort data in order. For example, it may be necessary to sort transactions in order by type of transaction. The following exercises demonstrate how to sort information in 1–2–3.

Sorting by a Primary Key

Create and save the file ABCSAL for use in this chapter. Refer to Figure 10–1 as a guide when creating the file.

Figure 10–1
Part 1

The file ABCSAL

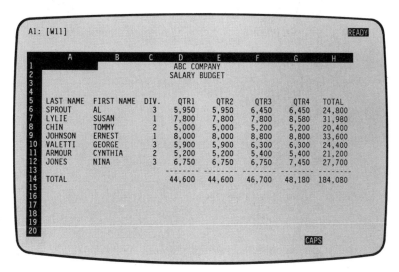

```
A1: [W11]                                                          READY

           A          B        C      D        E        F        G        H
 1                                     ABC COMPANY
 2                                     SALARY BUDGET
 3
 4
 5   LAST NAME  FIRST NAME  DIV.    QTR1     QTR2     QTR3     QTR4    TOTAL
 6   SPROUT     AL           3     5,950    5,950    6,450    6,450   24,800
 7   LYLIE      SUSAN        1     7,800    7,800    7,800    8,580   31,980
 8   CHIN       TOMMY        2     5,000    5,000    5,200    5,200   20,400
 9   JOHNSON    ERNEST       1     8,000    8,000    8,800    8,800   33,600
10   VALETTI    GEORGE       3     5,900    5,900    6,300    6,300   24,400
11   ARMOUR     CYNTHIA      2     5,200    5,200    5,400    5,400   21,200
12   JONES      NINA         3     6,750    6,750    6,750    7,450   27,700
13                                --------  --------  --------  --------  --------
14   TOTAL                        44,600   44,600   46,700   48,180  184,080
15
16
17
18
19
20                                                                   CAPS
```

Figure 10–1
Part 2

Cell Formulas for the file ABCSAL.

```
D1:  '   ABC COMPANY
D2:  '  SALARY BUDGET
A5:  [W11] 'LAST NAME
B5:  [W12] 'FIRST NAME
C5:  [W4] ^DIV.
D5:  "QTR1
E5:  "QTR2
F5:  "QTR3
G5:  "QTR4
H5:  ^TOTAL
A6:  [W11] 'SPROUT
B6:  [W12] 'AL
C6:  [W4] 3
D6:  5950
E6:  5950
F6:  6450
G6:  6450
H6:  @SUM(D6..G6)
A7:  [W11] 'LYLIE
B7:  [W12] 'SUSAN
C7:  [W4] 1
D7:  7800
E7:  7800
F7:  7800
G7:  8580
H7:  @SUM(D7..G7)
A8:  [W11] 'CHIN
B8:  [W12] 'TOMMY
C8:  [W4] 2
D8:  5000
E8:  5000
F8:  5200
G8:  5200
H8:  @SUM(D8..G8)
A9:  [W11] 'JOHNSON
B9:  [W12] 'ERNEST
C9:  [W4] 1
D9:  8000
E9:  8000
F9:  8800
G9:  8800
H9:  @SUM(D9..G9)
A10: [W11] 'VALETTI
B10: [W12] 'GEORGE
C10: [W4] 3
D10: 5900
E10: 5900
F10: 6300
```

Figure 10–1
Part 3

Cell Formulas for the file ABCSAL.

```
G10: 6300
H10: @SUM(TOTAL)
A11: [W11] 'ARMOUR
B11: [W12] 'CYNTHIA
C11: [W4] 2
D11: 5200
E11: 5200
F11: 5400
G11: 5400
H11: @SUM(D11..G11)
A12: [W11] 'JONES
B12: [W12] 'NINA
C12: [W4] 3
D12: 6750
E12: 6750
F12: 6750
G12: 7450
H12: @SUM(D12..G12)
D13: ' --------
E13: ' --------
F13: ' --------
G13: ' --------
H13: ' --------
A14: [W11] 'TOTAL
D14: @SUM(D5..D13)
E14: @SUM(E5..E13)
F14: @SUM(F5..F13)
G14: @SUM(G5..G13)
H14: @SUM(H5..H13)
```

Specifying the Data Range

In this exercise, records in the file ABCSAL will be sorted so that the records in the file are placed in order by division. Before sorting the spreadsheet, enter the menu options and specify the data range. The **data range** indicates where the database records are located on the spreadsheet. To specify the data range:

Press	/	(the command key)
Type	D	(for Data)
Type	S	(for Sort)
Type	D	(for Data-Range)

When prompted for the data range:

Move	the cell pointer to cell A6
Press	.
Move	the cell pointer to cell H12 ↵

All of the records in cells A6 through H12 comprise the data range. Note that only the records and *not* the field titles (LAST NAME, FIRST NAME, . . .) are included in the data range. If the field titles are included, they will also be sorted. Another common error made is to highlight only the column that needs to be sorted when indicating the data range. If this error occurs, only the column specified in the data range will be sorted; none of the data in the adjacent columns (e.g., LAST NAME, FIRST NAME) will be sorted with the appropriate division.

Specifying the Primary Key

To specify the primary key:

Type	P	(for Primary-Key)
Move	the cell pointer to cell C5 ⏎ (or any other cell in column C)	

The **primary key** indicates the column containing the field by which the database should sort the records. Since column C contains the data to sort by (in this example, by division), any cell in the column containing the division numbers can be the primary key. When prompted for the desired sort order:

Type	A	(for Ascending) ⏎

The two options for sorting are Ascending and Descending. **Ascending** order can refer to alphabetic order (from A to Z) or numerical order (from the smallest number to the largest number). **Descending** order can refer to reverse alphabetic order (from Z to A) or numerical order (from the largest number to the smallest number).

Sorting the Data

To begin the sort procedure:

Type	G	(for Go)

The records should be sorted in order by division number. The screen should look like the final illustration in Figure 10–2. Figure 10–2 displays the entire sort procedure.

*Figure 10–2
Part 1*

Step 1 of the Sort Procedure: Specify the Data-Range

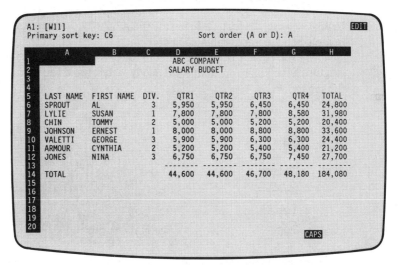

*Figure 10–2
Part 2*

Step 2 of the Sort Procedure: Specify the Sort Column and the Sort Order

```
A1: [W11]                                                    EDIT
Primary sort key: C6              Sort order (A or D): A

       A          B          C      D        E        F        G        H
1                                       ABC COMPANY
2                                       SALARY BUDGET
3
4
5    LAST NAME  FIRST NAME  DIV.   QTR1     QTR2     QTR3     QTR4     TOTAL
6    SPROUT     AL           3     5,950    5,950    6,450    6,450    24,800
7    LYLIE      SUSAN        1     7,800    7,800    7,800    8,580    31,980
8    CHIN       TOMMY        2     5,000    5,000    5,200    5,200    20,400
9    JOHNSON    ERNEST       1     8,000    8,000    8,800    8,800    33,600
10   VALETTI    GEORGE       3     5,900    5,900    6,300    6,300    24,400
11   ARMOUR     CYNTHIA      2     5,200    5,200    5,400    5,400    21,200
12   JONES      NINA         3     6,750    6,750    6,750    7,450    27,700
13                                 -------- -------- -------- -------- --------
14   TOTAL                         44,600   44,600   46,700   48,180   184,080
15
16
17
18
19
20                                                              CAPS
```

*Figure 10–2
Part 3*

Step 3 of the Sort Procedure: Select **Go** from the Sort Menu to Sort the
Database

```
A1: [W11]                                                        READY

         A          B        C      D        E        F        G       H
  1                                 ABC COMPANY
  2                                 SALARY BUDGET
  3
  4
  5    LAST NAME  FIRST NAME  DIV.   QTR1     QTR2     QTR3     QTR4   TOTAL
  6    JOHNSON    ERNEST       1     8,000    8,000    8,800    8,800  33,600
  7    LYLIE      SUSAN        1     7,800    7,800    7,800    8,580  31,980
  8    CHIN       TOMMY        2     5,000    5,000    5,200    5,200  20,400
  9    ARMOUR     CYNTHIA      2     5,200    5,200    5,400    5,400  21,200
 10    VALETTI    GEORGE       3     5,900    5,900    6,300    6,300  24,400
 11    SPROUT     AL           3     5,950    5,950    6,450    6,450  24,800
 12    JONES      NINA         3     6,750    6,750    6,750    7,450  27,700
 13                                --------  -------- -------- -------- --------
 14    TOTAL                        44,600   44,600   46,700   48,180 184,080
 15
 16
 17
 18
 19
 20                                                                    CAPS
```

Sorting by Primary and Secondary Keys

In this exercise, the records in the the file ABCSAL are sorted so that the names appear
in alphabetical order within each division.

This exercise has been written with the assumption that the results of the previous
exercise have just been completed and that the sorted records are currently visible on
the screen.

Specifying the Data Range

To specify the data range:

Press	/	(the command key)
Type	D	(for Data)
Type	S	(for Sort)
Type	D	(for Data-Range)

When prompted for the data range, make sure that cells A6 through H12 are highlighted
as a result of completing the previous exercise. If they are not, highlight cell A6 through
H12 at this time. With cells A6 through H12 highlighted:

    Press   ↵

Specifying the Primary Key

A common error at this point is to indicate that the Last Names column is the primary key. This would not be correct. In this case, when the database is sorted, the last names would be sorted correctly, but the divisions would be out of order. The Division column will remain the primary key so that the database is sorted *primarily* by division. The Last Name column will be specified as the **secondary** key so that the database is sorted *secondarily* by last name. This will cause the last names to appear in alphabetical order within each division. To specify the primary key:

Type   P   (for Primary-Key)

Cell C5 should be highlighted as a result of the previous exercise. If it is not, highlight cell C5 by moving the cell pointer to cell C5 at this time. With cell C5 highlighted:

Press   ↵

When prompted for the sort order, make sure that the letter A (for Ascending order) appears. The A should appear as a result of being selected in the previous exercise. If it does not, type A at this time. With A specified as the sort order:

Press   ↵

Specifying the Secondary Key

To specify the secondary key:

Type   S   (for Secondary-Key)
Move   the cell pointer to cell A5 ↵ (or any other cell in
                  column A)

Since column A contains the data to sort by (in this example, by LAST NAME), any cell in column A can be specified as the Secondary Key.
When prompted for the desired sort order:

Type   A   (for Ascending) ↵

Sorting the Data

To begin the sort procedure:

Type   G   (for Go)

The database should now be sorted so that the last names are in alphabetical order by division. The screen should look like Figure 10–3.

Figure 10–3   Sorting by Primary and Secondary Key

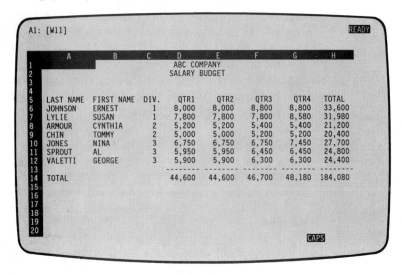

Note that Lotus 1–2–3 has only two sort keys—the Primary Key and the Secondary Key. Database packages (e.g., dBASE III PLUS, RBASE, Paradox) specifically designed for manipulating information in databases are a more viable option if extensive sorting features are needed. This is especially true if the user has large databases containing thousands of records. Note also that it is possible to translate records that were created and manipulated from a database package into Lotus 1–2–3 for spreadsheet analysis.

▉ QUERYING

At times the 1–2–3 user may need to perform a **query,** which is the process of searching through a file and selecting items based upon specific criteria. For example, one may wish to select all stores in a database file that have revenues in excess of $75,000 a year. The following exercises demonstrate how to perform queries in 1–2–3.

Querying with a Simple Criteria

In this exercise, the file ABCSAL will be queried to find individuals in the file that have a total salary greater than $25,000.

Retrieve the original file ABCSAL for use in this exercise using the **File Retrieve** command sequence. The results of the previous exercises do not need to be saved.

Placing the Criterion on the Spreadsheet

The query procedure in Lotus 1–2–3 requires that the **criterion** be placed somewhere on the spreadsheet. The criterion must consist of two cells. The first cell specifies the column heading (field title) which contains the data field relevant to the query (in this case, the relevant data field concerning salaries is under the field title TOTAL). The second line of the criterion must consist of a formula or line of data which specifies what the actual query is. To specify the criterion for the query:

Move		the cell pointer to cell H5 (the word TOTAL)
Press	/	(the command key)
Type	C	(for Copy)

When prompted for the range to copy FROM:

Press	↵

When prompted for the range to copy TO:

Move	the cell pointer to cell I5
Press	↵

To see the results of the copy command:

Move	the cell pointer to cell I5

The word TOTAL in the criterion must be listed exactly the way it is specified in the spreadsheet. It does not matter if the label is listed in lowercase or uppercase letters or whether a label prefix (^," or ') was used. However, TOTAL must match the field title TOTAL character for character; if an additional space is included anywhere in the cell, the query will not be performed. For example, TOTALS would not render the correct results because the S in TOTALS is not present in the field title in the database (in cell H5). To avoid any problems, use the Copy command. To indicate the second line of the criterion:

Move	the cell pointer to cell I6
Type	+
Move	the cell pointer to cell H6
Type	25000 ↵

The two cells required for the criterion—the field name (TOTAL) and the condition (+H6>25000) have been entered. (H6 is the first field in the column under TOTAL.) In this example, the criterion indicates that the query will be for cells under the field title TOTAL that contain data greater than 25000.

The number 0 appears in cell I6. This is not significant in terms of performing a query; 1–2–3 simply tested the condition +H6>25000 to see if cell H6 was greater than 25000. Since H3 contains 24,800, the test was false and a 0 was placed in cell I6. If the condition was true, the number 1 would have appeared in cell I6.

An optional step is to format cell I6 so that the formula, or criterion, is displayed rather than a 0 or 1. To format the cell to show the formula:

Move		the cell pointer to cell I6 (if it is not already there)
Press	/	(the command key)
Type	R	(for Range)
Type	F	(for Format)
Type	T	(for Text)

When prompted for the range to format:

Press	↵

Cell I6 now displays +H6>2500, which is not the complete formula.

In order to show the complete criterion, widen column A:

Press	/	(the command)
Type	W	(for Worksheet)
Type	C	(for Column)
Type	S	(for Set-Width)

When prompted for the column width:

Press	the right arrow key ↵

The formula +H6>25000 is now fully displayed.

Documenting the criterion is an optional step. To document where the criterion is located:

Move	the cell pointer to cell I3
Type	CRITERION ↵

Placing the Output Range on the Spreadsheet

Once the records matching the criterion have been located, it is possible to copy these records to another part of the worksheet. By specifying an output range, the desired records can be analyzed and manipulated without disturbing the database in which the records are contained.

In this exercise, the fields for the LAST NAME, FIRST NAME, and TOTAL for each record that satisfies the criterion (the amount under TOTAL is greater than $25,000) will be copied to another part of the worksheet. The field titles will be referred to as the **output range.** The records that match the criterion will be copied or "output" to the columns immediately beneath the output range. As illustrated by this example, note that column titles can be specified so that the entire records do not have to be copied; in this case, only the LAST NAME, FIRST NAME, and TOTAL will be copied. The information for the four quarters will not be copied.

To specify the fields to copy, the field titles from the spreadsheet must be copied to another area of the spreadsheet. The field titles in the output range must match the field titles in the spreadsheet character for character. For this reason, the copy command will be used. To specify the LAST NAME and FIRST NAME fields as two of the fields to output:

Move		the cell pointer to cell A5 (the words LAST NAME)
Press	/	(the command key)
Type	C	(for Copy)

When prompted for the range to copy FROM:

Move	the cell pointer to cell B5 (the words FIRST NAME) ↵

When prompted for the range to copy TO:

Move	the cell pointer to cell J5 ↵

To widen column J so that the column is wide enough to display all last names (an optional step):

Move		the cell pointer to cell J5 (or any other cell in column J)
Press	/	(the command key)
Type	W	(for Worksheet)
Type	C	(for Column)
Type	S	(for Set-Width)

When prompted for the column width:

Type	11 ↵

To widen column K so that the column is wide enough to display all first names (an optional step):

Move	the cell pointer to cell K5 (or any other cell in column K)	
Press	/	(the command key)
Type	W	(for Worksheet)
Type	C	(for Column)
Type	S	(for Set-Width)

When prompted for the column width:

Type   12 ↵

To specify the TOTAL field as another field to output:

Move	the cell pointer to cell H5	
Press	/	(the command key)
Type	C	(for Copy)

When prompted for the range to copy FROM:

Press   ↵

When prompted for the range to copy TO:

Move   the cell pointer to cell L5 ↵

To document where the output ranges are located (an optional step):

Move	the cell pointer to cell J3
Type	OUTPUT ↵

To copy the documentation OUTPUT to cells K3 and L3:

Press	/	(the command key)
Type	C	(for Copy)

When prompted for the range to copy FROM:

Press   ↵

Cell J3 has been selected as the range to copy. When prompted for the range to copy TO:

Move	the cell pointer to cell K3
Press	.
Move	the cell pointer to cell L3 ⌐

To see the results of the copy command:

Move	the cell pointer to cell L3

Documentation is optional; OUTPUT documents where the output range is located on the spreadsheet. The screen should look like Figure 10–4.

Figure 10–4

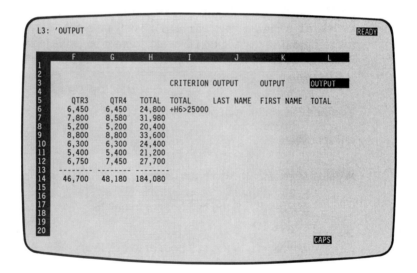

Specifying the Input Range through the Menu

Now that the criterion range and output range have been entered on the spreadsheet (see Step 1 in Figure 10–5), the following steps will illustrate how to access the menu and indicate through the Lotus 1–2–3 menu options where the records, criterion, and output range are located on the worksheet.

First, indicate the input range. The **input range** is the term for the field titles and data records located on the worksheet.

To specify the input range:

Press	/	(the command key)
Type	D	(for Data)
Type	Q	(for Query)
Type	I	(for Input)

When prompted to indicate the Input range:

Move	the cell pointer to cell A5
Press	.
Move	the cell pointer to cell H12 ↵

See Step 2 in Figure 10–5. Note that the input range includes the field titles (LAST NAME, FIRST NAME, . . .). If there are two or more lines of field titles, include only the bottom row in the input range and use only the words in the bottom line as the field titles. Remember that the first data record must be in the line immediately under the field titles without any rows separating the field title from the first record.

Specifying the Criterion Range through the Menu

To specify where the criterion is placed:

Type	C	(for Criterion)

When prompted for the Criterion range:

Move	the cell pointer to cell I5
Press	.
Move	the cell pointer to cell I6 ↵

See Step 3 in Figure 10–5. Cells I5 (TOTAL) and I6 (+H4>25000) make up one criterion.

Specifying the Output Range through the Menu

The following steps will show how to find and then copy the desired fields from the records that fit the criterion to another area on the spreadsheet. To indicate where to copy these records, the Output Range must be specified. To specify the Output range:

Type	O (for Output)
Move	the cell pointer to cell J5
Press	.
Move	the cell pointer to cell L5 ↵

See Step 4 in Figure 10–5.

Performing a Find

The **F**ind command highlights all records that fit the criterion specified. To determine whether the criterion has been specified correctly, the following steps demonstrate how to perform a "Find" that will locate and highlight the records in the database that match the specified criterion. To perform the "Find" procedure:

Type	F (for Find)

The first record that should be highlighted is that of SUSAN LYLIE on row 7. Since her salary total is 31,980 in column H, her salary total satisfies the criterion (being greater than $25,000).

To move to the next record that matches the criterion:

Press	the down arrow key

The record of ERNEST JOHNSON should be highlighted because the salary total is $33,600 and this amount matches the criterion.

To move to the next record that matches the criterion:

Press	the down arrow key

The record for NINA JONES is highlighted.

Press	the down arrow key

Lotus 1–2–3 "beeps" when no more records are in the remainder of the database that satisfy the criterion (not because Nina Jones is the last record in the database).

To exit from "FIND" mode:

Press	↵

The Data Query menu should be visible at the top of the screen.

Extracting (Copying) the Desired Fields to the Output Range

After the Input Range, the Criterion range, and the Output range were input on the worksheet and specified in the **Data Query** menu, the **F**ind option verified that the Criterion and Input ranges were set correctly. Lotus 1–2–3 located only the records in the database (input range) that matched the criterion. The records that matched the criterion can be copied to the area below the specified Output Range using the Extract menu option. Only the fields specified in the Output Range will be copied. Note that although the name of the menu option that will be used is Extract, the fields are not really *extracted*—they are *copied*; in other words, the fields are *not* omitted from the original database/spreadsheet.

To copy the desired fields to the output range:

Type   E   (for Extract)

To exit the Data Query menu:

Type   Q   (for Quit)

The last name, first name, and total are now listed for the specified criteria. The worksheet should look like the final result displayed in Step 5 of Figure 10–5. Figure 10–5 displays the entire query procedure.

Figure 10–5
Part 1

Step 1 of the Query Procedure: Enter the Criterion and Output Settings on the Spreadsheet

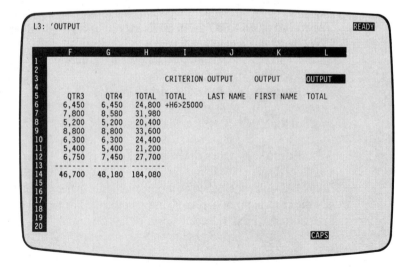

Figure 10–5
Part 2

Step 2 of the Query Procedure: Specify the Input Range through the Menu

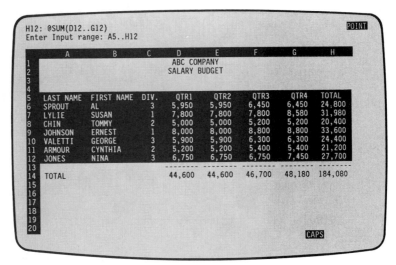

Figure 10–5
Part 3

Step 3 of the Query Procedure: Specify the Criterion Range through the Menu

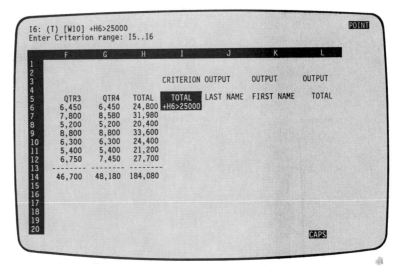

Figure 10–5
Part 4

Step 4 of the Query Procedure: Specify the Output Range through the Menu

```
L5: ^TOTAL                                                          POINT
Enter Output range: J5..L5

           F        G        H        I        J         K         L
 1
 2
 3                                  CRITERION OUTPUT    OUTPUT    OUTPUT
 4
 5         QTR3     QTR4     TOTAL    TOTAL  LAST NAME FIRST NAME   TOTAL
 6         6,450    6,450    24,800  +H6>25000
 7         7,800    8,580    31,980
 8         5,200    5,200    20,400
 9         8,800    8,800    33,600
10         6,300    6,300    24,400
11         5,400    5,400    21,200
12         6,750    7,450    27,700
13        --------  -------  --------
14        46,700   48,180   184,080
15
16
17
18
19
20                                                              CAPS
```

Figure 10–5
Part 5

Step 5 of the Query Procedure: Select Extract from the Menu to Extract the
Desired Records

```
L5: 'OUTPUT                                                         READY

           F        G        H        I        J         K         L
 1
 2
 3                                  CRITERION OUTPUT    OUTPUT    OUTPUT
 4
 5         QTR3     QTR4     TOTAL    TOTAL  LAST NAME FIRST NAME   TOTAL
 6         6,450    6,450    24,800  +H6>25000 LYLIE   SUSAN      31,980
 7         7,800    8,580    31,980            JOHNSON ERNEST     33,600
 8         5,200    5,200    20,400            JONES   NINA       27,700
 9         8,800    8,800    33,600
10         6,300    6,300    24,400
11         5,400    5,400    21,200
12         6,750    7,450    27,700
13        --------  -------  --------
14        46,700   48,180   184,080
15
16
17
18
19
20                                                              CAPS
```

Printing the Worksheet Using Condensed Print

To set the print range:

Press	/	(the command key)
Type	P	(for Print)
Type	P	(for Printer)
Type	R	(for Range)

When prompted for the print range:

Move	the cell pointer to cell A1
Press	.
Move	the cell pointer to cell L14 ↵

To set the appropriate code for condensed print (assuming that an Epson or Epson-compatible printer is being used—the code differs for other printers):

Type	O	(for Options)
Type	S	(for Setup)

When prompted for the setup string:

Type	\015 ↵

Because condensed print allows more characters per line, the margins need to be expanded. To change the margins:

Type	M	(for Margins)
Type	L	(for Left)

To set the left margin at 1:

Type	1 ↵

To set the right margin:

Type	M	(for Margins)
Type	R	(for Right)

To set the right margin at 132:

Type   132 ⏎

If the right margin is not changed past 80, the printout will not be correct. 132 is selected becuase this is the maximum number of characters that can be printed on a 8.5 inch wide piece of paper. To leave the Print Options menu:

Type   Q   (for Quit)

The primary Print menu should now be displayed. Make sure the printer is on and the paper is properly aligned. To print the spreadsheet:

Type   A   (for Align)
Type   G   (for Go)

To eject the printed page and an additional page (if necessary):

Type   P   (for Page) *twice*

To return the setup string back to the original setup:

Type   O   (for Options)
Type   S   (for Setup)

To erase the current setup string:

Press   the [Esc] key ⏎

To leave the print menu:

Type   Q   (for Quit) *twice*

The printout of the worksheet in condensed print should look like Figure 10–6.

Figure 10–6

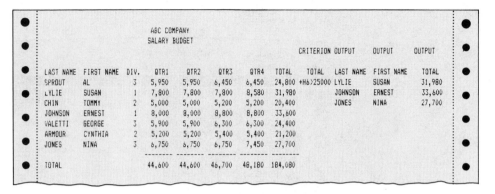

```
                        ABC COMPANY
                        SALARY BUDGET
                                                           CRITERION OUTPUT      OUTPUT      OUTPUT

  LAST NAME  FIRST NAME  DIV.    QTR1     QTR2     QTR3     QTR4    TOTAL    TOTAL  LAST NAME  FIRST NAME    TOTAL
  SPROUT     AL           3     5,950    5,950    6,450    6,450   24,800  +H6>25000 LYLIE     SUSAN        31,980
  LYLIE      SUSAN        1     7,800    7,800    7,800    8,580   31,980            JOHNSON   ERNEST       33,600
  CHIN       TOMMY        2     5,000    5,000    5,200    5,200   20,400            JONES     NINA         27,700
  JOHNSON    ERNEST       1     8,000    8,000    8,800    8,800   33,600
  VALETTI    GEORGE       3     5,900    5,900    6,300    6,300   24,400
  ARMOUR     CYNTHIA      2     5,200    5,200    5,400    5,400   21,200
  JONES      NINA         3     6,750    6,750    6,750    7,450   27,700
                                -------- -------- -------- -------- --------
  TOTAL                        44,600   44,600   46,700   48,180  184,080
```

Querying with Multiple Conditions Using #AND#

In this exercise, the criterion set in the previous exercise will be reset so that the criterion contains multiple conditions. In this example, the file ABCSAL will be queried to find individuals in the file that have a total salary between 20,000 and 22,000, including any salaries that are exactly 20,000 or 22,000. To perform this query, the logical operator #AND# will be used to combine two conditions.

Assuming that the previous exercise has been completed and is still visible on the screen, complete the following problem.

Changing the Current Criterion to the Desired Criterion

In this exercise, the current criterion will be changed from +H6>25000 to +H6>=20000#AND#H6<=22000. To change the criterion:

> **Move** the cell pointer to cell I6
>
> **Type** +H6>=20000#AND#H6<=22000 ↵

(The *first* line of the criterion (in cell I5—TOTAL) will remain the same).

To see the entire formula, column I could be widened using the **Worksheet Column Set-Width** command sequence. However, this step is optional and will *not* be done in this exercise. The entire formula in the criterion does not have to be visible on the screen in order to perform a query. The entire formula can be viewed by placing the cell pointer in cell I6 and looking at the control panel, which shows the contents of a highlighted cell. Assuming that the cell pointer is in cell I6, the screen should look like Figure 10–7.

Figure 10–7   The Criterion is Changed (the Results of the Previous Query Extract are
                       Still on the Screen)

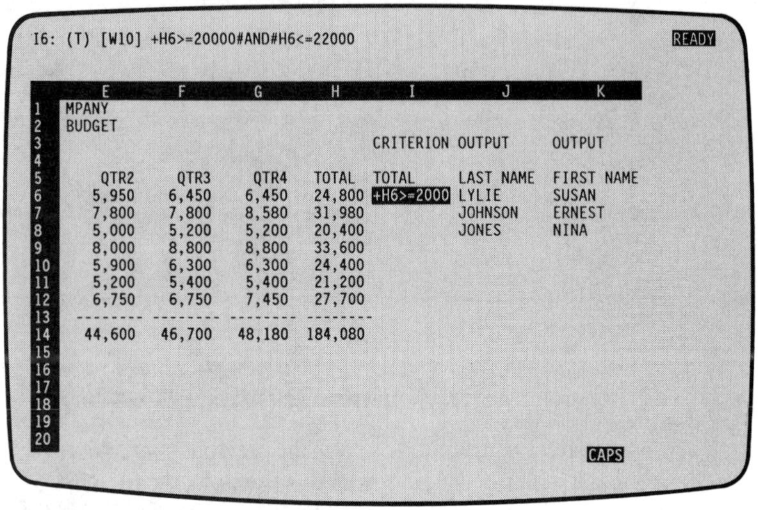

```
  I6: (T) [W10] +H6>=20000#AND#H6<=22000                           READY

          E        F        G        H       I        J          K
  1   MPANY
  2   BUDGET
  3                                       CRITERION OUTPUT     OUTPUT
  4
  5      QTR2     QTR3     QTR4    TOTAL   TOTAL    LAST NAME  FIRST NAME
  6     5,950    6,450    6,450   24,800  +H6>=2000 LYLIE      SUSAN
  7     7,800    7,800    8,580   31,980            JOHNSON    ERNEST
  8     5,000    5,200    5,200   20,400            JONES      NINA
  9     8,000    8,800    8,800   33,600
 10     5,900    6,300    6,300   24,400
 11     5,200    5,400    5,400   21,200
 12     6,750    6,750    7,450   27,700
 13   -------- -------- -------- --------
 14    44,600   46,700   48,180  184,080
 15
 16
 17
 18
 19
 20                                                   CAPS
```

In the previous exercise, the output range, input range, and criterion range were set. Although the criterion now being used is different, the *range* where the criterion is located is the same. To perform the query extract with the new criteria:

Press	/	(the command key)
Type	D	(for Data)
Type	Q	(for Query)
Type	E	(for Extract)

The desired data is now listed. Note that the data in the output range from the previous exercise using **Data Query Extract** was deleted completely and replaced with the data for the current **Data Query Extract**.

To exit the current menu:

Type	Q	(for Quit)

To see all of the extracted data on the screen:

Move	the cursor to cell L7

The screen should look like Figure 10–8.

Figure 10–8   After executing the Query Extract Command, the Results of the Extract
Procedure Using the New Criterion are Visible in the Output Range

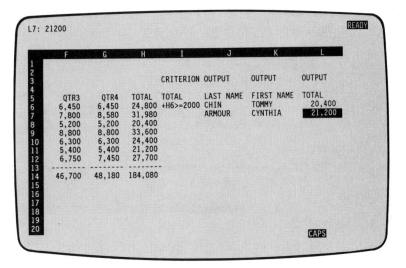

Querying with Multiple Conditions Using #OR# and Using the QUERY (F7) Key

Assuming that the results of the previous exercise are still on the screen, complete the following problem.

In this exercise, the file ABCSAL will be queried to find individuals that have a salary less than $22,000 or greater than $30,000 using the logical operator #OR#. The QUERY key (the [F7] function key) will be demonstrated as an alternative to using the **Data Query Extract** command sequence.

Changing the Current Criterion to the Desired Criterion

In this exercise, the current criterion will be changed from +H6>=20000#AND# H6<=22000 to +H6<22000#OR#H6>30000. To change the criterion:

Move	the cell pointer to cell I6
Type	+H6<22000#OR#H6>30000 ↵

(The *first* line of the criterion (in cell I5—TOTAL) will remain the same). Column I may be widened to see the entire formula using the Worksheet Column Set-Width command sequence. This step is optional and will *not* be done in this particular exercise. Because the same output range, input range, and criterion range that were set in a previous exercise will be used, they do not have to be reset. Although the criterion being used is different, the *range* where the criterion is located is the same. Because all of the ranges have been previously set, an alternative to performing the query through the menu can be used. Instead of pressing / **Data Query Extract**, the QUERY key (the [F7] function key) can be used. Providing that the output range, input range, and criterion range were previously set, pressing the Query key (the [F7] key) will perform a query extract and extract records that match the criterion to the output range. To perform a query extract using the new criteria:

Press   the QUERY key   (the [F7] key)

The desired data is now listed. Note that the data from the previous Data Query Extract exercise was deleted completely and replaced with data for the current query. Assuming that the cell pointer is in cell I6, the screen should look like Figure 10–9.

Figure 10–9

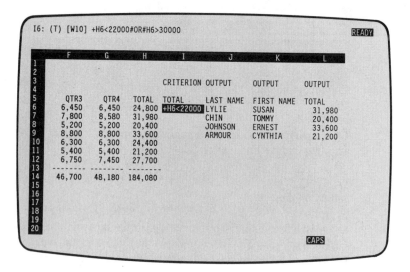

Querying with Multiple Criteria

In this exercise, the file ABCSAL will be queried to find individuals in the file that have a salary less than 25,000 and that are also in Division 3. Assuming that the results of the previous exercise are still on the screen, complete the following problem.

Changing the Current Criterion to the Desired Criterion

In this exercise, the current criterion +H6>=20000#AND#H6<=22000 will be changed to +H6<25000 (the first line of the criterion (TOTAL in cell I5) will remain the same) and will serve as the *first* criterion. A *second* criterion (DIV. and 3) will appear in cells J5 and J6, respectively. To change the criterion under TOTAL:

Move	the cell pointer to cell I6 (if the cursor is not already there)
Type	+H6<25000 ↵

(The *first* line of the criterion (in cell I5—TOTAL) will remain the same).

To insert a column so that the criterion for the desired division can be added:

Move	the cursor to cell J6 (or any other cell in column J)	
Press	/	(the command key)
Type	W	(for Worksheet)
Type	I	(for Insert)
Type	C	(for Column)

When prompted for the column insert range:

Press	↵

A blank column has now been inserted in the worksheet for column J. To enter the new criterion:

Move	the cursor to cell J5
Type	DIV. ↵

As an alternative to copying DIV. from cell C5, DIV. can be typed in cell J5 exactly the way it appears in cell C5.

Move	the cursor to cell J6
Type	3 ↵

To document the new set of criterion (an optional step):

Move	the cursor to cell J3
Type	CRITERION ↵

To widen column J by one space to see the criterion more easily:

Press	/	(the command key)
Type	W	(for Worksheet)
Type	C	(for Column)
Type	S	(for Set-Width)
Press	the right arrow key once ↵	

To select the proper criterion for the query:

Press	/	(the command key)
Type	D	(for Data)
Type	Q	(for Query)
Type	C	(for Criterion)

Notice that only the criterion in column I (cells I5 and I6) are highlighted from a previous exercise. Since the new criterion was placed in cells J5 and J6, these cells need to be highlighted also before performing a query for the desired data. To include the new criterion in the Criterion Range setting:

Press   the right arrow one time

Cells I5, I6, J5, and J6 should be highlighted. These cells contain the criterion displayed in Figure 10–10.

Figure 10–10   Using Multiple Criterion

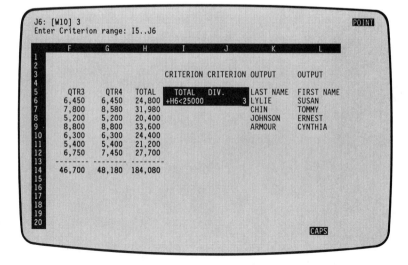

The results of the previous **Data Query Extract** are still visible on the screen. To accept cells I5 . . J6 as the Criterion range:

Press ↵

To perform the query extract:

Type E (for Extract)
Type Q (for Quit)

The data for the designated criteria should now be listed. The screen should look like Figure 10–11.

Figure 10–11

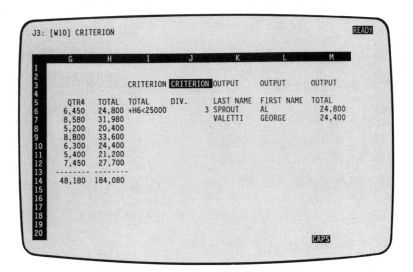

■ USEFUL DATA QUERY OPTIONS

In this section, the **Data Query Unique** command sequence and the **Data Query Delete** command sequence are demonstrated.

Using the Query Unique Command

Continue to use the file ABCSAL with the results of the previous exercise. For the purposes of this exercise, use the instructions below to alter the file so that it has a duplicate record.

Move   the cell pointer to cell A9

To insert a row:

Press   /   (the command key)
Type   W   (for Worksheet)
Type   I   (for Insert)
Type   R   (for Row) ↵

To copy Al Sprout's record from row 6 to row 9:

Move   the cell pointer to cell A6
Press   /   (the command key)
Type   C   (for Copy)

When prompted for the range to copy FROM:

Move   the cell pointer to cell H6

Cells A6 through H6 should be highlighted.

Press   ↵

When prompted for the range to copy TO:

Move   the cell pointer to cell A9 ↵

To execute a query:

Press   the QUERY key (the [F7] key)

The worksheet should look like Figure 10–12.

Figure 10–12

```
                     ABC COMPANY
                     SALARY BUDGET
                                                       CRITERION CRITERION OUTPUT    OUTPUT    OUTPUT

  LAST NAME FIRST NAME DIV.   QTR1    QTR2    QTR3    QTR4   TOTAL   TOTAL   DIV.   LAST NAME FIRST NAME  TOTAL
  SPROUT    AL          3    5,950   5,950   6,450   6,450  24,800 +H6<25000       3 SPROUT    AL        24,800
  LYLIE     SUSAN       1    7,800   7,800   7,800   8,580  31,980                   SPROUT    AL        24,800
  CHIN      TOMMY       2    5,000   5,000   5,200   5,200  20,400                   VALETTI   GEORGE    24,400
  SPROUT    AL          3    5,950   5,950   6,450   6,450  24,800
  JOHNSON   ERNEST      1    8,000   8,000   8,800   8,800  33,600
  VALETTI   GEORGE      3    5,900   5,900   6,300   6,300  24,400
  ARMOUR    CYNTHIA     2    5,200   5,200   5,400   5,400  21,200
  JONES     NINA        3    6,750   6,750   6,750   7,450  27,700
                           --------  ------- ------- ------- -------
  TOTAL                     50,550  50,550  53,150  54,630 208,880
```

Because the record for Al Sprout was duplicated in the database, the name Al Sprout appears twice in the output range in columns K, L, and M. In the following step, duplicate records will be deleted from the output range.

Press	/	(the command key)
Type	D	(for Data)
Type	Q	(for Query)
Type	U	(for Unique)

To leave the Data menu:

| **Type** | Q | (for Quit) |

In this example, the name Al Sprout appeared twice in the output range; after the **Data Query Unique** command sequence is executed, Al Sprout appears in the output range only once. The screen should look like Figure 10–13.

Figure 10–13

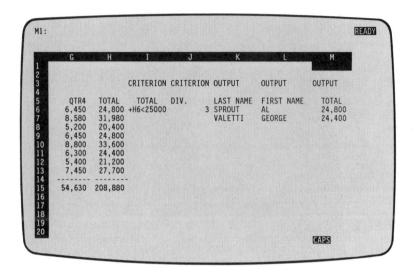

Press   the [Home] key

Note that this option does *not* delete duplicate records in the database itself, only in the output range. Al Sprout's record still appears twice in the database.

Using the Query Delete Command

In this exercise, the **Q**uery **D**elete command will be demonstrated. This command is *extremely powerful*, for it *deletes all records in the database that MATCH the criteria.* In this example, all individuals in the file ABCSAL that earn over $25,000 (represented as the criterion formula +H6>25000) will be deleted from the database. It is assumed that the previous exercise has just been completed and the results are still on the screen:

Press	/	(the command key)
Type	D	(for Data)
Type	Q	(for Query)
Type	D	(for Delete)

The Cancel Delete menu appears so that the user is given a chance to cancel this command or to go ahead and delete the records. To complete the process:

Type	D	(for Delete)

To leave the current menu:

Type   Q   (for Quit)

To see the database:

Press   the [Home] key (if necessary)

The worksheet should look like Figure 10–14. Notice that the output range still contains the names that were extracted from the database, but that the corresponding records from the database itself are deleted.

Figure 10–14

```
                            ABC COMPANY
                            SALARY BUDGET

                                                      CRITERION CRITERION OUTPUT      OUTPUT     OUTPUT

  LAST NAME  FIRST NAME  DIV.   QTR1    QTR2    QTR3    QTR4   TOTAL   TOTAL  DIV.  LAST NAME FIRST NAME  TOTAL
  LYLIE      SUSAN        1    7,800   7,800   7,800   8,580  31,980  +H6<25000    3 SPROUT   AL         24,800
  CHIN       TOMMY        2    5,000   5,000   5,200   5,200  20,400                 VALETTI  GEORGE     24,400
  JOHNSON    ERNEST       1    8,000   8,000   8,800   8,800  33,600
  ARMOUR     CYNTHIA      2    5,200   5,200   5,400   5,400  21,200
  JONES      NINA         3    6,750   6,750   6,750   7,450  27,700

                              --------  --------  --------  --------  --------
  TOTAL                       32,750   32,750   33,950   35,430  134,880
```

■ CREATING A FREQUENCY DISTRIBUTION

The **Data Distribution** menu option allows the user to determine the frequency distribution of any column or row of numbers. Retrieve the original file ABCSAL using the **File Retrieve** command sequence for use in this exercise. It is not necessary to save the results of the previous exercise.

In this example, the user will determine the frequency distribution of salaries based upon the "bin" range set up in cells I16–I20. The bin range is a column consisting of either numbers or formulas that specify the intervals desired by the user. The intervals in the bin range are determined by the user and must always be in ascending order. A blank column should exist to the right of this column (with an additional blank row below the last value in the interval range) where the results will be placed after the **Data Distribution** procedure is invoked through the menu. First, set up the bin range. Use Figure 10–15 as a guide to enter this information in cells B16 through B19, C16 and D20.

Figure 10–15

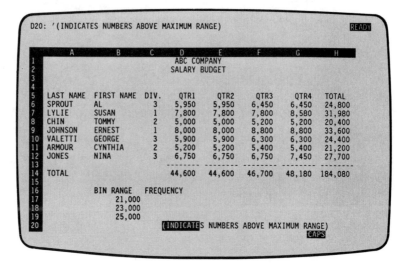

To find the data distribution for the salaries in this file:

Press	/	
Type	D	(for Data)
Type	D	(for Distribution)

The prompt "Enter Values range:" appears. Since the distribution for this example is for salaries, highlight the salary amounts:

Move	the cell cursor to cell H6
Press	.
Move	the cell cursor to cell H12
Press	↵

The prompt "Enter Bin range:" appears. Since the bin range chosen for this example is from 21,000 through 25,000, highlight the range:

Move	the cell cursor to cell B17
Press	.
Move	the cell cursor to cell B19
Press	↵

The frequency of the salary amounts should now be visible on the screen. Note that the number 3 which is listed in cell D20 indicates that three numbers were above 25,000 under TOTAL.

The 1 in cell C17 indicates the number of salaries that are less than or equal to 21,000.

The 1 in cell C18 indicates the number of salaries between 21,000 and 23,000, including 23,000.

The 2 in cell C19 indicates the number of salaries between 23,000 and 25,000, including 25,000.

The 3 in cell C20 indicates the number of salaries greater than 25,000.

The screen should look like the final illustration in Figure 10–16. Figures 10–15 and 10–16 display the entire Data Distribution procedure.

Figure 10–16
Part 1

Step One of the Data Distribution Procedure: Set Up the Desired Bin Range on the Spreadsheet

```
D20: '(INDICATES NUMBERS ABOVE MAXIMUM RANGE)                            READY

        A          B         C         D          E        F        G        H
 1                                   ABC COMPANY
 2                                   SALARY BUDGET
 3
 4
 5   LAST NAME  FIRST NAME  DIV.    QTR1       QTR2     QTR3     QTR4     TOTAL
 6   SPROUT     AL           3      5,950      5,950    6,450    6,450    24,800
 7   LYLIE      SUSAN        1      7,800      7,800    7,800    8,580    31,980
 8   CHIN       TOMMY        2      5,000      5,000    5,200    5,200    20,400
 9   JOHNSON    ERNEST       1      8,000      8,000    8,800    8,800    33,600
10   VALETTI    GEORGE       3      5,900      5,900    6,300    6,300    24,400
11   ARMOUR     CYNTHIA      2      5,200      5,200    5,400    5,400    21,200
12   JONES      NINA         3      6,750      6,750    6,750    7,450    27,700
13                                 --------   -------- -------- -------- --------
14   TOTAL                         44,600     44,600   46,700   48,180   184,080
15
16              BIN RANGE   FREQUENCY
17                 21,000
18                 23,000
19                 25,000
20                              (INDICATES NUMBERS ABOVE MAXIMUM RANGE)
                                                                        CAPS
```

Figure 10–16
Part 2

Step Two of the Data Distribution Procedure: Set Up the Desired Values
Range through the Menu

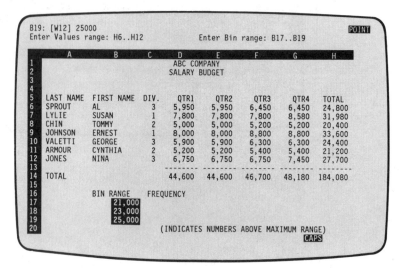

```
B19: [W12] 25000                                                      POINT
Enter Values range: H6..H12

        A         B        C      D        E        F        G       H
                                   ABC COMPANY
                                   SALARY BUDGET
 1
 2
 3
 4
 5    LAST NAME  FIRST NAME  DIV.   QTR1     QTR2     QTR3     QTR4    TOTAL
 6    SPROUT     AL          3      5,950    5,950    6,450    6,450   24,800
 7    LYLIE      SUSAN       1      7,800    7,800    7,800    8,580   31,980
 8    CHIN       TOMMY       2      5,000    5,000    5,200    5,200   20,400
 9    JOHNSON    ERNEST      1      8,000    8,000    8,800    8,800   33,600
10    VALETTI    GEORGE      3      5,900    5,900    6,300    6,300   24,400
11    ARMOUR     CYNTHIA     2      5,200    5,200    5,400    5,400   21,200
12    JONES      NINA        3      6,750    6,750    6,750    7,450   27,700
13                                 --------  --------  --------  --------  --------
14    TOTAL                        44,600   44,600   46,700   48,180  184,080
15
16               BIN RANGE   FREQUENCY
17                   21,000
18                   23,000
19                   25,000
20                              (INDICATES NUMBERS ABOVE MAXIMUM RANGE)
                                                                       CAPS
```

Figure 10–16
Part 3

Step Three of the Data Distribution Procedure: Set Up the Desired Bin Range
through the Menu

```
B19: [W12] 25000                                                      POINT
Enter Values range: H6..H12              Enter Bin range: B17..B19

        A         B        C      D        E        F        G       H
                                   ABC COMPANY
                                   SALARY BUDGET
 1
 2
 3
 4
 5    LAST NAME  FIRST NAME  DIV.   QTR1     QTR2     QTR3     QTR4    TOTAL
 6    SPROUT     AL          3      5,950    5,950    6,450    6,450   24,800
 7    LYLIE      SUSAN       1      7,800    7,800    7,800    8,580   31,980
 8    CHIN       TOMMY       2      5,000    5,000    5,200    5,200   20,400
 9    JOHNSON    ERNEST      1      8,000    8,000    8,800    8,800   33,600
10    VALETTI    GEORGE      3      5,900    5,900    6,300    6,300   24,400
11    ARMOUR     CYNTHIA     2      5,200    5,200    5,400    5,400   21,200
12    JONES      NINA        3      6,750    6,750    6,750    7,450   27,700
13                                 --------  --------  --------  --------  --------
14    TOTAL                        44,600   44,600   46,700   48,180  184,080
15
16               BIN RANGE   FREQUENCY
17                   21,000
18                   23,000
19                   25,000
20                              (INDICATES NUMBERS ABOVE MAXIMUM RANGE)
                                                                       CAPS
```

Figure 10–16
Part 4

Step Four: After pressing ↵ , the Frequency Distribution is displayed in
the Specified Bin Range.

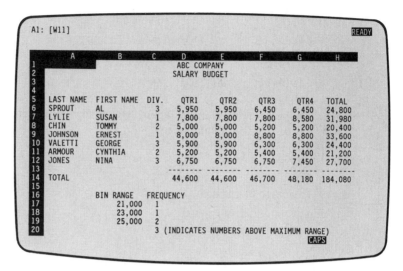

```
A1: [W11]                                                        READY

          A         B          C       D        E        F        G        H
 1                                           ABC COMPANY
 2                                          SALARY BUDGET
 3
 4
 5     LAST NAME  FIRST NAME  DIV.    QTR1     QTR2     QTR3     QTR4    TOTAL
 6     SPROUT     AL            3     5,950    5,950    6,450    6,450   24,800
 7     LYLIE      SUSAN         1     7,800    7,800    7,800    8,580   31,980
 8     CHIN       TOMMY         2     5,000    5,000    5,200    5,200   20,400
 9     JOHNSON    ERNEST        1     8,000    8,000    8,800    8,800   33,600
10     VALETTI    GEORGE        3     5,900    5,900    6,300    6,300   24,400
11     ARMOUR     CYNTHIA       2     5,200    5,200    5,400    5,400   21,200
12     JONES      NINA          3     6,750    6,750    6,750    7,450   27,700
13                                  -------- -------- -------- -------- --------
14     TOTAL                         44,600   44,600   46,700   48,180  184,080
15
16                BIN RANGE  FREQUENCY
17                   21,000   1
18                   23,000   1
19                   25,000   2
20                            3 (INDICATES NUMBERS ABOVE MAXIMUM RANGE)
                                                                        CAPS
```

■ GRAPHING A DISTRIBUTION

Assuming that the previous exercise has just been completed and is still on the screen,
complete the exercise by graphing the distribution of salaries.

For the X-axis on the graph, indicate the bin range. To document the cell indicating
the numbers above the maximum range:

Move	the cursor to cell B20
Type	">25000 ↵

By performing this step, >25000 will appear on the graph to indicate those numbers
beyond the bin range. (The double quote right justifies this label in cell B20.)

To create a graph depicting the results of the frequency distribution in the previous
exercise:

Press	/	
Type	G	(for Graph)
Type	T	(for Type)
Type	P	(for Pie)

For the X-axis on the graph, select the numbers in the bin range:

> **Type**   X   (for X-Axis)

For the X-axis:

> **Type**   B17.B20 ⏎

For the Y-axis, select the actual frequency indications. Choose the first data range for the Y-axis from the menu (menu option A):

> **Type**   A

For the data to go in this data range, indicate the location of the listed frequencies:

> **Type**   C17 . . C20 ⏎

To enter a title for the graph:

> **Type**   O   (for Options)
> **Type**   T   (for Titles)
> **Type**   F   (for First)

For the Graph title:

> **Type**   FREQUENCY DISTRIBUTION OF SALARIES ⏎

To exit the current menu:

> **Type**   Q   (for Quit)

To view the graph:

> **Type**   V   (for View)

The graph should look like Figure 10–17. (The screen display does not show the entire label ">25000", but the printout does.)

Figure 10–17

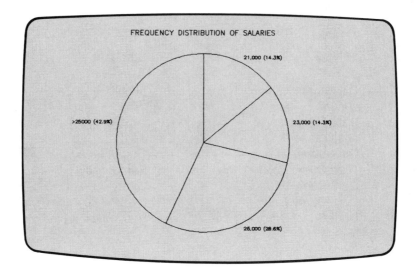

After viewing the graph:

Press ↵

To leave the current menu:

Type Q for Quit

For the purposes of this exercise, it is not necessary to save or to print the graph.

SUMMARY

In Lotus 1–2–3, a spreadsheet may be set up as a database, or a collection of related records. The **Data Sort** command sequence can sort records in a database with up to two sort keys chosen by the user. The **Data Query** can perform a query upon a database according to criterion specified by the user. The user must specify the database range, indicate the criterion, and may even specify an output range for the desired data. Additional **Data Query** options allow the user to delete duplicate records in an output range and also to delete specified records in a database (**Unique** and **Delete**).

Lotus 1–2–3 also contains a **Data Distribution** command that can determine the frequency distribution of data in a range specified by the user.

KEY CONCEPTS

#AND#
#OR#
Bin range
Criterion
Data **D**istribution
Data range
Data **S**ort
Data **Q**uery **D**elete
Data **Q**uery **E**xtract
Data **Q**uery **F**ind
Data **Q**uery **U**nique

Database
Data field
Field title
File
Input range
Key
Output range
Primary key
Query
QUERY key (the [F7] key)record
Secondary key

CHAPTER TEN
EXERCISE 1

INSTRUCTIONS: Circle T if the statement is true and F if the statement is false.

T   F   1. When sorting a database in Lotus 1–2–3, the data-range must include the field titles.

T   F   2. The field titles must be located in the line directly above the first record of the database for the **Data Query** command sequence to work properly.

T   F   3. It is appropriate to have more than one line consisting of field titles designated in the input range.

T   F   4. Each criterion consists of two cells (a field title and the actual criterion).

T   F   5. The input range, criterion, and output range must be manually set up on the worksheet and then identified through the menu options.

T   F   6. The output range allows the user to copy the desired fields that match the criteria to another area on the spreadsheet.

T   F   7. When designating the output range, the user may highlight only the field names that are desired; the records will appear directly below the field names on the spreadsheet in the output range when the **Query Find** is executed.

T   F   8. The QUERY key allows the user to perform a query based upon previously set ranges.

T   F   9. The criterion for a spreadsheet can be set by setting the bin range.

T   F   10. The **Query Unique** command deletes multiple records in a database.

CHAPTER TEN
EXERCISE 2
Sorting Records Using the Primary Key

INSTRUCTIONS: Create the file PERSON. Use Figure 10–18 as a guide.
Column A is 18 characters wide.
Column B is 11 characters wide.
Column C is 14 characters wide.
Column D is 5 characters wide.

Figure 10–18
Part 1

The file PERSON

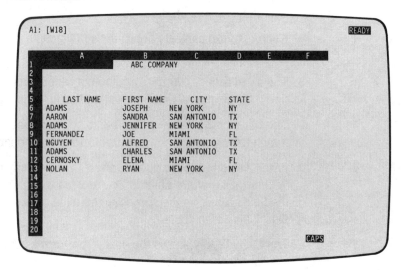

Figure 10–18
Part 2

```
Cell Formulas for the file PERSON

     B1:  [W11]  '   ABC COMPANY
     A5:  [W18]  ^LAST NAME
     B5:  [W11]  ^FIRST NAME
     C5:  [W14]  ^CITY
     D5:  [W5]   ^STATE
     A6:  [W18]  'ADAMS
     B6:  [W11]  'JOSEPH
     C6:  [W14]  'NEW YORK
     D6:  [W5]   'NY
     A7:  [W18]  'AARON
     B7:  [W11]  'SANDRA
     C7:  [W14]  'SAN ANTONIO
     D7:  [W5]   'TX
     A8:  [W18]  'ADAMS
     B8:  [W11]  'JENNIFER
     C8:  [W14]  'NEW YORK
     D8:  [W5]   'NY
     A9:  [W18]  'FERNANDEZ
     B9:  [W11]  'JOE
     C9:  [W14]  'MIAMI
     D9:  [W5]   'FL
    A10:  [W18]  'NGUYEN
    B10:  [W11]  'ALFRED
    C10:  [W14]  'SAN ANTONIO
    D10:  [W5]   'TX
    A11:  [W18]  'ADAMS
    B11:  [W11]  'CHARLES
    C11:  [W14]  'SAN ANTONIO
    D11:  [W5]   'TX
    A12:  [W18]  'CERNOSKY
    B12:  [W11]  'ELENA
    C12:  [W14]  'MIAMI
    D12:  [W5]   'FL
    A13:  [W18]  'NOLAN
    B13:  [W11]  'RYAN
    C13:  [W14]  'NEW YORK
    D13:  [W5]   'NY
```

Sort the data in the file PERSON in alphabetical order by city. When finished sorting, the screen should look like Figure 10–19.

Figure 10–19

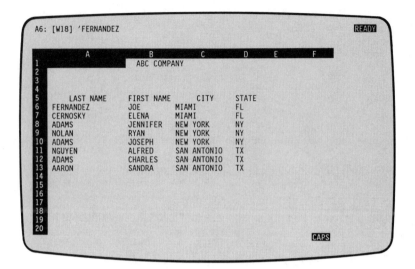

CHAPTER TEN
EXERCISE 3
Sorting Records Using the
Primary and Secondary Keys

INSTRUCTIONS: Sort the last names in the file PERSON in alphabetical order by city. (Assignment 4 will place JOSEPH and JENNIFER ADAMS in the proper order by first name).

The screen should look like Figure 10–20.

Figure 10–20

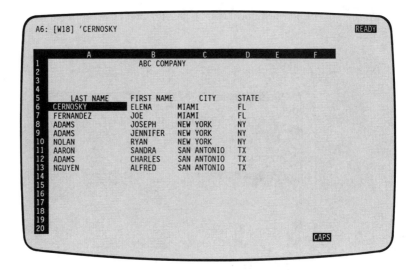

```
A6: [W18] 'CERNOSKY                                          READY

          A            B            C          D      E      F
 1                      ABC COMPANY
 2
 3
 4
 5      LAST NAME    FIRST NAME    CITY        STATE
 6    CERNOSKY       ELENA        MIAMI        FL
 7    FERNANDEZ      JOE          MIAMI        FL
 8    ADAMS          JOSEPH       NEW YORK     NY
 9    ADAMS          JENNIFER     NEW YORK     NY
10    NOLAN          RYAN         NEW YORK     NY
11    AARON          SANDRA       SAN ANTONIO  TX
12    ADAMS          CHARLES      SAN ANTONIO  TX
13    NGUYEN         ALFRED       SAN ANTONIO  TX
14
15
16
17
18
19
20
                                                      CAPS
```

CHAPTER TEN
EXERCISE 4
Sorting Records Using the
Primary and Secondary Keys

INSTRUCTIONS: Assuming that Assignment 3 has just been completed, notice that JOSEPH ADAMS and JENNIFER ADAMS from the city of NY are not in the proper order. To place these names in order:

Set the Data-range as cells A8 . . D9.
Sort primarily by last name and secondarily by first name.

The screen should look like Figure 10–21.

Figure 10–21

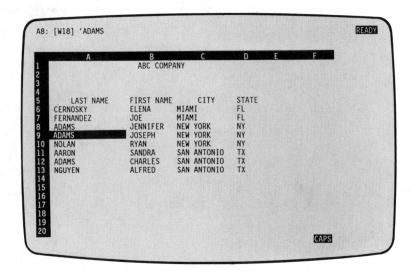

Since Lotus 1–2–3 has only two sort keys, the user may have to perform additional sorts in order to get the desired results, as illustrated in this exercise. Note that the solution suggested in this exercise will solve the problem, but would not be appropriate for a database that consisted of thousands of records. A database package would be a more suitable alternative if extensive sorting is needed.

CHAPTER TEN
EXERCISE 5
Querying Records Using One Criterion

INSTRUCTIONS: Retrieve the original file PERSON for use in this exercise.

Create the appropriate criterion and output range in columns A, B, and C to extract only individuals from the city of Miami. For the output range, request the person's last name and first name. Use Figure 10–22 as a guide.

Figure 10–22

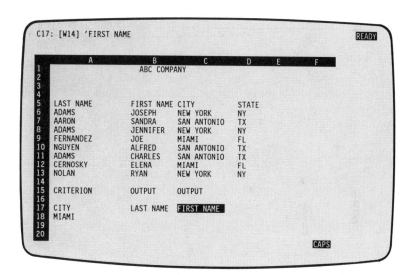

When finished, the screen should look like Figure 10–23.

Figure 10–23

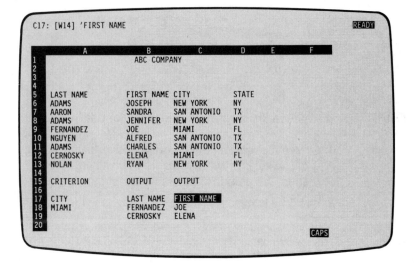

CHAPTER TEN
EXERCISE 6
Using the Data Distribution Menu Option

INSTRUCTIONS: Retrieve the original file ABCSAL for use in this exercise.

Use the **D**ata **D**istribution menu option to determine the number of people in each division in the ABCSAL database.

First, set up a bin range on the worksheet. Use Figure 10–24 as a guide.

Figure 10–24

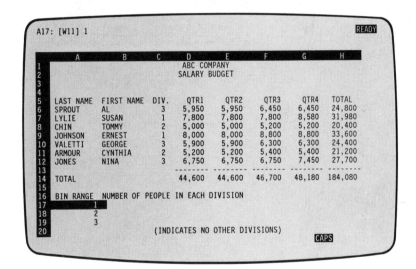

The Values range should be cells C6 . . C12.
The Bin range should encompass the division numbers in the database.

When finished, the screen should look like Figure 10–25.

Figure 10–25

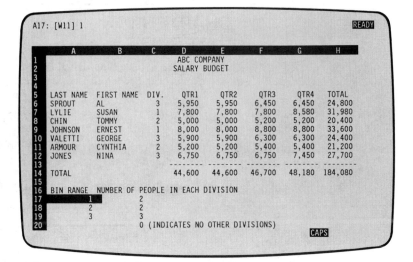

```
A17: [W11] 1                                                      READY

        A           B          C       D        E        F        G        H
 1                              ABC COMPANY
 2                             SALARY BUDGET
 3
 4
 5   LAST NAME   FIRST NAME  DIV.     QTR1     QTR2     QTR3     QTR4    TOTAL
 6   SPROUT      AL            3      5,950    5,950    6,450    6,450   24,800
 7   LYLIE       SUSAN         1      7,800    7,800    7,800    8,580   31,980
 8   CHIN        TOMMY         2      5,000    5,000    5,200    5,200   20,400
 9   JOHNSON     ERNEST        1      8,000    8,000    8,800    8,800   33,600
10   VALETTI     GEORGE        3      5,900    5,900    6,300    6,300   24,400
11   ARMOUR      CYNTHIA       2      5,200    5,200    5,400    5,400   21,200
12   JONES       NINA          3      6,750    6,750    6,750    7,450   27,700
13                                  -------- -------- -------- -------- --------
14   TOTAL                          44,600   44,600   46,700   48,180  184,080
15
16   BIN RANGE  NUMBER OF PEOPLE IN EACH DIVISION
17           1             2
18           2             2
19           3             3
20                         0 (INDICATES NO OTHER DIVISIONS)
                                                                CAPS
```

CHAPTER ELEVEN

SIMPLE TEXT PROCESSING

OBJECTIVES

In this chapter, the student will learn to:

- Write notes on a spreadsheet
- Manipulate labels to create a letter

■ CHAPTER OVERVIEW

Although Lotus 1–2–3 does not have "true" word processing capabilities, it does provide a way to perform simple text processing tasks by manipulating labels in the spreadsheet environment. The user can employ text processing to provide documentation in a spreadsheet or even to create a letter or memorandum. The first exercise in this chapter shows how to use 1–2–3 to include notes on a spreadsheet. The second exercise shows how to create a letter.

■ WRITING NOTES ON A SPREADSHEET

In the following exercise, notes will be entered below a spreadsheet. A printout of the final results is displayed in Figure 11–1.

Figure 11–1

```
                        ABC COMPANY
                          BUDGET


                QTR1     QTR2     QTR3     QTR4   YR TOTAL

   SALES        60,000   61,200   62,424   63,672  247,296

   EXPENSES
     SALARIES   35,000   35,500   36,200   37,000  143,700
     RENT        9,000    9,000    9,000    9,000   36,000
     TELEPHONE   1,000    1,050    1,103    1,158    4,311
     OFFICE SUPPLIES 750    800      850      900    3,300
     MISCELLANEOUS 1,000   1,030    1,061    1,093   4,184
                 -------  -------  -------  -------  -------
     TOTAL EXPENSES 46,750 47,380  48,214   49,151  191,495
                 -------  -------  -------  -------  -------
   GROSS PROFIT  13,250   13,820   14,210   14,521   55,801
                 ======= ======== ======== ======== ========


   You can create letters using Lotus 1-2-3.  If desired, you can
   also create notes below a spreadsheet.
```

Entering Text on a Spreadsheet

In this exercise, text will be placed on the previously created BUDGET file. To retrieve the file BUDGET:

Press	/	(the command key)
Type	F	(for File)
Type	R	(for Retrieve)

When prompted for the file to retrieve:

| **Type** | BUDGET ↵ |

To input the text:

| **Move** | the cell pointer to cell A22 |

At this point, the CAPS feature should be off.

Type   You can create letters using Lotus 1–2–3. If desired,
                  you can also create notes below a spreadsheet. ⏎

Do not attempt to correct any typographical errors at this time. The screen should look
like Figure 11–2.

Figure 11–2

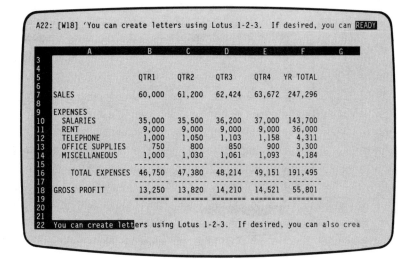

To justify the text:

Press   /   (the command key)
Type   R   (for Range)
Type   J   (for Justify)

When prompted for the range to justify:

Move   the cell pointer to cell F22 ⏎

With the justify range as A22 through F22, the text should be justified below the
spreadsheet.

Move   the cell pointer to cell A25

The text is justified. The screen should look like Figure 11–3.

If inserting text above a spreadsheet, be sure to highlight the entire range in which the text is to appear rather than highlighting only the first row when specifying the Justify range. If the Justify range is not large enough, columns in the spreadsheet may be disturbed when executing the **Range Justify** command sequence.

Figure 11–3

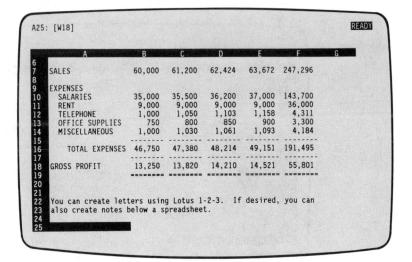

The following section has instructions for correcting typographical errors.

Correcting Typographical Errors

A summary of how to correct errors follows:

- Move to the line where the typographical error appears.
  The cell pointer must be in the column where the label was input. For example, if the label was input in column A; all editing will be from column A.
- Press the [Edit] key, which is the [F2] (function) key.
  When the [Edit] key is pressed, the label appears in the control panel so that it can be edited. If necessary, the [Edit] key can be used to continue typing after the last word entered on a line. For example, a paragraph exceeding 240 characters forces the user to press ↵ and justify the paragraph before continuing. Move to the last line of text and use the [F2] key to continue typing text.
- Use the directional arrow keys to move to the typographical error.
- To insert text at this point, begin to type the desired text. To delete text at this point, use the backspace key or the [Del] key. [Del] stands for "Delete."
  If using Release 2 or a later release of 1–2–3, press the [Ins] key to "toggle" between either inserting text or replacing text. [Ins] stands for "Insert." For example, to insert

text, press the [Ins] key. Begin to type. 1–2–3 is in "OVR" (overstrike) mode and all entered text will be typed over existing text. Press the [Ins] key again. Begin to type. All entered text is inserted without typing over existing text. Again, the [Ins] key works in this manner only with Release 2 and later versions of 1–2–3.

■ After editing the line, press ↵ .

■ Use the **R**ange **J**ustify command repeatedly to wrap words appropriately and to take into account any editing that was completed.

The steps above will have to be executed for *every* line that needs to be edited.

Editing the Text and Printing the Spreadsheet

If necessary, follow the instructions in the previous section to edit the notes below the spreadsheet.

Print the spreadsheet. If necessary, use the following instructions in this paragraph. To print the spreadsheet, highlight the area to print using the / **P**rint **P**rinter **R**ange command sequence. Make sure that the printer is on and on-line. Assuming that the print menu is still on the screen, choose the menu options **A**lign **G**o. After the spreadsheet and the notes are printed, choose the menu option **P**age twice to eject the paper from the printer. Select **Q**uit to exit the print menu.

The printout should look like Figure 11–4. If the printout is satisfactory, save the spreadsheet so that the print settings will also be saved. Name the file NOTES.

Figure 11–4

```
                              ABC COMPANY
                                 BUDGET


                       QTR1     QTR2     QTR3     QTR4    YR TOTAL

         SALES         60,000   61,200   62,424   63,672  247,296

         EXPENSES
           SALARIES    35,000   35,500   36,200   37,000  143,700
           RENT         9,000    9,000    9,000    9,000   36,000
           TELEPHONE    1,000    1,050    1,103    1,158    4,311
           OFFICE SUPPLIES 750     800      850      900    3,300
           MISCELLANEOUS 1,000   1,030    1,061    1,093    4,184
                       -------- -------- -------- -------- --------
         TOTAL EXPENSES 46,750  47,380   48,214   49,151  191,495
                       -------- -------- -------- -------- --------
         GROSS PROFIT   13,250   13,820   14,210   14,521   55,801
                       ======== ======== ======== ======== ========


         You can create letters using Lotus 1-2-3.  If desired, you can
         also create notes below a spreadsheet.
```

■ TEXT MANIPULATION USING 1–2–3

The following exercise demonstrates how to prepare a letter using 1–2–3. A printout of the completed letter is displayed in Figure 11–5.

Figure 11–5

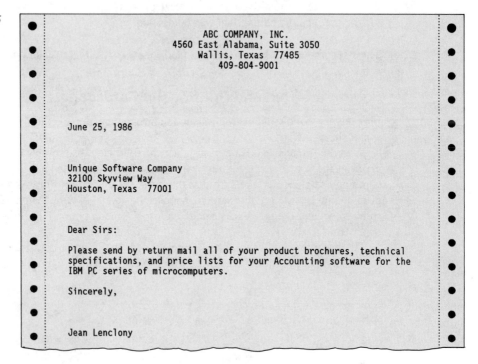

```
                           ABC COMPANY, INC.
                    4560 East Alabama, Suite 3050
                        Wallis, Texas  77485
                          409-804-9001




      June 25, 1986



      Unique Software Company
      32100 Skyview Way
      Houston, Texas  77001


      Dear Sirs:

      Please send by return mail all of your product brochures, technical
      specifications, and price lists for your Accounting software for the
      IBM PC series of microcomputers.

      Sincerely,



      Jean Lenclony
```

Clearing the Screen (if necessary)

To erase the screen before creating the letter, complete the steps below:

Press	/	(the command key)
Type	W	(for Worksheet)
Type	E	(for Erase)
Type	Y	(for Yes)

Widening Column A

The cell pointer should be in cell A1. To widen column A:

Press	/	(the command key)
Type	W	(for Worksheet)
Type	C	(for Column)
Type	S	(for Set-Width)
Type	72 ↵	

It is not necessary to widen column A to write a letter, but doing so makes it much easier to determine how many characters are on each line.

The screen should look like Figure 11–6. Only column A should be visible on the screen.

Figure 11–6

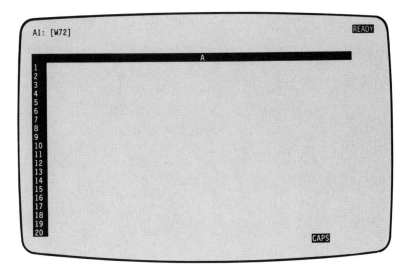

A1: [W72]   READY

                                    A

1
2
3
4
5
6
7
8
9
10
11
12
13
14
15
16
17
18
19
20
                                                          CAPS

Creating a Simple Letter

In this section, a simple letter is created using 1–2–3.

Entering the Return Address

To input the return address:

Move	the cell pointer to cell A1 (if it is not already there)
Press	the [Caps Lock] key (if CAPS is not already on)
Type	^ABC COMPANY, INC.

The ^ symbol centers ABC COMPANY, INC in column A.

Press	the down arrow key
Press	the [Caps Lock] key (to turn it off)

The following text will not be typed in capital letters.

Type	^4560 East Alabama, Suite 3050
Press	the down arrow key
Type	^Wallis, Texas 77485
Press	the down arrow key
Type	^409-804-9001 ↵

The address should now be entered in cells A1 through A4. The screen should look like Figure 11–7.

Figure 11–7

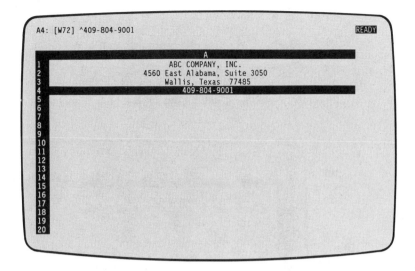

```
A4: [W72] ^409-804-9001                                              READY

                                A
 1                      ABC COMPANY, INC.
 2                4560 East Alabama, Suite 3050
 3                   Wallis, Texas  77485
 4                      409-804-9001
 5
 6
 7
 8
 9
10
11
12
13
14
15
16
17
18
19
20
```

Entering the Date, Company Address, and Salutation

To input the date:

Move	the cell pointer to cell A10
Type	June 25, 1986 ↵

To input the company address:

Move	the cell pointer to cell A14
Type	Unique Software Company
Press	the down arrow key
Type	'32100 Skyview Way

The apostrophe is a label prefix and is located on the key with the double quote. The use of the apostrophe is necessary for the entry **32100 Skyview Way** to indicate that the cell entry is to be treated as a label. If the apostrophe is not included, 1–2–3 will not allow the text to be entered (it will "beep" when ↵ is pressed). The "beeping" occurs because Lotus identifies cell entries as a value or a label by the first character. Since **32100 Skyview Way** begins with a value but also has non-numeric characters (Skyview Way, in addition to spaces), Lotus will not accept the entry as a valid value.

Press	the down arrow key
Type	Houston, Texas 77001 ↵

To input the salutation:

Move   the cell pointer to cell A20
Type   Dear Sirs: ↵

The screen should look like Figure 11–8.

Figure 11–8

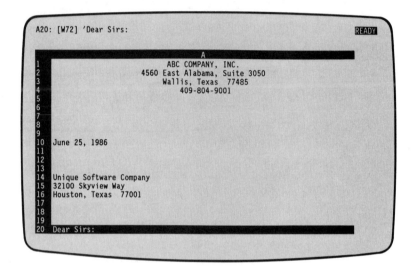

```
A20: [W72] 'Dear Sirs:                                                    READY

                                             A
 1                              ABC COMPANY, INC.
 2                      4560 East Alabama, Suite 3050
 3                          Wallis, Texas  77485
 4                             409-804-9001
 5
 6
 7
 8
 9
10  June 25, 1986
11
12
13
14  Unique Software Company
15  32100 Skyview Way
16  Houston, Texas  77001
17
18
19
20  Dear Sirs:
```

Entering the Body of the Letter

Without pressing ↵ , type the body of the letter:

Move   the cell pointer to cell A22

Type   Please send by return mail all of your product
              brochures, technical specifications, and price lists for
              your Accounting software for the IBM PC series of
              microcomputers.

As the text is typed, the text will "scroll" across the top of the screen. Do not attempt to correct any typographical errors at this time. When through typing the text:

Press   ↵

The text is entered as one long label in cell A22. The screen should look like Figure 11–9.

Figure 11–9

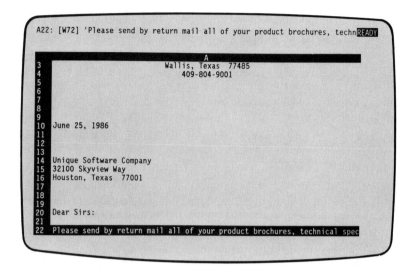

Justifying or "Wrapping" the text

To make the text "wrap" to the rows below:

Press	/	(the command key)
Type	R	(for Range)
Type	J	(for Justify)

When prompted for the range to justify:

Press ↵

To see the results:

Move the cell pointer to cell A25

The text has now "wrapped" to the rows below. The text now consists of three labels—one label in cell A22, A23, and A24, respectively. Except for possible typographical errors, the screen should look like Figure 11–10.

Figure 11–10

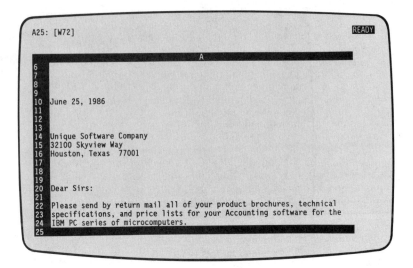

Entering the Closing

To complete the letter:

Move	the cell pointer to cell A26
Type	Sincerely, ↵
Move	the cell pointer to cell A30
Type	Jean Lenclony ↵

Except for possible typographical errors, the screen should look like Figure 11–11.

Figure 11–11

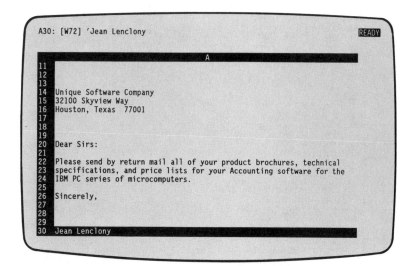

```
A30: [W72] 'Jean Lenclony                                              READY

                                        A
11
12
13
14  Unique Software Company
15  32100 Skyview Way
16  Houston, Texas  77001
17
18
19
20  Dear Sirs:
21
22  Please send by return mail all of your product brochures, technical
23  specifications, and price lists for your Accounting software for the
24  IBM PC series of microcomputers.
25
26  Sincerely,
27
28
29
30  Jean Lenclony
```

Editing and Printing the Letter

If there are errors that need to be corrected, follow the instructions in the section titled "Correcting any Typographical Errors" to edit the letter.

Print the letter. If necessary, use the following instructions in this paragraph. To print the letter, highlight the text to print using the / **Print Printer Range** command sequence. Make sure that the printer is on and on-line. Assuming that the print menu is still on the screen, choose the menu options **Align Go**. After the letter is printed, choose the menu option **Page** twice to eject the paper from the printer. Select **Quit** to exit the print menu.

The printout should look like Figure 11–12. If the printout is satisfactory, save the document so that the print settings will also be saved. Name the file LETTER. Note that 1–2–3 saves the letter as a spreadsheet file since the letter was created on a spreadsheet. The extension will be .WK1 on the file, just as it is on other spreadsheets.

Figure 11–12

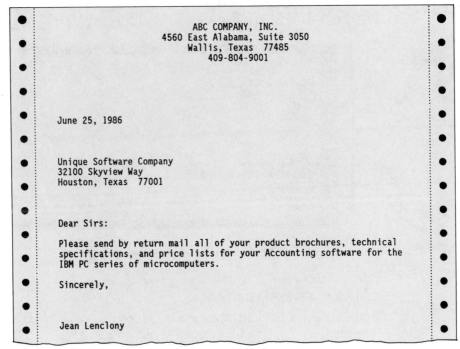

```
                    ABC COMPANY, INC.
              4560 East Alabama, Suite 3050
                  Wallis, Texas  77485
                     409-804-9001



June 25, 1986


Unique Software Company
32100 Skyview Way
Houston, Texas  77001


Dear Sirs:

Please send by return mail all of your product brochures, technical
specifications, and price lists for your Accounting software for the
IBM PC series of microcomputers.

Sincerely,


Jean Lenclony
```

SUMMARY

Simple word processing capability is available in Lotus 1–2–3. Letters or memos, and spreadsheet documentation can be written using the Range Justify command sequence to cause the text to "word wrap." The [Edit] key allows the user to fix typographical errors.

KEY CONCEPTS

[Alt]
[Ctrk] [Break]
Documentation
Macro
MACRO key
Macro range names
Tilde

CHAPTER ELEVEN
EXERCISE 1

INSTRUCTIONS: Circle T if the statement is true and F if the statement is false.

T   F   1. A column on the spreadsheet has to have a width of 72 before text can be justified.

T   F   2. Each line of text is a separate label after the Range Justify command is executed.

T   F   3. To edit a line of text that has been justified with the Range Justify command, use the [Edit] key.

T   F   4. If the Range Justify command is executed with text above an existing spreadsheet, the Justify range should include enough space to justify the text without disturbing the spreadsheet below.

T   F   5. The Range Justify command only works if the Justify range consists of one column and text is not displayed under other columns.

CHAPTER ELEVEN
EXERCISE 2
Editing Text

INSTRUCTIONS: Follow the instructions below to practice editing text.

Clear the screen (/ **Worksheet Erase Yes**).
Enter the following text in cell A1:

```
Now is the time for all good men, women, and children
to come to the aid of their country. ↵
```

Justify the sentence to appear across columns A–G (the actual text
consists of labels in column A).Copy the text to cell A6.
Edit the second sentence so that the sentence is as follows:

```
Now is the time for all good men and women to come to
the aid of their country. ↵
```

Justify the second sentence to appear across columns A–G. The screen
should look like Figure 11–13.

Figure 11–13

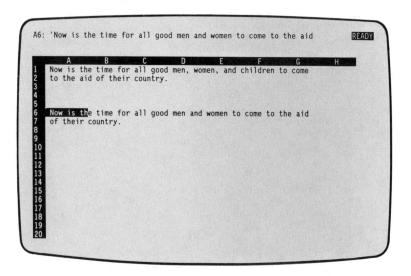

CHAPTER ELEVEN
EXERCISE 3
Creating a Memo

INSTRUCTIONS: Follow the instructions below to practice creating a memo.

Clear the screen (/ **W**orksheet **E**rase **Y**es).
Enter the following text beginning in cell A1. If needed, use
Figure 11–14 as a guide.

Figure 11–14

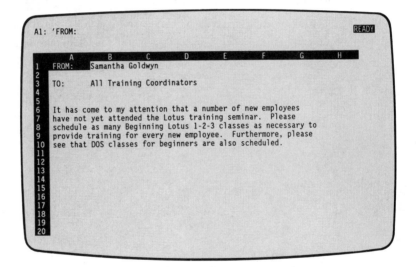

FROM:
TO:

It has come to my attention that a number of new
employees have not yet attended the Lotus training
seminars that are currently available. Please schedule
as many Beginning Lotus 1-2-3 seminars as necessary to
provide training for every new employee. Furthermore,
please see that DOS classes for beginners are also
scheduled.

Remember to press ↵ and enter the existing text if more than 240 characters are input. Then press the [Edit] key (the [F2] key) to resume typing.

Justify the text so that it is displayed in columns A–G.

In cells B1 and B2, please list "Samantha Goldwyn" as the author of the memo and "All Training Coordinators" as the recipients. Print the memo.

The printout should look like Figure 11–15.

Figure 11–15

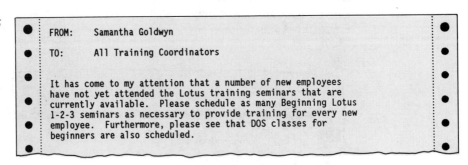

```
FROM:     Samantha Goldwyn

TO:       All Training Coordinators


It has come to my attention that a number of new employees
have not yet attended the Lotus training seminars that are
currently available.  Please schedule as many Beginning Lotus
1-2-3 seminars as necessary to provide training for every new
employee.  Furthermore, please see that DOS classes for
beginners are also scheduled.
```

CHAPTER TWELVE

SUMMARY

As mentioned in the Introduction, this book is designed for individuals who need to learn the basic capabilities of Lotus 1–2–3. Each chapter could be lengthened to include additional 1–2–3 capabilities for the features being discussed. An endless variety of applications could be added. However, each chapter is deliberately limited to the essential, basic concepts. Stressing the basics allows the user to concentrate on the main idea of each exercise without being distracted by a multitude of other issues. At the same time, the examples are comprehensive and thorough enough to provide the user with the tools needed to create larger, more complex spreadsheets. The next logical step for the user is to apply the skills learned in this book to his/her own applications.

APPENDIX A

THE DISK OPERATING SYSTEM (DOS) USED ON THE IBM PC

■ OVERVIEW

PC-DOS, the **Disk Operating System (DOS),** is the system software used on the IBM PC. **System software** is the set of computer programs used to get a PC started; DOS can retrieve and execute programs for specific applications, and load and retrieve data files. It is also used to perform utility operations such as preparing a disk for use and making copies or backups of files. DOS is necessary because it manages disks and disk files.

The rest of Appendix A contains instructions for starting the PC and using basic DOS commands. Users not familiar with the microcomputer and DOS commands should follow the instructions carefully. Users who are comfortable with the microcomputer and DOS commands will benefit by reading through the material for detailed explanations about each DOS command.

■ USING DOS TO START THE MICROCOMPUTER

*Note: The exercises in this book use two floppy disk drives (drives A and B). Fixed disks (typically designated as drive C) can be configured so many different ways that it would be impossible to predict how each user's particular system may be set up. The reader may wish to perform the following exercises on the microcomputer while reading this manual. Note that all actions are written in boldface so that it is clear when an action by the reader is needed (e.g., **Press, Type, Insert,** etc.).*

The following exercise describes how to load PC-DOS for the IBM personal computer. If using a computer that is compatible to the IBM PC or perhaps an older version of PC-DOS, a person can still use this exercise; however, the prompts and responses to the DOS commands may be slightly different.

The computer is assumed to be off. If the computer is already on, turn it off and continue with the instructions below.

Drive A is the primary disk drive. It is typically on the left when there are two horizontally or vertically placed floppy disk drives. Drive A is on the top when the drives are stacked on each other. If there is only one floppy disk drive available, the drive is also referred to as drive A.

When the computer is turned on, the computer will read the disk in drive A in order to perform DOS instructions. Before turning the microcomputer on:

Insert   the DOS System disk in Drive A
(disk label faces up on horizontally placed disk drives;
the label faces left on vertically placed disk drives)

Close   the disk drive door

The disk drive door must be closed whenever a disk is inserted.

Depending on which microcomputer system is used, the power switch may be located on the rear right panel on an IBM PC's central processing unit or on the front panel. (If the monitor has an on/off knob, be sure to turn on the monitor, also). Note that the word "disk" can be used to refer to a floppy disk (diskette) as well as a hard disk.

Turn the computer on (Figure A–1)

Figure A–1

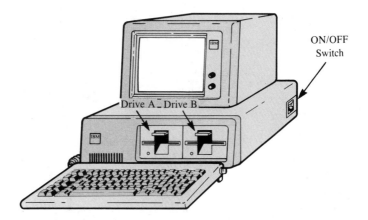

After several seconds, a message will appear on the screen which contains a prompt for today's date (Figure A–2). Depending upon which version of DOS is being used, the default date given may differ. *Default* means that if needed information is not given by the user, the computer has default information it will use. It is important to keep an accurate system date because files created in software packages are "stamped" or recorded with the system date when they are saved onto a disk. In this example, the date 1-01-1980 is used by the system if the user does not provide a date.

Figure A–2

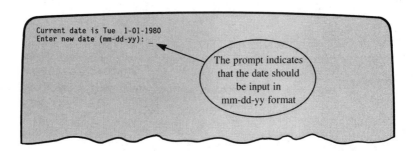

To enter today's date, use the numbers at the top of the keyboard and

Type   the current date, e.g., 5-8-88
Press   the Return key

Note that either the Return key or the Enter key can be depressed to enter data. The Return key appears differently on various keyboards (Figure A–3).

Figure A–3

The Return or Enter Key
(appears differently on
different keyboards)

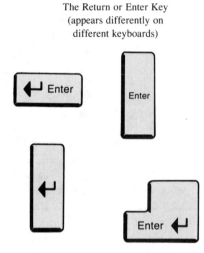

Throughout this book, the Return (or Enter) key symbol, displayed in Figure A–4, is used whenever the Return (or Enter) key should be depressed.

Figure A–4

Next, the system will display the default time on the screen (Figure A–5). The IBM PC uses military time, so 1:30 p.m. would be noted as 13:30 and not 1:30.

Figure A–5

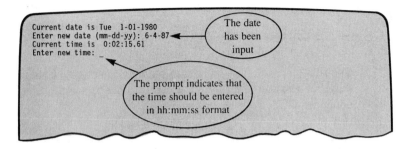

To enter the correct time:

Type   the current time, e.g., 13:30 ↵

The system will respond with the message appearing in Figure A–6. The letter A followed immediately by a "greater than" symbol (>) is referred to as an "A prompt". The system prompt followed by a blinking **cursor** indicates that DOS is waiting to receive commands from the user.

Figure A–6

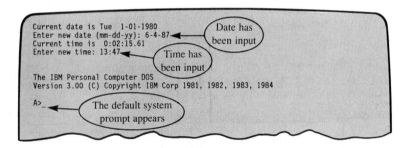

If the computer being used has a fixed or hard disk, it is possible to start the computer without using the DOS disk. This can be accomplished if the files on the DOS disk have been copied to the fixed disk. If a computer with a fixed disk is started, the computer first "looks" for a diskette to read in drive A. If a diskette is not present in drive A, the computer then reads drive C for DOS instructions. If the computer being used does not have a fixed disk and is started without DOS in drive A, the computer will come up in the programming language BASIC and will have to be restarted if applications depending upon DOS, such as Lotus 1–2–3, need to be run.

■ LOOKING AT FILES ON A DISK USING THE DIRECTORY (DIR) COMMAND

The files on a disk may be used to run a program (e.g., Lotus 1–2–3) or to store data (e.g., information input by the user). In order to see the files on drive A, the DOS command DIR can be used.

Note: *A DOS command may be typed in either lowercase or uppercase letters. To type text in uppercase letters, press the Caps Lock key once. To stop typing text in uppercase letters, press the Caps Lock key. Caps Lock works only for letters; all other characters (e.g., ?, !) require the use of a shift key. (Figure A–7). In this book, uppercase letters will be used for DOS commands.*

To correct a misspelled word, use the "Backspace" key. If the Return key has already been pressed and an error message appears, retype the command again and press the Return key (Figure A–7).

Figure A–7

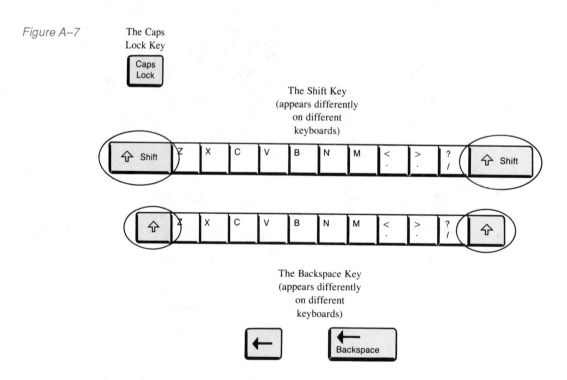

Type   DIR A: ⏎

DIR A: displays the files on the disk in drive A. DIR is the DOS command. A: is a *parameter* or *qualifier* specifying which disk to read. The letter A specifies the drive location and the colon indicates to DOS that the reference is to a disk drive. For example, to view files in drive B, type DIR B: and press the Return key. The directory for the disk in Drive B will appear on the screen. The DOS manual that comes with the DOS disks specifies numerous parameters for DOS commands. Parameters allow the user to be very specific when using DOS commands. After executing the DIR A: command, the screen displays the files on the disk in drive A (Figure A–8). If a different release or version of PC-DOS is used, the screen may show different files.

Figure A–8

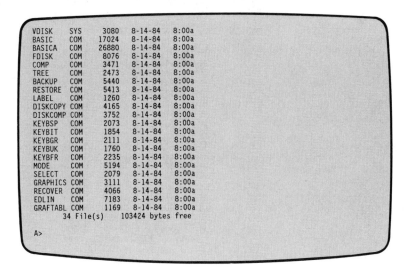

```
VDISK     SYS    3080    8-14-84   8:00a
BASIC     COM   17024    8-14-84   8:00a
BASICA    COM   26880    8-14-84   8:00a
FDISK     COM    8076    8-14-84   8:00a
COMP      COM    3471    8-14-84   8:00a
TREE      COM    2473    8-14-84   8:00a
BACKUP    COM    5440    8-14-84   8:00a
RESTORE   COM    5413    8-14-84   8:00a
LABEL     COM    1260    8-14-84   8:00a
DISKCOPY  COM    4165    8-14-84   8:00a
DISKCOMP  COM    3752    8-14-84   8:00a
KEYBSP    COM    2073    8-14-84   8:00a
KEYBIT    COM    1854    8-14-84   8:00a
KEYBGR    COM    2111    8-14-84   8:00a
KEYBUK    COM    1760    8-14-84   8:00a
KEYBFR    COM    2235    8-14-84   8:00a
MODE      COM    5194    8-14-84   8:00a
SELECT    COM    2079    8-14-84   8:00a
GRAPHICS  COM    3111    8-14-84   8:00a
RECOVER   COM    4066    8-14-84   8:00a
EDLIN     COM    7183    8-14-84   8:00a
GRAFTABL  COM    1169    8-14-84   8:00a
       34 File(s)    103424 bytes free

A>
```

The first two lines of the directory (which scrolled off the screen—refer to Figure A–9) indicate that the diskette was not given a particular name, and that the directory shown is that of drive A. The directory itself lists each file name, an extension to that name (typically three letters, such as COM), the size of the file in bytes, and the system date and time that the file was saved on the diskette. The last two lines indicate the number of files presently on the diskette as well as the number of bytes which are still available for storage on the diskette.

Figure A–9

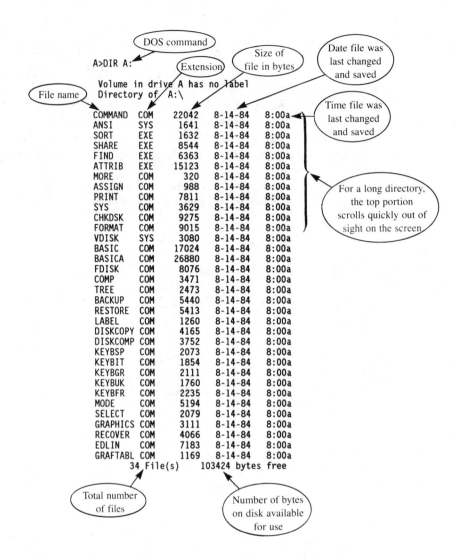

Using the Parameter /P to Show One Screen of Files at a Time

Note that it was not possible to see all of the files listed on the DOS disk because the first files quickly "scrolled" out of sight on the screen. The parameter /P can be added to the DIR command so that all of the files can be viewed easily.

Type   DIR A:/P ↵

A screen or page of files is displayed (Figure A–10); the system pauses. To continue displaying more files:

Press   any key

(to avoid problems, it is a good idea to use the ↵ key)

Figure A–10
Part 1

```
A>

COMMAND  COM    22042   8-14-84   8:00a
ANSI     SYS     1641   8-14-84   8:00a
SORT     EXE     1632   8-14-84   8:00a
SHARE    EXE     8544   8-14-84   8:00a
FIND     EXE     6363   8-14-84   8:00a
ATTRIB   EXE    15123   8-14-84   8:00a
MORE     COM      320   8-14-84   8:00a
ASSIGN   COM      988   8-14-84   8:00a
PRINT    COM     7811   8-14-84   8:00a
SYS      COM     3629   8-14-84   8:00a
CHKDSK   COM     9275   8-14-84   8:00a
FORMAT   COM     9015   8-14-84   8:00a
VDISK    SYS     3080   8-14-84   8:00a
BASIC    COM    17024   8-14-84   8:00a
BASICA   COM    26880   8-14-84   8:00a
FDISK    COM     8076   8-14-84   8:00a
COMP     COM     3471   8-14-84   8:00a
TREE     COM     2473   8-14-84   8:00a
BACKUP   COM     5440   8-14-84   8:00a
RESTORE  COM     5413   8-14-84   8:00a
LABEL    COM     1260   8-14-84   8:00a
DISKCOPY COM     4165   8-14-84   8:00a
DISKCOMP COM     3752   8-14-84   8:00a
Strike a key when ready . . .
```

After executing DIR A:/P the screen prompts the user to continue...

Figure A–10
Part 2

```
BASIC    COM    17024   8-14-84   8:00a
BASICA   COM    26880   8-14-84   8:00a
FDISK    COM     8076   8-14-84   8:00a
COMP     COM     3471   8-14-84   8:00a
TREE     COM     2473   8-14-84   8:00a
BACKUP   COM     5440   8-14-84   8:00a
RESTORE  COM     5413   8-14-84   8:00a
LABEL    COM     1260   8-14-84   8:00a
DISKCOPY COM     4165   8-14-84   8:00a
DISKCOMP COM     3752   8-14-84   8:00a
Strike a key when ready . . .
KEYBSP   COM     2073   8-14-84   8:00a
KEYBIT   COM     1854   8-14-84   8:00a
KEYBGR   COM     2111   8-14-84   8:00a
KEYBUK   COM     1760   8-14-84   8:00a
KEYBFR   COM     2235   8-14-84   8:00a
MODE     COM     5194   8-14-84   8:00a
SELECT   COM     2079   8-14-84   8:00a
GRAPHICS COM     3111   8-14-84   8:00a
RECOVER  COM     4066   8-14-84   8:00a
EDLIN    COM     7183   8-14-84   8:00a
GRAFTABL COM     1169   8-14-84   8:00a
        34 File(s)   103424 bytes free

A>
```

... before displaying the next portion of the directory

Using the Parameter /W to Show File Names Across the Screen

Information on files can be listed horizontally (file names and extensions only) by placing /W after the DIR command (Figure A–11).

Type   DIR A:/W ↵

Figure A–11

```
A>dir A:/W

 Volume in drive A has no label
 Directory of  A:\

COMMAND  COM    ANSI     SYS    SORT     EXE    SHARE    EXE    FIND     EXE
ATTRIB   EXE    MORE     COM    ASSIGN   COM    PRINT    COM    SYS      COM
CHKDSK   COM    FORMAT   COM    VDISK    SYS    BASIC    COM    BASICA   COM
FDISK    COM    COMP     COM    TREE     COM    BACKUP   COM    RESTORE  COM
LABEL    COM    DISKCOPY COM    DISKCOMP COM    KEYBSP   COM    KEYBIT   COM
KEYBGR   COM    KEYBUK   COM    KEYBFR   COM    MODE     COM    SELECT   COM
GRAPHICS COM    RECOVER  COM    EDLIN    COM    GRAFTABL COM
        34 File(s)    103424 bytes free

A>
```

Using the Ctrl-S to Temporarily Stop an Executing DIR Command

To temporarily stop the DIR command, type the following keystrokes (Figure A–12):

Type   DIR A: ↵

Press   the "Ctrl" key and while holding "Ctrl" down, press the the letter "S"

Release both keys

Figure A–12

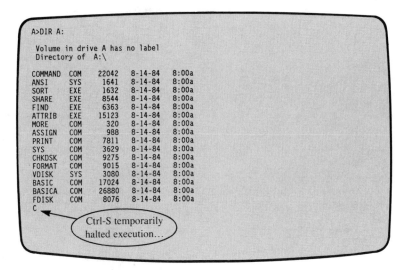

```
A>DIR A:

Volume in drive A has no label
Directory of  A:\

COMMAND  COM   22042   8-14-84   8:00a
ANSI     SYS    1641   8-14-84   8:00a
SORT     EXE    1632   8-14-84   8:00a
SHARE    EXE    8544   8-14-84   8:00a
FIND     EXE    6363   8-14-84   8:00a
ATTRIB   EXE   15123   8-14-84   8:00a
MORE     COM     320   8-14-84   8:00a
ASSIGN   COM     988   8-14-84   8:00a
PRINT    COM    7811   8-14-84   8:00a
SYS      COM    3629   8-14-84   8:00a
CHKDSK   COM    9275   8-14-84   8:00a
FORMAT   COM    9015   8-14-84   8:00a
VDISK    SYS    3080   8-14-84   8:00a
BASIC    COM   17024   8-14-84   8:00a
BASICA   COM   26880   8-14-84   8:00a
FDISK    COM    8076   8-14-84   8:00a
C
```

Ctrl-S temporarily halted execution...

Notice that the DIR command temporarily stops execution so that files can be viewed before they "scroll" out of sight on the screen. The screen stops listing files on the screen at the moment the "Ctrl" and "S" key are simultaneously depressed; in this example, the filename after FDISK.COM was interrupted while being printed on the screen. To continue execution of the DIR command and display the rest of the files, any key can be pressed. (Figure A–13):

Press   any key

Figure A–13

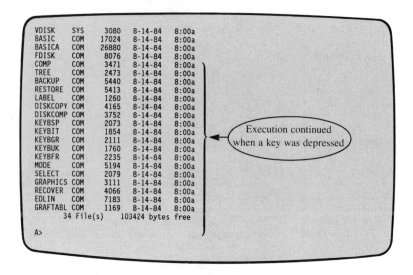

Using Ctrl-Break to Stop Executing DIR (and other DOS) Commands

To stop execution of the DIR command, the following keystrokes must be typed (Figure A–14):

Type	DIR A: ↵
Press	the "Ctrl" key and while holding "Ctrl" down, press the the "Break" key (listed on the side of the "Scroll Lock" key or "Pause" key)
Release	both keys

Notice that ^C appears at about the point when Ctrl-Break was pressed, indicating that the execution was cancelled. In this example, the filename after FDISK.COM was interrupted while printing on the screen; the DIR command was halted completely at this point.

Figure A–14

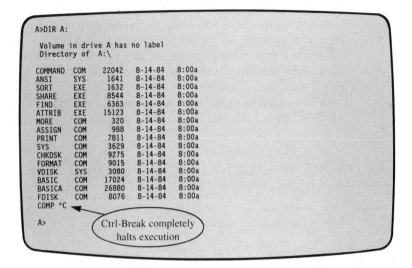

```
A>DIR A:

  Volume in drive A has no label
  Directory of  A:\

COMMAND  COM    22042   8-14-84   8:00a
ANSI     SYS     1641   8-14-84   8:00a
SORT     EXE     1632   8-14-84   8:00a
SHARE    EXE     8544   8-14-84   8:00a
FIND     EXE     6363   8-14-84   8:00a
ATTRIB   EXE    15123   8-14-84   8:00a
MORE     COM      320   8-14-84   8:00a
ASSIGN   COM      988   8-14-84   8:00a
PRINT    COM     7811   8-14-84   8:00a
SYS      COM     3629   8-14-84   8:00a
CHKDSK   COM     9275   8-14-84   8:00a
FORMAT   COM     9015   8-14-84   8:00a
VDISK    SYS     3080   8-14-84   8:00a
BASIC    COM    17024   8-14-84   8:00a
BASICA   COM    26880   8-14-84   8:00a
FDISK    COM     8076   8-14-84   8:00a
COMP ^C

A>
```

Ctrl-Break completely halts execution

■ INTERNAL AND EXTERNAL COMMANDS

Some DOS commands can be executed without needing to read information from the DOS disk. These DOS commands are known as **internal** commands. Internal commands are loaded into the computer's main memory when the computer is started with DOS. For example, if the DOS disk is removed from drive A after the computer is turned on, the DIR command can still be executed. Other commands need information from the DOS diskette; these are known as **external** commands. One example of an external command is the FORMAT command, which will be illustrated later.

■ EXECUTING A PROGRAM

A program consists of a series of instructions that the computer will perform to accomplish a particular task. The program resides on a diskette or hard disk. In order to execute a program using the two floppy disk drive system, the disk containing the program is typically placed in drive A. The command which executes the program is then typed and the ↵ key is depressed. For example, to execute the Lotus 1–2–3 program, the Lotus System Disk is placed in Drive A, the word LOTUS is typed and the Return key is pressed (this procedure is illustrated in Chapter Four). As will be seen later, it will take a few seconds for the program to be loaded into the computer's main memory before the initial screen for the Lotus program appears on the monitor.

Note that DOS is the operating system needed to execute many application software programs; however, the commands used to execute the programs are not DOS command words. For example, DOS is needed to run Lotus 1–2–3, but LOTUS is a command word designated by the creators of the software and specified in the Lotus 1–2–3 software manual.

DOS also has program files. The external files in DOS are program files; they require a DOS command word so that the file can be loaded into main memory.

■ CLEARING THE SCREEN USING THE CLEAR SCREEN (CLS) COMMAND

In order to clear the screen:

Type   CLS ↵

The A prompt will appear at the top of the screen (Figure A–15).

Figure A–15

A>

Screen is cleared
after CLS is executed

■ FORMATTING A DISK USING THE FORMAT COMMAND

Before using a new diskette, the diskette must be prepared for use with the DOS FORMAT command. FORMAT can be used for two purposes: to prepare a new diskette for first-time use, or to erase all files on an old diskette so the diskette can be reused. To format a disk, the DOS disk should be in drive A.

Type   FORMAT B: ↵

The word FORMAT and the letter B do not have to be in capital letters. This is true of all DOS commands.

A message appears with a prompt to insert a new diskette for drive B and to strike any key when ready.

Insert   a new diskette, or a used diskette that needs to be erased, into Drive B

Press   ⏎

The diskette in drive B will be formatted. The formatting process takes a few seconds to complete. After the disk is formatted, a message will appear. In response to the message to format another disk:

Type   N ⏎

On certain releases of DOS, pressing the Return key is not necessary after typing "N" for "No."

The FORMAT program ends and the A prompt appears on the following line (Figure A–16).

Figure A–16

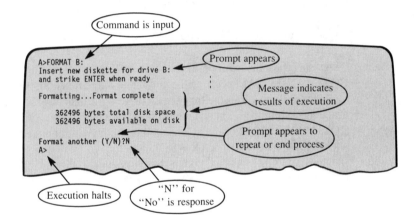

Remove   the disk from drive B

Using a felt tip pen so that the diskette is not damaged, label the data disk as follows: WORK DISK. This disk can be used to complete the exercises in this manual.

Reinsert   the disk in drive B

■ COPYING THE CONTENTS OF ONE DISKETTE TO ANOTHER DISKETTE

The COPY command can be used to copy a file from one disk to another. One of the primary reasons for using the COPY command is to keep a "backup" of files. If the original file is accidentally erased for any reason, the backup disk can be used. Backups are crucial, and should be made often. Since no files have been created, DOS files will be used for the following exercises.

Copying a File on One Diskette to a Second Diskette

In this exercise, the DOS file COMMAND.COM will be copied from the DOS disk to the work disk. Make sure that the DOS disk is in drive A and that a newly formatted disk is in drive B. If desired, type DIR A:/W and press RETURN to see the file COMMAND.COM on the disk in drive A. Type the following command exactly as it is written below; do not insert extra spaces.

Type   COPY A:COMMAND.COM B: ↵

A: specifies the **source** disk drive—the disk containing the file to be copied. **COMMAND.COM** specifies the file name and extension, which must be separated by a period. **B:** specifies the **target** disk drive—the disk to which the file will be copied. Since no name was specified after B:, the file name on drive B will also be COMMAND.COM; a new name could have been specified (e.g., COPY A:COMMAND.COM B:XXX.ABC).

The file COMMAND.COM now exists on the disk in drive B. If desired, type DIR B: and press the return key to see the file listed in the file directory (refer to Figure A–17).

Figure A–17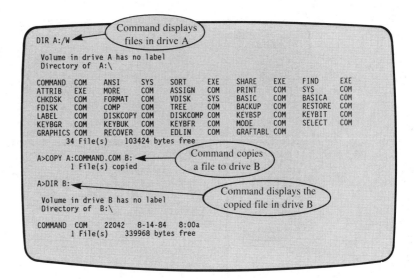

Copying All Files on One Diskette to a Second Diskette

In order to make a backup of all the files on a diskette at once, the COPY command is used with the *.* parameter. The asterisk (*) can be thought of as a "wild card" representing all characters.

Type   COPY A:*.* B: ↵

All regular files on the DOS disk will be copied to the disk in drive B. Note that COMMAND.COM already existed on drive B when the second COPY command was executed. In this case, the file COMMAND.COM was simply copied over itself.

The first "*" is a "wild card" for all file names. The second "*" is a "wild card" for all file extensions. If desired, type DIR B: to see the files listed in the file directory (refer to Figure A–18).

Figure A–18
Part 1

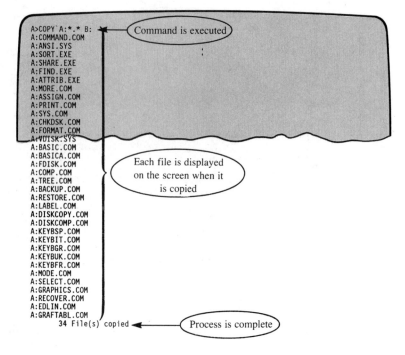

```
A>COPY`A:*.* B:
A:COMMAND.COM
A:ANSI.SYS
A:SORT.EXE
A:SHARE.EXE
A:FIND.EXE
A:ATTRIB.EXE
A:MORE.COM
A:ASSIGN.COM
A:PRINT.COM
A:SYS.COM
A:CHKDSK.COM
A:FORMAT.COM
A:VDISK.SYS
A:BASIC.COM
A:BASICA.COM
A:FDISK.COM
A:COMP.COM
A:TREE.COM
A:BACKUP.COM
A:RESTORE.COM
A:LABEL.COM
A:DISKCOPY.COM
A:DISKCOMP.COM
A:KEYBSP.COM
A:KEYBIT.COM
A:KEYBGR.COM
A:KEYBUK.COM
A:KEYBFR.COM
A:MODE.COM
A:SELECT.COM
A:GRAPHICS.COM
A:RECOVER.COM
A:EDLIN.COM
A:GRAFTABL.COM
        34 File(s) copied
```

Command is executed

Each file is displayed on the screen when it is copied

Process is complete

*Figure A–18
Part 2*

```
A>DIR B:

Volume in drive B has no label
Directory of  B:\

COMMAND  COM   22042   8-14-84   8:00a
ANSI     SYS    1641   8-14-84   8:00a
SORT     EXE    1632   8-14-84   8:00a
SHARE    EXE    8544   8-14-84   8:00a
FIND     EXE    6363   8-14-84   8:00a
ATTRIB   EXE   15123   8-14-84   8:00a
MORE     COM     320   8-14-84   8:00a
ASSIGN   COM     988   8-14-84   8:00a
PRINT    COM    7811   8-14-84   8:00a
SYS      COM    3629   8-14-84   8:00a
CHKDSK   COM    9275   8-14-84   8:00a
FORMAT   COM    9015   8-14-84   8:00a
VDISK    SYS    3080   8-14-84   8:00a
BASIC    COM   17024   8-14-84   8:00a
BASICA   COM   26880   8-14-84   8:00a
FDISK    COM    8076   8-14-84   8:00a
COMP     COM    3471   8-14-84   8:00a
TREE     COM    2473   8-14-84   8:00a
BACKUP   COM    5440   8-14-84   8:00a
RESTORE  COM    5413   8-14-84   8:00a
LABEL    COM    1260   8-14-84   8:00a
DISKCOPY COM    4165   8-14-84   8:00a
DISKCOMP COM    3752   8-14-84   8:00a
KEYBSP   COM    2073   8-14-84   8:00a
KEYBIT   COM    1854   8-14-84   8:00a
KEYBGR   COM    2111   8-14-84   8:00a
KEYBUK   COM    1760   8-14-84   8:00a
KEYBFR   COM    2235   8-14-84   8:00a
MODE     COM    5194   8-14-84   8:00a
SELECT   COM    2079   8-14-84   8:00a
GRAPHICS COM    3111   8-14-84   8:00a
RECOVER  COM    4066   8-14-84   8:00a
EDLIN    COM    7183   8-14-84   8:00a
GRAFTABL COM    1169   8-14-84   8:00a
        34 File(s)    141312 bytes free
```

The VERIFY Command

The VERIFY command can be used so that an error message will occur if a file is not copied accurately. To activate VERIFY, type VERIFY ON and press RETURN before using the COPY command. To see if the verify command is activated, type VERIFY and press Return; either the message "VERIFY IS ON" or "VERIFY IS OFF" will appear. An alternative method is to add the parameter /V; for example, COPY A:COMMAND.COM B: /V will verify if a file has not been copied correctly (Figure A–19). Note that a space before the parameter /V is optional; the same is true of other parameters (e.g., /P, /W).

Figure A–19
Part 1

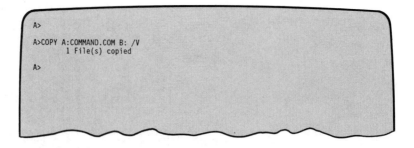

```
A>

A>COPY A:COMMAND.COM B: /V
        1 File(s) copied

A>
```

Figure A–19
Part 2

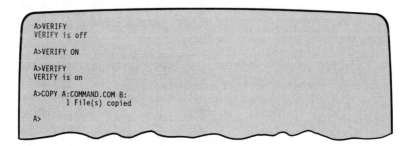

```
A>VERIFY
VERIFY is off

A>VERIFY ON

A>VERIFY
VERIFY is on

A>COPY A:COMMAND.COM B:
        1 File(s) copied

A>
```

■ CHANGING THE FILENAME USING THE RENAME (REN) COMMAND

In this exercise, the file COMMAND.COM on the disk in drive B is renamed to XXX.COM (Figure A–20).

Type   REN B:COMMAND.COM XXX.COM ↵

To return the filename XXX.COM to the filename COMMAND.COM:

Type   REN B:XXX.COM COMMAND.COM ↵

Figure A–20
Part 1

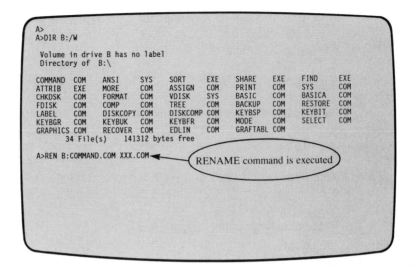

Figure A–20
Part 2

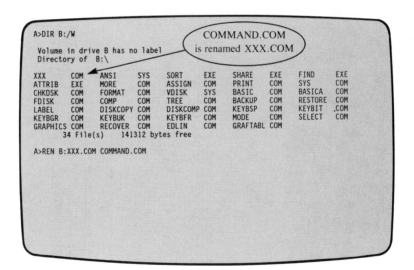

■ CHANGING THE CURRENT DRIVE

The current drive that DOS reads can be changed.

Type   DIR ⏎

Since DOS is using the A prompt, the files on drive A are displayed when a disk drive is not specified (e.g., DIR A: could have been typed to achieve the same result). To change the current drive that DOS reads:

Type   B: ↵

The new line displays the B prompt rather than the A prompt.

Type   DIR ↵

Notice that the directory of drive B is found rather than the directory of drive A. DOS now assumes drive B whenever a DOS command is used unless another drive is specified. (Figure A–21).

To return to the A prompt (Figure A–21):

Type   A: ↵

Figure A–21
Part 1

```
A>DIR

Volume in drive A has no label
Directory of  A:\

COMMAND  COM    22042   8-14-84   8:00a
ANSI     SYS     1641   8-14-84   8:00a
SORT     EXE     1632   8-14-84   8:00a
SHARE    EXE     8544   8-14-84   8:00a
FIND     EXE     6363   8-14-84   8:00a
ATTRIB   EXE    15123   8-14-84   8:00a
MORE     COM      320   8-14-84   8:00a
ASSIGN   COM      988   8-14-84   8:00a
PRINT    COM     7811   8-14-84   8:00a
SYS      COM     3629   8-14-84   8:00a
CHKDSK   COM     9275   8-14-84   8:00a
FORMAT   COM     9015   8-14-84   8:00a
VDISK    SYS     3080   8-14-84   8:00a
BASIC    COM    17024   8-14-84   8:00a
BASICA   COM    26880   8-14-84   8:00a
FDISK    COM     8076   8-14-84   8:00a
COMP     COM     3471   8-14-84   8:00a
TREE     COM     2473   8-14-84   8:00a
BACKUP   COM     5440   8-14-84   8:00a
RESTORE  COM     5413   8-14-84   8:00a
LABEL    COM     1260   8-14-84   8:00a
DISKCOPY COM     4165   8-14-84   8:00a
DISKCOMP COM     3752   8-14-84   8:00a
KEYBSP   COM     2073   8-14-84   8:00a
KEYBIT   COM     1854   8-14-84   8:00a
KEYBGR   COM     2111   8-14-84   8:00a
KEYBUK   COM     1760   8-14-84   8:00a
KEYBFR   COM     2235   8-14-84   8:00a
MODE     COM     5194   8-14-84   8:00a
SELECT   COM     2079   8-14-84   8:00a
GRAPHICS COM     3111   8-14-84   8:00a
RECOVER  COM     4066   8-14-84   8:00a
EDLIN    COM     7183   8-14-84   8:00a
GRAFTABL COM     1169   8-14-84   8:00a
       34 File(s)   103424 bytes free
```

Figure A–21
Part 2

```
A>B:

B>DIR

Volume in drive B has no label
Directory of  B:\

COMMAND  COM    22042   8-14-84   8:00a
ANSI     SYS     1641   8-14-84   8:00a
SORT     EXE     1632   8-14-84   8:00a
SHARE    EXE     8544   8-14-84   8:00a
FIND     EXE     6363   8-14-84   8:00a
ATTRIB   EXE    15123   8-14-84   8:00a
MORE     COM      320   8-14-84   8:00a
ASSIGN   COM      988   8-14-84   8:00a
PRINT    COM     7811   8-14-84   8:00a
SYS      COM     3629   8-14-84   8:00a
CHKDSK   COM     9275   8-14-84   8:00a
FORMAT   COM     9015   8-14-84   8:00a
VDISK    SYS     3080   8-14-84   8:00a
BASIC    COM    17024   8-14-84   8:00a
BASICA   COM    26880   8-14-84   8:00a
FDISK    COM     8076   8-14-84   8:00a
COMP     COM     3471   8-14-84   8:00a
TREE     COM     2473   8-14-84   8:00a
BACKUP   COM     5440   8-14-84   8:00a
RESTORE  COM     5413   8-14-84   8:00a
LABEL    COM     1260   8-14-84   8:00a
DISKCOPY COM     4165   8-14-84   8:00a
DISKCOMP COM     3752   8-14-84   8:00a
KEYBSP   COM     2073   8-14-84   8:00a
KEYBIT   COM     1854   8-14-84   8:00a
KEYBGR   COM     2111   8-14-84   8:00a
KEYBUK   COM     1760   8-14-84   8:00a
KEYBFR   COM     2235   8-14-84   8:00a
MODE     COM     5194   8-14-84   8:00a
SELECT   COM     2079   8-14-84   8:00a
GRAPHICS COM     3111   8-14-84   8:00a
RECOVER  COM     4066   8-14-84   8:00a
EDLIN    COM     7183   8-14-84   8:00a
GRAFTABL COM     1169   8-14-84   8:00a
        34 File(s)   141312 bytes free
```

Figure A–21
Part 3

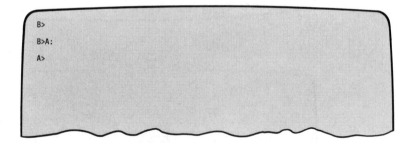

```
B>

B>A:

A>
```

■ ERASING INFORMATION FROM A DISK

The ERASE command can be used to erase a single file or multiple files from a disk.

Erasing a Single File from a Disk

It is assumed that the previous COPY exercise has recently been completed; the DOS disk is now in drive A and the data disk is in drive B. In this exercise, the DOS file COMMAND.COM is erased from the disk in drive B.

Type   ERASE B:COMMAND.COM ⏎

B: specifies the **source** disk drive—the disk containing the file to be erased. **COMMAND.COM** specifies the file name and extension.

The file COMMAND.COM is no longer available on the disk in drive B. To see that the file is not listed in the file directory, type DIR B: and press Return (Figure A–22).

Figure A–22
Part 1

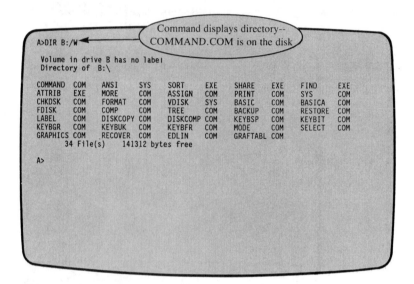

Figure A–22
Part 2

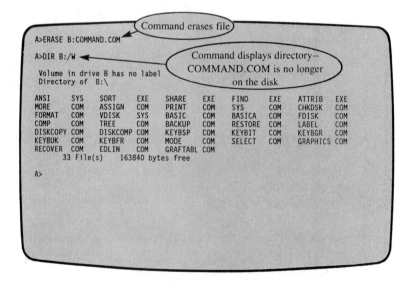

Erasing All Files on a Diskette

An alternative to using the FORMAT command to erase all files from an old disk is the ERASE command. The ERASE command can be used with the *.* parameter. The * can be thought of as a "wild card" representing all characters.

Type   ERASE B:*.* ↵

When "Are you sure?" appears on the screen.

Type   Y ↵

In some releases of DOS, the Return key does not have to be pressed after the letter "Y" for "Yes."

All regular files on the disk will be erased.

The first * is a "wild card" for all file names. The second * is a "wild card" for all file extensions. If desired, type DIR B: to see that all files have been erased (Figure A–23).

Figure A–23
Part 1

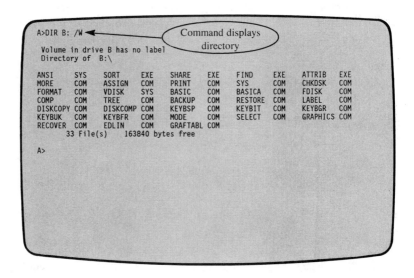

```
A>DIR B: /W                    Command displays
                                   directory
    Volume in drive B has no label
    Directory of  B:\

ANSI     SYS     SORT     EXE     SHARE    EXE     FIND     EXE     ATTRIB   EXE
MORE     COM     ASSIGN   COM     PRINT    COM     SYS      COM     CHKDSK   COM
FORMAT   COM     VDISK    SYS     BASIC    COM     BASICA   COM     FDISK    COM
COMP     COM     TREE     COM     BACKUP   COM     RESTORE  COM     LABEL    COM
DISKCOPY COM     DISKCOMP COM     KEYBSP   COM     KEYBIT   COM     KEYBGR   COM
KEYBUK   COM     KEYBFR   COM     MODE     COM     SELECT   COM     GRAPHICS COM
RECOVER  COM     EDLIN    COM     GRAFTABL COM
         33 File(s)    163840 bytes free

A>
```

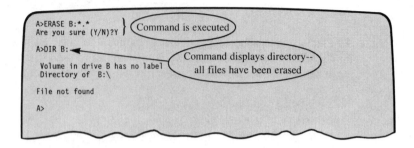

```
A>ERASE B:*.*
Are you sure (Y/N)?Y  }   Command is executed

A>DIR B:

Volume in drive B has no label        Command displays directory--
Directory of  B:\                      all files have been erased

File not found

A>
```

■ OBTAINING A PRINTOUT OF THE SCREEN DISPLAY

Two methods of getting a printout of the screen are as follows: using the PrintScreen key, and using the Ctrl-P keystroke combination.

Using the PrintScreen Key

The PrintScreen key (marked "PrtSc" or "Print Scrn" on most keyboards) allows a printout of the screen display. Note that special characters and graphics may not print accurately without additional instructions. To obtain a printout of the directory of the disk in drive A, make sure that the printer is on at this time. To place a directory of the disk in drive A on the screen,

   Type   DIR A: ⏎

To print the directory of the disk in drive A,

   Press   a shift key

While holding down the shift key:

   Press   the PrintScreen key
   Release both keys

The printer should print a copy of the screen's contents (Figure A–24).

Figure A–24

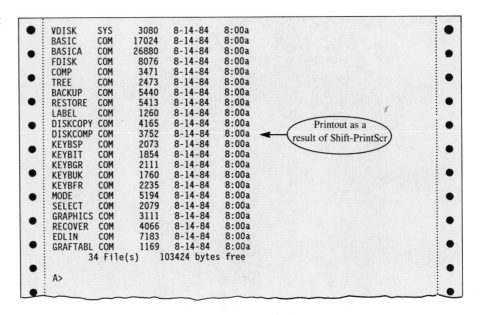

```
VDISK    SYS    3080    8-14-84   8:00a
BASIC    COM   17024    8-14-84   8:00a
BASICA   COM   26880    8-14-84   8:00a
FDISK    COM    8076    8-14-84   8:00a
COMP     COM    3471    8-14-84   8:00a
TREE     COM    2473    8-14-84   8:00a
BACKUP   COM    5440    8-14-84   8:00a
RESTORE  COM    5413    8-14-84   8:00a
LABEL    COM    1260    8-14-84   8:00a
DISKCOPY COM    4165    8-14-84   8:00a
DISKCOMP COM    3752    8-14-84   8:00a
KEYBSP   COM    2073    8-14-84   8:00a
KEYBIT   COM    1854    8-14-84   8:00a
KEYBGR   COM    2111    8-14-84   8:00a
KEYBUK   COM    1760    8-14-84   8:00a
KEYBFR   COM    2235    8-14-84   8:00a
MODE     COM    5194    8-14-84   8:00a
SELECT   COM    2079    8-14-84   8:00a
GRAPHICS COM    3111    8-14-84   8:00a
RECOVER  COM    4066    8-14-84   8:00a
EDLIN    COM    7183    8-14-84   8:00a
GRAFTABL COM    1169    8-14-84   8:00a
        34 File(s)    103424 bytes free

A>
```

Printout as a result of Shift-PrintScr

Figure A–25

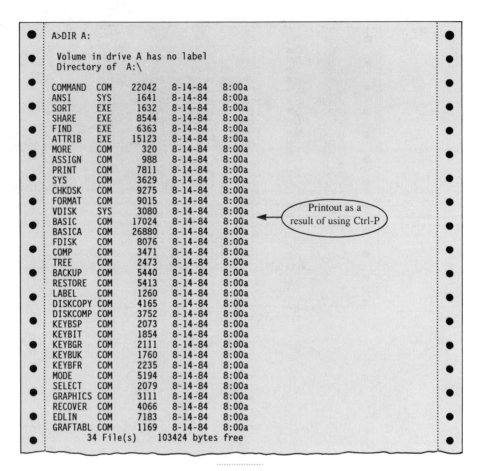

```
A>DIR A:

Volume in drive A has no label
Directory of  A:\

COMMAND   COM    22042    8-14-84    8:00a
ANSI      SYS     1641    8-14-84    8:00a
SORT      EXE     1632    8-14-84    8:00a
SHARE     EXE     8544    8-14-84    8:00a
FIND      EXE     6363    8-14-84    8:00a
ATTRIB    EXE    15123    8-14-84    8:00a
MORE      COM      320    8-14-84    8:00a
ASSIGN    COM      988    8-14-84    8:00a
PRINT     COM     7811    8-14-84    8:00a
SYS       COM     3629    8-14-84    8:00a
CHKDSK    COM     9275    8-14-84    8:00a
FORMAT    COM     9015    8-14-84    8:00a
VDISK     SYS     3080    8-14-84    8:00a
BASIC     COM    17024    8-14-84    8:00a
BASICA    COM    26880    8-14-84    8:00a
FDISK     COM     8076    8-14-84    8:00a
COMP      COM     3471    8-14-84    8:00a
TREE      COM     2473    8-14-84    8:00a
BACKUP    COM     5440    8-14-84    8:00a
RESTORE   COM     5413    8-14-84    8:00a
LABEL     COM     1260    8-14-84    8:00a
DISKCOPY  COM     4165    8-14-84    8:00a
DISKCOMP  COM     3752    8-14-84    8:00a
KEYBSP    COM     2073    8-14-84    8:00a
KEYBIT    COM     1854    8-14-84    8:00a
KEYBGR    COM     2111    8-14-84    8:00a
KEYBUK    COM     1760    8-14-84    8:00a
KEYBFR    COM     2235    8-14-84    8:00a
MODE      COM     5194    8-14-84    8:00a
SELECT    COM     2079    8-14-84    8:00a
GRAPHICS  COM     3111    8-14-84    8:00a
RECOVER   COM     4066    8-14-84    8:00a
EDLIN     COM     7183    8-14-84    8:00a
GRAFTABL  COM     1169    8-14-84    8:00a
    34 File(s)    103424 bytes free
```

Printout as a result of using Ctrl-P

Obtaining a Continuous Printout of the Screen Display

Pressing the Control (Ctrl) key in conjunction with the letter P sends a message to the printer to print all data sent to the screen. This process is illustrated by printing a copy of the directory of the disk in drive A. See Figure A–25.

Type   DIR A: ↵

To get a printout:

Press   the Control (Ctrl) key

While depressing the Control key:

> **Press**   the letter P
> **Release** both keys

To obtain the printout:

> **Type**   DIR A: ↵

The printer should print a copy of the directory.
To turn the printer "off" from printing:

> **Press**   the Control (Ctrl) key

While holding down the Control key:

> **Press**   the letter P
> **Release both keys**

The Control-P combination is used to turn the message to the printer on and off. If the printer continues to print, press Control-P again (Figure A–24).

■ CHECKING A DISK'S CONDITION USING THE CHECK DISK (CHKDSK) COMMAND

The CHKDSK command's function is to ensure that all files are recorded properly on the disk. It displays on the screen the number of files on the disk, the amount of disk space used, and how much disk space is available. It also indicates how much memory is presently being used and how much is available in the computer's main memory.

> **Type**   CHKDSK A: /F ↵

CHKDSK A: checks the disk in drive A for errors; /F will attempt to fix any errors found in the directory or to recover any lost file clusters. Files that have been recovered may have to be renamed by the CHKDSK program; the recovered files will have the extension CHK (Figure A–26).

Figure A–26

```
A>CHKDSK A: /F

    362496 bytes total disk space
     37888 bytes in 2 hidden files
    221184 bytes in 34 user files
    103424 bytes available on disk

    655360 bytes total memory
    618496 bytes free

A>
```

SUMMARY

As illustrated in this appendix, many DOS commands manage files on a disk. Appendix A can be used as a reference to manage the files created in Lotus 1–2–3 as well as in other application packages.

The DOS commands covered are some of the ones most commonly used. To learn more about these and other DOS commands, refer to the DOS Reference Manual.

KEY CONCEPTS

Check disk (CHKDSK)
Clear screen (CLS)
Copy
Disk Operating System (DOS)
Directory (DIR)
Erase
External commands

Format
Internal commands
PrintScreen
Rename (REN)
System software
Verify

APPENDIX A
EXERCISE 1

INSTRUCTIONS: Circle T if the statement is true and F if the statement is false.

T   **F**   1. DOS manages files on a disk.

T   **F**   2. DIR A: is a DOS command to look at the files on a disk in drive B.

T   **F**   3. DOS commands must be written in uppercase letters.

T   **F**   4. To copy the file HELLO.XXX from drive A to drive C, it is necessary
to type COPY A:HELLO C: and press Return.

T   **F**   5. The RENAME command is used to rename disks.

T   **F**   6. In the filename HELLO.XXX, .XXX is known as the parameter.

T   **F**   7. In the command COPY A:GOODBYE.XXX B:ALOHA.XXX,
GOODBYE.XXX was the source file that was copied to a second
disk and given the name ALOHA.XXX.

T   **F**   8. DOS commands will execute even if extra spaces are in the
command (e.g., COPY A: *.* B:)

T   **F**   9. If a disk is not present in drive A when the computer is started, the
computer system will then "look" for a disk in drive B.

T   **F**   10. It is not important to input the correct time on the computer system.

APPENDIX A
EXERCISE 2

INSTRUCTIONS: Explain what will happen when the following DOS commands are executed.

Problem 1:   A>DIR ↵

Problem 2:   A>B: ↵

Problem 3:   A>COPY A: *.* B: ↵

Problem 4:   A>DIR C; ↵

Problem 5:   B>ERASE HELLO.XXX ↵

APPENDIX B

LOTUS 1–2–3 COMMAND TREES

```
┌─────────────────────────────────────────────────────────────────────────┐
│ Worksheet  Range  Copy  Move  File  Print  Graph  Data  System  Quit      │
└─────────────────────────────────────────────────────────────────────────┘
```

The menu options listed above are on the top menu level in 1–2–3. Options that contain multiple menu levels are illustrated on the following pages.

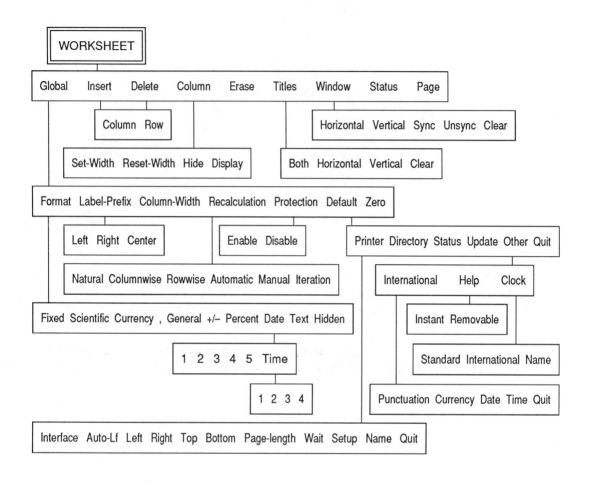

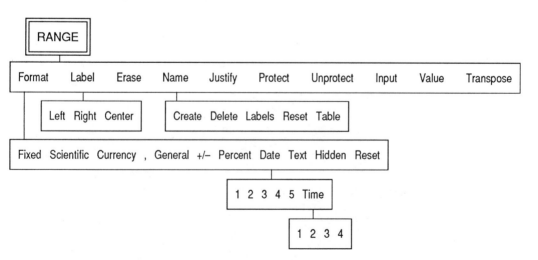

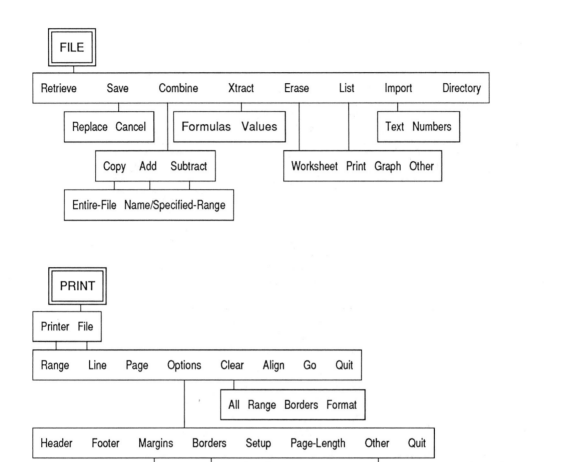

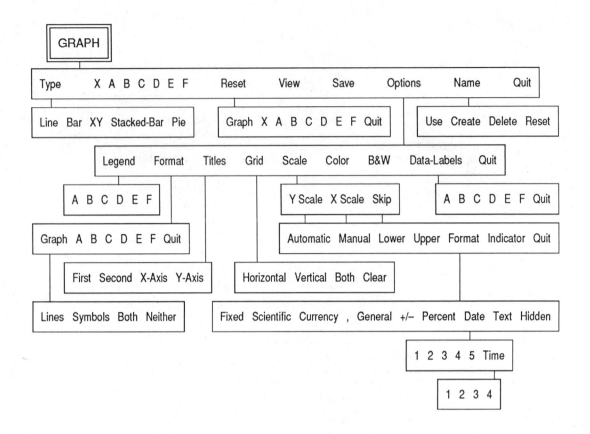

GRAPH

Type   X A B C D E F   Reset   View   Save   Options   Name   Quit

Line Bar XY Stacked-Bar Pie

Graph X A B C D E F Quit

Use Create Delete Reset

Legend   Format   Titles   Grid   Scale   Color   B&W   Data-Labels   Quit

A B C D E F

Y Scale   X Scale   Skip

A B C D E F Quit

Graph A B C D E F Quit

Automatic Manual Lower Upper Format Indicator Quit

First Second X-Axis Y-Axis

Horizontal Vertical Both Clear

Lines Symbols Both Neither

Fixed Scientific Currency , General +/– Percent Date Text Hidden

1 2 3 4 5 Time

1 2 3 4

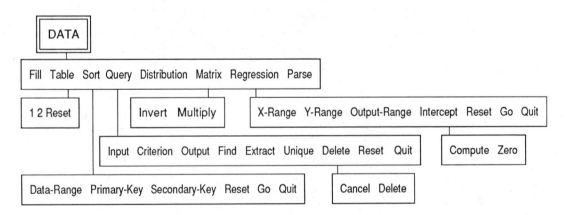

DATA

Fill Table Sort Query Distribution Matrix Regression Parse

1 2 Reset

Invert   Multiply

X-Range Y-Range Output-Range Intercept Reset Go Quit

Input Criterion Output Find Extract Unique Delete Reset Quit

Compute Zero

Data-Range Primary-Key Secondary-Key Reset Go Quit

Cancel Delete

■ SUMMARY OF COMMANDS COVERED IN THIS BOOK

As indicated by the previous diagrams, there are many types of commands available in Lotus 1–2–3. Below is a summary of the functionality of the commands covered in this book. This summary is useful when a person knows what needs to be done but does not know what command to use. A complete list of the functionality of the 1–2–3 commands can be found in the Lotus 1–2–3 reference manual that comes with the software.

The keystrokes required for each command sequence are in bold and a description of the command sequence are included.

Data Analysis

Determine a frequency distribution for some data in a range of cells

/DD   **/D**ata **D**istribution

Change formulas into values

/RV   **/R**ange **V**alue

Create graphs from data in a spreadsheet

/G   **/G**raph

Sort data in a spreadsheet

/DS   **/D**ata **S**ort

Modifying the Appearance of the Spreadsheet

Change the format of a specific cell or group of cells in the spreadsheet

/RF   **/R**ange **F**ormat

Change the default format for numeric values in the spreadsheet

/WGF   **/W**orksheet **G**lobal **F**ormat

Change the width for a specific column in the spreadsheet

/WCS   **/W**orksheet **C**olumn **S**et-Width

Change the column default width

/WGC **/W**orksheet **G**lobal **C**olumn-Width

Copy information from one portion of the spreadsheet to another section of the spreadsheet

/C **/C**opy

Show formulas instead of numbers

/RFT **/R**ange **F**ormat **T**ext

Erase a specific cell or range of cells in the spreadsheet

/RE **/R**ange **E**rase

Erase the entire spreadsheet

/WEY **/W**orksheet **E**rase **Y**es

Hide a column or group of columns in the spreadsheet

/WCH **/W**orksheet **C**olumn **H**ide

Insert a blank row or rows in a spreadsheet

/WIR **/W**orksheet **I**nsert **R**ow

Insert a blank column or columns in a spreadsheet

/WIC **/W**orksheet **I**nsert **C**olumn

Keep row labels or column headings on the monitor

/WT **/W**orksheet **T**itles

Move information from one section on the spreadsheet to another section on the spreadsheet

/M **/M**ove

Modify the arrangement of text in a spreadsheet

/RJ   **/Range Justify**

Display previously hidden column

/WCD   **/Worksheet Column Display**

Delete a row or rows from a spreadsheet

/WDR   **/Worksheet Delete Row**

Delete a column or columns from a spreadsheet

/WDC   **/Worksheet Delete Column**

Divide the spreadsheet on the screen into two parts or windows

/WW   **/Worksheet Window**

Suppress from view all cells that have a value of exactly 0

/WGZ   **/Worksheet Global Zero**

Copying Data

Copy information from one portion of the spreadsheet to another section of the spreadsheet

/C   **/Copy**

Change formulas into values

/RV   **/Range Value**

Include data from another spreadsheet file into the spreadsheet in the memory

/FC   **/File Combine**

Erasing Data

Delete a row or rows from a spreadsheet

/WDR   /Worksheet Delete Row

Delete a column or columns from a spreadsheet

/WDC   /Worksheet Delete Column

Erase the contents of one or more specific cells

/RE   /Range Erase

Erase the spreadsheet presently being used

/WEY   /Worksheet Erase Yes

Graphing Data

Indicate the type of graph desired

/GT   /Graph Type

Specify the data to appear on the X-axis in a graph

/GX   /Graph X

Specify the data to be graphed (six variables can be graphed at a time)

/GA   /Graph A
/GB   /Graph B
/GC   /Graph C
/GD   /Graph D
/GE   /Graph E
/GF   /Graph F

Display the graph on the monitor screen

/GV   /Graph View

Indicate various graphic settings

/GO   /Graph **O**ptions

Specify legend labels for variables being graphed

/GOL   /Graph **O**ptions **L**egend

Specify title lines for the graph

/GOTF   /Graph **O**ptions **T**itles **F**irst
/GOTS   /Graph **O**ptions **T**itles **S**econd

Specify labels for X-Axis and Y-Axis

/GOTX   /Graph **O**ptions **T**itles **X**-Axis
/GOTY   /Graph **O**ptions **T**itles **Y**-Axis

Place labels on data points

/GOD   /Graph **O**ptions **D**ata-Labels

Place horizontal, vertical or both horizontal and vertical lines on the graph

/GOG   /Graph **O**ptions **G**rid

Name a graph

/GN   /Graph **N**ame

Save a graph on a file for later printing

/GS   /Graph **S**ave

Print or plot the graph

Use the PrintGraph program

Reset or cancel some or all of the graph settings

/GR   /Graph **R**eset

List the graph files

    /FLG   /File List Graph

Hiding Data

Restrict the display of a column or columns

    /WCH   /Worksheet Column Hide

Display a column that had previously been hidden

    /WCD   /Worksheet Column Display

Suppress from view all cells that have a value of exactly 0

    /WGZ   /Worksheet Global Zero

Loading Data

Load a spreadsheet file into the memory of the microcomputer

    /FR   /File Retrieve

Include data from another spreadsheet file into the spreadsheet in the microcomputer memory

    /FC   /File Combine

Moving Data

Move information from one section on the spreadsheet to another section on the spreadsheet

    /M   /Move

Insert a blank row or rows in a spreadsheet

    /WIR   /Worksheet Insert Row

Insert a blank column or columns in a spreadsheet

    /WIC   /Worksheet Insert Column

Delete a row or rows from a spreadsheet

/WDR   /Worksheet Delete Row

Delete a column or columns from a spreadsheet

/WDC   /Worksheet Delete Column

Printing a Portion or an Entire Spreadsheet

Specify the range of data to print

/PPR   /Print Printer Range

Indicate top of page setting

/PPA   /Print Printer Align

Initiate printing

/PPG   /Print Printer Go

Advance printer paper to top of next page

/PPP   /Print Printer Page

Place spreadsheet on a text (ASCII) file

/PF   /Print File

Alter present printing settings

/PPO   /Print Printer Options

Specify margins for printing page

/PPOM   /Print Printer Options Margins

Print cell formulas instead of numeric values

/PPOOC   /Print Printer Options Other Cell-Formulas

Print what appears on the screen if cell formulas were previously used

/PPOOA /Print Printer Options Other As-Displayed

Insert a page break

/WP /Worksheet Page

Print or plot a graph

Use the PrintGraph program

Saving a Spreadsheet or Graph

Save a spreadsheet on a file

/FS /File Save

Save a graph

/GS /Graph Save

Database Commands

Indicate input range of the database

/DQI /Data Query Input

Indicate the criterion to be used

/DQC /Data Query Criterion

Indicate the information to be output if the criterion is satisfied

/DQO /Data Query Output

Find and highlight records in the database that satisfy the criterion

/DQF /Data Query Find

Copy the data from the records that satisfy the criterion to the output range

/DQE /Data Query Extract

Copy the data from the records that satisfy the criterion to the output range and eliminate duplicate data

/DQU   /Data Query Unique

Delete records from the database that satisfy the criterion

/DQD   /Data Query Delete

Sort records in a database

/DS   /Data Sort

Specify data range to be sorted

/DSD   /Data Sort Data-Range

Specify the primary sort key

/DSP   /Data Sort Primary-Key

Specify the secondary sort key

/DSS   /Data Sort Secondary-Key

Initiate sorting process

/DSG   /Data Sort Go

Reset data sort settings

/DSR   /Data Sort Reset

File Operations

Retrieve or load a file

/FR   /File Retrieve

Save a spreadsheet on a file

/FS   /File Save

Save a spreadsheet in a text (ASCII) file

/PF **/Print File**

Include data from another spreadsheet file into the spreadsheet in the microcomputer memory

/FC **/File Combine**

Display names of files in current directory

/FL **/File List**

Remove or erase a file

/FE **/File Erase**

Save a graph for printing at a later time

/GS **/Graph Save**

Using Named Ranges

Create a named range for a cell or group of cells

/RNC **/Range Name Create**

Delete a named range

/RND **/Range Name Delete**

Remove or delete all range names

/RNR **/Range Name Reset**

Working with Numeric Values

Modify the default format of all numbers

/WGF **/Worksheet Global Format**

Modify the format of a cell or group of cells

    /RF   /Range Format

Check the recalculation settings

    /WS   /Worksheet Status

Indicate how and when recalculation of formulas occurs

    /WGR   /Worksheet Global Recalculation

Suppress from view all cells that have a value of exactly 0

    /WGZ   /Worksheet Global Zero

Modify the column width when asterisks appear in a cell

    /WCS   /Worksheet Column Set-Width

Associate a range name with a number or set of numbers

    /RNC   /Range Name Create

Convert a cell or group of cells with a formula(s) to a value(s)

    /RV   /Range Value

Determine a frequency distribution for some data in a range of cells

    /DD   /Data Distribution

Miscellaneous Commands

Display amount of memory available and current default settings for format, column width, cell protection, zero suppression, etc.

    /WS   /Worksheet Status

Display current configuration for the printer, directory, margins, etc.

    /WGDS   /Worksheet Global Default Status

Change configuration settings for the printer, directory, margins, etc.

> **/WGD** /Worksheet Global Default

Change spreadsheet settings for format, column width, recalculation, protection, etc.

> **/WG** /Worksheet Global

Indicate how and when recalculation of formulas occurs

> **/WGR** /Worksheet Global Recalculation

Exit to the operating system

> **/S** /System

Quit using 1–2–3

> **/Q** /Quit

APPENDIX C

USING FORMULAS IN LOTUS 1–2–3

OVERVIEW

Lotus 1–2–3 allows the use of three types of formulas:

- Arithmetic formulas
- Text formulas
- Logical formulas

Various types of operators can be used in the formulas to indicate operations such as addition and subtraction. In this appendix, the types of formulas are discussed and the order in which operations occur in formulas is discussed.

■ TYPES OF FORMULAS

The three types of formulas that can be entered into a cell in 1–2–3 are arithmetic, text, and logical.

Arithmetic Formulas

Arithmetic formulas are used to compute numeric values using arithmetic operators. For example if the the cell formula, +A3–10 appears in B5, then the value 10 is subtracted from the number appearing in cell A3 and the result will appear in cell B5.

Text Formulas

Text formulas are used to calculate labels using the text operator (&). For example, if the text formula +C5&"EXPENSES" appears in cell K7, then the label that results from combining the label in cell C5 with EXPENSES will appear in cell K7.

Logical Formulas

Logical formulas are used to compare values in two or more cells using logical operators. A logical formula calculates a value of 0 (meaning false) or 1 (meaning true). For example, if the formula +C3<=25000 appears in cell D3, then the value 0 will appear in cell D3 whenever the value in cell C3 is greater than 25,000. A value of 0 will appear in cell D3 if the value in cell C3 is less than or equal to 25,000.

■ OPERATORS AND ORDER OF PRECEDENCE

1–2–3 uses various operators in formulas to indicate arithmetic operations. Listed below are the mathematical operators allowed in 1–2–3. The operators are listed in the order of precedence by which operations are completed.

Operator	Definition
^	Exponentiation
– +	Negative, Positive
* /	Multiplication, Division
+ –	Addition, Subtraction

The operators that appear higher on the list are evaluated prior to operators that are lower on the list. Exponentiation is the highest level operator. For example, if the arithmetic formula 10+5^2 appears in cell A5, then the result that appears in cell A5 is 35 (10 + 5 squared) not 225 (15 raised to the power of two).

1–2–3 can tell the difference between a + or – sign that means a positive or negative number as opposed to the + or – sign meaning addition or subtraction. For example, if the formula 10/–5+10 appears in cell B8, then the result that appears in the cell is 8 (–2+10) not 2 (10/5).

Multiplication and division operators are evaluated before addition and subtraction operators. For example, if cell C8 contains the formula 7–3/2, the value that appears in cell C8 is 5.5 (7–(3/2)) not 2 (7–3)/2.

The order of precedence can be overridden using sets of parantheses. If more than one set of parentheses are included in a formula, then the order of execution begins with the innermost set of parentheses and proceeds to the outer most set of parentheses.

Work the following set of example problems using the information provided to make sure the order of precedence is understood. Assume that cell A1=3, cell B2=4 and cell C4=8.

Formula	Order of Evaluation	Answer
+C4–B2*2	8–(4*2)	0
+B2–A1–C4/B2	4–3–(8/4)	–1
+B2–(A1–C4)/B2	4–((3–8)/4)	5.25
+A1/–3+3	(3/–3)+3	2
+A1–4*C4/B2^2	3–((4*8)/4^2)	1
(A1–4)*C4/B2^2	(3–4)*(8/4^2)	–0.5
+A1*B2/C4–10/2	((3*4)/8–(20/2))	–3.5

APPENDIX D

CHAPTER ONE/EXERCISE 1 ANSWERS

INSTRUCTIONS: Answer the following questions in the space provided.

1. Define the following terms:
   a. Row Numbers—the row of numbers on the left border of the worksheet screen.
   b. Column Letters—the letters that appear across the top border of the worksheet screen.
   c. Cell—the area on a worksheet that occurs at the intersection of a column and a row.
   d. Cell Pointer—rectangular item that is used to highlight a cell.
   e. Current Cell—the cell that is highlighted by the cell pointer. When information is entered into a worksheet, it is placed in the cell highlighted by the cell pointer.
   f. Cell Address—the location of a cell. It is defined by a column letter followed by a row number.
   g. Control Panel—the area above the column letter section of the worksheet.
   h. Mode Indicator—appears in the top right corner of the control panel of the worksheet.
   i. Status Indicator—specifies the condition of certain keys or of the program.
   j. Date Indicator—current date being used by Lotus 1–2–3 that appears in the lower left hand corner of the worksheet screen.
   k. Time Indicator—current time being used by Lotus 1–2–3 that appears in the lower left hand corner of the worksheet screen.
   l. Worksheet—a term that is used interchangeably with the word spreadsheet.

2. Describe the standard way of using the 1–2–3 menu structure.
   The first action is to press the / key (sometimes called the command key). The menu pointer is then moved to whatever menu option is desired and the ↵ (return or enter) key is pressed. The process is continued until the command sequence desired by the user is completed.

493

3. Describe the alternative method of using the 1–2–3 menu structure.
   The only difference in using the alternative method instead of the standard method is that the first letter of the menu option can be typed rather than moving the menu pointer to the desired menu option and pressing the ⏎ key.

4. Describe the purpose of using the function keys F1 through F10. The function keys have been "programmed" to perform specific operations. These keys let the user perform specific actions such as going to a particular cell without having to use the arrow (directional) keys.

CHAPTER ONE/EXERCISE 3 ANSWERS

Note: Exercise 3 does not require an answer key.

CHAPTER TWO/EXERCISE 1 ANSWERS

INSTRUCTIONS: Circle T if the statement is true and F if the statement is false.

T   F   1. One way to erase incorrect data is to move to the incorrect data's cell, retype the data correctly, and press ⏎ to enter the correction.

T   **F**   2. The formula SUM(A1..A7) will add the data in cells A1 through A7.

T   **F**   3. To round a number to two decimal places, use the Range Format command.

T   F   4. The **Worksheet Erase Yes** command sequence erases the worksheet currently in use from the microcomputer memory.

T   F   5. A print range must be specified before a spreadsheet can be printed.

T   F   6. The "@" character must precede special functions such as the SUM and ROUND functions.

T   **F**   7. Lotus 1–2–3 will automatically save changes that are made to a spreadsheet file.

T   F   8. To look at a previously saved file, the **File Retrieve** command is used.

T   **F**   9. "BUDGET 1" is an acceptable file name.

T   **F**   10. The letter "X" is the symbol for multiplication when using Lotus 1–2–3.

CHAPTER TWO/EXERCISE 3 ANSWERS
Correcting a Spreadsheet

A3: 'A1−A2
READY

	A	B	C	D	E	F	G	H
1	52							
2	30							
3	A1−A2							
4								
5								
6								
7								
8								
9								
10								
11								
12								
13								
14								
15								
16								
17								
18								
19								
20								

CAPS

1. What caused the error in cell A3?
   Because A1−A2 begins with an alphabetic character, the formula was read by Lotus as a label.

2. How can the error be corrected?
   Retype or edit the formula to be +A1−A2. Since the formula now begins with a numeric character, the formula will calculate correctly.

CHAPTER TWO/EXERCISE 5 ANSWERS
Correcting a Spreadsheet

A3: −A2
READY

	A	B	C	D	E	F	G	H
1	52							
2	30							
3	−30							
4								
5								
6								
7								
8								
9								
10								
11								
12								
13								
14								
15								
16								
17								
18								
19								
20								

CAPS

1. What caused the error in computing A1−A2?
   +A1 was typed in and ↵ was pressed before the formula was completely typed in; at this point, +A1 was entered as the complete formula. −A2 was typed and the ↵ key was pressed again, which resulted in −A2 being entered in cell A3. −A2 results in the answer −30, since 30 is the number in cell A2.

2. How can the error be corrected?
   Do not press ↵ before the entire formula is written.

CHAPTER TWO/EXERCISES 7 & 9 ANSWERS

Note: Exercises 7 and 9 do not require answer keys.

CHAPTER THREE/EXERCISE 1 ANSWERS

INSTRUCTIONS: Circle T if the statement is true and F if the statement is false.

T   F   1. Dependent formulas use numbers located elsewhere in a worksheet to perform calculations.

T   F   2. If the number in cell B1 is changed in a worksheet, the cell entry containing the formula +B1–260 will change when the worksheet is recalculated.

T   **F**   3. The cell entry 260–10 is an example of a dependent formula.

T   F   4. When assumptions in a worksheet are changed, the results can be printed without permanently saving the changes to the file.

T   F   5. Assumptions do not have to be printed if they are not included in the highlighted print range.

CHAPTER THREE/EXERCISE 3 ANSWERS

Note: Exercise 3 does not require an answer key.

CHAPTER FOUR/EXERCISE 1 ANSWERS

INSTRUCTIONS: Circle T if the statement is true and F if the statement is false.

T   F   1. An absolute cell reference means that the reference is kept constant, even when copied.

T   F   2. The [Edit] key allows the user to correct a cell entry without having to retype the entire entry.

T   **F**   3. Worksheet Titles allows the user to center titles on a spreadsheet.

T   F   4. Worksheet Window allows the user to view two different areas of a spreadsheet at the same time.

T   F   5. Worksheet Page creates a page break in a spreadsheet.

T   F   6. If column D is hidden on a worksheet using Worksheet Column Hide, column D will not appear if the worksheet is printed.

T   F   7. Worksheet Global Recalculation Manual is activated so that data can be entered without the worksheet recalculating after each new entry.

T   F   8. Changing the File Directory changes the drive designation or path to which Lotus saves and retrieves files.

T   **F**   9.   **File E**rase erases a file from memory.

T   **F**   10. The **System** command permanently returns the user to DOS.

CHAPTER FOUR/EXERCISE 3 ANSWERS
Making a Cell Entry Absolute

---

1. How can the formula in cell C1 be changed so that cells D1 and E1 also refer to cell B2 for the projected revenue rate?

    Change the formula +B1*B2 in cell C1 to +B1*$B$2 so that B2 is an absolute cell reference. This can be accomplished by editing the formula to add the dollar signs to B2. Another method is to reenter the formula and, while highlighting cell B2 (or typing B2), press the [Abs] key to add the dollar signs.

    After changing the formula in cell C1, copy the formula to cells D1 and E1. The screen should look like Figure 4–43.

Figure 4–43

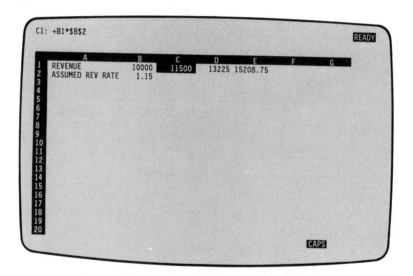

```
C1: +B1*$B$2                                                    READY

        A              B         C         D        E       F       G
   1  REVENUE        10000     11500    13225 15208.75
   2  ASSUMED REV RATE  1.15
   3
   4
   5
   6
   7
   8
   9
  10
  11
  12
  13
  14
  15
  16
  17
  18
  19
  20
                                                               CAPS
```

CHAPTER FOUR/EXERCISE 5 ANSWERS

Note: Exercise 5 does not require an answer key.

CHAPTER FIVE/EXERCISE 1 ANSWERS

INSTRUCTIONS: Circle T if the statement is true and F if the statement is false.

T   **F**   1.   In Lotus 1–2–3, a template file must be combined with another file containing data to generate a new spreadsheet.

T   F   2.   A template is a good way to keep detail spreadsheets standardized.

T   **F**   3.   When data is added to a template in memory, it is automatically added to the template file on the disk.

T   F   4.   A template can be used to create multiple files.

T   F   5.   When adding data to a template in order to create a new spreadsheet, save the spreadsheet under a new name rather than the template name so that the template file will not be altered.

CHAPTER SIX/EXERCISE 1 ANSWERS

INSTRUCTIONS: Circle T if the statement is true and F if the statement is false.

T   **F**   1.   The range name for a line of data must be taken from a label already existing on the spreadsheet.

T   F   2.   A template is a good way to keep range names standardized.

T   **F**   3.   A detail spreadsheet is used for summarizing data from several spreadsheets.

T   **F**   4.   File Combine Copy is used to add numbers together from various spreadsheets.

T   F   5.   If desired, the exact range location rather than range names can be specified when using the Named/Specified-Range command to combine data.

T   **F**   6.   File Combine Add can add numbers to existing numbers and formulas.

T   **F**   7.   The Range Value command can change values into formulas.

T   F   8.   The File Xtract command can be used to create a spreadsheet containing values from a spreadsheet containing formulas.

T   F   9.   File Combine Copy can copy formulas from one spreadsheet to another spreadsheet.

T   **F**   10. When files are combined, the original detail spreadsheet and summary spreadsheet are automatically changed.

CHAPTER SIX/EXERCISE 3 ANSWERS

Note: Exercise 3 does not require an answer key.

CHAPTER SEVEN/EXERCISE 1 ANSWERS

INSTRUCTIONS: Circle T if the statement is true and F if the statement is false.

T **F**   1. The range name for a macro must be taken from a label already existing on the spreadsheet.

T **F**   2. The range name for a macro must begin with a forward slash and a letter of the alphabet.

T F   3. A macro is a way to automate a repetitive procedure.

T F   4. Certain keystrokes in a macro must be enclosed in braces (the { and } characters).

T **F**   5. In a macro, the tilde (the ~ symbol) represents pressing the forward slash (the command key /).

T **F**   6. To execute the macro named \Z, the user must hold down the [Ctrl] key and tap the letter Z.

T F   7. A named range for a macro must contain the first macro step as the first line in the range.

T **F**   8. When entering data on a spreadsheet manually, the tilde can be used instead of pressing ⏎.

T **F**   9. Either apostrophe (the ' or the ') can be used to preface a macro step.

T F   10. Documentation should be included in a macro.

CHAPTER SEVEN/EXERCISE 3 ANSWERS

Note: Exercise 3 does not require an answer key.

CHAPTER EIGHT/EXERCISE 1 ANSWERS

INSTRUCTIONS: Circle T if the statement is true and F if the statement is false.

T   **F**   1. @MIN determines the minute for a given serial number.

T   F   2. Multiple items in a range may be listed individually (e.g., the syntax in the formula @COUNT(B1,B3,B4) is correct).

T   **F**   3. Arguments within an @ function may be placed in any order desired by the user.

T   F   4. Extra spaces are not acceptable within @ functions.

T   F   5. A label has a value of 0 and will be counted as such if included in a range for an @ function.

T   F   6. It is possible to alter an @ function with arithmetic operations to get the desired result (e.g., the formula @PMT(B1,B2/12,B3*12) is syntactically correct).

T   F   7. If a worksheet file containing the @NOW function (formatted to show the date) is retrieved from a file and actively recalculates, the @NOW function will display the *current* system date.

T   **F**   8. A single-cell item in an argument may not be entered directly into the formula (e.g., the formula @NPV(A1,B1..B6) cannot be entered as @NPV(.1,B1..B6).

T   F   9. More than one @ function may be used in a formula.

T   F   10. The @IF statement allows the user to test one or more conditions in a worksheet and provide appropriate responses for either a true result or a false result.

CHAPTER EIGHT/EXERCISE 3 ANSWERS
Using the Financial Analysis Functions

INSTRUCTIONS: Use the Financial Analysis Functions available in Lotus 1–2–3 to solve the following exercises. Each exercise provides the correct answer.

1. Compute the internal rate of return for the following cash flow stream using .15 as the guess rate:
   –1000, –500, 900, 800, 700, 600, 400, 200, 100
   The answer is .313959 or 31.4%.

2. Compute the net present value for the following cash flow stream using .10 as the discount rate:
   –1500, 900, 800, 700, 600, 400, 200, 100
   The answer is 1327.646 or 1206.951 depending upon whether the initial inventment of $1,500 is discounted.

3. Compute the future value if the payment per period is 500, the interest rate is 10%, and the term is 15 years.
   The answer is 15886.24.

4. Compute the present value using the arguments previously given in problem number 3.
The answer is 3803.039.

5. Compute the payment amount for a 100,000 loan that has an interest rate of 10% and is to be paid on an annual basis for a period of 12 years.
The answer is 14676.33.

6. Compute the *monthly* payment amount assuming all arguments in problem 5 stay the same except the time period is 30 years.
The answer is 877.5715.

Complete the following exercises if using Release 2 or a later release of Lotus 1–2–3.

7. Compute the straight-line depreciation for an office machine having an initial cost of $13,000, an estimated useful life of 8 years, and a salvage value of $200.
The answer is 1600.

8. Using the data given in problem 7, compute the depreciation of the office machine for the sixth year using the double-declining balance method.
The answer is 771.2402.

9. Using the data given in problem 7, compute the depreciation of the office machine for the sixth year using the sum-of-the-years'-digits method.
The answer is 1066.666.

10. Suppose $10,000 has been invested in an account that pays an annual interest rate of 10%, compounded monthly. Determine how long it will take to get $30,000 in the account.
The answer is 132.3820 months or about 11 years.

11. Suppose that $5,000 is deposited at the end of each year into a bank account. If 8% interest is earned per year, compute how long it will take to earn $20,000.
The answer is 3.607432, or about 3 1/2 years.

12. Suppose $15,000 has been invested in a bond which matures in 9 years to 25,000. Interest is compounded monthly. Determine the monthly interest rate.
The answer is .004741.

CHAPTER EIGHT/EXERCISE 5 ANSWERS

Note: Exercise 5 does not require an answer key.

CHAPTER NINE/EXERCISE 1 ANSWERS

INSTRUCTIONS: Circle T if the statement is true and F if the statement is false.

<u>T</u>   F   1. A Lotus 1–2–3 graph can contain up to six different data ranges.

<u>T</u>   F   2. To change a bar graph into a line graph, change the Graph Type from Bar to Line.

<u>T</u>   F   3. If numbers are changed on the spreadsheet, the graph will reflect the changes when the graph is viewed again on the screen.

T   <u>F</u>   4. If numbers are changed on the spreadsheet, the changes will be automatically reflected on any graph file that was created from the worksheet previously.

<u>T</u>   F   5. It is possible to create three completely different graphs with data from one worksheet.

<u>T</u>   F   6. If File Save is not executed after a graph is made, the graph settings will not be saved.

T   <u>F</u>   7. If a computer is not configured to show graphics on the screen, it is not possible to create and print a Lotus 1–2–3 graph.

T   <u>F</u>   8. A color graph on the screen displays the colors in which the graph will be printed on a color printer or plotter.

<u>T</u>   F   9. A pie graph displays the data in data range A.

<u>T</u>   F   10. An XY graph is different from other Lotus graphs because it graphs data for variable X.

CHAPTER NINE/EXERCISE 3 ANSWERS
Correcting a Graph

---

1. How can the graph be changed so that cells A1 through *A3* are graphed as seen in Figure 9–24?

Press / Graph **A**.
Highlight cells A1 through A3 and press ⏎ . (It may be necessary to press the Escape key to reset the data-range).
View the graph.

CHAPTER NINE/EXERCISES 5, 7, & 9 ANSWERS

Note: Exercises 5, 7, and 9 do not require answer keys.

CHAPTER TEN/EXERCISE 1 ANSWERS

INSTRUCTIONS: Circle T if the statement is true and F if the statement is false.

T   **F**   1.   When sorting a database in Lotus 1–2–3, the data-range must include the field titles.

T   F   2.   The field titles must be located in the line directly above the first record of the database for the **Data Query** command sequence to work properly.

T   **F**   3.   It is appropriate to have more than one line consisting of field titles designated in the input range.

T   F   4.   Each criterion consists of two cells (a field title and the actual criterion).

T   F   5.   The input range, criterion, and output range must be manually set up on the worksheet and then identified through the menu options.

T   F   6.   The output range allows the user to copy the desired fields that match the criteria to another area on the spreadsheet.

T   F   7.   When designating the output range, the user may highlight only the field names that are desired; the data will appear directly below the field names on the spreadsheet in the output range when the **Query Find** is executed.

T   F   8.   The QUERY key allows the user to perform a query based upon previously set ranges.

T   **F**   9.   The criterion for a spreadsheet can be set by setting the bin range.

T   **F**   10. The **Query Unique** command deletes multiple records in a database.

CHAPTER TEN/EXERCISES 3 & 5 ANSWERS

Note: Exercises 3 and 5 do not require answer keys.

CHAPTER ELEVEN/EXERCISE 1 ANSWERS

INSTRUCTIONS: Circle T if the statement is true and F if the statement is false.

T   **F**   1.   A column on the spreadsheet has to have a width of 72 before text can be justified.

T   F   2.   Each line of text is a separate label after the **Range Justify** command is executed.

T   F   3.   To edit a line of text that has been justified with the **Range Justify** command, use the [Edit] key.

T   F   4. If the **R**ange **J**ustify command is executed with text above an existing spreadsheet, the Justify range should include enough space to justify the text without disturbing the spreadsheet below.

T   **F**   5. The **R**ange **J**ustify command only works if the Justify range consists of one column and text is not displayed under other columns.

CHAPTER ELEVEN/EXERCISE 3 ANSWERS

Note: Exercise 3 does not require an answer key.

APPENDIX A/EXERCISE 1 ANSWERS

INSTRUCTIONS: Circle T if the statement is true and F if the statement is false.

T   F   1. PC-DOS manages files on a disk.

T   **F**   2. DIR A: is a PC-DOS command to look at the files on a disk in drive B.

T   **F**   3. PC-DOS commands must be written in uppercase letters.

T   **F**   4. To copy the file HELLO.XXX from drive A to drive C, one would type COPY A:HELLO C: and press Return.

T   **F**   5. The RENAME command is used to rename disks.

T   **F**   6. In the filename HELLO.XXX, .XXX is known as the parameter.

T   F   7. In the command COPY A:GOODBYE.XXX B:ALOHA.XXX, GOODBYE.XXX was the source file that was copied to a second disk and given the name ALOHA.XXX.

T   **F**   8. PC-DOS commands will execute even if extra spaces are in the command (e.g., COPY A: *.* B:)

T   **F**   9. If a disk is not present in drive A when the computer is started, the computer system will then "look" for a disk in drive B.

T   **F**   10. It is not important to input the correct time into the computer system.

INDEX